Elmer & Virginia

Elmer&Virginia

A World War II Romance in Letters

Compiled and edited by John Odell

QUICKFOOT BOOKS ■ **SAN FRANCISCO** ■ **2021**

Elmer & Virginia: A World War II Romance in Letters

by John Odell

Published by
Quickfoot Books
555 Ulloa Street
San Francisco CA 94127-1140

www.quickfootbooks.com

Contact the author at elmerandvirginiabook@gmail.com.

Excerpt from "Dulce et Decorum Est" by Wilfred Owen
printed with gratitude to The Wilfred Owen Association.

Frontispiece photograph by Charlie Williamson, used by permission.

Life Magazine cover on page 113 ©1942 Time, Inc.

"Pre-Flight Cadets Get To See Planes' 'Innards'" on page 172
© 1943 Montgomery Advertiser.

ISBN: 978-1-7365338-0-2 trade paperback
978-1-7365338-1-9 electronic book

Fourth printing

Design and composition: Dick Margulis, www.dmargulis.com

MANUFACTURED IN THE UNITED STATES OF AMERICA

Dedicated to the memory of my parents,
Elmer and Virginia Odell

Contents

Acknowledgments

M Y DEEP AND PROFOUND thanks to all who helped me create this book:

To Kristen Tate, my editor, whose keen eye, solid judgment, unfailing taste, deep sense of humor, and saint-like patience helped make what began as an amorphous plethora of transcriptions into a cogent narrative, and kept me sane in the process. To Dick Margulis, my book designer, whose artistry is evident on every page of *Elmer & Virginia*. To Stephen and Megan Kaminsky, for their amazing web wizardry. To Alena Scoblete of the Rockville Centre Public Library for her generous research into the archives of the *Nassau Review-Star*. To Gloria Kemp, for her early proofreading. And to my early readers and supporters, for their plentiful ideas and encouragement: Scott Buce, Dr. Carrie Evenden, Enid Goldstein, Pat Hunter, Jim Kelly, Marc and Marge Kenny, Elaine Kurka, Dana LaBrecque, Paige Lewis, Erin Meadows, Dan and Pat Odell, Betty Packard, Don Potter, Dan Redmond, Bob Rose, Veronica Rossi, Susan Seaman, Alan Schill, Brian Schill, Rachel Silverman, and Hazel Wilton.

Elmer & Virginia

Introduction

F OR MORE THAN HALF a century these letters—between my mother and father, and between my father and his parents—sat in shoeboxes at the bottom of my father's wardrobe closet. There are more than a thousand of them, opened but long unread. All of them were written between 1939 and 1944, the era of the Second World War. The telephone and telegraph were expensive and unreliable, so letters were the chief form of long-distance communication. Even if you went away on vacation for a week, you were expected to send at least a postcard. And during long separations, as in war-time, writing was a lifeline for people enduring fraught times. Letters were savored, saved, reread.

My parents were clear writers and gifted story tellers, and when I began reading these letters some time ago I was captivated by their first-hand accounts of those war years. Their letters brim with fears, frustrations, dangers, adventures, tears, and joys. They speak to their love of music, theater, and the written word. They're filled with anecdotes of everyday life and the tenor of the times.

The envelopes are frayed—ripped open in moments of need and desire, their backs used as notepads and score sheets. But inside are messages on quality acid-free paper, scribed with real ink.

They have endured, waiting—as many as eighty years—for more readers. I have gathered the best of them in this volume, and I hope you enjoy them as much as I have.

■

For nearly five years, beginning in October, 1939, Elmer Odell and Virginia Schill wrote to each other. Their correspondence, plus Virginia's diary entries and letters to and from his parents, forms the core of this tale. Here is a love story, told by the lovers themselves. It also chronicles their individual grails as they grew to adulthood in the years bracketed by the Great Depression and World War II.

Virginia was one of six children of a prosperous real estate developer, Mainard Schill. The Schills lived in a spacious home in the village of Hempstead,  Long Island, New York. Like her mother, Jeanette "Jet" McCarroll Schill, Virginia was of serious mien and a devout Catholic. She excelled in academics and had been the editor-in-chief of her high school newspaper—and was bound for a journalism degree at Syracuse University.

Elmer was the younger of two children of John Odell and Hazel Bamford Odell. They lived in a rented bungalow in Roosevelt, a working-class village adjacent to Hempstead. John Odell was a bookbinding foreman for the publisher Doubleday, after stints as a trolley conductor and a grocery store owner. Elmer was smart and a good student, but not a serious academic. He'd attended three years of Methodist studies, but the Odells were not regular churchgoers. Elmer favored

"le joi de vivre"—stylish clothes, parties, and dancing—especially the Lindy.

At the outset Elmer and Virginia seemed far from a match. They ran in separate social circles, and did not formally meet until after their graduation in 1939. But apparently Elmer and Virginia had spent some time in each other's company that summer, and not long after arriving in Syracuse, she sent him a postcard. He'd begun taking night business classes at the high school while job-hunting.

Getting Acquainted

WHEN ELMER AND VIRGINIA were sophomores, Japan invaded China. As they began their senior year, the Munich Pact was signed, avoiding war by allowing Hitler to annex part of what was then Czechoslovakia. "I believe it is peace for our time," said British Prime Minister Neville Chamberlain. Shortly before they began their correspondence, Germany attacked Poland, beginning the Second World War in Europe. These and other events ultimately would transform them, and their classmates, from carefree kids into totally immersed members of the Greatest Generation.

■

Elmer – October 4, 1939

Dear Ginny:

I received your card and was glad to hear from you. Everything in school is fine but Mr. Hayes and I do not agree. He believes in homework and I don't. That job I spoke of did not materialize but I have a couple of others lined up. I went down to the Brooklyn Navy Yard today but I guess I will not join the navy because I have

7

no desire to take a joyride on a torpedo. I'm in the same boat you are because I can't find anyone to "Lindy" with either.

As always, Elmer

P.S. Write again real soon and tell me all about Syracuse U.

SYRACUSE UNIVERSITY

October 24, 1939
3:30 P.M.

Dear Elmer,

If you have already begun to classify me with the rodents for not answering your letter before this, you ain't the only one! No doubt half of L.I. [Long Island] thinks evil things of me, judging from the pile of letters I must answer in the near future! My only excuse is a worn, tired, alibi:—I've been busy like the well-known bee! Much work they stack you with up here and many other things there are to do! Oh my yes! But if you'll break down and forgive me, I promise to mend my ways and answer letters quite promptly. O.K.?

No, don't join the navy! The uniforms might be pretty cute, but they *don't* stop a torpedo . . . Feet work better on land!

This letter gets crazier and sillier! Stiff upper lip!

I suppose Wally told you about hitchhiking here from Hamilton. Boy, what a surprise! I almost fell through to the cellar. It was swell to see someone you've known for more than 3 weeks! If you have nothing to do some weekend, take out your roller skates and come on up. I'd love to see you. [Wally Lister, a high school friend of Ginny's, was attending Brown University. He was

probably a bit sweet on her, as he signed his early letters "Love."]

Everything is hotsy-dandy at Syracuse. The kids are swell, the campus is the nuts, even the profs are nice. The only trouble I'm having is with Chemistry and the Lindy! Chemistry has me slowly going *mad*, and I *still* haven't found anybody who does the Lindy like it ought to be did! I came across *one* fellow who professed knowledge of it (all who claim this accomplishment are from N.Y.C. or L.I. The hicks up here are still *waltzing*, practically!), but he really wasn't good at it. Sorta did it half-heartedly! I'm really crusading up here to spread the Lindy around. "Let's Lindy" could be my motto, by-word, etc.! So far, all the girls in this cottage know it and *like* it. One girl (N.Y.C.) in particular is *good*, and the rest are coming along very well. I've been doing it, routines and all, every time something good comes on the radio. When I get home Christmas, will you come over a few dozen times? Too bad you can't fly up here. That would be *fun*!!

Tell Mr. Hayes for me that he should stop abusing you. Tell him I won't love him anymore! He's a *swell* guy, even if you don't agree with him about homework!

I hope you get one of the jobs you've lined up!

Write soon, pliz!! Ginny

[And on the back of the envelope] All the girls want you to come up. They want to see you Lindy!! Ginny

The Lindy, or "Lindy Hop," was named for aviator Charles Lindbergh, who flew the first solo nonstop crossing of the Atlantic in 1927. The dance is said to have evolved in Harlem in the late 1920s from a number of other dance forms. It included dancing as a couple plus breakaway solos. Words cannot describe the joy of this—watch it on YouTube. The Lindy was all the rage in the late 1930s and early 1940s, and my father, Elmer "Crazy Legs" Odell, was a master practitioner—a whirling dervish on the dance floor.

November 10, 1939 – Virginia turns eighteen

Elmer – November 12, 1939

Dear Ginny:

Well go ahead, call me it. Call me a cad, a low life, a dog, etc., etc. I deserve every bit of it, no doubt. I should have written sooner.

 I too have been working. Unbelievable as it sounds I've landed a job. And what a job! In a bank of all places. Not only that but in the largest bank in the country, Chase National. At last I'm out of the red and into the blue. Socially I'm in the mud. I have no one to Lindy with but my sister. I'd love to come up to Syracuse, and show those dudes how the "Lindy" really should be done but now it's impossible because I have to work half a day on Saturday (fooey, nuts, and other ejaculations of dismay).

By the way, Wally was home one weekend and we went to the Sophomore Soirée together. Afterwards we went out on a rampage. There were about fifteen of us. First of all we went over to the Garden City Hotel [a swanky place where Charles Lindbergh stayed the night before his historic flight]. Well you know that hotel on a Saturday night: a bunch of old fogies sitting around in evening clothes. We all trooped up to the bar, amid a volley of dirty looks from waiters and patrons alike, expecting to stay there for the evening but as luck would have it the bar was closed for alterations. On the way out three of the fellows got spinning in the revolving door and couldn't get out. Well I dare say we left that place in a hurry.

As always, Elmer

P.S. Good luck in your campaign to make Syracuse "Lindy" conscious."

Elmer – November 21, 1939

Dear Ginny:

A week ago last Saturday night, Norman and I were bumming around, looking for something to do, when we heard of a dance over in the New York Agricultural School. Having nothing else to do we went over there and found that it was a barn dance and also that they wanted four bits a person to get in [fifty cents, or about $8.50 today]. We found a back door and entered in a truly slinky mannerism, and got away with it. Before we left Norman and I had all the apples we could eat and all the cider we could drink, and on our way out we took a big pumpkin with us. Some fun, eh kid? [Norm Hilmar, a son of Danish immigrants, was a classmate and close boyhood friend. He called El's parents "Grammaw & Grampaw."]

Last Saturday night Norman and Marie [Quantrell, Ginny's childhood best friend, a woman of wry wit], and my sister and I went over to a dance at the "Y". Evie, that's my sister, and I shone doing the "Lindy". (The first time I've really "Lindied" in weeks). Am I boring you? No? I'm sorry, I thought I heard you yawn. I must have been the termites in this place.

Well, my little cream-puff [maybe he'd been drinking?], I will close this message of nothing-in-particular, and stagger back into the world of reality until such times (in the near future I hope) when I shall receive, from your beautiful little hands, a joyous message of good tidings fresh from Syracuse U. Ta, ta and stuff. (This typewriter writes the craziest stuff.)

As ever, I remain, Elmer

Virginia – November 26, 1939, 12:20 p.m.

Dear Elmer,

Gee, am I ever overwhelmed! Two letters of yours to answer! Now I'm the so-and-so. But here's the long-delayed letter so quit your crabbing! (Can't imagine you crabbing, but it was a pretty thought!)

I put out the flag (you know the one!) when I received the information that E.W. Odell was *working*! That's really swell, though. When you get to be president (only with a *capital P*) of Chase National (Inc.?), I'll probably be around to borrow a few thousands. Just for old time's sake, of course. No fooling, though, a fellow can get promoted pretty fast—if he's good, works hard, keeps away from wine, women, and song, and brushes his teeth regularly! (Do you?) Good luck from me! Whenever you feel you need one, I  can round up a good cheering section with extra-special vigor to root for—Rah, rah,—Elmer! I'm rooting alone now up here—but *rooting*, nevertheless. (Ain't that nice?)

Please don't mention Wally coming home for the Soph Soirée! That's a very sad thought for me! *I wanted to go too!!!* I do like to hear about these things but it's a little hard to take. Still haven't uncovered a fellow who can Lindy. What a place this is!

Glenn Miller's "Wham" is a swell number, as is his "In The Mood." Oh boy! I heard "Little Brown Jug" Thursday (Thanksgiving Day) for the first time since Sept.! I get plenty of *practice* on the Lindy— every girl in the house does it now, and it's spreading to the other cottages!—but I can't remember a couple of the breaks you do. Besides, I'm getting pretty tired of dancing with *girls*! (only 20 more days until I see Hempstead again!)

Terribly surprised to hear that the G.C. Hotel fogies didn't appreciate your lively company! Maybe they hadn't taken their Carter's Little Liver Pills [a popular patent medicine] that day! You don't hear that [commercial] up here, by the way. But then, you can get *very little* on the radio in this burg anyway.

Colgate weekend and the week before it was *noisy* but nice. They staged rip-roaring pep-fests every night, and Sat. night, after we'd won 7-0 (three cheers), all the alumni who came back to get drunk and all the students who stayed drunk for the occasion, proceeded to wreck the city. One of the tricks for Colgate night is—rent a hotel room and throw water, bottles, and other small or large objects down on the passersby. The streets around the hotels looked as if it had been raining—and it hadn't, except for the liquids the merry-makers had let fly. Gee, what a mess. The pep-fests were almost as riotous too. They poured gasoline in the trolley tracks and set them on fire. (Very pretty sight!) The little kiddies also bounced (yes, I said *bounced*) cars (which were parked along the street) out into the middle of the road, and did various other things to keep the cops in complete frustration. These things are slightly crazy practices but a lot of fun to *watch*. (Just have to see that *you* don't get killed or wounded!)

Tsk! Tsk! Sneaking into the Aggies' dance! Ain't you 'shamed? (No? I don't blame you!) It was pretty profitable, wasn't it. Did you have the pumpkin in the form of pie or are you saving it for next Halloween?

That certainly must have been termites you heard yawning during your letter. Catch *me* being bored with a letter!!! Some nerve—to think I don't like your letters!—This epistle is getting out of hand, so I'll finish here. Watch out for the Martians!

Ginny

For nearly two years beginning in January 1940, Virginia kept a diary. Although it's not very introspective (there's a lot about the weather) it provides fill-in information about periods when Virginia was home and not exchanging letters with Elmer. It also lets us track the disintegration of her relationship with George Hall, whom Virginia had begun dating during her junior year in high school. George, the son of an apparently overbearing chemical industry executive, had attended St. Paul's Academy, a prestigious prep school in the upscale neighboring village of Garden City, and was studying at Rensselaer Polytechnic Institute in Troy, New York—the state's preeminent engineering university.

A poem Ginny wrote around this time speaks of her attraction to George:

Wish
I'd like him for my own.
His ruddy cheeks
And curly hair,
That cunning smile
The devil-may-care
Look in his deep blue eyes.

How I wish they all were mine!
And his funny nose.
Though best of all
Is the fact that he's
More than six feet tall!

At the end of Christmas break, she writes in her diary that saying goodbye to George was so hard "she could have died." At the end of January she made another trip home, for her mother's sixtieth birthday. Her diary chronicled fights with George and a great deal of dancing with El. This time, on the train ride back to Syracuse, she tells us, "George felt pretty bad. I, not too awful."

While the Schills were financially comfortable, the Great Depression wore on. And while Virginia took on odd jobs such as proctoring to supplement whatever support she received from her father, a round-trip ticket between Syracuse and home cost the equivalent of about two hundred and fifty dollars today. The trip took about nine hours each way, if everything went well. This may be why, although she's listed in her yearbook as headed for the University of Wisconsin, she ended up at Syracuse. Madison may have been just too far.

And Syracuse may have been the better choice for another reason. Founded in 1870, it was a co-ed institution from the beginning, a policy scorned by administrators and students of nearby all-male colleges, where it was thought that educating women was a waste of resources. And Syracuse's admission of women wasn't just a sop. The first matriculating class was split evenly between men and women. So it was likely a more nurturing environment for a lass who was the first in her family to attend college.

January 7, 1940 – Food rationing begins in Great Britain

Elmer – February 5, 1940

Dear Ginny:

I really have been busy this past week. Monday, after I left you, I went bowling; Tuesday I had to work late and when I got home I went to the movies; Wednesday I had a bunch of fellows over to smoke, drink beer and play cards; Thursday I stayed in Brooklyn to attend some sort of a Methodist conference (very boring); Friday I went swimming with some fellows after work; Saturday I went to a dance over [at] the "Y"; and Sunday I went to an exceptionally good concert up at Hempstead High.

I went bowling Monday but I couldn't keep my mind on the game. (See what you do to me.) I wrote this "Masterpiece of Misery" in the bank so if it seems slightly disjointed in spots it is only because I have had to stop writing occasionally and do some work.

Guess what! I got a couple of new records Saturday and are they killeroos. One is Glenn Miller's "On a Little Street in Singapore" with "This Changing World" on the back and the other is Jimmy Dorsey's "A Man and His Drums" with "Cherokee" on the other side. Believe me "A Man and His Drums" is strictly out of this world! About ¾ of it is just a hot drum solo and is it good!

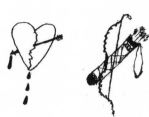  

Only Jitterbug in captivity

Me

Well, I will have to close this hunk of "lucid literature" because it is just about my lunch time.

As ever, Elmer

Virginia – February 9, 1940 12:30 a.m.

Dear El,

I intended to start this sooner this evening, but first it was French, then Glenn Miller and Bing Crosby, followed by a group of at least *eight* in my room! It was a delegation, come to discuss one of the members of Parker Cottage (this fair living center!) who has been making herself generally disliked. Charming girl. You ought to meet her!

Have you heard Miller play "Tuxedo Junction"?!! Boy, that is good! He played it a week ago and tonight, too. Both times I almost folded up. Erskine Hawkins sounds sad after Miller's arrangement. !!!!!! ← Indicating enthusiasm. Crosby was good tonight as usual. He sang "Indian Summer" and I missed part of it! He also ran through "I Thought About You," and he can certainly do that up neatly!—Pardon my ramblings about radio programs. That's a chief form of amusement for me, though.

Thursday classes started again and Friday I got my feet slightly frost bitten! What a life! I took a walk to inspect the snow sculpture, which was part of the Winter Carnival, and the day was rather *cool*. Anyway, my feet got a bit chilled. The doctor says I'll live.

I did it! I went skating—yes, *ice* skating! Strange as it seems, I *didn't* wipe up the pond. In fact, it wasn't bad at all, except for a slight bending inward of the ankles, the right one—particular! As soon as I get the blasted things to stand up, I'm sure I'll be a demon or better!

Tuesday I went swimming again—involuntarily—it's a life saving class!—and the work-out almost killed me. I guess I'll be another month getting back into condition! Today (or yesterday) wasn't *bad*, but it was very *wet* and *tiring*. Can't understand it. Could be that a little sleep would help—but that's just a theory.

You don't have to convince me that your new records are good. I heard Miller's "Street in Singapore" the other day and it *is* good. As for J. [Jimmy] Dorsey's "Man & His Drums"—I heard that one midnight on the radio while I was home. What drumming! Amazing! I thought they'd never stop. How's his "Cherokee"? Barnet's [Charlie] is *swell*, I know that. It is my secret desire, now, to get Miller's "Tuxedo Junction," if he's made it. Also Bing Crosby with "18th & 19th On Chestnut Street."(Not to mention a few dozen other choice selections!)

Methinks I oughta get to bed. There's a neat little chem. Lab scheduled for tomorrow morning. Halogens and stuff!! Nice?

Haven't figured out all the artistry at the bottom of your epistle. Either Valentine spirits have gotten you or else you were just *awfully* sad. The jitter bug was the only happy idea around! I have him in a bottle on my desk, and he takes off every time I bring a radio in the room!

All right, so I'm no crazier than most people! (I won't say— write again or I'll slug ya! It wouldn't be nice!)

Ginny

As is clear here, music was an important part of Elmer's and Virginia's lives. The "Big Band" era was in full swing, and the Dorseys, the Crosbys, Glenn Miller, Xavier Cugat, and the rest were all the rage. Their shows were first broadcast live from New York on AM radio, with fairly broad, if static-prone, reception. Virginia could listen from Syracuse—most of the time, depending on atmospheric conditions.

To meet further demand, the songs were recorded and pressed onto shellac or vinyl 78 rpm records; new releases were eagerly anticipated around the country. Although brittle and prone to breakage, their quality was far better and more consistent than what could be heard over the airwaves, though a far cry from what we expect in today's digital era.

On February 14, Virginia reports in her diary that she got a Valentine's Day telegram from George "and later the very same one from El! I'm *surprised* and a bit *skeptical.*"

Elmer – February 17, 1940

Dear Ginny:

Please forgive me if I seem a little ornery in this letter but it is because I am in a mean frame of mind. Listen to this and see if you blame me. Last night I was going to the Grand Ballroom of the Hotel St. George, to a dance the Bank was giving. Evie (that's my sister) and I were going to shine in the "Lindy." And then what happens. A blizzard! Foo!! So what did we do? We stayed home and played bridge. Now do you blame me for being a wee bit on the "Jersey Side." [This is an expression of New York snobbery— from 'inferior' New Jersey, not the "Big Apple."]

I have heard Glenn Miller's "Tuxedo Junction" and I think it's about his best. I've ordered it but it won't be released till this afternoon or Monday.

In your last letter, you mentioned an obviously detestable girl from Parker Cottage and you said I ought to meet her. What makes you think I would like to meet her if she is such a @!!!*— blank@??...*tsk! Tsk!

Virginia, if you saw me now you wouldn't know me. I swear, I'm a new man. You see I gave up smoking and drinking for Lent. I don't know whether this new individual that I am now is better than the old one. It's really too early in Lent to tell.

Well the firelight is waning and now I am writing by the light of the embers so I shall discontinue these prattling's until the next time.

As ever, Elmer

Virginia – February 20, 1940 1:45 p.m.

Dear El,

I've just come back from the Varsity Swing Shoppe (pronounced Shoppee and I didn't say sloppy!) where you can go and listen to records. You can also *buy* them but that's a minor point! Anyway, after hearing T. Dorsey's "Song of India" and "Marie," Miller's "Wham" & reverse side and "Tuxedo Junction," I'm in the mood! We bought the last and tenderly brought it home. *Ah!* I don't need to say what I think of it!

Jeepers—this whole letter will be records and Miller if I keep on this way. Cut it out now!

Thanks a lot for your telegram (I did get it!) [the Valentine's Day message]. It was *swell* of you, El, and if I could, I'd probably blush profusely, or something! Anyway, *merci beaucoup*, as they say in la belle France! I'm very flattered, to say the least.

Now hang on to your hat awhile, El! That "obviously detestable girl" isn't *that* bad! And I didn't mean that you ought to meet her because you'd *like* her! What do you think I think of you? I just said you ought to meet her—for the heck of it. She's a riot, really, if you can stand her. (I usually can't.) Today I almost let her have one. She was *singing* (can you call it that?) with the band in Dorsey's "Deep Night," and I *don't* like good music mutilated by accompanists!

So I wouldn't know you if I saw you now! Maybe you should wear an identification tag? But I *think* I'll be able to recognize you

Easter. That's pretty good giving-up you're doing for Lent!! Keep up the good work!! It isn't easy! If you do and I don't recognize you, *I'll* take the blame. O.K.?

Sincerely, Ginny

February 21, 1940 – Poll shows 77 percent of Americans opposed to US military intervention in Europe

---

Flash: Late report has it that the Irish-tempered Schill just lit into the Blonde Bombshell of Parker Cottage. Blondie, reputed for consideration and well-loved by her pals at Parker (!), had been carefully *murdering* all the music she knows by beating the piano to a pulp. In the meantime all other inmates were trying to sleep or study. So—throwing discretion and tact to the wind (which is pretty strong today!), Ginny of the Schill clan stormed out to the living room and handed Ria the last small piece of her mind. (To prove it *was* the last piece, witness this letter!) This Baldwin blonde, as Ria is known, had formerly won the love and admiration of the girls by endeavoring to relieve her cottage-mates of their dates—using, of course, her feminine charm. Today's encounter (Schill vs. Schuld) was only one of many. Feeling ran high last night, alas, as the proud beauty *sang* all evening with her sand-papered voice!

(Ed. note : You gather I don't care for the girl?)

Last Sat. night I was amused by the brother of a girl I met at freshman camp. We went to an informal frat dance. It was a vic [RCA Victrola automatic record player/changer] dance—a recording system with heaps of the latest and oldest *good* records. All would have been almost well, *but* Tom, I fear, was *very* partial to *one* step. He did that *one thing all night* until I thought I'd tear hair and beat on the walls!! Moses, how I wished *you* were there to show these sad people how to *dance*! The natives up here are the *lousiest* dancers I've ever found. When they played "Begin the Beguine" and like snazzy numbers—oh how I wanted to Lindy!!! The best things about the whole darn dance were the music (although tantalizing!), the root beer, (!) and the fact that I finally got inside a frat house up here! Otherwise the *dance* smelled—to me, anyway. Why don't you come to Syracuse and start a dancing school? They sure need one!

How are your Lenten resolutions holding out? You have me in the cheering section, pulling for you. That's a nice piece of giving-up you're doing—if you're still doing it!

I'm slipping in with this volume of scribbling a few pictures taken up here, in the hopes that they'll stir you to send *your* long-promised photos! You can keep that silly one of me with my mouth hanging open and I'd like an equally charming snapshot of you. The one you showed me—standing in water, pants rolled up, mouth hanging open, laughing—I like. Either that or another little thing like it. O.K.?

I'll be dogging the postman until next time!

Sincerely, Ginny

P.S. If the silly picture of me is too crazy, return, and I'll send you another model!

The day after this letter, Ginny asks her diary, "Wonder how near to love my feeling for him is?" The "him" in question was George, not Elmer. Her Easter vacation included excursions with George to the movies and the aquarium, as well as bowling and dancing with El. One of these excursions resulted in "a bit of a fight" with George. At the end of the week, in an entry she titled "The fateful Sunday," Ginny reports that George handed her a note suggesting "maybe we shouldn't go steady etc." Days later, back at Syracuse, she muses in her diary, "Miss George like the devil. Sometimes I wonder if I do love him!"

April 9, 1940 – Germany invades and occupies Denmark and Norway

---

Virginia – April 15, 1940 [a greeting card
that asks, "Why Not Write"?]

Wanted! ✳ Information on what has become of *Elmer ("El") Odell* (Name) When last seen looked like this→[the card includes a mirror] .Was last heard from about *March 1, 1940!!* In the vicinity of *Roosevelt, and Hempstead.* Is known to be subject to writer's cramp. Can be identified by: dry condition of fountain pen, absence of stationery, and as evidently having less than 3¢ in possession. Is believed to be fairly intelligent. Anyone with information notify *Ginny Schill Immediately* ! ✳ Pin this up in a prominent spot.

If sick, get well quick—If dead, sympathy—If married, congratulations—If not, why "censored" don't you write!?!?!??! *Or*—if *mad*, why Please??

Elmer – April 16, 1940

Dear Ginny

Knock! Knock!—Who's there?—

Elmer—Elmer who?—Elmer Odell—What the *!!@??* does *he* want!

He should be ashamed to show his face after not keeping his promise to write promptly—He wants to apologize for not writing sooner. He says he's sorry and that he doesn't think it will happen again.—Well, if he's really sorry, let him come in.—Silly, isn't it.

I just received your little poster and it's very cute. Thank you. The only thing that's missing is the amount of the reward. Answer to your little quiz on the bottom of your posted.

> Not dead;—apparently
> Not sick;—feeling fine
> Not mad;—why should I be?
> Not married;—although it's not a bad idea
> No writing;—no excuse

El and Jack

Everything is pretty dull around this burg now, but the future looks promising. For instance, Wednesday, Sid and I are going to see "Hellza Poppin." Sat. nite Jack and I are going to the Senior play (What a Life). [Jack LaMar, another close boyhood friend, was a "ladies' man." He referred to El's mom as "Mother #2".] Then in a couple of weeks there is a prospective week-end party coming off out in Jamesport. So you see the immediate future looks pretty bright. Oh yes, I forgot, we are beginning to rehearse our play [at the bank] which comes off late in May or early June.

As ever, Elmer

In an April 19, 1940 diary entry, after attending "a peace convo," Virginia writes, "Gee, I'm scared to death that we might get into this war! I want to do something to make other people *think* and realize the horror and the probability of our entrance—but I don't know what to do!" A couple weeks later Elmer appends to a letter, mostly about music, these lines from a poem he wrote about the World War, titled "I've Been Told":

Mothers and fathers gave their sons
To be quickly slaughtered by foreign guns.
Fearless youth, so recklessly bold;
I don't remember but I've been told.
Once more the Allies cry for men.
So pray to God we don't fall again.
T'was a bloody ordeal when the war drums
   rolled.
I don't remember but I've been told.

Virginia – May 2, 1940 11:30 a.m.

Dear El,

    This weekend is hot stuff up here. It's Spring weekend, officially, and that means a lot of things. Friday, that's tomorrow night, Mal Hallett (supposed to be pretty good—popular in New England) is playing for a dance. I even get a *1:30* [curfew] permission which is cause for celebration in itself! Saturday is Women's Day or Moving-Up Day—I become a superior sophomore with 10 o'clock permissions on week nights instead of the usual 8! Sat. a.m. at 6 (!) heralds gallop around on horses with bugles (the girls have the bugles, not the horses). Their main idea is to make racket enough to make students, weary as always, get up to throw a brick at them. Once the student is out of bed, he realizes what day it is, calms himself, also dresses himself, and takes same self over to the Chapel for an outdoor breakfast of strawberries in cream, etc. Nice, no?

After breakfast there's a parade of floats and in the afternoon all the women get together and put on a pageant. I hear it's a riot, especially the costumes they get rigged out in. My English prof describes their activities as "cavorting" so you can imagine!

Sat. night, along with other things (traditions, etc.), the sororities, frats, and some living centers have open houses. Anybody can waltz in, dance around a while, and trip out when they please. It's all very lovely.

♫♪♯♫♪♯ department: I've heard all the records you bought except "No Name Jive" which no doubt is a killer. G. Miller's "Penna. 6-5000" is *!!!!!!* It folded *me* up too the first time. Now I just melt! His "Polka Dots and Moonbeams" *is* beautiful. Did I mention before B. Goodman's "Beyond the Moon"? That is one *mellow* disc!

About your poem—all I can say is "them's my sentiments exactly"! I get so *mad* whenever I think of the World War and then realize that they're doing it *again*! And I *do* pray to God we won't be suckers again. Gee, I get so sore about it, but I don't know anything I can *do* to make other people realize how stupid any war is! Let's get together and purchase a large soap box. We can take turns exhorting the mob to *think* instead of just *feel*!

I'm glad you're one of the ones who doesn't get all hopped up about "killing those awful Germans"—oh no, it's Hitler we're all against, isn't it? Not the German people, oh no! Those are the very same lines they used in the last one!

We read some darn good poetry in English, written by the war poets—the fellows who were actually in it, Wilfred Owen, Siegfried Sassoon, & Robert Graves. Owen is the best. Here's one of *his* best:

If in some smothering dreams you too could pace
Behind the wagon that we flung him in,
And watch the white eyes writhing in his face . . .
My friend, you would not tell with such high zest
To children ardent for some desperate glory,
The old Lie; Dulce et Decorum est
Pro patria mori.

"Dulce et Decorum Est"—from that old Latin line of Horace—"It is sweet and honorable to die for one's country."

Write again soon, Ginny

As you may have surmised by now, Elmer, like the great majority of Americans then, held strong isolationist views. He was also a Republican, and although at that time too young to vote, was distrustful of President Roosevelt's intentions for his country vis-à-vis the war in Europe. On May 10, 1940, Germany invaded Belgium, Luxembourg, and Holland, prompting Virginia to note in her diary, "War seems *so* imminent, people so darned *dumb*, willing to go—I get so *mad, worried, scared stiff* we will enter!" In late May, the British began evacuating troops from Dunkirk, France, and a few days later Churchill declared in a speech before the House of Commons, "We shall fight on the beaches, we shall fight on the landing grounds, we shall fight in the fields and in the streets, we shall fight in the hills; we shall never surrender . . ." By June 14, the Nazis had occupied Paris.

During this same period, Elmer turned eighteen, while Virginia finished her first year at Syracuse and headed home for the summer. Her diary shows that both George and El continued to compete for her attention, while Virginia remained uncertain of her feelings, lamenting, "Wish I *knew* that I love George (or don't)!" Virginia got a summer job at the *Nassau Daily Review-Star* as a correspondent. By July George ceded the field, taking a summer job in Charleston, West Virginia. A few days after his departure, Virginia declares, "I'm quite sure now that I'll never love him and he's not the one for me. I'm rather upset about it all."

Virginia saw a lot of El over the summer. "El came over this aft. With his car he just bought. It's a very nice jalopy." "El called

this a.m. We spent the day Lindying & swimming at Hempstead beach. Good time. He came over later tonight. We danced, went out for a soda, danced, talked. Had a swell day." George returned in early September, and she tells

Elmer with his sister and mother.

him, "*when* he asked, that I *didn't* miss him much this summer," and gives him an ultimatum: "He's going to work this year, learn something, be somebody. If not, it's all over."

On that note, Virginia returned to Syracuse for her sophomore year, delivered there by her parents, who were, unusually for the time, embarking on a cross-country road trip to California and back. In her first letter to El after her return, she thanks him for "a *lot* of good times this summer."

On September 7, the German Luftwaffe began bombing London and other civilian targets in England, and on September 16, the Selective Service Act, establishing the first peacetime draft in US history, for men between the ages of twenty-one and thirty-six, was signed into law by President Roosevelt.

Virginia – September 22, 1940 2:30 a.m.

Dear El,

Here's an idea I thought up the other day: I noticed that the weekend after the 7th, when you planned to come up, is Colgate weekend, 16th, which is a traditionally "Big" weekend. I must have told you about it last year. Anyway, we play Colgate, and everybody gives his right eye to win, *and* there's a dance that night. Of course, that Monday isn't a holiday for you which is what makes the problem. I was wondering if perhaps you'd rather come for Colgate weekend, *if* you could get that Saturday off. Since it's your job and your boss, I don't know. I'm just suggesting. Colgate weekend *is*, though, the high point of the football season. What do you think?

Keep up the penwork, El. It's swell! Good morning!

Ginny

Elmer – September 24, 1940

Dear Ginny:

Your suggestion of my coming up there Colgate weekend sounds very excellent, delectable, delicious, beautiful etc; the piéce de resistance as it were. I'll try my darnedest to get that Saturday off. Hey, I just happened to think, (astounding, isn't it?), I might just cruise up into New York State, and, if that is the case, I will undoubtedly stop off in Syracuse. So, who knows, you may see me some time in the middle of next month.

Last Saturday Norman and I went swimming down to Point Lookout. Well, the water was warm, the sun was shining, everything was beautiful, until we started for home. Then it began to rain. I say it rained. This is about the grossest understatement I have ever uttered. Driving along the parkway was like swimming under water. And then it happened. With a gurgle and a gasp, and a choke, my motor stopped dead. So Norman and I stripped down to our bathing suits and pushed the car up on the grass. Then, having nothing better to do we had a water fight in a mud puddle in the rain. Some fun! After we were out in the rain a while, we came back to consciousness and I walked about a mile to a phone where I could call my Pop and have him come give us a push. All ended happily except for the fact that my Pop was just a wee bit aggravated.

Jack and Norman & I went for a ride Sunday and I had the roof down for the first time. I really looked schnazzy.

Well, I've taken up too much of your time already, so, like the Arab, I quickly fold my tent and silently slip away into the night.

As Ever, Elmer

**September 27, 1940 – Germany, Italy, and Japan
sign the Tripartite Pact, creating the Axis Alliance**

Virginia – September 28, 1940 8:30 p.m.

Dear El,

Was the undersigned glad to hear you're coming up next month!!! Of course, you didn't say you were *definitely*, but it's a very nice thought! Will you let me know if and about when you expect to hit Syracuse while "cruising through N.Y. state"? The cottage is planning a hay ride and dance (of a sort) and if I know when you're coming, I'll try to maneuver the date conveniently.

Gee, I wish I could have been in the water fight with Norman and you. I've always wanted to get *soaking* in a lovely downpour (of cats & dogs, of course)—but I was always *slightly* afraid that the boys from Islip [referring to the psychiatric hospital] would be after me if I were seen standing alone, drooping, and *dripping* on our front lawn!

I've been reading the paper religiously to follow the campaign of the stupid Mr. Willkie. Sorry, El, but I *do* think he's dumb—at least *politically*. He no more knows how to act or what to say than N.Y.C.'s lowliest street-sweeper! Well, he's not a smart politician, anyway! And guess what I did today? Joined the Democratic party here! I'll be doing various things until election time—I don't know just what it'll be though. We got the opportunity to work with the party through our Political Science II course. I've never been so convinced that W. Willkie has *nothing* to offer, as is realized with the question "Just what one part of F.D.R.'s program will he amend or change in any way?" Answer: Not *one*!

Listened to an album of Jimmy Yancy doing wonderful Boogie Woogie numbers. It was swell! All this happened at the Varsity Swing Shop where, as I've probably told you before, you can go and hear all the platters you want. Heard G. Miller's "Blueberry Hill" while I was at it. I think that's the best one of it. Have you heard Lionel Hampton's "Central Avenue Breakdown"? Dancing reminds me that I've been having classes in the Lindy lately. About everyone in the house knows it now and outsiders are asking to learn it! Maybe I'll convert 'em yet! They're all waiting (with bated breath) for you to come up. They seem to have heard *somehow* that you can dance like nobody else I know! Marvelous this grape-vine system!

So write again soon, honey boy. Don't *ever* think you're
"wasting" my time!—And what a *book* this has turned out to be!!
["honey boy"? That's a first.]

> Ginny

Elmer – October 7, 1940 2:30 p.m.

Dear Ginny:

I thought of you last night; (Not that I'm not always thinking of
you); Artie Shaw and his new band was on the Fitch Bandwagon
[radio show] and he played "Begin the Beguine." Perhaps you
heard him? If not, you really missed something swell. He played
his new "Concerto For Clarinets"—kinda smooth—wow! I was
disappointed;—he didn't play "Frenesi."

I feel kind of ashamed of myself. Here I boldly take my
pay envelope from the Bank every two weeks and practically
give nothing in return; so I'll close this letter and try to ease my
conscience with a little work.

> As ever and with love, Elmer

Virginia – October 12, 1940 midnight

Dear El,

Ain't this an awful hour for me to be up? And, worse than
the hour, I've been drinking *cider* [hard, apparently] until I'm
almost *out*! Oh, it's awful, this college life! Going straight to the
hounds!

What a night! (Here you may hear a soft, slow whistle
through the teeth [Virginia had a gap between her upper fronts],
indicating the type of night!) About 5/8 of a moon, warmishly cool

(isn't that definite?), soft breeze slapping all the leaves (slightly dead) together and producing a sound like rain,—and me, crying into my cider. And why? Why must I dilute my cider thus? Is it because I can't take it so strong? No, the stronger the better, is my drunken reply. It *might* be because of the long delay in writing (I mean *my* long delay) that I shed bitter tears. Or it might very well be the "I'm sorry for myself." I can think of better places to be on nights like as to this'un! With sadness I recall that moonlit night (here a quavering voice causes me to pause, take a long swig of that potent brew, and go on) when we pursued "They Drive By Night" [Humphrey Bogart movie]—and didn't we though!!

Oh, cut out the foolishness, Schill. (Aside to myself!) (Soliloquy, you might say!) Get on to saying something!—All right, all right!!!

Did you perchance, hear G. Miller larst Wednesday night. His program sounded like a request program—request coming from you or me. It included (to make you mad if you didn't hear it "Beat Me, Daddy, . . ." (too slow but not bad), "Blueberry Hill," the new "You Got Me This Way" (cute), and "Bugle Call Rag" (I think). Veddy nice!

I've gotta go over Wednesday a.m. to the Student Union (where we're holding the thing) and see if I can inveigle the man what changes the records on the juke box to put in some good ones for ye dance. We'll probably have a pile of nickels stacked up for use but what's the use if the records aren't so hot for dancing? [They were popularly called nickelodeons for that reason.]

I saw some kids Lindying tonight!! Sorta jumping, or bouncy Lindying, but *Lindying*. The people up here coitny [county] are no-good dancers!

Suppose I told you about my democratic activities. Yesterday three of us did some canvassing for Roosevelt, asking people if they'd registered yet, handing out propaganda, etc. Poor as the section was, despite the *holes* that they were living in, (we were working in a slum area, more or less) nevertheless they were more polite, friendly, and more decent than people of the middle class were to door-bell ringers. It was darn interesting.

Can you guess? (Ginny)

The stamps on Elmer's letters now begin appearing upside-down, a semaphore of love. Virginia notes in her diary about this time, "Wondering what happened to George and telling myself I don't care."

Elmer – October 15, 1940 9:45 a.m.

Dear Ginny:

I came to work happy as a lark because this is my last week of work before vacation. My spirits soared even more when I opened the mail and saw your letter among the rest. And then I opened it. Immediately my happiness deflated and I descended to the lowest depths of despondency. Your reminiscing took me back to the moonlight flooded night when we searched, almost in vain, for an open gas station. I too became melancholy, only I have no cider to cry into.

But that mood passes and I am happy again, when I think how soon I shall be in Syracuse. My jalopy is straining at its leash and raring to go.

Ginny, I'm glad I'm not coming up this week; you really wouldn't know me. My nickname should be changed from "Carnation Kid" to "Scarface." I have been marred by a nice long gash running from the outside corner of my left eye to the bottom of my nose. Really quiet fetching. The latest thing in men's wear this year. How did it happen, you ask? Football. You see, I had just tackled a fellow in the accepted method, but some of my teammates didn't think I did such a good job. The guy was still alive. So a few of them promptly piled on, feet first, and a shoe, with a cleat on one end, and a leg on the other caught me in the kisser. Well, this may not be exactly how it happened, but I did get a cleat in the face, playing football. My mother is adverse to football so I told her I was watching Norman chop wood and a piece flew up and struck me. She even believed me.

Did you hear Glenn M. last night? W.J.Z. 7:30 to 8:*00*. He was playing from the Café Rouge, and he played "Stonewall Jackson." Mellow! I'm glad to hear you found someone "Lindying" up there. It shows we're making progress in other sectors.

Well I must be off. I have a bit of work to do so I'll see you later.

Love, Elmer.

Virginia – October 18, 1940 5:25 p.m.

Dear El.

I woulda writ last night to you, scarface dear, but it was too far *not* night—or, to put it simply, it was morning and the urge for sleep was overpowering. Even now, I greatly fear this will be interrupted while I eat what is called dinner.

1:20 a.m. *See*—what did I tell ya! And if you're wondering how much I could eat in 13 hours, I might say other events intervened. After eating, I became very glamorous (no laughter, please) in that tomato-red dress I was telling you about (once), and hied myself to a Sigma Alpha Epsilon pledge dance. It was veddy nice—good orchestra, nice people—but I can't say a lot for my date's dancing ability. I think I'll be doing the box in my sleep!! Gad zooks! (Where have I heard that.?)

I'm really sorry to have taken the wind out of your happy sails with my melancholy story of last letter. No cider tonight, no moon (hope it doesn't rain tomorrow), no reminiscing—only looking into the future.

Fie for shame, for so deceiving your mother about the cut on your face! Ain't you 'shamed? No? Well I hope it's O.K., anyway.

                              Ginny

Elmer's visit, chronicled in Virginia's diary, was a whirl of dancing, football games, roller-skating, and classes—made even more hectic by a surprise visit from Virginia's parents, on their way back home after their cross-country trip. A few days later, Virginia reports in her diary, "wrote a letter to George, finally, and told him how he stands. What now? I wonder."

October 28, 1940 – Italy invades Greece

                              Elmer – October 31, 1940

Dear Ginny:

I wish I was back in Syracuse. Nothing doing around here. Mom won't let me take my car out until I get the brakes fixed, so I'm pretty well stranded. Gad zooks, I'd like to be seeing Charlie Barnet [bandleader] up there with you tonight.

Ginny, I can see now that I should never have left home. While I was away someone has been conducting subversive activities around here, and come home to find my mother has become pro-Roosevelt. Now I am alone in my beliefs. Everyone here is against me.

Ginny, could you get me some literature on Syracuse U.? Such as tuition, fees, subjects, etc. I want to go to school next fall, and I'm seriously considering Syracuse. Guess why?

Gee I had fun up there. I'd like to spend about nine months of the year up there. Hmm maybe I will yet. Who knows?

Well, Mom just decided she wants some painting done so I'll be moving along.

Love, El.

P.S. Write soon. Gad zooks but I miss you.

Virginia – November 1, 1940 11:45 p.m.

Dear El,

Congratulate your mother for her intelligent reformation. She will also enjoy my Democratic propaganda now! Just wait! Some very optimistic Willkie fan tonight bet me 50¢ that he'd win! Can you imagine it? I also expect to win about 10 cokes from a fellow Daily Orange [Syracuse University's student-run newspaper] reporter. Poor deluded beings!

I'm both glad and sorry that you miss the Salt City (and me, if I must say it!). The reason why I'm glad is obvious, and I'm sorry because it's hardly a happy state.

Instead of class on Tues., we're to go to a polling booth (pronounced boot) and watch the proceedings, legitimate and otherwise. Good fun!

Sure 'nuff I could get you literature on S.U.! I'll start a "Literature for El" collection tomorrow and have them piled and ready for you Nov. 16. Or do you want it sooner? Anyway I'll be very happy to assist you in your research. Bye the way, aren't you a Methodist? This was originally a Methodist school. Maybe you could even get a scholarship of one kind or another. There are a number of church scholarships, I think.

I ought to go to bed.—The time from Friday (2:15) to Tuesday (5:37) was wonderful! I had a swell time, El. Next star on my calendar, Colgate weekend!

Ginny

This is a revised edition or addition to last night's letter.

Miss Walberg [cottage-mate] has a huge "fun book" and among other games, etc., in the thing are directions for reading handwriting. After doing a few and finding that most people's

How is everyone in ~~to~~ Wilbur? How is the girl with the bad throat? Is she out of the infirmary yet? I hope,

are the same, I concluded that it was screwy. Anyway, you, according to the book and your handwriting, are "straightforward, dependable, honest, lacking initiative or active ambition,* subject to prejudices (this last based on slope of writing and it adds that: this slope reflects pessimistic mood, although it doesn't necessarily follow that the writer's nature is habitually pessimistic"!). The next installment in your character (à la handwriting) will be sent upon request! [We'll spare you further analysis.]

*One of the better parts!!!

Missing you, Ginny

The following few weeks were eventful ones: on November 5, Roosevelt was re-elected, by an overwhelming margin, to an unprecedented third term in office. In a letter, Elmer congratulates Virginia on the victory, warning, "Don't get drunk on all those 'cokes' you won." He also reports receiving a promotion at the bank.

On November 10, Virginia turned nineteen and on November 16 she welcomed Elmer and his father to Syracuse for Colgate

weekend, reporting in her diary: "Game— and a wonderful one, although we lost to Colgate 7-6!! Then to the Hotel Syracuse for dinner with Mr. Odell. We danced and got attention—a crowd & the spotlights!!! That wasn't all. A marvelous band, good singer, made the Soph dance swell—and we put on."

Virginia – November 18, 1940 2:45 p.m.

Dearest El,

Gloomy Monday! What a bleak, cold day! And even if the sun were out in all its glory, I'm sure I'd feel just as bad.

There's really no reason why I should write now. There's nothing to say that you don't know already. I had a perfectly *wonderful* weekend. Everything was swell—all because you are. Now I'm just going to work and try to get through 4 weeks and three days as quickly as possible. If they go by like this last weekend, I'll be home next week!

Please write immediately if not sooner. I am missing you very much and so far today have spent all my waking hours thinking about you and the weekend. The kids in the house think I've lost a large part of my mind. I can't even carry on an intelligent conversation! Just mumble blankly. Sad case!

Gloomily yours, Ginny

Elmer – November 19, 1940 9:40 p.m.

My dearest Ginny:

You say you miss me. I am glad to hear this but I don't see how it can compare with the emptiness of everything around here now that I'm not with you.

When I got to work yesterday morn I was about as unhappy as I have ever been in my life, and I must have showed it. Everyone in the bank thought I was still sick from Saturday [he'd called in sick to go to Syracuse]; so that wasn't so bad. I made more errors on adding machines yesterday! I would look on the keyboard for a number, but all that would be written on the keys was Ginny, Ginny, Syracuse, Ginny. I've got it bad.

I'm glad you had a good time Sat. & Sun. I know I never had a better time in my life. There was only one thing wrong with it. It was too short.

Well I shall stop living and go back to merely existing until I hear from you again. So—

All my love, Elmer

Virginia – November 24, 1940 2:00 p.m.

Dearest El,

Unhappiness again! I went to an engineer's semi-formal at the Onondaga Hotel Friday night and again almost or could have died because the music was so good and you were in Roosevelt. Gee, I wish other fellows could dance as well as you do, or you didn't, or you were here, or something. Honestly, El, dancing with anyone else is worse than just listening to good music and not having anyone to dance with! It's maddening! I don't even care about going to dances anymore! What a sad condition! [Virginia expressed these same thoughts in her diary, adding, "I like to dance only with El, I'm afraid!"]

Whenever you might think on the Salt City or the undersigned, you can bet dollars to doughnuts I'm thinking of you.

Inexpressibly, *Ginny*

Elmer – November 26, 1940 9:00 p.m.

My Dearest Ginny:

It's snowing. It reminds me of Saturday, morning, Nov. 16 (as if I have to be reminded!) I've got all the symptoms. I wander around in a daze whenever I think of you, and the wonderful times we've had together in Syracuse.

Did you ever notice that bad luck comes in bunches. I am in the throes of one of these bunches. Most of it concerns my jalopy. First of all I spent a buck [$17.25 today] for anti-freeze. Then my wagon blew a manifold gasket and when the mechanic fixed it, he broke the wall of the water jacket in the block and later all my anti-freeze ran off into the street. So I had to buy some more. Thanksgiving afternoon Norman and I were out riding and as I was passing another car on the right (tsk! tsk!) he (the other driver) decides to pull into a driveway on the right. Wham! Net result; one battered running board. Everything settled happily. Then Saturday night, Norman and Jack and I were ripping along Grand avenue in Baldwin, when some guy makes a U-turn in front of me. You guessed it. Wham! Net result; one crumpled fender for him, one *pleated* fender; one drooping bumper (which eventually fell off); one bent steering assembly; one license plate (lost in transit) for me. We couldn't decide whose fault it was, so we decided the expense would be dutch treat. Everybody happy. (Oh yeah!). But the worst of my hard luck I consider is my not being able to see you. Oh woe.

All my love, Elmer

Virginia – December 1, 1940 2:15 a.m.

Dearest El,

Two accidents in three days is more than *anybody* needs! Maybe Mr. Odell should not pass on the right! Jeeps, if you're not careful, you'll be driving a skeleton of a car, what with everything else beaten off!! And maybe you, too, will be somewhat skeletonized, if you see what I mean!

Your condition, though a sad one, makes me not the least bit unhappy. I figure it's 'cause I'm naturally cold-hearted. However, considering the two accidents and the probability of future mishaps if no remedy is effective, I'm worried. Even this anxiety, though, isn't enough to make me tell you to stop thinking of me. I suggest you get a few good books or study chemistry or something—thereby directing your attention to worthwhile subjects. (And seriously, if you've never read Shakespeare's love sonnets, you ought to. They're beautiful.)

Your state of heart makes me, in this wilderness, feel much better. About every other minute I think of something I'd like to do with you—from sliding down the path from H L [Hall of Languages] to reading Shakespeare! El, how I wish you were here! I miss you very much.

Ginny

Virginia – December 5, 1940

Dearest El,

It's been snowing almost all week. Furthermore, it was *cold* like anything yesterday—3 below. Lovely weather we're having!

I'm disgusted with the infirmary. Last year I got my feet frost bitten and took them over there for inspection. The good doctor looked at me in shoes (you've heard of those things, haven't you?) and ankle socks and says, "I'm not at all surprised. Look at the way you're dressed! You should be wearing—etc, etc, blah!" And he concluded, "Keep your feet warm & dry." So, I leaves.

This year I again suffer foot trouble. For a couple of weeks the right appendage has been unhappy, so again, I trudges thru snow to the infirmary, hoping that *this* time it will be something really serious. What happens? "It's no wonder," monsieur le docteur says, "your foot hurts." It gotten too cold—etc.—and you should wear boots, overshoes, stockings, etc!" Very disgruntled am I! I left, but I'll be darned If I'll wear huge clumsy boots all over the place, reasons being 1) every other coed in seven counties has a pair *just like* I'd have to get, 2) They'd look almost as silly on me as knee socks, 3) and besides, my foot isn't in *that* bad a condition!

To work, to work, I'm afraid. When I get home, I expect to catch up on a half a year's sleep. Picture of me now:

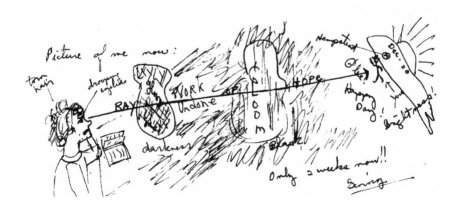

Only two weeks now, Ginny

Elmer – December 8, 1940 9:15 p.m.

Dearest Ginny:

I am so overcome I can hardly write. I have just been listening to
G. Miller and I have never heard him play a better set of numbers.
First of all he started off with "Wham." Need I say more? Then I
sat ~~spl~~ spellbound as Eberle sang "A Nightingale sang on Barkley
Square." Man Alive! Did I wish I was with you then. To top things
off he swung out with his arrangement of the "Anvil Chorus."
Would Wagner turn over in his grave if he could hear that.

   This afternoon, Jack & I went over to La Guardia field to
watch the planes come zooming in and go zooming out. While we
were there I had an ~~awe~~ overwhelming desire to sneak in a plane
and fly to ~~Seyr~~ Syracuse, but I thought Mayor La Guardia might
not like it and anyway I can't fly, so I had to be content to come
home and re-read some of your letters and answer your latest. We
went into the Kitty Hawk Cocktail Lounge at the airport. What a
schnazzy place that is. The bartender actually asked me to remove
my hat while standing at the bar.

   You will notice as you wade through this letter, that every so
often you will find a word very sloppily crossed out. I wish to point
out that this is not ~~do~~ due to poor spelling. It is due, I might add,
to the fact, that for some unaccountable reason, every so often the
pen I am using will not write a word exactly as I think it, but shoots
hither and yon over the paper of its own accord, so that when I do
get control of ~~its~~ it again, I have to go back and ~~croos~~ cross off the
~~dama~~ destruction it has wrought. Sounds absurd, doesn't it? But I
assure you it is true.

   All my love, El

Elmer – December 12, 1940

Dearest Ginny:

Fate dealt me a terrible blow. I bought Will Bradley's "Scrub Me Mamma" and played it on my portable. Well, I figured as long as I had my vic out, I might as well play some of my other records. I picked up Bob Chester's "Easy Does It." Zooks! Big chunks were missing from this platter. For a moment I stood aghast, then a terrifying thought struck me. "suppose more records were broken?" I examined them and my worst fears were realized. G. Miller's "Slow Freight"—cracked; Artie Shaw's "Begin the Beguine"—hunk missing; Miller's "Indian Summer"—hunk missing; Miller's "Pa. 6-5000"—cracked; disheartening, isn't it? That's the last time I lend my records to friends (?)

I've just got my chug-buggy fixed. It's been laid up for more than a week with a run down battery. It runs now but it's a pretty sorry looking mess. I really think it's ashamed to go out on the street with other nice new cars. Yesterday morning I went out and found it crying. No, I'm wrong. It was just the radiator leaking.

Well, I think I've been raving long enough so I'll just throw in a period and say good night, good afternoon or good morning, whenever you happen to get this letter.

Thinking of you constantly, love, El

Virginia – December 15, 1940 10:30 a.m.

Dearest El,

Gee—that's awful about your records! Six records ruined! Zounds! I'd throw a fit or two for the benefit of the "friends" (?)! They should be kicked to death by rabbits or chewed by red ants or something equally as pleasant. You have my deepest sympathy.

I'd suggest that you take your "chug-buggy" aside some day and lecture it quietly on the beauties of old age—philosophically of course! After all, this inferiority complex shouldn't go on. Part of its broken spirit is your fault, you know! How would *you* like someone to knock *your* fenders, bumpers, and running board (or their analogies) battered by two accidents? All right then!

Friday, about five, coming back from the Student Union we were looking at a gorgeous sunset and when we turned around, there was the full moon, just above the horizon, in a sky of deep purple. It was actually breathtaking! What beauty! Ever since then that same moon has haunted me. Last night—the moon, almost blinding it was so bright, stars all over, dark blue sky, and *cold!*—I could have died a not-too-happy death.

Ginny

On December 20, Virginia returned home from Syracuse for the holidays—reuniting with relatives and friends, partying, dancing, staying up late. George made a visit, and they returned the jewelry they'd given each other over the years. "Decided we could still go out, but the thrill is gone for me."

Despite that, perhaps grasping at straws, George gave her a leather correspondence case for Christmas. Elmer gave her the novel *Oliver Wiswell* (which he reported reading in an earlier letter, telling her approvingly that it "takes sides with the Tories and considers the revolutionists a bunch of worthless rabble") and a Waterman pen and pencil set. She gave him a cigarette lighter.

A couple of days later Elmer and Virginia went club-hopping, ending up at the Biltmore in Manhattan, where they danced to music by Will Bradley and his band. "Had a lot of fun. El told me he loves me!"

Falling in Love

ELMER AND VIRGINIA SPENT New Year's Eve like many young couples—more parties, dancing, staying up late. Virginia reports in her diary, "Getting very mellow with El. We went for a ride about 4:30, watched it get light near the water—a wonderful time!—then got home at *seven*. Mom & Pop returned [New Year's is a Catholic Holy Day, and they had gone to Mass.] and I was taken down a peg or two by Mom. She was undoubtedly worried and I'm awfully sorry about being the cause. We both broke down and then made up."

George was still waiting in the wings too. Virginia reports, "George called this afternoon. I got so mad at him I hung up—he made some not-too-complimentary remark about Marie. The more I see of him, the less I like him."

And the war in Europe raged on. The Luftwaffe air raids on London and other English cities continued into 1941, and U-boats controlled the Atlantic. War crept inexorably closer to America. On January 6, FDR gave his "Four Freedoms" speech, calling for freedom of speech and worship, and freedom from want and fear.

Virginia returned to Syracuse on January 5. "Classes were sleepy but I soon got to feel as though I'd never been home, even

though it was only last night El was with me. Hard to believe—
so near chronologically, but geographically—!"

Virginia – January 6, 1941 7:00 a.m.
[Her upside-down stamps begin now.]

Hello Honey!

Gee, El, I can't stop thinking of you and the wonderful time I had
these last two weeks! Every minute I was with you was swell, and
I'm not kidding. All the way up here "♫ I thought about you ♫,"
even during the few hours I slept. What a life! Perfect for two weeks
and grinding for three months! They'd better go fast or I'll go
crazy!

Wishing with all my heart you were with me, I'll try to sleep
for an hour. I would have so liked to take the next train to New
York!

Deep sigh of longing at this point.

Love, Ginny

Elmer – January 6, 1941 1:35 a.m.

My Dearest Ginny:

Here I've only been away from you about an hour and a half, and
I miss you like the devil already.

I had a swell time the past two weeks. I only hope you
enjoyed yourself half as much as I did. It's going to seem pretty
dead around here from now until Easter.

Now I want you to forget about me and Hempstead and
concentrate on your studies. I will be very disappointed if you don't
get a straight "A" on your exams. You keep your mind on your

work and I'll think about you and also think about me for you. Okay?

All my love, El

Virginia – January 7, 1941 9:15 p.m.

Dearest El,

I got your letter this morning at 8. I read it before going to class at 9 and I was *happy* going to zoology lecture, which is an unusual condition for me. Thanks for making me happy, *not* an unusual thing for you. However, there are a couple of things I must tell you.

1) *I can't forget you!!* What a silly idea! Forgetting Hempstead, impossible as it is, is a *cinch* compared to driving El out of the gray matter! Please don't ask it of me. Thanks for offering to do my thinking about you for me, but I'll be happy enough if you just think about me once in a while. I'll do my own "thinking" anyway, so you may as well not bother!

2) It is *very* doubtful whether I can get a straight "A". Journalism and poli sci are the two *main* worries and zoo. is very weak. For you, though, and also for myself, Mom & Pop, of course, I'll do my best. You can say a prayer or two. Maybe that will help.

I miss you very much, El, Ginny

Virginia – January 9, 1941 1:15 p.m.

Dearest El,

My pen writes simply *"sharply"*! I'm glad the things it writes are satisfying to you, also. Your pen does very well at making me happy! Everybody who's seen the set has admired it, which is hardly strange. Every time I look at them, I like them more. If things go on this way, my love for them will forbid me to use them and I'll be spending my spare time polishing them and arranging them in a plush-lined box! Well—that's a rough idea!

    I just thought that I'm *glad* it's snowing. Now I won't be bothered with that darn moon that's been beaming brightly at me. Why don't we have a moon on Long Island now and then?

Love, Ginny

Pen sets were an important part of this writing culture. This was before the advent of ballpoints or rollerballs, so these were fountain pens. Filled from an ink bottle, they fed ink to the paper via a metal quill not much different than the split bird feathers used to sign the Declaration of Independence. The other writing instrument in the set was usually a mechanical pencil.

But not only were their pens distinctive. Their stationery was as well. Special-ordered in colors like ecru or soft blue, each page was embossed with three letterhead initials, and the envelopes bore the writer's return address on the back flap. This was serious correspondence!

About this time there was some back-and-forth teasing discussion of drinking. Elmer suggests a cure for insomnia: "First of all you take a large size water glass and fill it to the brim with fine old Johnny Walker Black Label Scotch. (Red Label will not do.) Then taking the glass gently between thumb and forefinger of the right hand, take a good healthy draught of the contents. After this is done fill the glass with refreshing bubbling soda and sip at leisure. If this prescription is carried out to the letter I guarantee that you will never want to sleep again."

Virginia's retort: "In zoology lecture, this morning, we heard about the horrors of alcoholism. If I were a drinkin' woman, I'd be worried. From what the good prof says, it ain't good! A veddy interesting study—alcohol! And don't go reading things into my words, sir!'"

Virginia — January 20, 1941 4:30 p.m.

Dearest El,

I don't suppose you heard the president's inaugural address. It was good, very inspiring, and, as usual, able to be interpreted and appreciated by practically everyone. [And it's worth reading for its prescience for our times: "There are men who believe that democracy, as a form of government and a frame of life, is limited or measured by a kind of mystical and artificial fate, that, for some unexplained reason, tyranny and slavery have become the surging wave of the future—and that freedom is an ebbing tide. But we Americans know that this is not true."] If you give him credit for nothing else, you must admit the man's an *ace* at oratory. And what do you think of Willkie's seemingly friendly relationship with the administration? I should think the Republicans would burn!

Love, Ginny

Elmer — January 22, 1941 10:30 p.m.

Dearest Ginny:

This week I register for school. I will go on Wednesday nights from 5:45 to 9:30. This semester I take Economics I and Bank Org. I. They seem pretty dull but I'll see what I can do with them. The only thing wrong with night school is that too much emphasis is placed on homework. I write too few letters now. It will be even worse when I have homework to worry about.

All my love, El

P.S. I'll have to talk to the President and have him change Easter to February. I miss you too much.

At the end of January, Virginia came home for her semester break, deciding to surprise Elmer, reporting in her diary, "Train ride was long and I couldn't get much sleep. I was home about 7:30. Called El and he almost died. El came over. We listened to records until 11." And a few days later, "El had dinner here. Then we listened to records, played ping-pong for a while. Had a movie preview of Mom's first moving picture taking attempts [in Kodachrome, introduced in 1935]. Not at all bad. The West is gorgeous! What colors! I'd love to travel out there in a trailer!"

Virginia – February 4, 1941 1:20 p.m.

Dearest El,

I'm still not certain about whether it is better not to come home at all! At least, it would be a lot easier on my emotional status if I stayed here until May! Coming home is so wonderful but the price—going away from you again—is steep.

I think you should write a nice letter to Mr. Chase (the elder) and talk up the idea of a Syracuse branch with Odell as head of the block department. Never have I heard a better idea!

Love, Ginny

Elmer – February 6, 1941 10:15 p.m.

My Dearest Ginny:

Your suggestion that I speak to Mr. Chase (the elder) on the idea of
a Syracuse Branch is a good one but you see, I'm afraid Mr. Chase
(the Elder) will be indisposed for quite some time. As a matter of
fact, he's dead. Anyway, he had nothing to do with the founding of
Chase Bank. He was Sec. of Treasury under Lincoln and the bank
was merely named after him. However, I'll speak to Mr. Aldrich
(Chairman of the Board), and if you see a new building going up
around there, you'll know Chase is coming to Syracuse.

All my love, El

Virginia – February 6, 1941 3:45 p.m.

Dearest El,

I wonder how one person can be so unhappy! *Nothing* has
seemed right since Monday night. I don't feel like going to school
or working on the paper. I don't even feel like eating! Sleeping
even isn't very attractive. Doubtless I'll snap out of this blue state—I
always have before—but this one has lasted too long. All I want
to do or seem to be able to do is think of one El Odell—doggone
ya'!! Will April *ever* come? It looks hopelessly far away right now.

Yesterday afternoon Kathy [college housemate and lifelong
friend] and I saw "Gone With The Wind" for a second time. I
don't know why, exactly. It was as good as before, though *long* as
before, also.

For speech next Thursday we have to do some memory work
and I'm going to play around with Poe's "Raven," so maybe Easter

I can recite the lovely thing for you. It certainly is beautifully eerie and sad.

Love, Ginny

Virginia – February 7, 1941 11:10 p.m.

Dearest El,

Winter Carnival weekend! Ha! It rained all day today, making heaps of lovely slush for skiing and oceans of clean, fresh water for ice skating! The snow sculpturing, though, has mostly crumbled sadly.

I have gotten out of that awful "poor me" state, thank goodness. I've told myself I'm going to work and be somebody, now and in the future. Fame and fortune is what I want and that means work. So, I take things as they come and do my derndest each day. Some philosophy! Every now and then it gets lost in the sadness of partings but I manage to drag it out again, still shining and bright.

Oh well. To bed, "to sleep, perchance to dream." No complaints if of you, however!

Love, Ginny

Elmer – February 9, 1941 12:45 a.m.

My Dearest Ginny:

I received your letter dated Feb. 6 and it makes me both happy and sad. Happy because you say you think of me and sad because your peace of mind is in a very sad state. Unfortunately, Dr. Odell cannot prescribe a remedy for this disease, for you see he is suffering from the same symptoms.

I writ a poem:

Dreamers dream of things they love.
A summer breeze and stars above
A harvest moon and sparkling dew.
Me too; I dream of you.

All my love, El

Virginia – February 9, 1941 9:45 p.m.

Dearest El,

Not to be outdone in the literary or poetic field, I wrote this instead
of the usual message.

If I should say in one short line—I miss you—
And sign my name without another word,
You'd doubtless overlook the meaning in it
That would be obvious to you, were it heard.
If you could hear me tell you that I dream nights,
On the blue-skied days and grayish days, of you,
Then certainly you realize I want you.
I hope you would. With all my heart, I do!

Good night for a while!
Love, Ginny

Virginia – February 13, 1941 1:00 p.m.

Dearest El,

I do want to say Happy (or it may be merry, I'm not sure)
Valentine's Day. You should know, if you possibly don't, that I like

you as a gentleman, and—although I can think of a long list of things, when I try to drag them out into words on paper, they look silly and different from what I mean. Well, among other things, I like you because you like good music, because you like to learn, because you like good literature, yes—because you're a wonderful dancer!—maybe I could include it all by saying, because you like everything fine about life and living.

Anyway, feeble as this attempt is, I hope you now know I'm very much aware of you and your admirable qualities—now and all the time.

Love, Ginny

Elmer – February 14, 1941 9:30 p.m.

My Dearest Ginny:

I just received your latest letter a couple of hours ago, and it was the nicest Valentine I ever received. It had more thought behind it than any silly old card, and I really appreciate it.

Ginny, that poem of yours was very good. It really affected me deeply. Any further poetic attempts will be most graciously welcomed.

I can't write as fluently as you can or use the beautiful phraseology you do, but I have tried, in my letters, to let you know how I feel toward you. I think I have succeeded.

All my love, (and I mean it) El

In her diary, Virginia reports that she received a Valentine's card and letter from George: "I think the old feeling is creeping in on him, if it had left. Don't know as I feel anything, but I'm afraid I did it in my last letter. Better be careful, or I'll be in a very uncomfortable position!"

Virginia – February 15, 1941 9:55 p.m.

Dearest El,

Proctoring again! This time it's at one of the freshman cottages (9-12:30 35¢ per hr.!) and they certainly have been raising the devil. Nothing so noisy as frosh!

I'm listening, or trying to listen, to Toscanini conduct. The reception is pretty poor, though. He is certainly marvelous. He can get more cooperation from those 50 or so men than anyone alive.

!!?! Frosh!! A girl and her date just came in and turned off the symphony!! I can't complain, of course, but I could wring their necks, anyway, even if it's quite understandable!

Tuesday I heard Bertha Damon [author of the bestselling 1938 memoir *Grandma Called It Carnal*]. Although she was funny, I didn't like what she said, this being little enough! She's one of those "oh-this-younger-generation" age, sort of. At least, she's longing for or advocating a return to the principles of "the good old days" or her darn "grandma." The "simple things of life" are best. I have a funny feeling that "grandma" and her neighbors had one heck of a time popping corn of an evening, not so much because they *loved* popped corn but more because they didn't have a shiny car to hop into and go to a movie! She also intimated that the "young people of today" must have "made" entertainment, with which idea I violently disagree—or are you one of those awful youngsters who doesn't enjoy the woods on a beautiful spring day? Well—I do, too—and I'll bet most kids do, doggone her! She continually dealt in the *typical* and *trite*. But she did tell some very funny stories.

Sigrid Undset [Nobel Prize–winning novelist and refugee from Nazi-occupied Norway] was interesting but she was so obviously prejudiced, and biased, and full of *hate* for Germany,

Germans, and everything to do with them, that you couldn't believe anything she said in its entirety. For half of her lecture, I couldn't understand her, what with her accent and throaty voice. When I got used to that, she was a moving, very personal speaker, but oh-so-bitter. She said the Norwegians ask "Is it true or is it German?"!!

[Virginia's touchiness about Germans likely stemmed from her ethnic background. Her paternal grandfather, John Schill, emigrated from Germany. Her father Mainard, it was said, suffered feelings of shame for his German heritage during the First World War and the beginnings of the Second].

We're now hearing "No Name Jive"! Hmmm! At least I can think of you enjoying "Voices of Spring" and Strauss!

Love, Ginny

February 23, 1941 – The element plutonium is identified by scientists at the University of California at Berkeley

Elmer – February 24, 1941 10:30 p.m.

My Dearest Ginny:

I sit here writing with a pen in one hand and a can of ale in the other. You shouldn't send me things like that; you'll make a rummy out of me. Not that I don't appreciate it, the sentiment is beautiful, but you know I'm not a drinking man. Thank you very much anyway. It's a good thing you didn't send it after Wednesday. I'm giving up smoking and drinking for Lent.

I consider myself lucky to be here to write. Saturday Norman and I went for a hike and ended up around the foothills of Huntington or Syosset. We were pretty tired by then and we sat on a railroad trestle dangling our feet into space. In the distance we hear a train whistle but it sounded about a mile away. We sat there awhile and suddenly I looked up and saw a locomotive tearing around a bend, straight at us. Never have I seen two individuals move as fast as Norm and I did then. When the train passed, it was so close I could almost hear the engineer swearing at us.

Sunday I was a good boy and stayed home studying and listening to the New Philharmonic. I missed Toscanini Saturday night. I don't care too much for Wagner anyhow. He's a mite deep for me.

All my love, El

As you have by now surmised, Elmer and Virginia's taste in music was not confined to "Swing." And their love of classical music continued throughout their lives. At breakfast each morning they would tune to WQXR, "The Radio Station of the New York Times," and introduce their children to symphonic music.

Virginia – February 24, 1941 2:00 a.m.

Dearest El,

I wasn't too happy about the prospect of a night at the Castle [headquarters of the college newspaper] & publishing company. I got down there and found the night editor in a most upset physical condition. Indeed—he was not glowing with health, and this state kept up all night. So—although he stayed down, despite offers of relief from other junior editors—I was more or less official and took the paper through. He had made up the layout of the paper and a bunch of good writers had piled down to the office for no good reason. They zipped off the heads in beautiful order and we went to the publishing co., leaving the ed. to rest a while. Anyway, I had great fun actually putting the type in the chase, making type corrections, etc. I really felt as though it were my paper and happy was I about the whole thing. For a time, though, I was afraid the printer's ink would never come off my hands!

Did I tell you part of the journalism course this semester is 20 hours work at the Post-Standard, one of the two city dailies? The kids who've already worked say they run you ragged—but I still think it will look very fancy on a letter of application this summer—"work on a city daily"—wow! [From another letter we learn that her work for the *Post-Standard* was writing for the "women's dept."]

You are a fine, upstanding fellow to give up smoking and drinking, especially the first, for Lent. No cinch, I might say (referring again to the first, sir, *of course*!!) I'm eliminating a few things (like desserts) and doubtless I'll die a horrible death before Easter.

I did discover a freshman who can play boogie-woogie piano very prettily (!), though, while I was snooping around the basement of the main library. I heard 8-to-the-bar stuff coming from the depths somewhere and followed my ear, which might have looked funny but I never *could* hear with my nose! Must have that attended to!

Monday night, I listened attentively to a round-table discussion on "Has Religion the Answer?" There was a Jew, the (Methodist, I think) head of the Chapel, and the Catholic counselor on hand for information. It was veddy interesting and they carefully avoided all controversial subjects. We also decided that to be religious, in the most prevalent and original sense of the word, one must go to church. I was roped in on an old-fashioned square dance number and it almost ruined my health for life! Gad—better

I should run races! With atmosphere, and other stuff, lacking, square dances shouldn't be!

P.S. If not out of pity for my lonely state were you very dead, then out of consideration for the mess you'd undoubtedly be—pulease, keep out of the paths of trains! They're not gentle to minor obstructions such as people!!!

Love, Ginny

Elmer – February 27, 1941 11:30 p.m.

My Dearest Ginny:

I would have liked to sit in on that discussion on "Has Religion the Answer?" What conclusion did you come to? *Has* Religion got the answer? (Personally, I doubt it). If I may I should like to disagree on the point that one must go to church to be religious. In my mind (this is original and does not reflect the ideas of the denomination to which I belong) religion is purely a psychological effect. That the church is merely an instrument whereby a man can formulate his own conceptions and beliefs of religion, but that it isn't the only instrument he may use. It's hard to express myself on paper. We'll have to have a long discussion on the subject some time.

Ginny, you seemed to dislike the square-dance in your last letter. Just what is wrong with the square-dance? Fundamentally it is the same as the "Lindy" and you like the "Lindy." I can't understand it.

I'm not living now. I'm merely existing. No Ginny, no cigarettes, no candy, no beer. (Especially the first). What a life.

All my love, El

Virginia – March 1, 1941 4:00 p.m.

Dearest El,

Thursday was a lulu. A trip to the infirmary after lunch started things—a physical test is necessary before they'll let you in the School of Journalism, it seems. First they inserted a fine needle in my only left arm and let out of the needle juice for a T.B. test. Well—all right. *Then* they punctured my right arm with a not-so-fine needle and drew out into a lovely glass tube a goodly quantity of bright red blood—Wassermann test [for syphilis]! Both holes were all right Thursday. In fact—the right arm puncture is fine but the other one! They must have put in the fiercest and most vicious tubercula bacilli they had around the place because Friday—much soreness, stiffness, big red splotch, swollen! "Hmm-mm," I said, "I like this not. Better I should have T.B.!"

Well, like they told me, I went back this a.m. and they takes one short look at my disabled arm and says—"Very positive, isn't it!" That's fine, I thought! A tuberculosis case! Then they took a lovely x-ray and I'm to return in a week to find out the results. It's *great* fun sitting around, waiting to find out whether to reserve a room in Farmingdale [the Long Island TB sanatorium]! But seriously, though my arm is very unhappy, I hear the skin tests are often positive but it don't mean a thing if you ain't got the spots—shown on the x-ray. Anyway, I *hope* so! [Tuberculosis, also called "consumption," was a then-incurable, often fatal disease, mostly of the lungs. Elmer's maternal grandmother, Isabella Bamford, died of it in 1909. Even since the introduction of antibiotics, it still kills about a million and a half people globally each year.]

Managed to get the money back on the leaky boots that I'd returned several years ago and never heard anything more about. With part of the money, I bought an option on a lovely pair of *ice skates*! Yes! I said ice skates! They're *brown* leather and quite the nuts. Now maybe I will learn! I bought them in a very purty store—leather goods almost exclusively—and the beautiful luggage and other hide things they were displaying made me favor, for a time, a more equal distribution of the wealth—in my direction!

Today, all afternoon, the kiddies from Freshman cottages have been tramping through our house, looking at rooms. It's been wonderful! Maxine put on an act about leaks, calling loudly to Evy or Fran, asking whether the leaks in their rooms had been fixed; we assure them that there are no seniors to move out; we are as uncomplimentary to Wilbur [their residence cottage], poor hole, as possible—mostly so *we'll* be here next week and *they* won't!

El, if the square dance is to be compared to the Lindy, I'm leaving! Maybe fundamentally they're the same. I don't deny it because all dances are the same basic 8 steps at heart—either one or two of the 8 or varieties of them. But fundamentals aren't everything. Unless you're feeling *very* jovial and have a mountaineer or farmer atmosphere, all I can see in the square dance is rapid racing around to a steady, unvaried, and usually corny beat. It's too darn simple! The trickiest part of it is in being able to form circles and double circles and then partners again! Maybe I'm wrong and just don't know the finer points. Very likely, I admit. But right now, I'll continue with the more modern dances. Can you understand it now? If not, we *have* found something to disagree on!

If it weren't for the above very profound and serious disagreement (!) we should have a real one in the question of religion having the answer. I think if religion hasn't the answer we certainly can fold up our tents and die. But I'm as sure that it has as I'm sure that there's a God—which sureness is absolutely *positive*. I don't say the man who goes to church is the only honest, religious man. But without church services, group worship of God, men lose a lot of the inspiration, reassurance, finer feelings that come with a belief in a Supreme Being. It's different with Catholics, this question of going to church, because one isn't a practical Church member unless he does go to church (mass) every Sunday, etc. But with Protestants and Jews—a very simple argument for church going is that it can be likened to our own much-worried-about democracy. If men took their own little pieces and went off to their private homes with them, never coming together in an assemblage of common feeling, I doubt whether democracy would live long. Wouldn't it be likely to die of starvation? And a religion, if its believers don't regularly assemble and sense the spiritual uplift of common worship it is very likely to get lost in the shuffle. Men are that weak. No, I don't say church-going is the only way to get a feeling of religion. A tramp in the woods might be a way for many. But the *group* idea, one man assuring the other of their mutual agreement (and perhaps their only subject of common feeling), is what is necessary for the life of a religion. Maybe— I hope—you know now what I mean. If not, we *will* have to discuss it sometime. I'd like to anyway.

> Missing you as much as ever—
> Love, Ginny

> Virginia – March 3, 1941 2:15 p.m.

Dearest El,

Got a letter from Brod [her brother] today with several clippings about Pop and the Democrats. He certainly has a good time in politics. Too bad he didn't get the nomination for mayor (although I doubt he wanted it much). He'd never have won (he sees too much) but it would be a good fight. [In her diary, Virginia added, "It's a good thing. A lot of trouble and no pay. Besides, he's too honest to get along with a lot of men he'd have to as mayor."]

Six army pursuit planes came zooming down from the sky Thursday between 9:50 & 10:00 a.m. They were traveling like the wind (of a cyclone) and, after circling once or twice & power diving with unbelievable speed, they left, leaving half the campus kids staring after them; and many of the fellows were left in a very enthusiastic pro-air pilot mood—you know, oh what a wonderful thing to be flying one of those beautiful, silver-pencil affairs! And they were a thrilling sight—shining in the sun. But the war boys should be told that an air demonstration is even better than a brass band for getting the mob in uniform. Anyway, to get away from these world implications or what-have-you, the planes (pilots) were saluting, dipping their wings to a recently-killed buddy pilot, who came from here, graduated from here. What has amazed me, though, ever since, is that they made it from Mitchel Field [near her home on Long Island] to Syracuse in *28* minutes!!! Could you manage to get yourself an army pursuit plane? I'd like that!

Love, Ginny

Elmer – March 4, 1941 12:30 a.m.

Dearest Ginny:

I am deeply concerned over the results of that T.B. test. Will you let me know the outcome as soon as you possibly can.

Did you happen to hear Gene Krupa [renowned drummer and band leader] on the Hotel Bandwagon, Sunday eve? He rapped out a Boogie number called "Drum Boogie." Plenty of hot boogie piano and solid drumming. Also bend an ear to Barnet's "Redskin Rhumba," sort of a sequel to "Cherokee."

Education: Last week I received a very nice letter to the effect that I did not receive a high enough mark on that English Proficiency Exam to warrant my skipping the course. So next semester I'll be taking English. Also we have been informed that this Wednesday is the mid-term exams so I have been busily reviewing (this is a good excuse for not writing).

All my love, El

Virginia – March 10, 1941 8:45 p.m.

Dearest El,

Attended the town hall debate Thursday night. The topic was "If Germany wins the war—what?" It was good but not very encouraging. I think now, more than ever, that the British haven't much of a chance. Hitler holds all the aces. As soon as he gets going in Greece & in Libya—poor Britain & her allies! To say the least—these are not happy times!

Oh yes, you can cancel the room reservation at Farmingdale. They told me the x-ray showed nyetting and I'm all right. Now I'm waiting patiently for my disabled arm to heal.

Barnet's "Redskin Rhumba" is O.K. but *awfully* like Cherokee and not as good. I haven't heard "Drum Boogie." In fact, I'm sorta corny as far as new tunes go. I just "don't know nothing"!

Love, Ginny

March 11, 1941– FDR signs the Lend-Lease Act, authorizing aid to countries fighting the Axis, and asks Congress for $7 billion to fund it

---

Elmer – March 16, 1941 10:50 p.m.

Dearest Ginny:

Never have I felt more depressed than I did today and I have no explanation of it. This afternoon Norman and I were over on the sound [Long Island Sound]. It was about four o'clock and there was a light mist over the water but never have I seen the sound so calm. There wasn't a breath of air stirring and it was deathly quiet. There was a solitary duck swimming alone on the water and a gull cried mournfully somewhere. I don't know how to explain it but Norman and I both felt it. The whole setup seemed like a foreboding of something beyond our control, something on a gigantic scale that would involve both of us. It made me feel small and insignificant. But let's leave this macabre mood.

All my love, El

Virginia – March 18, 1941 5:15 p.m.

Dearest El,

We had a lulu of an assignment (in poli-sci) for today. Write a paper (2-5 pages) on the present defense status of the United States! Fun!

I almost saw the sound, myself, from your description. But don't let a dreary scene get you down. Invariably we read into nature our own feelings and it doesn't help *at all*. I'd prefer to think of that scene you pictured as more peaceful, quiet, calming, than foreboding of evil. Or maybe I wouldn't be able to judge— not having been there. All I can remember is the way it was when I first saw it. Your description sounded like *that*, but it doubtless had another feeling in it. Still, don't let that make you morose. There are *plenty* of more tangible, actual reasons for moroseness (?) if you want to look for them!!

I *still* haven't heard "Boogie Woogie Bugle Boy, Co. B." that everyone's raving about. I'm an icky!! Even Wally (I got a letter yesterday) likes it and has *also* bought a record of the Andrews gals doing it. Gad, I've got to hear that soon or bury myself completely!

Love, Ginny

Virginia – March 28, 1941 9:00 a.m.

Dearest El,

The sophomores on the staff have taken over the Orange—putting it out almost entirely. I've been news editor (that's work on the desk—handling & copy-reading stories in the daytime) this week. We're beginning to feel official now. It's a lot of fun having a paper of your own to put through. Work, too!

Zoo. lab this afternoon and I think we're going to investigate the inner machinations of a crayfish. Oh what good fun!

Love, Ginny

April 6, 1941 – Germany invades Greece

Elmer – April 6, 1941 9:30 p.m.

My Dearest Ginny:

Only five more days! It's almost unbelievable, the time has fairly flown. It's a good thing, too. The return of robins and warm weather has made me mighty lonely for someone. You guess who.

Let me know the details of your triumphant return to civilization and I will be on hand.

Have you noticed the moon lately? If you haven't; do so immediately. You will notice that it is about ¾ full, and waxing rapidly. By difficult astronomical calculations, I have come to the conclusion that toward the end of the week, it should be pretty good. This is very encouraging, because that lunar body has been pretty dark all the other times you were home.

All my love, El

Spring break for Virginia featured dates with both Elmer and George, and left her once again conflicted. She writes in her diary, "I wonder if I'm not a heel about both El & George. But I don't know what the score is in my heart!"

Virginia – April 21, 1941 11:10 p.m.

Dearest El,

The train last night (seems ages ago!) had hardly gotten going when I was dozing. The nice conductor came bellowing by, looked at my extended ticket, and grunted, "Syracuse! You're on the wrong train! You should be on the one that left from the other track. This goes only to Utica!" "Well," I said, "What am I supposed to do?" and he calmly and gruffly said that I *might* catch my train in Albany! So what am I to do? I thought. No use worrying! If you catch it—good. If not—well, you don't! And I went back to sleep!

Pretty soon from my reverie I hear noises like "Syracuse you train you Syracuse!" and soon came to enough to understand that the train I was supposed to be on was on the next track in Harman. So I gathers up my junk and tore across to the right conveyance. There I found Kathy, who'd been thinking I'd missed it. After exchanging bare bits of conversation with her, I returned to my former occupation and slept most of the way up. It wasn't bad at all.

I've completely lost that vacation glow of loafing and having a good time. All work now.

Love, Ginny

Elmer – April 21, 1941 9:45 p.m.

My Dearest Ginny:

Well, here I am back again in the humdrum existence of a bank clerk. For a little more than a week I was very happy but now; Oh well—only a few weeks waiting this time.

I timed myself going home last night and I didn't exactly stand still. From Lexington and 43rd St. to my garage [27 miles] in *51* minutes ain't what you'd call slow time. Just a cowboy at heart.

You know, Ginny, there must be some way you could go away a little at time. This sudden change is almost too much to bear. Sunday, all happiness and sunshine because I'm with you; Monday, "Gloomy Sunday" only a day late. Very discouraging.

All my love, El

**April 27, 1941 – Athens falls,
with 7,000 British Empire troops captured**

Virginia – May 4, 1941 5:00 p.m.

Dearest El,

On the gloom side of the ledger, much work to do on the Orange this week—night editor Wed. (I think) & assistant another night. My new beat, though good, gives me many stories, meaning many hours.

But the brighter side is more obvious, on second thought: The new beat is more chance to show what you can do and perhaps (I can dream of it, can't I?) get to be a senior editor. (Yes—I'm a *junior* now—since yesterday morning when the Chancellor moved all the classes up.) I like the choice of senior editors for next year and ought to have no trouble with them.

Being interviewed by journalism profs as prerequisite to entrance into the School of J., I was led to believe by one that my reading is negligible—but *negligible*! Seems I get time to read only the N.Y. Times and I *should* read the local paper, the journalism periodicals, *and* books. So—I'm going to read *2* daily papers from now on (final in j. is on current events, I hear!) and I've made a few resolutions besides. He recommended getting a little of a lot of things instead of specializing so much. A good newspaperman should know economics, etc.   . *So*—this summer I'm going to try to learn economics, banking, & finance. *Also* a method of shorthand and improve my typing as well. If I find I can't learn the stuff, even with your help (please!), I'll have to take a course up here. I've been thinking about learning something about art & music, too. I'll be an all-around scholar if it kills me! Therefore, I'm dedicating this summer—or a good part of it—to school on my own. Will you help me keep on the narrow & straight? A part of every day I've *gotta* be learning something.

I was so engrossed at the Castle Friday afternoon that
I completely forgot I should have been working at the Post-
Standard! I'm sort of wondering what will be the consequences of
"forgetting" to go to work! Sounds good, no?

Wow! The Dodgers won again—in second place! Also the
Yankees! What teams—good for my money to take the pennants (I
hope!). Then the Yanks will smear the Trolley-dodgers.
Wouldn't that be a wonderful series! (Or are you a faithful
Brooklyn rooter, even so far as to rate them above the Yankees?)
[They did meet in the World Series in 1941. The Yankees won it in
five games.]

I'm sorry about screaming to you to write. I forgot about
your exams. I'm glad you got the better of them. It's my turn to
apologize now. Reason: unbelievable busity (my own word!).

Love, Ginny

Elmer – May 6, 1941 11:30 p.m.

My Dearest Ginny:

Do you have trouble starting a letter? Gee, I do. I get as far as the
date, the hour and "My Dearest Ginny" then I'm stumped. I sit for
ten or fifteen minutes before I get an idea how to begin. From now
on I'm going to start in the middle.

Boy, is our block department a mad-house this week. We're
working with a skeleton crew. One fellow is out with the grip and
today the bank doctor sent another fellow to the hospital to have
his tonsils yanked.

There's a carnival in the empty lot across the street this
week. I can hardly hear myself think, what with the merry go round
etc.

Ginny, I will be more than happy to help you with Eco. and
Banking this summer. I still have my texts; they should prove a

great aid. I was just thinking. We could go down to the beach on
Sundays, and study in the sunshine.

All my love, El

Virginia – May 7, 1941 1:00 a.m.

Dearest El,

I was supposed to take the paper through tomorrow night but it's
going to be an 8-pager—which means "they won't get home until
morning" and we mean *morning*. So, I'm elected for Friday night
instead. Fri. as I see it will be Post-Standard from 1:30 – 5:30 and
D.O. from then on. Collitch is peachy.

Even at this time the Joe Colleges are ripping by every now
& then blowing horns, yelling, and having a gay old time. Must be
the season—or the sultry weather. [Back then 'gay' meant 'joyful'
or 'festive.']

This afternoon I delved into the inner parts of a crayfish and
then dropped in on a tea given by my English prof for a few of her
charming Stooges.

This has been the excitement since Sunday.

Love, Ginny

Virginia – May 9, 1941 1:00 a.m.

Dearest El,

"'Tis late in ♪ the evening, ♫ the kids are all sleeping, ♪ I wish I
were nearer a bar!"♫

Well—something like that! Frustrated is the word for
me—I just ain't got TIME to go to classes anymore! Either I quit
this college business and devote my life to the Daily Orange or
study now and then and become a rotten reporter. All I want

to find is the guy who first said "What an easy life is that of the college student." I'd make him eat every word—printed on heavy cardboard!

The story is that tomorrow I ought to write an editorial, *have* to write a long story, *should* read some 50 pages of English (Matthew Arnold's essays)—and all this before 10 a.m. Reason? 10-11 Latin; 11-12 journalism lab; 12-1:00 English; 1-1:30—yes, I still eat!; 1:30-2:30, a few more interviews for journalism. Of course, from 1:30 to 5:30 I'm working at the Post-Standard and the D.O. takes on the occupation of my idle hours from then—. Otherwise, tomorrow will be slow. Sad, I'm going mad like a loon!

Sunday Wilbur et al. has planned a lovely picnic which I wish I could avoid in favor of some *little* study at least. Finals are fairly hours away and when I think...! Call the wagon, boys, and chain 'er to the wall—she may get violent!

Lighter side: I had a couple of features in today's paper. In fact, I'm beginning to feel like a real junior editor—which means *tired*, for one thing. Sometime this summer I'll tie you down and crow as I push my pet papers and stories under your nose for you to read. Warning in advance! Don't say I didn't!

Love, *Ginny*

May 10, 1941 – The last major Luftwaffe bombing of London kills more than 1,400

Elmer – May 12, 1941 9:30 p.m.

My Dearest Ginny:

I just finished a session with the "Chamber Music Society of Lower Basin Street." It's the first time they're back on the air since we heard them together that night. Harry James [a famous band leader of the era] was their guest conductor. Wow! what a trumpet. If you possibly can, listen to them next Monday, for Maestro Will Bradley is to be guest star with a couple of his "bouncing boys," which probably means Señors Slack & McKinley. Bradley will introduce a new number aptly titled, "The Basin Boogie-Woogie."

On to more dreary subjects: I haven't received my marks from school yet and I am beginning to get slightly anxious. I'm afraid to come home every night because my marks might be here. If they send your marks home it means you flunked but if they send them to the bank, you passed.

Speaking of the bank I find I have another small promotion coming in two weeks. One of the boys is leaving to get a job in another bank so I am moving up a notch.

Enough of me. I judge by your letters, that you are pretty well stacked with work. I'm on the sidelines rooting for you.

I miss you more and more as the days go by and send—

All my love, El

Elmer – May 13, 1941 9:45 p.m.

My Dearest Ginny:

I am very unhappy. Today I find the new position is all off. The bank gave the job that I was to get to a girl who has only been in the bank since April 4th. They're giving the better jobs to girls so they won't be up the creek when the fellow gets called in the draft. This is the first time I have been personally affected by conscription and I don't like it in the least.

In a measure I have been recompensed. Today I got my marks from school, and I did much better than I thought I would.

Opening my little brown envelope I found an A- in Economics and a B in Bank org.—Wonder of wonders. Now I feel capable of helping you in these subjects this summer.

> I send all my love and good luck on your finals—El

May 14, 1941 – First large-scale round-up of Jews in Paris

Virginia – May 17, 1941 9:30 p.m.

Dearest El,

For the last three weeks I've been working on the Orange for a living. Guess I told you that. Things haven't changed. On a feature in today's paper I got my first D.O. byline. Think I'll frame it!

I took a quiz in tennis—my last gym period for all college life—joy!

I saw a couple of pieces of baseball games this week—NYU & Colgate games, good ole Syracuse taking both. The bat boys have done very well this season, although the infield smells, to put it bluntly.

Yesterday I did get to the Post-Standard to work, having missed 2 afternoons! Same old stuff—social news.

Golly, El, your marks are swell! If I do as well, we can put out the flag and blow the trumpets when I get home!

Love, Ginny

May 18, 1941 – Elmer's nineteenth birthday

Elmer – May 19, 1941 9:30 p.m.

My Dearest Ginny:

I got your little brown package tonight and I can't tell you how happy it made me. Gee, I think you're swell Ginny, and I thank you profoundly. It's a swell wallet; the first time I ever saw anything made of ostrich skin.

Mom and Pop got me two new tires for my car, so I'll soon have the old jalopy running.

Don't feel sorry about my promotion, for I find that it was all for the best. You see the boss is going into the army in a month or so and I will move up two notches instead of one. I'll be the boss downtown in the morning, with two fellows under me, and will be third man in the block. Just call me dictator Odell.

All my love, El

Virginia – May 24, 1941 8:40 p.m.

Dearest El,

Guess what I've been doing lately? More fun! Comes Wednesday. Hmm—mm! What did we do? There was a small matter of zoo. to take—it was not pleasant. In fact, it was awful. And to make it worse, the other half of the zoo. stooges took the *same* exam the following day—after having learned the answers carefully !! I only hope he's not as stupid to be unaware of the excellent grape-vine system on campus.

Thursday—I was up quite *early* that a.m. with the big blue book in front of me. The final was only *14* pages of true-false numbers. Yes—fourteen. Simply charming. After the 10th, I wondered if some little guy wasn't adding pages on the back of mine as I finished one. *Unending* it seemed. When the last page was turned, you were too tired of "encircling T if true and F if false" that you didn't care about looking—even *glancing* at the ones you'd left out for further thought!

Awful as the grind was, I'm happy about it today. They told me at the office that my term mark is A.

Then yesterday!—I *couldn't see* after 2 a.m. so I went to sleep, intending to get up at an unholy hour to study 8 chapters of journalism. So—I wake up at 7:15! The exam's at 8! Well I zipped through the book—the stuff we'd had this semester—and got to the final at 8:15. But that darn exam! They asked *lots* of little questions on *last semester's* work! Also stuff on a booklet dear Dr. Bird had never given us! Now I'm worried about getting into the School. Without a B in journalism it won't work.

This morning Kathy and I went to the N.Y. Central R.R. station and I now own a pretty little yellow *1-way* ticket to N.Y.C.!

Watch out for a girl with Syracuse stickers on her bags at 9 at the info. booth in G.C.T.!

Love, Ginny

Summer Break

O N MAY 27, 1941, Virginia reports in her diary, "Packed my trunks & suitcases tonight. Awful thunder & lightning exhibition about 3:30. I love it." Once she returned home, as before, her diary provides our sole narrative. It didn't take but a few days for her to hit the dance floor with Elmer: "We went to Madison Square Garden for the dance carnival opening—Benny Goodman, Larry Clinton, & Charlie Barnet bands playing. It was wonderful! Amazing to see so *many* people all jumping! Crowd! Swell music! Small floor! We had a good time and danced ourselves to rags. *Then* he ran out of gas on the way home & we had to *walk* from the Southern State pkwy—a goodly distance. More things happen!"

But she saw George as well: "George and I went to the movies—I am attracted to him, rather irresistibly. Maybe it's love—I wish I knew. I don't know what's going to happen about this business. My feelings for George are much stronger than mine for El—but I don't know how intelligent and how emotional—that is, physical—they are. I feel like a dirty 2-timer—but I'm not— the way I see it!" However, it turned out that George had also been seeing other people. A few days later, she reports, "George called & came over. I was unpleasantly surprised to find—he told me—that he likes the girl he's been going with no little bit—in fact, he's undecided between the two of us! I didn't know it was so serious and, since I feel pretty strongly for him, I don't like it much. Goodness knows when it'll clear up." Her exasperation with him comes through even more clearly in an entry a few days later: "George was supposed to come over tonight—was late, as per, and then had to leave for home early—his father's orders! (Soon he'll be twelve and can wear long pants!)"

A few weeks later she muses after a beach excursion with Elmer and some of his friends, "I could see a similarity in the

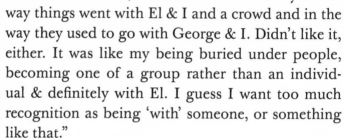

way things went with El & I and a crowd and in the way they used to go with George & I. Didn't like it, either. It was like my being buried under people, becoming one of a group rather than an individual & definitely with El. I guess I want too much recognition as being 'with' someone, or something like that."

Elmer – June 21, 1941 7:05 p.m. [Sent from a Catskills resort where he was vacationing with his friend Norman.]

My Dearest Ginny:

Hello honey. Please excuse me if you find a burp in the envelope, but I just got up from the dinner table, and what a meal! Everything from soup to nuts. I could just about stagger into the writing room.

A couple of times on the way up, I thought my jalopy wouldn't make it. One tire decided to go flat every few miles so I finally had to stop and change it. Also we had to put water in the radiator, and once it blew up like a geyser. Outside of that, it was a very pleasant trip.

Norman and I both have a very good case of tan acquired riding up with the top down.

Well, I'll say so long for a while. We have a big softball game coming up in about 15 minutes.

All my love, El

June 22, 1941 – Nazi Germany invades Russia

Virginia – June 22, 1941 1:00 a.m. [Sent to Elmer at the resort.]

Dearest El,

Hope you and Norman had a good trip. If the sun shone on you going up the way it was beating down here all day El has a sunburn *now*! (All this is taking it for granted you two girls wore the top *down*.)

On the radio I'm listening to the news of the German declaration of war on Russia. Hitler and the boys have finally gotten around to polishing off the Russians. This ought to be interesting, even if not much trouble for the efficient Panzer divisions. [Not a very good reading of the crystal ball here. This invasion is generally considered to have begun the undoing of the Third Reich.]

Only a little while ago I heard Saint-Saens' *Danse Macabre* and Tchaikovsky's *Romeo & Juliet* overture on the same little invention—the wireless [radio]. Certainly get a variety of programs!

The music, crumby as it is, is forever being broken into with "flashes" that "the news rooms" just "picked up" and I'm getting weary of it all.

Greetings to Monsieur Hilmar and best wishes to bote of youse for a veddy excellent vacation.

I may even write again!

Love, Ginny

Virginia – June 23, 1941 9:40 p.m.

Dearest El,

I'm listening to a crazy rhumba by Xavier Cugat. He just played "Night Must Fall" (remember that?) which he wrote himself. I didn't know until they announced it.

Funny tonight! Very peculiar feeling, as of mixed-up emotions and thoughts, yet over all, a pervading orderliness. Wish I could write. I get ideas for stories and before I even get them worked out I've decided they're trite and quite worthless. Times like these I greatly doubt my ability beyond this very triteness.——

Sorry to have run on like this. Very drab.

Lovingly, Ginny

Virginia was having very little luck finding a summer job. On June 18, she records in her diary: "More job-seeking today. More 'Sorry, we can't use summer help.' Very discouraging." Finally, she landed one at Jones Beach, first as cashier in a candy booth and afterward working as a switchboard operator and typist, after which she would often go out dancing or drinking with Elmer. On August 4, she reports, "Hung around until the west bath house closed, when we went to the Mariner's Rest. At first I thought I wouldn't have any fun at the party, but things got going, beer flowed and I had a swell time, dancing, talking, and getting gay. By 3:30 at home, I felt I'd had *plenty* to drink." The next day was a "tough" one at work, "after all that beer and no sleep (3 hrs.!)."

There are also hints of flirtations with her new coworkers. When her working hours were changed to 4:00 p.m. to midnight, she worried she wouldn't like it, but reports, "Working at night is all right! Less work (I wrote 2 letters!), more fun (no Mr. Rosenberg to do a lot of ordering around and more of one *Bill Lennox*, a very interesting person who might be called the head office boy.)" A few days later: "To work at 4 and I didn't get home until about 3. Reason: I got a ride to Freeport with a few (8!) of 'the boys.' Of course we stopped for a beer and a dance at Gintz' in Freeport and so forth. I was mainly with Tommy Kinsella, a carver and a good enough fellow, but he drinks too much."

September's big event: Virginia's father bought a brand-new Buick Roadmaster. Virginia declares it "gorgeous" and reports, "Took Claire & Nadine to a club meeting—in Pop's new car!"

In her diary, Virginia reports on her last few days at home before returning to Syracuse: "El came over tonight. We walked, looking at the Northern Lights display. Wonderful and awfully beautiful." And two days later George came over: "We drove out to our usual 'talking' spot. Same ole stuff. I don't know whether I want him or not."

September 8, 1941 – The German siege of Leningrad begins

Prelude to War

Dearest El,

Realization comes late. It was exactly 6 a.m. yesterday morning when I began to feel the severance part of coming back. This going-away-to-school business certainly uproots attachments—with force and often.

I was hardly here before activities on the Orange started with a staff meeting. I spent this afternoon on the desk down there so by now I feel as though I'd never been away. It certainly takes but little time to get back into the old groove.

Thanks again for the candy, El. Why don't you ever do things to make me hate you *more* instead of less??!!

Love, Ginny

Virginia – September 27, 1941 7:05 p.m.

Dearest El,

Besides classes I've also neatly inscribed the hours I work on the NYA job I got yesterday. [The National Youth Administration was a New Deal jobs program.]

Very handy. I work in the Castle for the secretary of one of the profs—doing anything and everything. Most times I've been slave for BPI (Bureau of Public Info.) office—the people who send all the news of the local boy making good at S.U. to the local papers.

As soon as I get enough money, I think I'll buy some western boots (cowboy style) for the winter. You'll love them!

Wilbur and its kids are O.K. We have three new girls who seem nice enough, and we happily lost one I distinctly dislike. The student dean is sho' nuff a southern girl who now 'n then calls y'all honey or sugah!—but I figure she'll be all right when I get used to her. Syracuse? It's still as swell (to me) as ever. Last night and the throngs of orange lidded Frosh—*millions*, it seemed—swarming out of the stadium to trot around the field at the half—the old gang and the old fun at the D.O. office—the smell of fall and the football season spirit—it's all as it was and I'll never get tired of it.

Your assignments aren't exactly easy, are they? [He'd described them in a previous letter.] But I suppose that they'd have to be heavy at night school to get the material covered. I too have assignments already—in editorial interpretation, in American lit. (for whom I have Prof. *Snook*—cute? who'll probably be very erudite but *awfully* tiring) *and* in Shakespeare (and this prof is really swell—I could tell just by looking at him!) These last two courses have books that are worthwhile keeping. You don't even mind buying *new* ones.

Honey, after this letter you oughta send me one of your 500-word themes in an envelope! But I'll settle for something shorter *sooner*!

Love, Ginny

Elmer – September 29, 1941 11:45 p.m.

My Dearest Ginny:

I'm going to have to cut this short. I've just finished my
English theme, after having run about 2500 checks today (no-
exaggeration) so by now I don't think my writing is very legible.

But first, some good news. I spoke to the boss, and Colgate
week-end is in the bag. So I'll see you 9:20 a.m. Nov. 15, 1941.

You know, I sorta miss your telling me how much you hate
me, even though I don't think you mean it. (I hope).

All my love, El

Virginia – October 4, 1941 10:40 p.m.

Dearest El,

This is some night! I'd give a bakery window full of jelly doughnuts
to be out celebrating our holding Cornell to a 6-0 score and
otherwise playing a good game of feetball. There's a perfectly
drooly full moon showing through slight haze and hanging in the
tall trees.

Monday night I took the Orange through and it wasn't
too bad. We were delayed about an hour waiting for a picture,
though.

Since then I've spent the afternoons in classes, labs, or the
D.O. office. Had a couple of good stories break right for me this
week and on the whole I'm happy with me on the Orange during
the past 6 days. If it keeps up, I'll be happier, being as my chances
for a senior position will increase.

Here, if I were less weary, I'd insert three rousing cheers on
accounta El's coming for Colgate. As it is, I'll just inform you that
the tickets are already spoken for (I hope they're better'n last year!

We were on the 50-yd. line today, first row!) And I'm working on a new & better curse (for Colgate's undoing, of course) to insure an Orange victory.

But El—what conceit you show! What *ever* made you believe I was kidding when I said (if I said it once...!) I hated you? I just *can't* understand it!! (And if at this pernt you're wondering if maybe I *do* mean it, you should be kilt for sheer thick-headedness!)

Ha! Mom sent me the shoes I'd been trying to get (mainly because they're men's style & I couldn't find a store with them in 7) and they're lovely! [A standing joke among the Schill sisters concerned their large feet.] Wonder if you'll approve!?! I do have such trouble with you and my shoes!

You should see the flask Carol brought me—a souvenir or something. The glass is enclosed in leather and they've inscribed stuff on it. Trouble is, it's quite empty.

Please don't knock yourself out by too many "hard days at the office" followed by grueling sessions of school. I want something to be left of you. Really I do!

Love, Ginny

P.S. Is your father coming with you? (Wondering if I should get him a date!)

Elmer – October 7, 1941 11:25 p.m.

My Dearest Ginny:

I have just finished my English assignment for this week, so by this time I have nearly developed house-maid's knee of the right hand, if such a thing is possible.

Now about those shoes. I can tell without seeing them that I ain't gonna like ' em. Why can't you buy regular shoes like other girls do? Hoy Gee! You gotta be different! And be sure that flask *stays* empty. Remember, total abstinence is the only sure way to eternal glory. Sister, has you seen the light?

Dad doesn't know for sure whether he is coming up this year or not, but you better keep in touch with a couple of blondes, just in case.

All my love, El

While Virginia and Elmer were making plans for his visit in November, she took advantage of a cheap train ticket to come down to Long Island for a weekend. On October 14, she writes to Elmer, "if you're around G.C.T. about 6:30 or 7 this very Fri. eve, I wouldn't be annoyed atall, atall."

Elmer – October 22, 1941 9:15 p.m.

My Dearest Ginny:

Will you please, Miss Schill, at your earliest convenience, write to me and tell me definitely whether or not you were in Hempstead and vicinity this past weekend? I heard rumors that you were home and I think I saw you once or twice, but the time went so fast that I am not at all positive.

In the heart of metropolitan Roosevelt there is an ice-cream parlor. In the heart of this ice-cream store there stands a jukebox. In the innards of this jukebox is a record. In the middle of the record is a label, in the center of which is writing which reads "'You and I' recorded by Tommy Dorsey." I put about a quarter in that jukebox tonight, playing one song, #5, "You and I" by T.D. because for some intangible reason, it reminds me of you. Maybe it's because I seem to hear it whenever I'm with you.

Ginny, about your smoking. I realize I have no right to tell you what to do and what not to do, but personally I don't think much of the idea. I'll grant you more & more women smoke every day but I still know plenty who don't. My sister is a noteworthy example. She has never smoked and probably never will. Go ahead, ask me why don't I practice what I preach. But, in a measure it's different with a fellow.

Well, Sugar, I've got to outline various court rulings on the legality of the devices used by labor organizations to gain their ends, and I think I better get started.

I can't think of any fancy ways of phrasing it so I'll merely say I really miss you.

All my love, El

Virginia – October 26, 1941 4:30 p.m.

Dearest El,

Yes, I know. It's been a while since the last like this but I've started to read the textbooks I've had for a month. Takes time, too!

Wednesday night I went to a reception given by Theta Sigma Phi, women's journalism honorary, and I expect to be a pledge of same in a couple of weeks.

Nope, El, you have no right to tell me what to do and I don't care how many women do or do not smoke. I fact, I don't think your little sermon was necessary because I don't smoke enough to warrant it and I really don't expect to go on. The only reason I ever started was probably for the variety of it, making it an entertainment in an otherwise very solid routine of living. I really don't have much of a social life up here you know—or do you? I don't admire the practice any more than you do, in fellows or girls, it makes no difference to me. The physical damage it inflicts, which is the best argument against it, is no less with a fellow than with a girl. Analysis of my smoking gets me to the conclusion that it was a semi-subconscious attempt to get out of a rut I'm in.

But that's beside the question—am I going to continue you probably want to know? If I get anything out of the practice, yes. But because indications so far are that I don't, because I admire health *and* individuality, and also because I have some regard for what you and Mom & Pop think about it—well, you guess. [She would be an almost lifelong smoker, finally giving it up for good in her early sixties. Elmer quit in his late fifties.]

Love, Ginny

Elmer – October 27, 1941 9:30 p.m.

My Dearest Ginny:

You needn't apologize for not writing more often. I realize that it's getting on towards mid-semester and things must be piling upon you.

You seemed rather explosive on the subject of smoking. I'm sorry I brought the matter up, and had I known at the time how you felt about it, I assure you I wouldn't have. So let's forget the whole business.

Yesterday Norman, Jack and I went horseback riding. I wish you could have been there. It was really funny. We started late in the afternoon out at Belmont Park and the horses were reluctant to leave the stables but very anxious to return after they left so I dare say we had more than a little trouble keeping them under control. Norman had an immense job by the name of "Steel" which he said would look better in front of a plow, Jack had a brown devil and I had a frisky and temperamental mare, which, like most women, had a mind of her own. When we got to a certain point on the bridle path, the horses would go no further, and no amount of persuasion would change their minds. Coming back was a different story. They were more than eager to go. Norman's horse broke into a trot and Norman, not knowing how to post, bounced all over the saddle and ended up by flinging his arms about the horse's neck and hanging on for dear life. My horse must have thought she could have made better time without me because when she decided she wanted to go home, she put her head down, threw her hind feet up in the air and shook. The fellows said when she bucked, my hat went up in the air and came down on my head again. She didn't throw me, though I still don't see how I stayed on. Our riding wasn't too successful but we got a good laugh out of it.

All my love, El

November 5, 1941 – Japanese admiral Isoroku Yamamoto issues secret plan for the attack on Pearl Harbor

---

Virginia – November 9, 1941 4:30 p.m.

Dearest El,

I have procured a room for you—a room which will be warmer than last year's, I think. It is small but otherwise nice and the $1.50 it will cost includes towels. The landlady, Mrs. Friends, has sympathy for people who must carry in their suitcases wet wash cloths, she told me! Anyway—you won't have to sleep in Thornton Park. I'm now working on a system whereby you can be gotten out of bed Sunday morning! Thinking of rounding up a battery of alarm clocks and setting them at five-minute intervals!

Love, Ginny

November 10, 1941 – Virginia's twentieth birthday

Elmer – November 11, 1941 10:15 p.m.

My Dearest Ginny:

Happy Birthday, honey! I got your letter today and I am glad to hear that you have a place for me to hang my hat while in your friendly city. It's nice to know I don't have to spend all Saturday morning trooping around looking for a place to sleep.

All my love, El

Elmer – November 17, 1941 11:05 p.m.

My Dearest Ginny:

I've seen blue Mondays and I seen even bluer Mondays, but this is the bluest Monday I have ever encountered in my short life. Gee but it's horrible to be back in my accustomed rut. If I could only find words to tell you how much I enjoyed myself this past, too-short weekend, and how super-swell I think you are.

I saw Jack this evening and he is all hopped up over an idea he and his cousin have got to join the R.C.A.F [Royal Canadian Air Force]. They have even written to Royal Air Force Headquarters in Montreal, P.Q. [Provence de Quebec]. Jack asked me to go with them if they go, and the way I feel today I wouldn't take much coaxing to make me say yes.

All my love, El

Elmer – November 21, 1941 9:25 p.m.

My Dearest Ginny:

Just as I was about to start this letter, Jack came in with a letter.
The answer to his request for information on the R.C.A.F.! It was a
very nice letter thanking him for his interest in the Royal Air Force,
and it was accompanied by a ten-page manual of requirements,
wages, and different branches of the service, etc. I read it all
through and it sounds mighty good. I spoke to my folks about it
and they don't exactly relish the idea, especially Mom. However if I
made up my mind to go, I don't think they'd really try to stop me.
We'll see what develops.

Ginny, in your last letter you said that all you can do now
is look back and reminisce. I tried that. It doesn't work. It is very
discouraging to look back and realize that such a wonderful
week-end is over. So I try looking ahead, and truly the prospects
are much brighter. December 19th isn't really very far off, and
Christmas vacation is a lot longer than a week-end.

All I've been doing today is wishing that time would turn
back one week. This time last week I was making last minute
preparations to go to Syracuse.

Honey, if I were to say I miss you, it would sound hollow
on paper, but my vocabulary doesn't embrace the words to say it
more fluently, so I hope you realize that I do. Physically I am here
in Roosevelt, but my thoughts are always in Syracuse, and with
them is—

All my love, El

Virginia – November 24, 1941 1:30 p.m.

Dearest El,

I'm in one of my unaccountable and therefore maddening
(to me) "lows." Guess it started this morning when, on top of my

usual reluctance to get out of bed, was added the bleakness of *snow.*

But I got out the boots I bought Saturday—you probably won't like 'em!—and trekked to my 8 o'clock. I took a look at the Daily Orange schedule for the week. Guess who's taking the paper through tonight? Right.

Even your letter made me droop. For heaven's sake, what are you considering the RAF for? What, all of a sudden, has put the love of England into *you*? [He believed, like many Americans, that the British were trying to drag the US into another war.] And I can't understand Jack's thinking of giving up his job for that—or is he interested in flying? I dunno! Maybe you are too—I just didn't know about it until now. My gosh, you have a job and where do you suppose you'll be, if alive, after the war as an RAF pilot? Huh? I'd first join the Army air force. Anyway, if you're at all serious about this thing, an explanation would help me comprehend. I don't get it.

Guess I'll finish this tonight, whenever I get home.

Nov. 25, 5:00 p.m.

It was two when I got home last night! And 3:30 when I finished my editor's reports.

Seems the paper was a big one to start out. Things were going about the usual way—until about 10:30 or so. Then I started getting phone calls (at the publishing company now) about a Phi Psi committing suicide. First I was afraid it was an exaggerated account of an accident but the story came through and the fellow—a 19 year-old sophomore in Applied Science—died shortly afterwards in the hospital. Shot himself through the head with a Winchester rifle belonging to another fraternity brother. The whole affair was pretty unhappy—especially for the Phi Psi's, who have to live there and who had to almost see it happen. The fellow, a straight A student last year, was worried about his marks, which hadn't been so good this year.

Of course, the front page of my paper had to be ripped up and made to accommodate the big story. All of which takes time and therefore I was *very* tired and no little depressed when I got in.

So that's the story for today, honey. I'll write again soonly.

Love, Ginny

Elmer – November 27, 1941 7:00 p.m.

My Dearest Ginny:

In your last letter, you asked for an explanation of the reason I suddenly wanted to join the R.C.A.F. For a complete explanation, you would have to delve deep into human psychology, but I will try to give you a rough idea.

First of all, occasionally I go into a state of—(call it what you will) unrest, uneasiness, despondency, at the prospect of spending the rest of my life at a job, no doubt good, but still a job, where for only two weeks out of fifty-two a year I can do the traveling that I would like to do before I'm too old to enjoy it. I know that is sort of a juvenile idea and I also know that I am steadily outgrowing it but even the thought of losing the *desire* for travel makes me shudder. Now, I was in one of these moods, possibly caused by my return from even the short trip to Syracuse, when Jack approached me with the idea of joining the R.C.A.F. At the time it sounded as a darned good escape but now that this mood has passed I can see the foolishness of the idea. As for my love of Britain, that is negligible.

If I were going to join an army to fight, I'd just as soon join the Chinese army. The Canadian Air Force just happened to be nearest, that's all.

As a matter of fact, I enclose a poem that pretty well describes my feeling toward England in her relations to this country. [It was published anonymously in the *New York Journal-American* on November 26, 1941; this is an excerpt.]

This is the war John Bull built,
And this is the propaganda, studied and shrewd,
Conceived to deceive and made to delude,
And further the war that John built.

Ginny, from this letter you may get the idea that I'm a pretty moody fellow, but honestly honey, I'm not. Only it gets you some times when you realize that you're chained to a desk till the time you cash in your chips and take a gamble on the great beyond.

The progress I am making in the bank helps to stop these fits of melancholia. They are beginning to teach me the head bookkeeper's job. You see the bookkeepers are girls hired for that one job and they will never go any higher but they must have a head bookkeeper and that is the job I get next. I probably won't get it for a year or more, but still I am being groomed for it.

All my love, El

Virginia – December 6, 1941 11:30 p.m.
[Postmarked December 7, 1941 8 p.m., Syracuse N.Y.]

Dearest El,

Tonight I'll probably go to bed with my right (or write—ha, ha!) hand in a sling. I'm chief proctor and door-opener tonight and I've spent the evening trying to soothe into peaceful submission the many people I've owed letters for *weeks*! It's gonna be a most thrilling feeling, owing *no one* a letter for a day or so!

Did you hear Glenn Miller tonight? Played on the Coca-Cola program and ran through "Chattanooga," "Tuxedo Junction," "Everything I Love" (a purty new one), and "Moonlight Sonata" (wonderful arrangement—even Beethoven wouldn't mind, I'm sure!).

Seems that one of my profs won't meet his 8 o'clock class. Therefore I only have *one* class Fri. a.m. & one Saturday. I'd always expected to leave here Friday, cutting only the Sat. class. However, since this news and also some doubt about the N.Y. Central having an Orange special Friday (the soldiers get leave and the trains will be much used for them), I figure I may as well leave Thursday.

About that poem you sent—whether or not "John Bull built this war," (it *is* debatable) the outcome nevertheless vitally affects us. If you don't believe it, I'll try to convince you some time!

Love, Ginny

After Pearl Harbor

THE NEWS OF THE air attack on Pearl Harbor on December 7, 1941 prompted Virginia to pick up her diary once more: "This is the first insertion in months but I am greatly disturbed in mind. Japanese planes today bombed Honolulu, and Japan later declared war on the United States. I doubt if my powers of concentration will conquer the rumbling echoes of this news I find in my mind. Right now they're hawking an extra 'Japan Declares War on U.S.' outside. Crouse [Hall] chimes played 'God Bless America' & 'My Country 'Tis of Thee.' Can I *sit here* and *study*???" This was her last diary entry. The United States declared war on Japan the following day.

Virginia – December 11, 1941 1:20 p.m.

Dearest El,

So many things have happened since Saturday night that I hardly know which is my life and which are those things very much related to but yet outside of my everyday routine.

War! First Japan—and all its implications and losses right away—then Germany & Italy today. [When the US declared war on Japan, Germany and Italy subsequently reacted by declaring war on the US.]

You begin to be quite confused. I don't know—trying to keep my mind on my work, school and the like, seems to be burying your head and being quite blind—but when I think about the war, I want to do something and am quite frustrated—because I *can't* do anything. Efforts to keep balanced must be huge—at least I can't think about them all without school being thrown into the corner in regard to comparative importance.

I don't mean I want to leave—as so many are foolishly doing, or thinking about. But finishing will take concentration I'm not sure I'm capable of. When Japan attacked Hawaii Sunday, I was studying Shakespeare for an hour exam Monday. Imagine— with tales of destruction of American lives and property, I had to read Shakespeare! Believe me, it wasn't easy.

Love, Ginny

Elmer – December 11, 1941 10:45 p.m.

My Dearest Ginny:

Now it's my turn to make excuses for not writing, but I fear that I haven't any. Just events of the past week have sort of upset a normal routine.

Speaking of the events of the past week, after 1:30 p.m. Sunday I was sorry I sent you that poem. Seems now John Bull wasn't the cause of our getting into this war. As a matter of fact, a lot of my attitudes on this country's foreign policy have changed since Sunday.

The war certainly has affected my job. Two of the boys in the block have been called by the Naval Reserve. Today I heard that the entire block department in our Garfield Branch quit en masse and joined the Marines.

You no doubt have heard about our air raid alarms Monday afternoon and Tues. morning. I didn't see or hear anything, but our messenger said it was pretty exciting.

All my love, El

Virginia returned to Hempstead for the Christmas holiday, so there are no letters until January.

January 2, 1942 – Japanese occupy Manila

Virginia – January 5, 1942 12:10 p.m.

Dearest,

This is gruesome, coming back here to everything related to work, leaving everything—like you. I think it will be my ambition fulfilled when I can have both in the same place at the same time.

Things aren't too bad, of course. Even an eight o'clock and following classes didn't seem too strange. And I'll be getting used to this tired feeling all too soon. But I'll *never* get used to the empty feeling that comes when vacations end—when I have to start counting days and weeks again until I see you.

After every vacation, the way I wear memories out by repeated fondling makes me feel like a miser with his gold. But it's the only method I have for remaining a half-way happy person.

Otherwise, I have nothing to tell you, except that I miss you *very* much. But thinking about it only blurs my vision.

Love, Ginny

Elmer – January 5, 1942 10:45 p.m.

My Dearest Ginny:

I was glancing through a copy of Milton's "Paradise Lost" this evening, and I come across a line that fit my mood.

"Farewell happy Fields, Where Joy forever dwells: Hail horror, hail Infernal world, and thou profoundest Hell Receive thy new Possessor!"

Ginny, how many hours were you home? Four or five it seemed like. Your leaving has shattered my morale. This is the toughest time of the year in the bank, but while you were here I didn't mind it because I had something to look forward to when I got home. Now it's different. So I work all day. So I come home. So I do homework. So what. Back in a very depressing rut.

Honey, I want to thank you for a *very* enjoyable fort-night and also for your broad-minded attitude toward my conduct New Year's Eve. I am very much ashamed of that incident. [It is not known what that was.]

All my love, El

Virginia – January 7, 1942 1:30 p.m.

Dearest El,

Why I should write to you right now is beyond me! I have only a few minutes before class time, I have nothing of interest and news to relate—but I just want to talk to you.

For a while my mood was bluer than anything imaginable but I got over it. Something happens—don't know what—and I think of the brighter side. It's funny, but little things mean a lot to me along this line. I try to pick out a high point in each day to look forward to. Back of all these minute bright spots, of course, is the time when I'll be with you again. Maybe you could try it, honey. If the thought of dinner at home or reading a good book is pleasant to you, try working with that time in mind. That way, every day has some good thing in it.

Your most welcome letter today showed me you work on the same principles I do, so maybe this system of "brightening the day" will work with you too—not *always*, I realize, because it *doesn't always* work for me, but most of the time.

Love, Ginny

Virginia – January 14, 1942 1:30 p.m.

Dearest,

Today so far has been a beaut.

A couple of days ago I got a card from the appointment office, asking me to report as soon as possible. I went over this morning to learn that the old _____who's in charge of NYA, etc, didn't approve of what I'd been quoted in the Orange as saying about the NYA and its probable curtailment. Seems I'd said I used the money for "spending money," which to her means money to throw around, I guess. Anyway, she gave me a little lecture and said I'd have to stop working until she'd "referred it to the board." O.K., I think. So I know she's a so-and-so. But I got mad anyway. Then, a bright idea, I guess.—she said I could write a letter to the editor, explaining the thing and that would do the trick. So, burning with a desire to spit in her glassy eye, I left, to go to work. However I didn't work the scheduled 2 hours. Instead, after beginning to explode to one of the girls in the office (where I type stuff) I broke in several pieces and cried, as though I'd just

heard the death sentence of my mother. It was awful. I *was mad.*
But I can't understand why it should've affected me so *strongly.*
When I couldn't stop—it really was awful—I got even madder,
now at myself, for being so foolish. The reaction (of what powerful
physiological causes, I haven't yet figured out)—finally ceased and
I tried to get rid of my *red*, white, & blue eyes.

Now I feel like a beat-up rag. Also, the more I think about
it, the more like a fool I feel. I wish I didn't have any feelings, or
at least not such painfully sensitive ones. I also wish I had more
money so I could write the _____ a letter to stand her head on
end. As it is, I wrote a fairly innocuous and simple letter, doing as
she wants. Now *certainly* will become a charter member of the
"Oh-Mrs.-Allis,-how-we-hate-you" club. And don't think there isn't
one. She's well-known for tricks like that.

Sorry to pour out the sob (very literally) story to you, honey,
but it had to be done—and you may as well know the awful truth.

A horrible habit, or fear of overestimating my very strong
feelings, keeps me from writing more than

Love, Ginny

Virginia – January 15, 1942 1:00 p.m.

Dearest,

Exams start Wednesday, with Monday & Tuesday termed block
week (I don't know why) when some classes are held as usual
but you don't have to attend. They're mostly for review. My first
exam is Saturday the 24th, Shakespeare. That's going to be
one of the toughest. The next *three* (count them, 3!) come on
the 27th, Tuesday. I have editorial interpretation, copy reading,

and American literature. This should be a red letter day, because both the first & last of the three are going to be *good*. On the next day, at *8*, I have the typography final and the last exam, advertising, falls on the last day, the 29th. So you see what fun it will be. I doubt whether I'll see Hempstead before April 3 or 4 [Easter break]. But if you came up before then, it'd be almost as good as my coming home! I say *almost* because you can't bring Schill Chateau & inmates with you. Maybe it's a good thing (?) you're not up here these days. The girls, many of them anyway, have taken to wearing slacks to keep warm. You'd be grumbling continually!

I didn't hear the philharmonic Sunday. Sundays I try to bury myself in my room and get a lot of back work done. I'd *love* to read the papers and listen to symphonies but I just can't. Sunday's are days of perseverance for me, and last Sunday I succeeded in getting a big assignment (for this afternoon's lab) finished.

The letter I wrote about the NYA business was published today. I hope the old bat is happy now—(correction) not happy—*satisfied*.

Latest flash—I've been appointed head of the publicity department in the women's volunteer work for defense on campus. (Here I bow slightly.)

What do you think about the submarine off Montauk Point?? More business for the upstate summer resorts! [This was a German U-boat captained by Reinhard Hardegen. On January 14 it sank the Norwegian-crewed oil tanker *Norness* off eastern Long Island. Over the course of his two tours, U-boats under Hardegen's command would sink or cripple eighteen more merchant vessels.]

It's a small word, honey, but its portent is great.

Love, Ginny

Virginia – January 18, 1942 4:20 p.m.

Dearest El,

If anyone had told me that Thomas Paine's "Rights of Man," with
its dusty, seldom-read look about it, would be interesting, I'd
have laid it to the fact that they were English or poli. Sci. majors
and therefore naturally of a distorted viewpoint on such subjects.
But, since I began a few days ago to read it—required as it is
with a report due ever since—I am astound [*sic.*], aghast, and
furthermore delight. It really is good, punchy writing. Diatribe,
ridicule, and various other juicy editorial features are all used by
Paine to prove his many arguments. I repeat, it's a good book.

Nonetheless, I wish the last 100 pages were *read* already and the report written.

You're in my thoughts all the time.

Love, Ginny

[On the reverse, next to her drawing]: All right—so I won't try to put my pictures on paper anymore—unless it be in words alone. I promise!

Elmer – January 18, 1942 10:00 p.m.

My Dearest Ginny:

If I had to write with any part of me except my right arm, I couldn't do it. That's the only place I'm not stiff. Last night I was skating at Brierly Field with Norm, Jim Hunter and a bunch of other fellows. I say skating; I'm wrong. It was more like a football game. I'd be peacefully skating along minding my own business and someone would come roaring up and throw a flying body block on me. Naturally I would have to reciprocate. Most of us were horizontal more than we were vertical so you can understand why I creaked when I got up this morning. I guess we're just gluttons for punishment because Jim and I went skating again this afternoon.

Well, both my finals are over and that English was a lu-lu. Write, write, write till deep in the night. I'll send you the results as soon as I get them.

All my love, El

Elmer – January 19, 1942 10:00 p.m.

My Dearest Ginny:

Dismal day. Rain all day long and tonight—fog. Nice clammy, thick fog. Perfect night for a murder if one is so inclined. Personally, I'm not, unless it's a Japanese soldier; but that's neither here nor there.

Ginny you keep right on drawing pictures on your letters. I find them very amusing and they do convey a message. However I would like to comment on a few items. First of all, why did you give me wings? I don't think they're exactly appropriate. Also you have my hair falling all over my forehead when you *know* it's always neatly combed. Lastly I think you would be much more becoming in a skirt rather than those sloppy-looking slacks. I just happened to notice. You've got my hair parted on the wrong side! Ginny, how could you overlook anything so obvious!

I leave you with a hot tip. No, I have nothing good in the 5th at Tropical [the local racetrack] tomorrow. Just keep Saturday, Feb. 21 in mind.

All my love, El

Virginia – January 21, 1942 7:30 p.m.

Dearest,

Not only a letter, but sunshine in it—and today we could use it here. Did you possibly mean, by your "hot tip" that you *can* get the Saturday (21st) off? Don't keep me in suspense this way!!

P.S. on this subject: you just better *not* have "something good in the 5th at Tropical"!!!

Every good artist has "commentaries" written about his work, to clear up questions in the layman's mind. I'll write my own commentary.

Appreciating Miss Schill's latest, "Girl Dreaming at her Study," requires an active imagination. Although the uninitiated would call her touch crude, without feeling and depth, the true connoisseur of modern art will understand it as something beyond the usual. The first glance shows one a cloudy mess of discordant line and shades. Obviously, this conveys the mood of the girl pictured. She has transcended the commonplace, above routine and ugly things, or, as they say on the street, "out of this world." Closer perusal tells why. Study may be her real object, but a vision is haunting her every minute. It is the vision of a boy and his image counterbalances the weight distribution (color and size) in the self-portrait. He is given an ethereal tone. The realist questions the meaning and truth of the wings sprouting from the boy's shoulders. Here we scornfully explain that, since only one human type of beings, namely angels, are pictured with these appendages, it is quite obvious what position the boy holds in the student's affections.

Aside from this minor digression, Miss Schill's self-portrait is strictly realistic. Slacks, sometimes considered ugly by prejudiced conservatives, hair of both subjects awry, as (I speak with intimate knowledge of those pictured) is often the case, and other accurate features. Judging the whole, we conclude that the artist has given up a concise, easy-to-understand picture of her daily life.

(As for you, El, if you can't *see* that I was looking in a mirror at the time and *naturally* got your hair parted on the wrong side,—well, you'll just *never* be an art lover if you won't try to fathom out simple things!!!)

Love, Ginny

Virginia – January 24, 1942 9:05 p.m.

Dearest,

I hope like anything you're listening to the symphony now. Toscanini is right now doing a wonderful job on Overture to a Midsummer Night's Dream. I must get this. I *love* the violin part. They're *so* dainty and fairy-like. Mendelssohn must have appreciated Shakespeare thoroughly. It's a *perfect* musical reproduction of the atmosphere in the play.

The mention of Shakespeare brings vividly to my mind the final this afternoon. It was a beaut—*entirely* on Hamlet!! Of course I'd spent *hours*, working my eyes red, white & blue over all the background material and the other plays we read this year. But was there anything about these things? Not attall, *attall*.

All right! All right, be a skeptic! Doubt my word! If you think that when you're on my mind, it's so lightly, so imperceptibly, that it can't be seen in any self-reflecting (oops, sorry) mirror, you can go on belittling my power of concentration (on you) and see where it gets you! Be careful what you say to me! Your wings will fall off!—And this last, I don't believe will *ever* happen, angel.

Love, *Ginny*

Elmer – January 26, 1942 9:50 p.m.

My Dearest Ginny:

The way everything is being speeded up in this war effort, you would think that time would speed up accordingly. It's fairly creeping. Seems like you've been gone for months when in reality it has only been a couple of weeks.

Last night I went to a Church supper. There is only one thing
wrong with Church Suppers. They don't give you enough to eat.
After the supper Mom & Pop stayed to hear a lengthy report by the
District Superintendent but I had to leave early and go down to the
diner for a couple of hamburgers. I was still hungry.

Today we had an air-raid practice in the bank. Everything
went off like clock-work. We had every negotiable instrument in the
bank in the vault, the ledgers put away and everyone in the bank
up on the 3rd floor within *five* minutes. Did I tell you I have been
appointed an air-raid captain?

They really are beginning to trust me in the bank. This
morning one of the officers called me up to his desk and gave me
a check for $5,000 [about $78,000 today]. He told me to deliver
it to a certain Mr. Endres but not before the gentleman in question
could identify himself to my satisfaction. They left it to my judgment
whether the gent was who he was supposed to be. He was.

Honey if you keep calling me angel I will continually be
glancing over my shoulder to see if I really am sprouting wings.

All my love, El

Virginia – January 31, 1942 8:30 p.m.

Dearest El,

This has been a day of leisure and I can't say I've enjoyed it.
Everyone has left—not only Wilbur, but all of the campus,—and
the *deadness* hovering all around gives me the jumps. [She'd
stayed on campus for winter break.] I slept until 12:30 today. That
was wonderful. But since I got up it's been awful. I read a book
this afternoon and tonight (later) it will be some tales of Poe. This is
O.K, I guess, but when I think of all this time when I *could* be with

you and how much I'd love doing these things with *you* instead of alone—well, I'll be sort of glad when classes start and I'm again pressed for time to sleep.

Last night Kathy & I *did* go skating. The ice was good, my skates are lovely, and my *skating's getting better*! In fact, with a little more practice I wouldn't mind skating with anyone who can *skate*—like you.

Well, honey, I know the news about the American lit. B, plain and simple. I console myself with the knowledge that *dear* Mr. Snook *notoriously* begins his alphabet with B. Still...!

Very gay scene here. Kathy knitting. Miss Madden knitting. Chris reading. Very exciting. *Quiet*. Jeepers, I wish *this* weekend were *the* weekend. You'd be here now. And there's a beautiful moon. Deep sigh. But all I can do *now* is *send* my love to my angel, you.

                         Ginny

                         Elmer – February 2, 1942 11:05 p.m.

My Dearest:

Today was a blue Monday to end all blue Mondays. The first of the month always is a heavy day but to make matters worse, one of the boys was out today. None of the blocks would prove; customers were making errors on their deposits which kept us from proving; I'm breaking in a new and very unintelligent girl to the block work; and to top it all off, the tellers were late in striking a figure, without which my proof-sheet won't balance, and this made me just late enough to miss my train. You can see why I was tearing my hair out in large clusters when I came home tonight. Then I looked on the book-case and there sitting very quietly were two letters. Honey you can't realize what a lift those two letters gave me. One would have been enough to pull me out of the dumps but two sent me into a beautiful—reverie, shall we say, and all my blues were forgotten.

Honey, did you happen to see last week's issue of Life Magazine. Beautiful pictures of United States War Planes, in full color, too! And among them was *the* ship. Republic's new high-altitude fighter P-47. [The "P" was a hold-over from World War I, when they were called "pursuit" planes. It was later changed to "F" for fighter.] What a plane! Powered by a 2,000 H.P. Pratt & Whitney motor that pulls it along at a paltry 450 M.P.H. It has power dived at 680 M.P.H.! Which ain't hay. That's what I want for Christmas. A P-47 and a commission as a 2nd Lieut. in the Army Air Corps.

© 1942 Time, Inc.

All my love, El

Virginia – February 3, 1942 11:30 p.m.

Dearest,

All day yesterday I batted out stories on the ball. The ball-goers voted on the four senior ball queen finalists and elected a queen (Cinderella this year) so I had to write *four* leads to my main story *and four* feature stories on the Cinderella for today's paper! *But,* I wrote only 3 features because I figured one of them didn't have much of a chance. It was *very* good she didn't win!

The ball? Ah yes. Well, frankly honey, I had only a mediocre time. James' [Harry, famous trumpeter and band leader of the time] music was quite good, though noisy at times. He really has several good arrangements and his sax section is excellent.

But I *do* have James' autograph on the very nice leather program and I *did* get to the Senior ball!

Love, Ginny

P.S. You ought to hear James' "Flatbush Flanagan." Very good!

Virginia – February 6, 1942 8:30 a.m.

Dearest El,

Last night I saw a color and sound movie on Airacobra [the P-39], that very pretty but very destructive pursuit plane with a small cannon mounted in the nose and machine guns in the wings and the tail, *all*  operated by *one* man, the pilot, from his controls! Bell Aircraft, who make the Airacobras, put it out.

And I did see those pictures in Life. In fact, I'm saving them for posterity or further reference or somebody.

P.S. You *cannot* have a P-47 *or* the commission as 2nd lieutenant in the Army air corps. If you get *that* for Christmas, *I* expect a P-40 so I can commute!

I'm very unhappy. The mail just came and no letter from El. Black curse of Cromwell [ancient and powerful Irish oath] be on him!

Love, Ginny

Elmer – February 10, 1942 10:05 p.m.

My Dearest:

Your last letter wounded me deeply. A wound that I doubt even time can erase. Here I've been hovering between life and death for the past few days [he had a cold] and you call me a bum for not writing! Oh! What a stab in the back!

Back to work today, after a nice long rest. The bank doctor, who the boss insisted I see, said, after close examination, that there is really nothing wrong with me. Just a case of acute consumption. He gives me from three to four weeks to live. That's good. I'll have time to go to Syracuse and see Ginny.

How do you like the new war daylight saving hours we're on? I think it's wonderful in the afternoon. It's still light when I get home from work! But in the morning! Seems like I get up in the middle of the night. When I drove to the station this morning the moon and the stars were shining brightly, with just the faintest hint of dawn in the east.

It's been quite a few letters since I told you how much I miss you. By now you should realize it goes without saying.

All my love, El

Virginia – February 12, 1942 8:15 p.m.

Dearest,

I've tried and it's no use. At least the words don't come out as I hear them inside. Maybe there are no words to go with these feelings.

The thing is, that after a vain session with paper and pencil *early* this morning—all I can write now, in the way of poetry, is the jingle type—I decided to say it in prose.

Remember the letter I wrote you last year? This, again on Valentine's Day, will be about the same, except now I'm even more sure you're wonderful.

Angel. Because of many things. Because you don't get mad and yell. Because you seldom even get mad! My angel—ever since that *awful* day when you were so sweet about everything anyone else would've gotten disgustingly drunk over. [It's not known what this was about.] Because you work so hard—not only in things any fellow would, his job, but also at schoolwork where the results are so intangible.

You're never bored. You're interested in subjects and you can talk about subjects *anyone* just wouldn't know the first thing about.—I can't remember *ever* hearing you say anything unkind about anybody. You're not that way.

Even if you don't like my shoes, honey, or most unorthodox trends in the way of clothes. I'm very satisfied with the way *you* look—just for fun, some day, I'd like to see you when you *weren't* neat, clean, and freshly brushed looking!

This isn't a quarter of how I appreciate you. You like woods and streams and out-of-the-way places. You like Tchaikovsky and Thornhill, Dvorak and Dorsey. You like dancing, swimming, skating—everything. You like to read Sunday newspapers, see a New York show, sit quietly in some softly-lit restaurant and argue pleasantly over scotch and soda.

Every time I see a beautiful sunset, outlining Crouse towers and the Castle, I think of you and wish *you* could see it. Tonight the sky was deep blue and the tree branches, silhouetted and accentuated with snow, seemed to be tangled with stars—they were never that near and bright. I wished you could see it with me.

It must be because the same feelings, the same motives, the same goals and ideals that I call my own I often find in you.

How could I ever sum it all up in one letter and explain why it's Love, Ginny!?!

Elmer – February 16, 1942 10:15 p.m.

My Dearest:

I got your Valentine and honey it was the sweetest, most thoughtful thing a man could ever receive for Valentine's Day or any other time. You'll never know how deeply that letter touched me. However, the things you said more closely described you than they do me. Every nice thing you wrote is something I have, at some time or another, thought of you; only I haven't the faculty to express them. Aside from the nice things you said there are other sterling qualities you possess that I greatly admire. The first is intelligence and ability to converse intelligently. I have, on occasion, gone out with other girls and honey I find they can be put into one of two classes. Either they refrain from conversation altogether and act like a bump on a log or else they chatter incessantly about nothing in particular. Not so with you. You can carry on an intelligent conversation with ease and also you're a good listener which is another reason I think so much of you. The second is forbearance. I ask you. How many girls would act the way you did New Year's Eve? Any other girl would never have spoken to me after my conduct that night. Incidentally, I wouldn't have blamed them. I could go on and on—.

All my love, El

Virginia – February 18, 1942 8:00 p.m.

Dearest,

This war has stymied me. I called the U.S. Weather Bureau tonight
to find out what the weekend's weather is to be but—"We can't
give out any information" was all I got. He was very pleasant and
seemed to realize I wasn't a spy, but still, no weather forecast.
[Weather reports were considered of potential use by the enemy,
and the Code of Wartime Practices forbade their dissemination.]

    I won another dollar (plus small leather wallet affair) for an
ad I wrote in advertising—a dollar in credit at the store, it is. Now
I've told you that and there's nothing left.

    But I can't think of anything but Saturday and you anyway!

Love, *Ginny*

February 19, 1942 – President Roosevelt
issues Executive Order 9066,
beginning the forced internment of Japanese Americans

Virginia – February 24, 1942 9:00 p.m.

Dearest,

Everything without you is lonely. This morning was the bluest
Tuesday I've ever seen. Besides the fact that it was *snowing* (!!)
There was also the thought of everything just *finishing*, with an
awful long wait for the next time. I felt and must have looked like
walking worry. After the second class, though, hope returned. I'd
met a few people who knew you'd gone and sympathized with

me. I'd had a few assignments piled on and the prospect of much business from here on in.

It was a wonderful weekend, dearest. I'll dream of it, talk of it, think of it for the next five weeks. And all because there's so much of me in the rather small word I always send you—

Love, Ginny

Elmer – February 25, 1942 10:00 p.m.

My Darling—

Please, please forgive me for not writing last night. I just couldn't do it. I fell asleep right after supper. You see I spent nearly ten hours on the New York Central. I never would have made the 1:40 if it hadn't been late. It came into Syracuse 25 minutes late. That was only the beginning. Between Syracuse and Albany we lost 3 ½ hours! A bearing burned out on one of the Pullmans. The train staggered into New York at 11:20 a.m., exactly 3 hours and fifty minutes late. You can see why I was tired last night. I told them at the bank exactly what happened. They didn't say anything.

Honey, you speak of a blue Tuesday. You cannot possibly have had as blue a Tuesday as I did. The first reason it was blue was naturally leaving you. This was the reason for 99% of my blues; but accompanying this reason were others. One was that my trip was a change of scenery and I hated to get back into my rut.

Ginny, I want to thank you for showing me a really swell time while I was up there. You seemed to have something planned for every minute and believe me, I really enjoyed myself. However,

I have got one complaint to make. Why didn't you think of a way to make the week-end last longer.

All my love, El

Virginia – February 26, 1942 10:00 p.m.

Dearest El,

Glenn Miller just played Beethoven's Moonlight Sonata and of course I'm thinking now of the College Inn with you. Hope you know, honey, what the weekend was to me.

Paul Robeson sang a spiritual and "It Ain't Necessarily So" on Crosby's program tonight.

I wish you were here.

The dreadful precipitation stopped after yesterday's session, when I was at the brink of insanity. It's wonderful today—the comparison alone is!—and very like spring. Darling, you *must* come up here in the spring! Could you be quite, *quite* ill the morning of May 9? I'm giving you plenty of time to arrange this! It would be spring weekend and, although the junior prom is *Friday* night, I would gladly settle for you on Saturday morning. That weekend is neither at the beginning nor the end of the month so the bank should be *glad* to see it my way, no? It isn't even the *middle* of the month!

News: I'm on the dean's list in the School of Journalism (also Liberal Arts as I'm dually enrolled). In English 119 (American Lit.) this a.m. I got into an excellent political argument with the usually boring prof. It was the first time in weeks I've been able to break down his careful routine of lectures!

Not news: I love you. Ginny

Elmer – March 4, 1942 10:30 p.m.

My Dearest—

About twenty minutes ago I was walking home from an errand for Mom when I quietly said to myself "Hmm, spring is almost here," for no reason whatsoever. It's not warm out; as a matter of fact, there is a thin crust of ice on the damp ground. The sun is not shining; it's nighttime. Birds are not singing; if there are birds around, they are sleeping. Anyway something made me feel that spring was trying to put in an appearance. Maybe it was a clean, earthy smell that did it; or maybe it was a chill-less breeze that whispered in my ear. This feeling gave way to a feeling of utter serenity and peace. I have a clear conscience, and there is no reason why I shouldn't be calm and serene, but this was different. More or less a deep contentment. Please excuse my ramblings, but my feelings were odd. I hope I have been able to express them as I felt them.

All my love, El

March 7, 1942 – The initial class of five Tuskegee airmen graduates, becoming the first Black military aviators

---

Virginia – March 8, 1942 3:00 p.m.

Dearest,

Although it was snowing yesterday morning, thus dashing my ideas of spring to pieces for a while, today makes me feel *much* better. It really looks, feels, and *smells* like the wonderful season has come.

Right at this point in the calendar everyone (junior editors) on the Orange is breaking his neck to make the best of the last few weeks before election of the senior staff. Up to a while ago, my hopes were very slim indeed, but I have a scheme under way that even *I* hardly dare *think* about in terms of results. All I can do is work and hope.

Love, Ginny

March 11, 1942 – General MacArthur escapes the Philippines

The Army Calls

Elmer – March 12, 1942 11:00 p.m.

My Dearest—

I was talking to our asst. credit manager the other day and he tells me that he is well acquainted with the officer in command of the Army Air Force in the New York Area. He told me that if I wanted to join the Air Corps he could probably help me out. This is a very nice thing to know, but I won't act upon it until the fall. I have too good a summer in the offing.

All my love, El

Virginia – March 15, 1942 11:20 a.m.

Dearest,

This week has been hectic and I'm looking forward to similar ones for the next three. Since Tuesday I've been cultivating my new beat, the Radio workshop. It's fairly interesting and I'm learning a few things about radio, but I've liked beats more!

The senior editors problem is still the thorn in all junior editors' flesh. At Friday's junior staff meeting we were told about the writing of our letters of application. I intend to *apply* for editor-in-chief with editorial page director as second choice. This means I've got to plan what I'll do with the paper if I should get it because you must include such info. in the letter and must elucidate said plans before the publications board when election time comes around! Great fun. It's a nerve-wracking problem, really. *Every thing* you do in the office, almost every move you make you feel is being watched. I took the paper through Friday and, so far as I can see, it's a good enough paper.

Depending on when I decide to leave this place it's only 18 or 17 days to go [until Easter break]—which really won't be long—I hope. I want to take about six hours off and listen to all my records and I want to go to the woods I mentioned once before and wade in the streams.

Love, Ginny

Elmer – March 23, 1942 10:45 p.m.

My Dearest—

Home from my weekly Mon. night gym and swim session. This systematic exercise is great for one's constitution. Very exhaustive though.

I wish you hadn't told me the program for next week's symphony. Now I am disappointed because I have to miss it. I am an usher in a special Palm Sunday Cantata in church next week.

No class in accounting tonight and I think fate had something to do with it. I got home in time to hear Bing Crosby and I think his program was meant just for you and me. He sang

"I Remember You," "Blues in the Night," "A Couple in the Castle" "Miss You;" and the orchestra played "A String of Pearls." What a program!

All my love, El

March 26, 1942 – Nazis begin deporting Jews to Auschwitz

Virginia – March 28, 1942 9:20 p.m.

Dearest,

Speaking of Crosby, we've been crossed up, honey! Thursday night, not only was I taking the paper through with the first sophomore being trained for the job, but also that was the night for the city (5-county, to be exact) black-out! So—I couldn't get to the radio and if I had, it was being used to report blackout proceedings! I'm glad you heard it though. It certainly was a star program!

Last night we had our spring formal. *I* spent the evening plotting—for the coming election of senior editors! Irene & I did paste-up jobs, samples of what we'd do with the paper if, etc. I'll be so glad when it's all over!

Darling, if I didn't have so much to do I'd wish today were Wednesday, but there's so much to do before I go and it's such wonderful pleasure anticipating being with you and home again— well, for the short time, I almost enjoy it, do you understand? Sort of like lingering over a delicious-looking morsel before tasting it!

Now, to my various & sundry tasks so the week home will be as near perfection as possible. Let me know what train I should get immediately, if not sooner!

Love, Ginny

Pardon me sir, have you seen the moon?

Elmer – April 16, 1942 7:30 p.m.

My Dearest—

Honey your going back to school affects me in a strange way.
Somehow it makes me want to join the Army as soon as possible.
While you were around I was content to wait in anticipation of
the summer, but since you went away everything seems dull
around here and I want to leave. You have no cause to worry
though, Mom won't sign up for me yet. [At this date, recruits had
to be twenty-one to volunteer without parental permission, or
to be drafted. On November 30, Congress lowered that age to
eighteen.]

I miss you my sweet
and I love you very much, El

**April 18, 1942 – Lieutenant Colonel James Doolittle
leads a B-29 bombing raid on Tokyo, taking the war to Japan
and giving Americans a big morale boost**

Virginia – April 19, 1942 4:45 p.m.

Darling,

I really have news today. I've been pledged to Eta Pi Epsilon,
senior women's honorary on campus. It's got me quite excited—it
really is an honor, although I hate to be the one to be telling you.
Only 15 were pledged this year.

For those evenings when you get to feeling like joining
the army, I suggest that you read "Moby Dick" by one Herman
Melville. Only one thing—you must *not* then want to be a sailor!!

Seriously, honey, I wish you weren't so anxious to join the air
force—still I'm awfully glad you do feel that way. But *first*, I wish

that you were less fidgety. It's an awfully somber note, darling, but an awfully real one when I suggest that after you leave it may be for good. So please—and it's very selfish of me, I know—consider this summer as already planned for?

I love you so, El, that everything I do, everything I think and say has to be associated with my love. It's far too great to fit into one heart. So I dwell on it, the newness and wonderful happiness of it.

Did I say "my" love? But that's not really right, because I never think singly in this matter.

It's always El and Ginny

Elmer – May 1, 1942 9:45 p.m.

My Dearest—

Honey here is some news. I think El is going to put in his application for Army Air Cadet within the week. Now don't get sore—Let me explain. You see, Bob and Jack have had their applications in for at least a month and have been accepted, yet they still haven't been inducted. When they do get inducted, they will then be given a 30 day furlough before being sent away. All in all there is a lapse of almost three months from the time your application is presented 'till the time you are sent away. This means that if I wait until Sept. to present my application, I will not be sent away until winter, and I don't want to leave in winter; but, if I enroll now, I will leave around August 1st which seems like a good time to me. Please let me know what you think of this idea.

I miss you terribly
and love you very, very much. El

May 4–8, 1942 – The Battle of the Coral Sea, the first in history conducted entirely between carrier-borne aircraft, thwarts a major Japanese advance

Virginia – May 1, 1942 12:10 a.m.

Dearest El,

I have yet to hear about the senior staff for the Orange. The publications board met Tuesday afternoon. We five (applicants for the editorship) were interviewed and returned to sweat for a few hours. Comes 5:30 or so, the board files out of the room. "No decision."

Yesterday at 3 again they convene, and the little tale is repeated, but without the interviews. They (the board) reached no decision but decided to take the deadlock to the Chancellor. The latest news today has it that the board will re-assemble Monday with the Chancellor's advice on the subject to go by. So *perhaps* we'll know by Monday.

In the meantime, the juniors in question are slowly going mad, the rest of the staff is disintegrating, and a general mess seems to be prevailing. All great fun!

Love, Ginny

Virginia – May 8, 1942 1:00 a.m.

Dearest,

It all started, of course, Monday. That weekend I don't recall very much of. It was nervous—but Monday was worse than anything I've been through. The board met at 3, talked for about an hour,

called in three of the five candidates, then discussed some more after they'd been questioned. Finally, when my hands were quite cold and my insides quite in a turmoil, the ex-editor came out and said, "Miss Schill." [She was only the second woman to be appointed editor-in-chief of the *Daily Orange*.]

I don't believe I've gotten over it yet. It wasn't all surprise—though that had a part—because I'd dreamed of such things. It just didn't seem true!

First headache came with my staff. The fellow who was deadlocked with me for the editorship refused the executive editor's position. He wanted to be managing editor or nothing. I'm glad now he's not on the staff. Such childishness and pride are not commendable—and are very unusual in D.O. workers.

Anyway, I got my staff, it was announced officially today, and today I *conferred* with the Dean who was furious that I hadn't consulted him about the staff. Things have been very unlovely today. Some days you'd do better to stay in bed!

By Monday, however, the old staff will be completely evacuated so *perhaps* things will run smoother. As it is, everything is as confused as possible. I miss an average of one class and 2 meetings per day.

And I *still* don't want you to sign up with the air corps right away! Just because Jack's had a long wait is no surety for you of the same! It could as easily happen one way as the other. So there!

Still thinking of you, though not so agile with the pen!

Love, Ginny

A week before his twentieth birthday, Elmer writes to Virginia to tell her that he has his application for the Air Corps—news he buries on the second page of the letter. Virginia responds in her next letter, "I'd like to know what the score is with this air corps stuff you've been handing me! Thought you were going to be home this summer?!? Hmmm!!" The effects of the war began to be felt more broadly in the US with the rationing of commodities such as gasoline and sugar.

Elmer – May 29, 1942 11:15 p.m.

My Dearest—

No doubt you received my telegram. So I will go on to explain. When you wrote and told me to wait until Fall to sign up, I conducted an investigation and found that the average waiting time between induction into the Air Corps and departure for a training station was from three to four months. I figured if I joined now, I would go just about the time you went back to school. So I put in my application, and Wednesday they called me down for my mental exam; which incidentally was a lulu (3 ¾ hours). Sixty three out of 125 passed and I was lucky enough to be one of the former group. Those of us who passed were told to report back the following morning (yesterday) for our physical. Bright and early they marched us down to the ferry and shipped us over to Governors Island [then a US Army fort in New York Harbor]. The exam took from 8 am to 1 pm and how they did tear us apart. They split us up into small groups so I can't say for sure but I understand that more than 50 % flunked the physical. So you see I haven't got the Transylvanian crud after all! In the afternoon we were brought back to the mainland for a character interview with an officer. During the course of this interview, I asked the Captain how long it would be before we went away, and he said from 2 ½ to 3 months. It's reasonably certain that I will be around most of the summer. You see why neither of us have heard from El recently. He has been studying and sleeping.

Darling, I hope you're not angry with me for not waiting. I hated to go against your wishes, but I couldn't see any sense in signing up in the fall and then having to wait until winter before going away. Still love me honey?

El

Virginia – June 2, 1942 3:30 p.m.

Dearest,

Thanks for the telegram. Of course I was glad you passed the exams, and especially since they're no cinch!

No, silly, I'm not mad at you for signing up! Christmas! I just wanted you to be home this summer, and if you will—good! You're only to be congratulated for passing the exams, honey. You didn't *really* think I'd be annoyed, did you?

I would have written sooner about your becoming an army man but there were too many exams staring me in the face.

Love, Ginny

Elmer – June 3, 1942 10:20 p.m.

My Dearest—

I received three letters today. One from Ginny, one from the War Department [as the Department of Defense was then called] and one from the Department of Internal Revenue. The War

Department told me to appear at 39 Whitehall Street [the Armed Forces induction center] at ten A.M. on June 5 to be sworn into the United States army, after which I will be on reserve until called. The Department of Internal Revenue gently reminded me that I owe the government $8. in income taxes.

These last few days are passing much too slowly. However they must eventually pass and then I will be able to tell you how much I love you, and not have to be content with writing it on a piece of paper.

All my love, El

Virginia returned home to Hempstead in early June, so there is no correspondence until she returns to Syracuse in September. On June 7, the US emerged victorious from the Battle of Midway, which effectively eliminated Japan's aircraft carrier force and any realistic hope that the Japanese might prevail, though the war raged on for more than three years.

Virginia – September 18, 1942

Darling,

I've been thinking of you all day—and if this is a criterion,—as I know it is, you'll never be off my mind. Gad—the poor fate of the Orange!

Went out for a coke with Irene and felt like I'd walked into a canteen instead of The Varsity. What a slew of uniformed men— CPT [civilian pilot training] pre-flight and other pre-flight students. This is a camp, not a campus!

I'll write you again tomorrow, dearest, to tell you I love you. There's not enough room for the subject here!

Love, Ginny

Elmer – September 21, 1942 7:15 p.m.

My Dearest—

Jack had to report to 39 Whitehall Street today for orders. He came home on the 5:12 with the gang tonight and it seems he has to leave 10:00 Friday [five days later] for Nashville, Tenn. They don't give you much notice, do they?

Incidentally, Honey, it may interest you to know that after Jack leaves I am going to give up smoking and drinking so that I'll be in prime condition when my time comes.

Yesterday [we] took a ride out East. It seemed almost a luxury to travel some distance by automobile. The only reason we went riding was because Jack has a lot of gas coupons he wants to use up. How unpatriotic!

The fellows in the bank feel as though they know you better than I do, I talk about you so much. Gee, Honey a lot of the joy of loving someone is in praising her to other people.

All my love, El

Elmer – September 24, 1942 8:15 p.m.

My Dearest—

Oh! Am I glad there aren't many more of the gang going into the army!! Last night we tossed a Stag affair for Jack over at Pat's. None of us got really drunk just extremely happy, but you should have seen the bunch on the train this morning. They looked like they'd been through a war. Even *I* had a head. I woke up bright and early to-day and felt fine. Then I got out of bed and stood up. Wham! Somebody hit me with a brick.

Jack was over here for the last time, tonight. He was pretty darned excited about the whole thing. Except for you, honey, I wish

I were going with him. Jack says if he could go into the army about twice a year, he would be set for life. Seems as though everyone is giving him a going-away present. Better than Xmas.

I got a new girl in the department the latter part of last week. I say girl; that's not quite correct. She is twenty-four and married. I can't complain though; she is interested in her work and quick to learn, so that there is not much difficulty in breaking her in to block work.

My right hand man leaves tomorrow and I am getting an experienced girl to take his place. I only hope she is half as good as Dick was.

All my love, El

Virginia – September 30, 1942
12:10 p.m.

Dearest El,

Got a ticket to hear Dr. Igor Sikorsky downtown so I went. He spoke mostly of his latest invention, the helicopter, and explained its workings. Really a marvelous machine! Goes almost any way you can mention, and is very easily handled. He showed movies of his first ship (helicopter) and the trial flights and tests. Most ungainly looking machine—closely resembles a huge insect of some sort—but is amazingly flyable (if that's a word). He predicted mass use of them after the war.

Rough sketch → *[rotor, propeller]* But I'm still not sure which is the front !!

I love you. Ginny

Elmer – October 6, 1942 8:15 p.m.

My Dearest—

Got a letter from Jack today. He's doing pretty good in Nashville. He said at first he had a little difficulty with the marching drills; kept wandering off by himself. But he's catching on to it now. He mentioned the good food they're getting down there. Yesterday for lunch, he said they had fried chicken, green peas, mashed potatoes and chocolate pie. For *lunch* mind you.

Nassau County had a surprise blackout last night. I was just coming out of the eye doctor's when the alarm sounded, so I went back in and chewed the fat with doc till it was over. His office is right in the heart of Freeport village, and did that place get dark quick. In a matter of seconds, every light in the village was out. Very effective.

Jim got a letter from the draft board yesterday. He is to report for induction on the 15th of October, probably the same day that Bob leaves. After that, I will be the only one of the old gang left. So then it won't be so bad leaving.

All my love, El

Elmer visited Virginia at Syracuse the weekend of October 10, and they became engaged, but kept it a fairly close secret, likely because they wished to announce it to their parents in person.

Virginia – October 13, 1942 12:55 p.m.

Darling,

It's wonderful being engaged to you, honey, unofficial though it is. I told Carol and I'm going to tell Kathy when she comes up—I want to see her face when I do!—but otherwise it will be unknown. I feel like telling everybody, but I don't think I'd better when Mom &

Pop don't know, among other reasons. You see what I mean, don't you?

I gotta get to work. I'm taking the paper through (with the juniors, of course) tonight, so I won't be able to write where I said I would. Forgive me?

I love you, El. Ginny

Elmer – October 13, 1942 8:30 p.m.

My Dearest—

I get back home to find that the only other fellow in the bank, beside myself, got his notice to report to headquarters for instructions.

Darling, I felt miserable about leaving you and of course I miss you very much; but under this misery, I feel an almost buoyant happiness, brought about, no doubt, by the knowledge that you are willing to wait for me and that you want to marry me as much as I want to marry you. I swear, I've been walking around above everyone's heads today. As a matter of fact, the boss said to me today, "Odell, if you don't come down off the ceiling, you're going to get fired!"

All my love, El

Elmer – October 22, 1942 7:30 p.m.

My Darling:

Yesterday I went down to Air Corps Headquarters again to see if I could get any concrete information on my departure. Their answer was very clarifying and satisfactory. I leave approximately the 20th of November for Nashville, Tenn. Now the only trouble is, I won't be in Nashville during Christmas vacation. Where I go from there remains a mystery. Possibly Montgomery, Ala., possibly San Antonio, Texas. Who can tell?

All my love, El

October 23, 1942 – The decisive second battle of El Alamein begins; the British victory prevents German control of Egypt

---

Virginia – October 23, 1942 9:00 p.m.

Darling,

I don't doubt the Norm has by now told you of his expectations in regard to being sent overseas—before Christmas, he told me, since armorers are in great demand. I'm sure he didn't mean to conceal anything from you.

You'll let me know, practically the *very minute you* know, when you have to leave, won't you!

That's a darn good idea—taking the pre-induction course being given, by the American Legion, I believe. [He'd written that he'd signed up for weekly training in the "fundamentals of drilling and the manual of arms" at the Hempstead Armory.] Just another of the things you do that I admire. You're so enthusiastic, so eager to learn and work at whatever you have to do.

You're wonderful, darling. Ginny

Elmer – October 25, 1942 9:30 p.m.

My Darling—

I am aware that your birthday will soon be here and I've been wracking my brain trying to think of something to give you. I have decided I would like very much to give you a diamond and make our engagement official. What I want to know now is how you feel about it. Do you want an engagement ring at this time? Or would you rather wait. Personally I could think of no better time to get engaged than during Colgate Weekend. If you want a ring now, shall I go up and speak to your father. Give me some idea of the procedure. You know I don't get engaged very often. That one custom I'm not up on.

All my love, El

Virginia's letter in response to Elmer's proposal of a ring is missing from the collection, but she did not get a ring for her birthday.

Elmer – November 1, 1942 8:00 p.m.

My Darling—

I read and reread your letter and it sounds like sound judgment. I realize now that it would be selfish of me to make an issue out of the question. I guess it would be better for us to wait, at least for a few months anyway. Oh well, it was an idea. I love you so much, I guess it clouds my judgment.

About your getting home or my coming up more than once, I am as much in a fog as you are. It all depends on the Army. You see I don't want to leave the Bank until I get my notice and I don't know exactly when that notice will be forthcoming.

All my love, El

Virginia – November 1, 1942 11:45 p.m.

Darling,

Seems like I haven't seen you in years. Dearest, how can I possibly stand a whole long war away from you? I think I'll work very hard, try to be clever, and get a job as foreign correspondent. (Some order, huh?) Then at least I'll be seeing something too. I hate to think of staying home, out of everything, *waiting*, and doing the little that we can. [They had discussed in several letters whether she should come home to see him before he left.]

Indecision is awful. My marks certainly don't warrant it and I *prefer* to be on hand for every publication, but this can't be the main issue when you're concerned—you and the limited time you'll be around. So   !

If you don't hear from me, you'll be seeing me—very soon. Because I love you very much.

Ginny

Virginia came down to Hempstead on Thursday, November 5th and returned on Sunday the 8th.

November 8, 1942 – The beginning of "Operation Torch," the first American landings in North Africa

Virginia – November 9, 1942 1:05 p.m.

Darling,

Just to let you know I'm here and thinking of you. I didn't take the 11:45. There wasn't any room on the lousy freighter, so I took the 11:55. First there were about 3 (sounding like 30) potted soldiers making everyone know they had vocal chords. Then it was fairly quiet but also fairly *cold*. The cars didn't have the double windows on yet and the breeze certainly blew in! Hope my nose isn't going to run long!

All in all, it wasn't so bad. Just not very comfortable and not at all happy. If you'd been there, I would've enjoyed riding the rails.

Got in about 5:45 and grabbed a couple of hours sleep in bed. I'm beginning to come alive again now.

I can't believe that I'm lucky enough to have you in only a few days. Dearest, I do love you *so* much! What happened to this past weekend? I only caught a glimpse of you!

I love you, El,Ginny

November 10, 1942 – Virginia's twenty-first birthday

Elmer went up to Syracuse on Friday the 13th and returned to Roosevelt on Monday the 16th.

Virginia – November 15, 1942 11:00 p.m.

Darling,

What to say to you? Just a few minutes ago I could hear your voice. An hour ago I could kiss you. Now you're only a few blocks away—but as good as in New York. What a system!

But I certainly couldn't have had a more wonderful weekend, dearest. I'm luckier than a lot of girls right now, I suppose, but as humans do, I want everything, all the time. That means you. Some day, God willing, I won't always have to see you leave me but instead, be able to go with you wherever you go.

Wrote to Mom & Pop yesterday. I told them that we are considering ourselves engaged, and I explained about the ring. I'm rather anxious to hear their reactions.

I love you, darling. Ginny

Elmer – November 16, 1942 10:00 p.m.

My Dearest—

The trip down wasn't too bad, except at first I thought I made a mistake and boarded a troop train. So many soldiers I have never seen. A few of them were boisterous but I managed to get a little sleep.

As I predicted, everybody in the office wanted to know how I felt today. "Oh, I'm feeling better, but I'm not quite in top-notch shape yet." I said dramatically, with my fingers crossed.

Darling, I want to thank you again for a very wonderful week-end. You have given me many beautiful memories that will come in very handy when I am far away from you and home.

Although I know it will be the last time for quite a while, I can't wait to see you again. I love you so much, dearest.

All my love, forever, El

This was his last letter from Roosevelt. He was called up later that week, and phoned Virginia with the news.

Virginia – November 18, 1942 1:55 p.m.

Darling,

All day long I've been chasing a circle mentally. Considered going home this afternoon, and the temptation is still great, but then I thought of the more sensible aspects. And it really wouldn't help matters very much, I suppose. But oh, darling, it's so hard to think of you leaving—for 8 months!

With a little work on myself, I think I'll be able to keep going fairly happily and enjoy the present separation. It won't be easy, and *enjoy* isn't the right word, of course, but I'm going to 1) consider your going as the start of something great—the wings and commission, 2) get to work on my studies and make a better average, 3) look forward to Christmas, perhaps, or my graduation, or your "graduation" as a time when I'll *really* be very happy.

So my dearest, all my love, wherever you are always, and know always that I'm cheering for your success.

I love you, darling. Ginny

November 19, 1942 – The onset of the Battle of Stalingrad, which marked the beginning of the end for Nazi Germany and its army

---

In the Army

ELMER BEGAN WRITING TO Virginia as soon as he departed, sending two postcards and a letter during the train journey to Nashville for boot camp, where the army turns civilians into soldiers. This training would also determine which men got to continue in the Air Cadet program and which would be sent to the regular army. His mood was cheerful at first (he reports "the food on this train is really fine" and that "the time is passing rapidly and enjoyably") and then weary (he is looking forward to fresh air during a stop "after chewing soot for the past 20 hours").

Elmer – November 23, 1942 3:10 p.m. Central War Time

Dearest—

So now I'm in the Army. We arrived in Camp about 8:30 last night and it was raining! After standing around the station about ½ hour, we marched about ¾ of a mile to our area. Then came more standing before mess so that we finished supper about ten-thirty. We were assigned to barracks in the next hour, so that we were asleep by 12:00.

They got us up at 5:30 this morning. Five and one half hours sleep after spending about 34 hours on a day coach.

The Commanding Officer of this camp is General Mud. [He was kidding.] I swear I never saw so much mud in my life. Everything is covered with about a foot of the stuff; and it's not ordinary mud. It's nice sticky, gooey, slurpy stuff. You walk in it for about five minutes and you grow about four inches.

We haven't been issued uniforms yet. They'll probably be sent up tomorrow. All we've done today is eat and sleep. I guess the work-out starts tomorrow.

Darling, missing you is all that keeps me from enjoying Army life. The food is good, the fellows are swell, the bunks are comfortable. What more could I ask for except you. Although I look forward to the great experience ahead of me, I still wish this war was over and I could come home to you.

All my love, El

Elmer – November 25, 1942 1:00 p.m.

Dearest—

Yesterday we received our uniforms. I swear, you wouldn't know me honey. Now I really feel like a soldier.

Honey, I'd like to make this longer, but I have a lot to do. They're beginning to keep us busy. We have to drill in about ten minutes and after that comes a lecture on Military Courtesy.

All my love, El

P.S. Today was the first time the sun shined since I've been in Nashville.

Virginia – November 21, 1942 1:15 a.m.
[mailed November 27]

My Darling,

This letter, by the time you get it, will undoubtedly be a lulu, because from now until the time you send your address, I'm going to write and write and *write*. After I get the address, I'll write on the envelope and start in again on the paper. You'll be able to wallpaper all the barracks with my letters—or stuff every body's shoes with them! I'll leave the choice up to you—depends on whether you're esthetic or practical minded.

I'm lying in bed, thinking of you of course, and I'm picturing you asleep right now. The horrible thought has entered my mind, however, of your plight at reveille. How, my sound slumbering dearest, will you *ever* wake up to a mere bugle or sergeant's shout? It has me worried no little bit. Should I get you an air raid siren for an alarm clock—a Christmas gift, I mean?

I heard from Mom today—she always writes, for herself and Pop. After relating all the unimportant incidentals, she gets to a mention of our engagement. She said: "Your special letter to Pop & I was indeed a great surprise to us both. We had no idea you were contemplating anything of this nature. I have been speechless for the past few days. My thought was that you were so wrapped up in your career that marriage was a thing of the future. However, if you know that you are right in your choice, and you must be sure before you take such a serious step, it is perfectly O. K. with me. El is a fine lad, intelligent, a perfect gentleman, and I like him a lot, but this was the last thing I thought of for the time being. I knew, of course, sooner or later, the time would come for you to make your choice, that is only natural. I quite agree with you about the ring, announcing the engagement, etc.; after you graduate is of course the proper time to do that."

After a few other matters—including the fact that you came in to say goodbye—she goes on: "Have not said a word to the girls [Virginia's sisters] about your special letter and will keep it a secret for a while. I am very glad you have confided this information to us and hope you will not be hasty in the matter, and wait until after this awful war is over before you marry. Pop does not approve of war marriages, one takes too many chances, in many ways. Think it over."

So you see, honey, it's O.K. I was even surprised that they were surprised! I figured they would have guessed, but maybe after this summer, they rather wondered if it was definite. And I knew they'd mention not to get married before the war ended, even though I reassured them that it was far from our intention. As for my "career," as they put it, I don't have any idea of dropping it, and, had I expected to as soon as I was married, I'd *still* have plenty of time ahead of me in the professional world. (I hope that isn't true, I sincerely do—you know that—but I don't like to hope for a quick peace and be disappointed. I'd rather be pleasantly surprised.) Did you note that Mom thinks some of the same things about you that I do? Only she doesn't love you as I do—that's an *awful lot*.

November 26, 1942 8:00 p.m. Thanksgiving Day

Tuesday night I started a map reading (maps and blueprints) course. It's one of the many civilian defense night courses and it's one of the few really *good* ones. At least, after only one class, I think it's good.

It's very interesting. Some guy in Chattanooga, Tenn. read of this class in the Daily Orange (plug!) and wrote to the dean of women offering them (the girls taking the course) jobs when they were finished! And I also heard that the government is going to start a more involved course in the same work for senior coeds only, with jobs at $1800 [about $27,000 in today's dollars] when they complete it! The reason I'm taking it, though, is mainly to learn something more and perhaps be useful if needed. I wouldn't *want* to drop newspaper work, but I would if necessary. How far is Chattanooga from Nashville? (See the way my mind runs?)

Forty-eight WAACS moved in on campus Sunday morning and gave the place a very military air. They're really sharp looking, and some very good looking girls among them. March about at a brisk pace and in general act very efficient, as undoubtedly they are. More are coming later.

Today wasn't a very good day for me. I'm getting tired of Thanksgivings away from home. I hope your Thanksgiving was pleasant, at least. With all our dinner, I thought of how wonderful a sandwich would be if you were with me. I love you very much, dearest.

Ginny

Elmer – November 27, 1942 1:00 p.m.

My Dearest—

Just came back from a lecture on the divulgence of military information. It seems that the contents of our letters now will have to be confined to non-military subjects. This order limits me but I will try to make my letters as interesting as possible.

This morning our barracks had our first day physical exam. This consisted of an interview with a psychiatrist, a blood type, a small-pox injection, a chest x-ray and a Wassermann [for syphilis]. Right after that came lunch and an hour and a half of drilling. After that a quick shower and then this lecture. This is the first chance I've had to sit down since 5:30 this morning. This army really keeps one busy.

I wish they'd stop this examination business and let me start training so that I could get in and finish this war and come home and marry you.

All my love, El

Elmer – November 28, 1942 7:50 p.m. Central War Time

Dearest—

I finished up my physical exams today. I think I made out alright too. Boy, I thought that exam I took at Governors' Island was tough. This one was ten times tougher. A great many fellows have to go back for a re-check or something or other. I don't have any re-checks; that's what makes me think I made out alright.

There really is a great bunch of fellows down here. Because we are still in quarantine, we can't go to church tomorrow, so a few of us in our barracks got together and planned a non-sectarian service. It sorta gives one a warm glow to know that the fellows that one is going to live with for quite a while are that kind of guys.

Funny thing happened to me last night. I was running from our squadron day-room to our barracks when a voice from behind me yelled "Hey, Mister." (That's how they address us cadets down here.) I turned around and found I was being addressed by our Commanding Officer. I walked up, snapped to a salute and said "Yes sir." He wanted me to go to all the barracks and see that they turned on all the outside lights. I said "Yes sir" again, saluted again and carried out his orders, walking on air. It was the first time I had come in contact with the C.O. and he had addressed me personally.

All my love, El

November 29, 1942 – Coffee rationing begins

Elmer – November 30, 1942 7:15 p.m. Central War Time

Dearest—

I can just about see to write this. We had a seven (7) hour written exam today on everything imaginable, from celestial navigation to airplane identification. Tomorrow I take a coordination test that takes about four hours. After that, all I have to worry about are my shots.

I got some good news about an hour ago. The sergeant told me that because of my C.M.T.C. training, I stand a very good chance of being made an acting corporal in command of a platoon. I know it isn't much, but it's a step in the right direction.

Our Sunday service turned out very well. We had to see the C.O. to get permission, and he thought it was such a good idea that he let us hold it in the day room and announced it at mess call yesterday morning. We had a pretty large turnout.

Dearest, I'm glad your folks took the attitude they did toward your momentous news. How could they help it, though. Anyone can see how much we love each other, and your folks are very understanding people.

All my love, El

December 2, 1942 – First self-sustaining nuclear chain reaction is initiated at the University of Chicago, by a team of scientists led by Nobel Laureate Enrico Fermi

Elmer – December 2, 1942 9:50 p.m.

Dearest—

Yesterday I had my last exam. That coordination test I was telling
you about. Boy what a lulu. Everything under the sun from playing
with blocks to intricate machines to test your reflexes. Now all I
can do is wait. I'll let you know as soon as I get classified. They tell
us we will ship out of here in about three weeks, which will be just
before Xmas.

Honey, I'm exhausted. What a day today. After chow we
had a lecture on current events and chemical warfare. Then came
calisthenics. And I mean calisthenics. We ran about a mile to the
drill field, did an hour of exercise and ran back again. Believe me
some of the older fellows were really sucking air. Boy, am I getting
into condition. After lunch came 2 hours of drilling!

Darling, I am enclosing a pair of wings to help you
remember me. If for any reason you don't get them, let me know
and I'll send you another pair.

All my love, El

Elmer – December 4, 1942 9:15 p.m.

Dearly Beloved—

We have been told that we are in Nashville, Tenn. but we doubt
it very much. We have come to the conclusion that we have been
duped and sent to Montreal. It snowed all day yesterday and now

the ground is covered with about four inches of the stuff. Reminds me very much of Syracuse. It has other good points too. Keeps us from running and drilling. We can use this respite. Everyone in the squadron is tightened up with stiff muscles.

This morning we had a very good lecture on, in strictly army terms "Latrineograms" or rumors that usually issue forth from the latrine. Most of these rumors are unfounded and the C.O. set us straight on them.

I just got back from the Post Exchange. A couple of fellows and myself went down for a bottle of beer and did it taste good. It was only 3.2 (all that the state law allows) but it was the first I've had since I left home.

Dearest, the prospects for Christmas are pretty glum. I doubt very much if we will get a furlough and I don't think it will be possible for you to come down here because I think we will be moving out.

All my love, El

Elmer – December 5, 1942 8:20 p.m. [To his parents]

Dear Mom & Dad,

Mom, I am not an ordinary soldier, I am a cadet and consequently we are treated like kings and do not have to do our own washing. We get our laundry done very reasonably. Not only that but we are well supplied with sox and underwear. We were issued nine pair of sox, six sets of underwear, six shirts and six pair of trousers, so we are pretty well supplied. Pop, I told you a couple of letters back to join up right away [John had considered enlisting in the Navy], but since then I have been thinking it over and I retract that statement. Pop, I'm very proud of you, (more than you should be of me) for even thinking of doing this [he was forty-five years old and had not been drafted during the First World War], but I think you could do the family more good by staying home where my letters can reach you and Mom together and you two could collaborate on writing me. You know, when I was a civilian, I thought this bond buying campaign was a lot of propaganda and I took it rather lightly, but since I've been in the service, my attitude has changed, and I think you could do more good for your country by investing every penny you can spare in War Bonds. That's the quickest way of getting me back home where I belong. I swear, I really have changed already. I'm not the scatter-brained kid that left home two weeks ago. Mom, you don't seem to believe me when I say I'm happy. I assure you it's true. As a matter of fact I have never been happier in my life as I am right now. I just had a good meal, took a hot shower and to top it off, today I was classified as *Pilot!!!! Yippie!!!*

All my love, El

Virginia – December 6, 1942 2:00 p.m.

Dearest,

Thank you for the air corps insignia. I have it on the lapel of my camel hair jacket. But I *don't* need any help remembering you, honey!

I got elected to Phi Kappa Phi, national honor society (average & activities), recently. The invitation (to please pay 10 bucks!) came Friday. Glad to get it, of course, but I didn't make what I *really* wanted—Phi Beta Kappa. It's no surprise. I was just hoping, because my average *isn't* really good enough, after last semester. So, I tell the parents,—who would have been very happy, more than I, if I had—that "you can't have everything," Oh well.

Darling, the mail's going to be collected soon. Remember that I love you.

Ginny

Elmer – December 7, 1942 6:55 p.m.

Dearly Beloved—

This morning the morale at this post was the lowest it has ever been. Everyone was sick from tetanus and typhoid shots, the mud was getting everyone down and most of us were down with colds. I didn't write yesterday because I couldn't lift either arm and I was flat on my back with typhoid fever. I had chills and fever alternately and thought I was going to die then and there. Today I'm much better thank you. Getting back to morale, this afternoon it rose to unprecedented heights, simply because the classifications were posted. Yes honey, I have been classified. I am now slated for pilot training and am I happy. The only way I could be happier would be to be with you.

You ask about my courses and practical work. Honey I can't write about these subjects simply because I don't take them. This is merely a classification center; our studying begins in a couple of weeks when we go to pre-flight. I promise to let you know what I'm doing as soon as I start doing something.

Today it's raining again. We can't drill or do calisthenics so we get lectures. Three today. One this morning on sex hygiene, one on the conduct of officers and cadets, and a surprise quiz on the Articles of War. I did pretty good on the quiz. Second highest out of about 150. Guess I was lucky.

All my love, El

Virginia – December 7, 1942 10:10 p.m.

Dearest,

My glum feeling of yesterday and Saturday is gone. It's when
I don't have anything but studying to do that I get down in the
dumps. Maybe it's a lot of things. But I'd like to spend all of my
time on the paper—or all on classes, but preferably the former.
When I can't do assignments as well as I can or as well as
they should be done, I get discouraged or annoyed—generally
disgruntled, let's say. Doing things half way gets under my skin.

News of the day is that we're not having any Saturday
classes on the 19th. This change in vacation is supposed to be
lightening the transportation burden [due to troop movements] on
that weekend, somewhat. Probably by Easter we won't be able to
get home.

Also in tomorrow's paper will be the news that the University
is going to admit high school students who've finished 3 years
and are in high scholastic standing, etc. Big stuff. [Syracuse had a
shortage of enrolled male students because of the draft.]

Your mention of latrine rumors reminded me of what one
of the WAACs told me. They call rumor, l.r., but they also said
these l.r.'s are often soon to become truth. But I can imagine very
well how the c.o.'s frown on this stuff. Even on campus, students,
supposedly intelligent, take the wildest ideas they "hear" from
somebody and believe them—or at least spread them, until half
the campus is scared stiff or bitterly aroused, depending on the
nature of the rumor. We're trying to catch these things and get the
truth, then publish it. Helps some, but it doesn't eliminate it. We
have a Rumor Clinic on campus, but that deals mainly with war
propaganda. Good business, though. People are *so* gullible.

Pearl Harbor day—and I remember how we felt last year. If
we have to witness another December 7, at war, I hope it will be

more of a celebration, in anticipation of peace. And I pray that we'll be together.

I love you, El, Ginny

Elmer – December 10, 1942 7:40 p.m.

Dearly Beloved—

Honey, if you saw me now, I don't think you would know me. You see, yesterday I got a G.I. haircut. My hair is approximately ½ inch long. It's kind of chilly and it does not look so hot but boy is it convenient. No trouble keeping it combed and it dries fast after a shower.

Dearest, right here on post there is, in my mind, one of the major tragedies of the war. On the highest hill in the camp, in the midst of a grove of locust trees is a house, the like of which, I have always dreamed of owning. It's a brick affair with white clapboards on the second floor and a large chimney at each end and it stands majestically overlooking the beautiful countryside. The government bought it when they took over this section and it is about to be demolished. Whenever I look at it, empty and forlorn I think of how unhappy someone must have been to leave it, and it makes me hate Hitler all the more. I hope that someday you and I can live in a house like it, somewhere on a similar hill, and we can be together forever and not have our happiness interrupted by another war.

All my love—El

Virginia – December 11, 1942 1:15 p.m.

Darling,

I was *very* glad to hear about your pilot's classification! I'm almost as happy as you must be, darling. It's wonderful! Now I *really* can look forward to seeing you get wings and a commission. And I *do* hope to see it.

Setting the pace for your platoon! And are you acting corporal yet? Gee you're wonderful, honey! I'm so proud of you— but it's hardly a new feeling. I've always been.

Love you, dearest. Ginny

Elmer – December 16, 1942 3:50 p.m.

Dearly Beloved—

I was on K.P. yesterday; from 4:30 in the morning to 7:30 at night with 15 minutes off for each meal. What a day! I did everything from peel about 100 lbs. of onions to scrub floors. Luckily I wasn't put on the "China Clipper" (the dishwasher). This is a lousy detail. Imagine washing mess kits for over 1000 fellows!

I have twenty-four hour guard duty tomorrow. We are on duty for two hours, then off for four and so on for twenty four hours. What a system! How I wish they would send us out of this mud-hole. Everyone is slowly getting fed up with this place.

All my love, El

Virginia – December 19, 1942 2:45 p.m.

Darling,

Wednesday & Thursday *were* as bad as I thought they'd be. I can hardly remember what happened—but I do know that I was a dead bunny when I got on the train for N.Y.—such a dead bunny, in fact, that a couple of scotch & sodas made me quite unhappy. Probably due to lack of food & sleep, but it certainly was sad.

Darling, how I missed you at the station and how I miss you now—all the time. Everywhere I go around the house I'm reminded how often you've been there. But I can stand it by looking forward to the day we'll start being together always.

A whole column of sailors piled out of the track alley (or whatever it's called) singing. Certainly made me feel proud to be an American. So many things make me feel that way.

I love you, El. Ginny

Virginia – December 20, 1942 12 (midnight)

Dearest El,

Eddie Rickenbacker [the World War I flying ace] made a good speech on the radio this afternoon. Hope you heard it—but I mainly hope the selfish *grabbing* part of the population heard it, because he made plain, ordinary civilian work seem easy— comparatively easy.

Today all I did was eat and read the papers and listen to the radio. These last two occupations only made me feel droopy—the papers with stories of "Christmas in New Guinea" and the radio with carols that *insist* on your being with me for full appreciation. I do love you so, honey. When's the war going to be over?

I love you, Ginny

Elmer – December 22, 1942 11:25 p.m.

Dearly Beloved—

We are finally on orders and our squadron moves out Sunday morning. Pray that they discharge me from this place [he was quarantined in sick bay with a bad cold] in time to go with my squadron. I think they will. I'll only be in here a day or two more.

Gee, I wish I could get home for Xmas. You can't image what it is like to be away from home this time of year. Not only from the folks but away from you too. That's what hurts. Every night I pray that this war will be over quickly. Dearest, how can I tell you on paper how much I love you. In my spare moments I have been planning our future. Drawing plans for a house, planning gardens and stuff like that. Oh for the day when we can carry out our plans together.

All my love, El

Pre-flight School

PRE-FLIGHT SCHOOL WAS WHERE the freshly minted air cadets were taught just about everything about flying airplanes without actually flying one. They would dip into aeronautics, navigation, the mechanics of engines, and so forth. It was all bookwork, except for the strenuous calisthenics.

Elmer – December 28, 1942 7:30 a.m.

Dearly Beloved—

Yesterday morning we moved out of Nashville, the happiest day of my life. We are now at Maxwell Field, Montgomery, Alabama.

I got my discharge from the hospital Saturday morning, and by rushing my head off, I just made this shipment. If I had missed it, I would have been sent to Santa Ana, California.

Honey, from now on I expect to be pretty busy, so if you don't hear from me quite as often as you'd like, try to forgive me. I shall try to keep you posted as to what I am doing all the time. I know you are interested.

I'm about 1200 miles away from you now, but the further away I go, the more I love you and paradoxically enough, the nearer you seem to be to me. I hope you feel the same way.

All my love, El

Elmer – December 29, 1942

Dearly Beloved—

Today we really started working. This morning we had drilling and calisthenics; this afternoon we had classes. Classes include code, mathematics and map and chart reading. We get plenty of homework in all subjects and since taps is at 9:30 p.m., we have very little time for writing.

All my love, El.

Elmer – December 31, 1942 7:55 p.m.

Dear Mom & Dad—

Up at Nashville with my acting corporal rating, I was pretty well off. Down here I am just a lowly "Zombie" (term applied to underclassmen). We really take a riding from upperclassmen. When we eat we have to sit at the table at attention with our eyes fixed on a point on the other side of the table. If we want something we have to say "Sir, does anyone care for the butter? Please pass the butter." When we are on formation an upperclassman can come up to us and say "Mister! Sound off." Then we have to say "Sir, New aviation cadet Odell, E.W., 12084872, Roosevelt, New York Sir." There are a hundred and one things they can do to us. It's a lot of fun though.

All my love, El

Virginia – December 24, 1942 3:30 p.m.
[mailed on January 1, when she got his address]

Dearest El,

I've been seeing a lot of Jean [her sister] since I got home. I think she's trying to make me feel less lonesome for you. She's asked me over for dinner tonight, and has done other little things. I told her (and Bert & Claire) about our engagement—I'd like to tell a million people, it makes me feel so good saying it!

Christmas eve I had dinner with Jean & Charlie [Jean's husband], looked for a Christmas tree with Charlie, and then went to midnight mass with Mom & Pop. (Pop was so annoyed with a woman behind him, coughing, that he left early! So like him!) When I got home I opened your present [likely a symphony recording] and played the whole thing—until 2:30 a.m. Darling it's wonderful, and I'm looking forward very much to the time when we can listen to it together.

I love you so, El!

[Part two—mailed the same day in a separate envelope]

The clock is striking twelve, and with every stroke I pray that you'll be with me next year, and all the years after that.

Just fixed myself a scotch and soda. Maybe that will make my eyes feel drier.

Came into N.Y. Monday morning and dropped in at the N.Y. Times & the Herald-Tribune offices. Of course, there's little hope of my getting a job there in May, but if I can, I will. The Times personnel mgr. told me to come back when I was ready to work and the Trib mgr. explained, unnecessarily, that it was difficult to break into metropolitan newspaper work without experience. He added that there might be copy girl positions open by May, but little else. I'll probably work with a local paper first, but I'm going to write several letters between now and May. It's not so easy to remember how all this vacation went, but it certainly has gone. I don't seem to have done anything, but it's almost time to return to the Salt City. I'm taking the afternoon train this time, because you, the main reason for my taking the midnight job, are not here. There's no question on that point. You are definitely not here!

Have you heard the very pretty tune "You'd Be So Nice to Come Home To"? I like the melody and the words—and Dinah Shore's rendition of it.

I'll write more tomorrow, darling. I love you.

Ginny

Elmer – December 31, 1942 11:30 p.m.

Dearly Beloved—

Happy New Year darling.

It is 1943 in New York but it won't be '43 here for a half hour.

Dearest, I really miss you tonight. Events like this get us to thinking of home and it's almost unbearable. Let's hope that this is the only New Year's Eve that we have to spend apart.

From that last paragraph, don't get the idea that I'm dissatisfied with this place. I'm really happy. This Maxwell is 1000% better than Nashville. I'll write tomorrow and tell you about life here. I gotta close now.

All my love, El

Elmer – January 2, 1943 7:20 p.m.

Dearly Beloved—

We were issued gas masks this morning and the first thing we did is have a gas mask drill. They marched us over to the gas chamber and had us put on our gas masks. Then they took us into the chamber which was filled with tear gas. That was o.k., we had our masks on. Then they took us out, made us take off our masks and go back in the chamber without them. We stayed in the chamber about a minute, and when we came out we were pretty bad off. Did you ever even sniff tear gas? It's wicked stuff. One can't imagine what it does to one's eyes, nose and throat. When we came out of there, we were all crying like babies. They weren't satisfied yet. They made us go back into the chamber and put our masks on in there. It was wicked, but it really made us respect our masks. I wouldn't part with that thing for a million dollars.

Honey, I'm doing pretty well down here. My average for the week in studies is 95%. And I hope that I can keep it up there.

The weather down here is perfect. For the past two days it was actually *hot*. Yesterday a couple of us went for a hike around be the airfield in athletic *shorts* it was so warm. Imagine walking around in shorts on New Year's Day. I pity you poor people up north in the cold.

All my love, El

**January 3, 1943 – The US Selective Service warns
it will begin prosecuting draft dodgers**

Virginia – January 8, 1943 12:30 a.m.

Dearest El,

Guess I told you about the military map making course I've been thinking about taking. Well, I'm almost decided not to, after consultation with the woman who knows. My regular schedule will be heavier next semester and includes *3* required and stiff journalism courses. These, in addition to the other things I'm trying to do, will probably keep me from doing a good job on the map making course. So, I think I'll sit in on as many classes as I can and let it go there.

I love you, honey. But darling, please stop gloating about the fine weather in Alabama! Today was the first clear day in more than a week! It's been snowing, *snowing*, *snowing*! Sound familiar?

Guess whom I heard from the other day?!?! You'll *never* imagine, and I was definitely surprised. None other than Sgt. George M. Hall!! I figured that after he was married, he'd stop writing, but he assures me he "just wants to be friends—will I write?" Gad—what a soldier won't do for mail! Think I'll ask him if his wife wants me to be so "friendly"!!

> So sweetheart, remember I love you.
> Ginny

Elmer – January 8, 1943 1:50 p.m.

Dearly Beloved—

I put my code to use—

••/•—••, •••, •••—, •/—•——, •••, ••— [I love you]

Our room, (six men) has a bunch of interesting fellows. One fellow is an ex-coal miner from Pennsylvania (a strapping Russian); another is a service man who transferred from the Coast Artillery. He was stationed in Bermuda but originally came from Miami, Fla. The third was a dairy farm hand from Vermont; the fourth a French Canadian lumber man from New Hampshire and the fifth an art student from Brooklyn. The sixth one you know pretty much about. He's the fellow that loves you so doggone much.

The boys in the room think I am going crazy. I find myself talking aloud to your picture and your expression seems to understand what I'm saying. For instance, when I leave for classes or something I look at your picture and say something like—"So long honey, I gotta go to school; I'll see you later."

Yesterday they called us out on formation and our tactical officer gave us a little talk. A small epidemic of measles has broken out in the lower class and we have to be segregated from the upper class. The upper classmen can't even talk to us so consequently they can't haze us. It's wonderful. We eat by ourselves, drill by ourselves, do calisthenics by ourselves. Heaven.

We are getting a series of lectures on "Tropical Sanitation" and how to prevent tropical diseases. They must be going to send us to the Solomons for combat. Seems a little early in our training for that sort of thing.

All my love, El

Elmer – January 9, 1943

Dearly Beloved—

They don't fool around down here, especially where the Honor System is concerned. Last night at about 11:45 we were awakened and told to get dressed and get out in formation as soon as possible. We thought the war was over or Maxwell had been bombed or something. The tactical officer said something like this—"At 11:00 p.m. this date, Jan. 8th 1943, Cadet _____ was found guilty by a group board of making a false statement to an officer. Cadet _____ has been broken from the Cadet Corps and his name will never be mentioned on this post again." We were dismissed then, to go back to bed. Within two hours after he was found guilty, that fellow was on a train bound for the regular Army Corps. They didn't even let him go back into his barracks. They are shipping his belongings after him. It seems like extreme measures but it sure does keep the rest of us on the ball.

    I wonder if my map course is anything like yours. I guess not, though, we are concerned with aeronautical charts with plotted radio beams. Darned interesting course.

                          Gotta make up my bunk.
                          I love you darling. El

                          Elmer – January 11, 1943 8:45 p.m.

Dear Mom & Dad—

We had a crash out here this morning. A Cessna Bomber Trainer hit a bunker on the golf course and dove into the Alabama River. We were on cross-country running and we saw the ambulances and crash wagons around the bank of the river. The pilot was killed and the student was injured. Some excitement. I got a bawling out in drill today for making a mistake in a flanking movement but that doesn't bother me. I'm not in the Army to march. I just want to fly.

                          All my love, El

**January 14, 1943 – Japan lands a rearguard force
to begin its withdrawal from Guadalcanal,
the start of an island-by-island retreat in the South Pacific**

John Odell – January 15, 1943

Dear Son.

Your mother just *rooted* me up from the couch, to write you a letter.
The reason I didn't write before was that I gathered all the news I
could and mother did the writing.

Glad to hear you are doing so well in your studies, but was
somewhat shocked to hear you were reprimanded in Ground Drill
you may never use, but it is very essential for timing and habit
coordination. Remember everything the army has you do is a
detail and a combination of details makes for perfection, so try
and master everything they give you. So much for the lecture front.
Now for questions. Is Alabama a dry state, or can you get beer?

Dad

Elmer – January 17, 1943 7:15 p.m.

Dearly Beloved—

Today for the first time I came in contact with airplanes since
I've been in the air corps. They had a show for the Cadets in the
1st and 6th groups out on the field. There were two multi-motor
trainers (AT-9, AT-17) a double wing Stearman trainer, three AT-6's
and a P-40E at our disposal. There was an instructor in each of
them and we were allowed to climb all over the planes and ask all
kinds of questions. You should see the instruments on that P-40.
Sometime when I have about five hours I'll write a nice long letter

explaining, with diagrams, one of these panels. Later a Major took up an AT-6 and did a few snap rolls, lazy eights, etc. It was really an interesting afternoon.

I have been mentioned as a candidate for a Cadet Officer's position when I become an upper classman because of my academic average, but I doubt if I will because I am a "feather merchant" and preference goes to previous service men. However I'll let you know what develops.

All my love, El

Virginia – January 19, 1943 12:45 a.m.

Dearest El,

I miss you so,—and have ever since you left,—that I don't believe I'll know what to do when I see you again. It won't seem real. And I'm trying to get used to the idea that it won't be El in civilian clothes, but El in a uniform. Gee, dearest, I hope you'll be so much the same that you'll shine right through your G.I. suit, because I just *can't* imagine you being in a uniform. Is it silly? I wonder if every other girl has gone through the same thing, anticipating the first time she sees her boyfriend in his khaki—or navy. Maybe I haven't explained exactly what I mean. But you might be able to see if you'll try to think of me in a WAAC or WAVES uniform. Sort of hard taking someone out of one category and picture in your mind and putting him in an entirely different picture.
Maybe I could be assisted in this job if I had a *picture* of El!! (HINT!!)

Darling, I don't want the boys to think you're crazy—but I like to think of you talking to me. Think how crazy Carol [her roommate] thinks *I* am when I talk to *nothing*!!

Very interesting bunch you're with! Golly, the variety is *wonderful*—but it's echoed in the variety of America itself. An American is everything. You've certainly a group there that represents one of the things we're fighting for—the ability of different men to live together in peace.

I love you, dearest. Ginny

Elmer – January 20, 1943 8:10 p.m.

Dearly Beloved—

Maybe you think I'm crazy. Maybe I am. I have been studying aircraft recognition and my mind is in a whirl. Positive dihedral, elongated nacelles, inverted gull wing, parasol type, diamond shaped wings, swept back leading edge, PBY's stinger type tail, TBF, power turret, F4UI, rounded dorsal fin. Here I roll my eyes, tear out my hair, and make like a moron.

The math is getting tougher too. We're studying vectors now. Given: heading 180°; wind 30 M.P.H. from 310°; air speed—175m.p.h. Find ground speed and track. It's not so bad when you catch on to it, but it took me a while to catch on.

We ran the "Burma Road" today. Perhaps you have never heard of Maxwell's "Burma Road"? It's an obstacle course about two miles long and it is up and down hill all the way. You have to jump fallen trees, run across streams on logs, crawl under bushes, etc. Before we ran it we had about an hour of tough calisthenics and ran about two miles on level ground. The army is really whipping your man into good shape, but he was really down after that workout.

All my love, El

Virginia – January 22, 1943 12:05 a.m.

Darling,

I went to the Varsity for coffee with a girl from the house. Sitting in a booth directly in front of me was a girl with an air corps officer, a *pilot*. And I could've screamed or thrown a sugar bowl through the front window before they left. Just seeing the uniform and the silver wings made you closer in my mind and so very much farther away in reality.

I love you, Ginny

Virginia – January 22, 1943 10:10 p.m.

Dearest El,

I sent you some Daily Oranges yesterday, including those of recent date concerning one Westbrook Pegler [prominent conservative columnist]. The issue was over a column he wrote attacking the OPA [Office of Price Administration] administration of the "no pleasure driving" edict. We objected to his premise—that the gasoline is the *right* of the citizen—and also to his method of criticism, common with him, that of name-calling, calumny, diatribe, vitriol, etc. So an editorial was written. Well—that editorial caused more stir, talk, and excitement than any six we've printed in the past! *We* didn't send it anywhere, but faculty members sent it to various places, including to the Post-Standard [city morning daily] and to Pegler—if he by any chance should care to read it! The Post-Standard reprinted the editorial and wrote one of their own about—and differing in opinion with—our editorial. Then started letters to the editor from campus, city, out of town, both to the D.O. and the P.-S. Great fun! If nothing else, though, we got a few people talking and thinking about the question.

Although I'm only using my imagination and what little information I could glean from your use of the term, I take it that "feather merchant" means "cadet what was formerly a lowly civilian." It's wonderful that you've been mentioned for cadet officer, even if you don't get it, darling. But *you're* wonderful and I love you.

Ginny

Virginia – January 23, 1943 8:15 p.m.

Darling,

My favorite day dream is one in which I try to picture when and where we'll be when we meet after the war, meet without the thought of parting again, ever. I've imagined so many *small* things about our future life, but it's hard to put in the main outlines. Guess I'm afraid to do that. I love you very much, and sort of hate to lose all these days—and I say *lose* them, because they *are* partly lost when you're not with me.

Don't ever forget how much I love you, darling.

Ginny

Elmer – January 26, 1943 12:30 p.m.

Dearly Beloved—

Yes, it's true. I have the measles; but the funny part of it is that I am not sick. I never felt better in my life, the only trouble is that I'm covered with a rash. The rest of the fellows in the ward are the same way, so we have quite a time. We have a radio, crossword and jig saw puzzles, all sorts of books and magazines, checkers, chess, and every afternoon four of us have a hot bridge game. What a vacation. The only trouble is that I'm worried about the school work I'm missing. I probably can make it up but it means I'm gonna hafta work like the dickens.

I'm sending a couple of clippings. One, from the "Montgomery Advertiser" is a shot of that air show I was telling you about. I am very apt to be in the foreground. I spent a good part of the afternoon around this P-40.

I became an upperclassman officially yesterday. Our underclass comes in Friday. That's the day I'm scheduled to get out of this prison. Then the fun begins.

All my love, El

Pre-Flight Cadets Get To See Planes' 'Innards'

© 1943 Montgomery Advertiser

AIRMAN'S HOLIDAY—You might call it that, anyway. Here pre-flight cadets at Maxwell Field get their first close-up of planes they will get to fly when they reach primary school.

January 27, 1943 – The first US air attack on Germany, targeting a submarine base at Wilhelmshaven

Virginia – January 28, 1943 6:45 p.m.

Darling,

I hope you haven't a bad case of that foolish-sounding disease—measles. Wish they'd send you home to recuperate. *I've had* measles!

The postman won't be at peace until I get word from you that you're all right again.

Darling, you're driving me nuts! *Why* did you send me a picture in which you *"might* be in the foreground"? Of course I can't distinguish the faces of *any* cadet, so I think that *"this* one may be El—or maybe that one—but here's one that looks like him, a little"! Really, it isn't fair to send a puzzle picture! But I do enjoy the picture of the cadets, even if you *aren't* among them. I can imagine one of them may be you and, if not, you'd been there before and were wearing the same kind of uniform, looking at the same plane. Makes you seem very close.

I love you, darling. Ginny

February 2, 1943 – The Germans surrender at Stalingrad

Virginia – February 2, 1943 1:00 p.m.

Darling,

Yesterday (last night) the Independent Women's association put on a lecture with a WAAC and a WAVES officer as speakers. A few of us met them and had dinner at Shrafft's. They were both *wonderful* girls, or young women, and they looked it. I got, I think, a little of that feeling men must get during those times when they, in civilian clothes, see men in the armed forces. No matter how important their civilian work is, they must feel lacking when they're among uniforms.

Anyway, I felt a little that way and I really think I'd like to join one of the services (necessarily the WAAC because of my eyes) but for the fact that what I intend to do *will* be taking a man's place, the purpose of these women's branches. I thought perhaps it was rationalization—an excuse for furthering my own career rather than sacrificing my time to the war effort *directly*. It isn't, though, I'm pretty certain, because I consider newspapers essential to a democracy, especially one at war, and if I can take a man's place on some staff, it will be both relieving a man for the service and working indirectly for the country. This last reference may seem to stretch a point somewhat (or a lot) but I'm sure of that fact—the necessity of newspapers—and I'll explain it some time to you if you don't see it entirely. So, although I have, for the first time, a sincere desire to join a women's service branch, I won't, because it seems clear to me that I'll be worth a lot more to a newspaper staff.

All the above rambling is a summary of what went on in my mind most of the last evening. What do you think of it?

I love you, honey. Ginny

Elmer – February 6, 1943 10:05 p.m.

Dearly Beloved—

I got your telegram [about phoning] today and thank you very much. I never expected such an immediate response. The only trouble (and it's driving me crazy) is that I can't get to a phone tonight or tomorrow. I drew guard duty for the weekend. I'm a super-numerary in the S.O.D.'s (Senior Officer of the Day) office. That's one good point. At least I'm not toting a rifle all night long. This army is trying its darndest to try and get me down. Tomorrow would have been the first chance I have had to get into town, and I draw guard. Do you realize I haven't been off a military reservation since the 19th of December?

There is one thing here in the Army that is really miraculous, and that is the way the barracks seem to clean themselves up for Saturday's stand-by inspection. Every Saturday morning a group of officers comes through inspecting the barracks and men. Everything must be in place and in spotless condition. About an hour before standby we start washing windows, cleaning sinks and woodwork, scrubbing floors, shining shoes, etc. About five minutes before inspection, everything is about half done and most of the fellows are still in fatigue clothes when they should be in full dress. The last five minutes pass and when the officers come through, everything is in perfect order and everyone is in full dress, standing at attention. You wouldn't believe it unless you could see it. There must be a good fairy working for Uncle Sam.

I don't like to seem boastful honey but I did something yesterday of which I am very proud. We had a final examination on "Safeguarding Military Information," a subject about Codes and Ciphers, cryptograms, what constitutes military information and how it is classified and bunch of other stuff I can't go into because it is restricted. Anyway I took that exam and got 100% on it. Not only that, but mine was the only 100 in our academic section (about 75 fellows). I really felt good when I found out.

Darling, I've been doing a lot of daydreaming myself recently. Most of all I've been dreaming about our home when we're married after this mess is all over. We want to build our own home, don't we honey? Just imagine the fun we can have, planning and decorating; and we must not forget landscaping.

All my love, El

Virginia – February 7, 1943 8:50 p.m.

Darling,

I'm in a very nervous state. I'm not sure whether by "next Sunday" in your letter you meant *today* or Feb. *14*. I sent the telegram with my phone number and when I'd be home today but I'm not sure you got it.

So I'm sitting here in the living room, on the love seat you've often occupied with me, and my heartbeat's faster, my hand unsteady, and my mind very unsettled. I haven't been so jittery since the morning I waited for a call that would mean you *weren't* coming up for the last time before leaving. Gee, it's awful!

And for days I've wondered what to say when I hear you. I know when it's over I'll have said nothing but "I love you."

Did I tell you about bouncing two junior men from the staff? It wasn't a pleasant task—calling them to tell them they were no longer junior editors—but it had to be done and should have been on many counts. The two who were on the desk Tuesday night were 1) drinking on the job and in the Castle 2) taking the whole thing as a big joke, the plant and the paper as their playground, and 3) giving a very undignified and distasteful opinion (to the many underclassmen working that night) of the Daily Orange as a whole. It wasn't easy to ask fellows, who are rather likeable, or *definitely* likeable, boys to leave after 2 ½ years of work—but their evening of fun was only the culmination of several weeks of dogging it,—generally avoiding work in other words. Wednesday wasn't a joyful day for me.

So it's now 11:30 and I guess you didn't mean tonight. Oh well. We all make mistakes.

I love you, Ginny

To say that the telephone system in the 1940s was more primitive than today would be serious understatement. To begin, only about 40 percent of US households had phones. Every phone call was carried over wires; cell phones weren't introduced until the mid 1980s. Long-distance connections were made manually by telephone operators, mostly women.

In the first years after America's entry into the Second World War, while men were in training and not yet deployed overseas, demand for long-distance connections was intense. Youngsters in military training, often away from their homes and family for the first time, craved the connection that the telephone provided, and the lines were almost always jammed. Civilians were encouraged to avoid using their phones during early evening hours, to keep limited capacity open for soldiers and sailors.

The letters between Elmer and Virginia during these weeks are full of references to missed connections. On February 9, Elmer reports, "I've been trying for the past three days to call you. Sunday night, right after Guard mount I had a call in for two hours but it didn't come through. I tried again last night from 7:15 until 9:25 and it didn't come through." A few days later, Virginia writes that an operator had been able to track her down to the Castle, the office of the *Daily Orange*: "Trying to keep calm, I get on the wire and *wait*. After listening to frazzy operator voices for a while, one of them tells me, in a southern accent, that the party has left the phone booth, or something like that." It would take them until February 25 to finally connect.

Elmer – February 11, 1943 8:15 p.m.

Dearly Beloved—

I have been haunting the switchboard since last Sunday night.

Speaking of time, I thought you might like to know how we read it in the air corps. (If you don't already know.) Nine [*sic.*, he meant eight] o'clock is 2000 pronounced twenty hundred. We go from twelve noon to thirteen hundred and so on until 2400 or midnight. At one A.M. the time is written as 0100. Or a fraction of the hour, for instance 835 would be written 0835. Pretty tricky system.

Things are going along smoothly now that I've caught up to my class, and at last we are beginning to realize that we will soon be flying. Yesterday they gave the upperclass a form to fill out. On it we were to give our preference as to what type plane we wanted to fly. There were about ten types of ships and we could give our three most desired ships. I chose single engine fighter, double-engine fighter, and light bombardment in that order. This is not definite we can change later if we want to or if we are more adapted to another type ship, but it does bring us closer to the time when we will be in the air.

All my love, El

Elmer – February 14, 1943 8:50 p.m.

My Dearest—

Happy Valentine's Day darling. I love you.

I went into town last night for the first time. It isn't a bad town but it's sorta small. The capitol is a nice building but that is about all there is to Montgomery. A roommate and I went down to the Cadet Club in the Jefferson Davis hotel. I was drinking scotch and soda for the first time since I was in Syracuse. Good scotch too. Black and White. About midnight we decided to stay in town overnight (It is permissible on Saturday night). We went down to the U.S.O. and asked if they could get us a room. They sent us to a private home on the outskirts of town. What a swell place it was. An elderly widow lived there alone. She gave us a big room with a bed and innerspring mattress, for only $1.50 each. You have heard of southern hospitality. I have never seen it quite as clearly as in the case of this woman. We slept till 1100 this morning and she drove us into town at noon. She told us to come again and next time give her a little notice and she would make us some fudge and sandwiches. It was swell.

I went to the G.I. dentist last night. It really is an impressive sight. Dentistry on a mass production basis. Those fellows don't mess around either. Boy, are they rough.

Yesterday afternoon about twenty of us from "K" squadron went up in the high altitude chamber to test us under low pressure. I volunteered to be a subject. They took us up to 5 thousand feet (in the chamber of course) and then brought us down again to see if we could equalize the pressure in our ears. Then they took us up again. At ten thousand feet the rest of the fellows put on their oxygen masks but I didn't. They used me to show how lack of oxygen affects pilots. They had a photo-electric cell attached to my ear to show oxygen amount in my blood. At 15 thousand feet I felt a little giddy, but at about twenty thousand feet I felt fine again. They took us up to twenty five thousand and stayed there. My lips and finger nails turned blue. They told me to count backwards from 100 by sevens. I started out O.K. but in the sixties I began to waver. They told me to write my name and serial number over and over. I started out o.k. but after a while it became illegible. All the time I felt good and thought I was writing alright. Later they told me that after about three minutes I slumped forward and the instructor put my mask on and I was alright again. We went up to 28,000 and then came down again. Very interesting experience.

All my love, El

The apple doesn't fall far from the tree. Elmer's oldest son (me), not knowing his father had done the above, was the volunteer for the same experience while going through Navy pre-flight training some twenty-five years later!

Virginia – February 18, 1943 2350 (11:30 p.m. right?)

Darling,

I'm almost asleep in bed. I was awfully tired, so I stayed home all evening—didn't even go to the Castle for a while. Of course, the night I stay in, Alabama doesn't call! Gee, honey, I wish you'd get me soon!

Here's a pome {sic.}: (or reasonable facsimile)

Starkle, starkle little twink
Who the hell I are you think?
I'm not under the affluence of incohol
Although some thinkle peep I am.
I fool so feelish
I don't know which is me
The drunker I sit here, the longer I be!

Just a little thing to relax with. I like the sound of the first line.

I love you, dearest, Ginny

February 19, 1943 – US and German tanks engage in the Battle of Kasserine Pass, Tunisia, where the Americans are badly defeated

Elmer – February 21, 1943 8:20 p.m.

My Dearest—

Yesterday morning we went out on the firing range. My ears were ringing all day. Everything is quiet, and then the order is given— Ready on the right—Ready on the left—Ready on the firing line. Then all hell breaks loose. What a racket. I fired a Thomson .45 calibre sub-machine gun, a Browning stationary .30 cal. machine gun and a Springfield .30 rifle. What a kick that rifle had. I had fifteen shots. Five standing, five kneeling and five prone. That gun almost tore my shoulder off. I don't know why they give us this stuff. We're not in the infantry. That .45 cal sub-machine gun is a sweet weapon. It fires about 10 slugs in one second and it has no kick at all. I just wish there had been a couple of Japs on the range.

We'll be moving out next Saturday or Sunday. We haven't gotten our shipping orders yet but two squadrons in our group have theirs. They're going to Ocala, Fla.

All my love, El

Elmer – February 23, 1943 1:45 p.m.

My Darling—

I love you very much.
Society Note:
"Mr. E.W. Odell is spending the remainder of the winter in Avon Park, Florida." Yes honey, it's true. I'm sorry K squadron

isn't getting furloughs, and I can't get home to see you, but this is a really good break. Avon Park is reputed to be the best and most luxurious Primary School in the Southeast Training District. It used to be a flying military school and it has the best instructors available. Avon Park is right in the center of Florida, just north of Lake Okeechobee. It's only about 60 miles from West Palm Beach and a little more from Lakeland, Tampa and Clearwater, so the climate should be great this time of year. I'm only sorry you can't be here to share it with me.

Gotta close now, it's just about time for calisthenics.

All my love, El

February 27, 1943 – Norwegian commandos blow up the German heavy water factory at Telemark, Norway, sabotaging Nazi efforts to build an atomic bomb

---

Primary Flight School

P RIMARY FLIGHT SCHOOL WAS where air cadets found out if they "cut the mustard" to fly military airplanes. They were introduced to the Stearman Model 75, an open cockpit tandem two-seater biplane with a 7-cylinder 220-horsepower air-cooled radial piston engine mounted on the nose. Mastering this primitive flying beast was a ticket to Basic and a step closer to wings and a commission. But although the Stearman was a forgiving aircraft, the rate of student attrition was high. After a month, Elmer was feeling confident, writing to his father, "I don't fly with my mind, I fly by the seat of my pants."

Elmer – February 28, 1943 2130

Dearest—

We got in Avon Park at 2:30 this afternoon and we've been on the go ever since. What a beautiful place this is! The barracks is a large hotel and there are two men to a room with a private bath. There's a lake just outside of the front door with boats and diving boards, etc. It is like mid-August down here. The walks and drives are lined with palm trees, blooming petunias and pansies and many other beautiful flowers. All this in February. I forget to mention we have inner spring mattresses on the beds. The field is three miles away from here and we are taken there by bus so that it's not so noisy at night. I swear I have never been in such a place in my life.

Gosh but that phone call made me happy Friday. Just hearing your voice made a new man of me. I just wish you could

be down here to share the beauty of this place with me. The further along in my training I go, the further away from the war I seem to become. This will change though. I'll know there is a war all too soon. But it will be all over some day and I will be back with you darling, and we can be married as planned.

All my love, El

Elmer – March 4, 1943 2050

Dearest—

Honey, everyone is making sacrifices for the war effort, and I am afraid I will have to ask you to make one more. I think you will have to be content with a few less letters. I thought I was busy at Maxwell, but that was a vacation compared to what we have to do here. We are up at 6:10 and meet reveille at 6:20 [flag raising, then breakfast]. From 7:00 to 7:20 we clean up our room. 7:25 we go to the flight line. We are there all morning either flying or having blackboard lectures with the instructor. We return to the barracks at 12:10. At twelve-twenty we drill until 1:10. At 1:20 comes mess formation [to lunch]. Two o'clock finds us lined up to march around the lake to school for three hours instruction in Aircraft Engine, Theory of Flight, Aircraft

Identification, Meteorology, and Navigation. At five fifteen we fall
out for 1 ½ hours of calisthenics. At 7:20 p.m. we assemble for
retreat [flag lowering] and supper mess until 8:00. After supper
we are confined to our rooms until taps at 10:30 to do homework.
Of course this last period I could use to write (as I'm doing now)
but you see at this field one out of every two cadets wash out and
I want to be in the 50% that goes through, so I am afraid I will
have to forgo the pleasure of writing to you so often. When you
stop and think of it, it is a shame that we have to go through such
rigorous training just to kill or be killed. Such a waste of time and
money. But I am looking beyond the war and therefore I take my
training seriously.

Had my first flight today. The instructor took the ship up to
2500 feet and gave me the controls. You know the hardest thing to
learn at first is straight and level flight? The nose has a tendency to
sink or raise and the wings want to dip or climb. He had me do a
few banks and turns and then he brought the ship back in. So now
I have thirty-six minutes of flying time logged. It really is wonderful.
I'd never be content in any other branch of the service. The country
around here is beautiful from the air. It is dotted with hundreds
of lakes and then the regular rows of trees in the orange groves
makes a wonderful sight from the air.

I know it is selfish of me and illogical at the same time, but I
wish we could be married before I have to go overseas. However
before I can even think of this I must finish my training and get my
wings. I'll be here a couple of months after graduation and I can
ponder the question then.

Well darling I have to get back to my "Theory of Flight"
textbook. Remember I love you and always will—

All my love, El

Virginia – March 6, 1943 10:15 p.m.

Darling,

Well—so I got home, after a week without word from my darling—but the thought of your telephone call, the sound of your voice, will make me happy for a long time. I hope my memory holds out until I can see you.

Tuesday night, before I left, the army air corps arrived—750 privates who may, if they qualify, be a/c's [air cadets] after the training at Syracuse. They expect more before long and by April the total's supposed to be 2100. Gee, it was thrilling seeing them come in! Julie (managing ed.), the reporter, & I went to the station. The troopers pulled in about 9 p.m. and got a taste of real Syracuse weather. It was snowing, and not very warm. They "fell in" and marched up to campus singing the air corps song and other old favorites. Good looking bunch of fellows and very nice boys, at least those I spoke to were. Julie & I were taking pictures. Since then, I've seen them, shouting cadence as they marched, going across campus, down University place, etc. It's wonderful to have them—because it means Syracuse is really doing something, because it means the U. will survive the war, and because it gives the campus a more warlike atmosphere.

The addition of the air crewmen came when we'd lost almost 500 men to the army via the army enlisted reserve corps. The ERC called its men this past week and there was a general exodus taking place on campuses all over the east. It was getting me down, too, because it's not easy to say goodbye to fine fellows, especially when it may be the last time you'll see them. The paper's being hard hit, too. From the sports staff alone, there are 6 or 7 men gone! That leaves us with a skeleton staff, but definitely. Frankly, I don't know what we'll do. Everything's up in the air. Think we'll work a plan with the army on campus, whereby they get one page of the paper for their news.

I'm enclosing a clipping I read in the Post-Standard before I left. Did you see the mess? I *hate* to read things like that. Why should they lose so many ships and men *in this country*? [Datelined Avon Park, Fla., the headline reads, "5 Killed in Crash of Army Bomber".]

I love you—always, darling. Ginny

March 7, 1943 – US Major General George Patton arrives in Tunisia

Elmer – March 7, 1943 2005

Dearly Beloved—

About ten minutes ago they started playing records over the P.A. system and they just played Cugat's "Night Must Fall." I almost went crazy. It vividly brought to my mind all the wonderful evenings I spent with you in your cellar, especially the night we got together again after those many agonizing weeks apart.

What a time I had flying yesterday. When we went up the wind was blowing very strong and the air was bumpy as the dickens. The sky was overcast but it was broken. We climbed to about 3000 feet and got over the clouds. It's beautiful up there. The clouds look like big hunks of loose cotton thrown around under the plane. For about ten minutes the instructor had me doing climbing and gliding turns. Then the ceiling closed in and we lost all visible contact with the ground. The instructor took over the plane and started searching for a hole through the stuff. In about fifteen minutes he found one about the size of your living room. He did a wing over and dove through it like a bat out of you know where. We pulled out at 500 feet and I thought my stomach was going through the bottom of the plane. When we got under the stuff it was o.k. but the air was rougher, so I thought we would land. Instead he gave me the controls and told me to do some coordination turns. (Make a left turn, level off and go right into a right turn, level off and then a left turn and so on.)

The air was so bumpy I couldn't tell if the nose was level in the turns or not and I thought I was doing lousy. In about twenty minutes he took over and we landed. As we walked back to the pilot room he casually remarked "That was damned good flying for the weather we had up there." Boy! That made me feel good!

All my love, El

March 8, 1943 –Allied bombers launch a major attack on Nuremberg

Virginia – March 9, 1943 1:30 p.m.
[from Hempstead, home on a school break]

Darling,

Did I tell you how wonderful it was to hear you on the phone? Gee, sweetheart, I walked around on a cloud, grinning foolishly, for the whole evening. Even the next day there was still at least a foot between me and the ground when I walked. It was so swell to hear your voice—but it certainly made me want you even more than before.

You know, I'm almost as thrilled as you must be about your first flying time! How many hours do you have when you're through primary? And please keep telling me as much as possible about your instruction, particularly in flying. Remember, I'm going to fly someday too!

I love you, El,Ginny

Elmer – March 10, 1943 8:30 p.m.

My Dearest—

As to where I'm going from here, I haven't the slightest idea. If I don't wash (I say this because more than 50% of our upper class has washed out) I will be here for eight weeks more and I won't know for seven weeks at least where I will be sent for basic training. A furlough between here and basic is almost out of the question. As a matter of fact it is almost positive that I won't get one for six months. So if I am going to see you, you will have to come where I am. Oh, I hope that you can. When would you though? After graduation?

My flying is coming along fine. I'm getting to the point where I can take off and land by myself. It's the most wonderful feeling to give a plane full throttle, have it roar down the runway, give it a little forward stick to keep the tail up, and when it gets up air speed, to ease the stick back, and have it leave the ground and bite into the air.

We have been practicing stalls and spins yesterday and today. There is no way to describe a spin. Just imagine flying along at say 4000 feet, then pulling the nose up to say 45° over the horizon and when it loses air speed and starts to drop, kick hard on the right rudder and spiral nose first toward the ground. What a sensation to see the earth come spinning up at you. To pull out, you push hard on the opposite rudder and when it stops spinning, ease back on the stick and gun it at the same time to pull out.

A stall is the same thing only you don't spin. You get the nose up until it will climb no more and as it loses its air speed it hangs in the air for a fraction of a second then the nose comes roaring down and you go into a dive. There are six kinds of stalls. I have gotten so that I can do them all and the spin. But this is only the beginning. In about four or five more hours I should be soloing.

All my love, El

Virginia – March 11, 1943 11:45 p.m.

My darling—

Today was hard for me. I spent the whole of it shopping with Mom—an easy enough assignment, you'd say—except that you were there all the time; that is, the lack of you was there, in my mind, and everything seemed to emphasize the fact. Writing cases—and I wondered what to give you when you become 21. Curtains—and how I wished I could buy some for *our* home. So it went in every department. Then we went to the movies and the love scenes in "Casablanca" made me want you terribly. Missing you grows harder to take every day.

I'm leaving [for Syracuse] Sunday afternoon and the only good things about the trip are that I won't have to part from you and it will be the last trek "back to the grind" (which it certainly will be this time—with the journalism comprehensive exam looming). Sometimes I say, "To hell with the worries—I'll let tomorrow take care of itself"—and other times, usually, in fact, I groan and do the last minute cramming and hope. With additional worries of who's going to take the paper (editorship) next year, what the setup will be, how our staff will hold out, if the army will cooperate—well you get the idea—I don't have gumption enough at present for the "to hell with it" attitude.

I love you, El. Ginny

Virginia – March 13, 1943 12:30 a.m.

Dearest,

A very important thing I forgot to say last night—how happy I am and how proud of you when you tell me things like your instructor's compliment to you after doing coordination turns in bad weather. Darling, only the best should come to you, according to my estimation, and these things prove it. Do keep up the good work—but I know you will. My prayers are for you, El.

Mom and I picked out a watch which is to be a graduation present—so I don't get it until then! But it's a gorgeous job—an Elgin, and I'm dying to wear it. Mom, however, remains adamant. I'll wait until May 9!

Never forget that *I love you*, darling, *always,*Ginny

Elmer – March 16, 1943 2105

My Dearest—

Well, my hours in the air are piling up. I now have seven hours and thirty seven minutes to my credit and I expect to solo tomorrow

or the next day. The washing machine is starting to grind. About
fifteen of the lower class have washed out already and about
six more are going up for their final check tomorrow. (This final
check is just a formality before washing out. Only one cadet in the
history of this field has ever passed a final check.) Despite the high
washout rate, I am not particularly worried. My instructor seems
highly satisfied with my work and progress. I now feel that I am
master of the plane and it is no longer master of me. I went up
about 8:00 this morning and it was beautiful. The air is smooth
early in the morning and there was still a mist hanging over the
swamps to the south. I can't describe scenes like these, you have to
be up in the air yourself to appreciate them. You will too, someday,
alongside of me. As a matter of fact you'll be my co-pilot for life.
Will that day hurry up?

A few of our class have soloed already, but most of them
have had previous time. The first fellow that soloed, ground
looped and completely demolished a wing. These Stearmans are
really good at ground looping because the wheels are so close
together. A ground loop is caused by not landing straight. As the
wheels hit the ground the plane has a tendency to turn rapidly to
one side. If this is not corrected immediately by prompt rudder
action, the plane will continue to turn and centrifugal force will
raise one wing and dig the other into the ground. So many wing-
tips are lost this way that the school is awarding a bonus of fifty
dollars to the instructor whose students do the least damage to the
planes over a certain period of time. Don't worry though honey, a
ground loop isn't serious. No one has ever been hurt in one.

My academics are coming along fine also. Had a final in
aircraft recognition yesterday and ended up with a 94% average
in that subject. All kinds of planes too. Japanese, American,
British, German and Italian. Navigation is what is getting
tough. Pilotage, dead reckoning, radio navigation and celestial

navigation are starting to weigh heavily on my poor shoulders. But enough of me.

Darling, in your last letter you seem to be somewhat disgruntled over your schoolwork. Honey, don't let it get you down. Just keep plugging, that's all you can do. Before I got into the army I couldn't give this advice, because I think I was the most lackadaisical guy going, but since I have a goal to shoot at, I have changed. Just do your best, that's all they can ask of you. I gotta cut this out, I sound like a Dutch uncle.

Darling, taps will blow any second so I gotta say good night for now. Remember that I love you dearest, more and more each day.

All my love, El

Virginia – March 16, 1943 10:30 p.m.

Darling,

We have to get out of Wilbur! Yes, after 2½ years of one room & one roommate in the same house, we have to move. Got the good news when we got back Sunday night—and we were rather

surprised. We'd figured the army wouldn't want this small house, but we were wrong. And it is the army air crewmen who are causing our being "turn out," too. I told you about the pre-aviation cadets here. (There are about 1000 here now.) They're really taking over. It's swell to have them, though, in my estimation. Maybe

their presence will make the ostriches on campus realize there's really a fight going on. In addition to that, they add a military and very alive aspect to the place. Singing as they march to and from campus, or shouting cadence during drill, they can be heard at all times of the day.

Gad, do they *sing*!! Today one of the ditties was (to the tune of "Battle Hymn of the Republic"):

When the war is over we will all enlist again [repeated twice]
We will, like Hell, we will!

Gee, what problems we're having on the paper—personnel & other difficulties. Think we'll give what used to be the sports page to the army. I'm going to see the public relations officer tomorrow. In a couple of weeks we'll no longer be senior editors of the D.O. Elections will be held shortly—I haven't decided the exact date yet—and I'll be a has-been. Probably I'll feel like a lost soul without the paper, but I'll certainly need the time to get my work caught up.

I love you, always. Ginny

Virginia – March 22, 1943

Darling,

The office will no longer be my almost perpetual residence after Friday, if the publications board is quick about making up its mind. The idea of it being almost over, with everything gone but the memories, practically, is on my mind. Certainly loved it. Don't know whether I'll write a swan song or not. Probably will. That will not be easy.

Dearest, I hope you don't mind the typing. I'm in a terrible rush and have it handy. If you object, I'll never do it again. But if you have any regard for your eyes ATALL, you'll like this.

When will I ever get time to write you a real letter???

I LOVE YOU.Ginny

Virginia – March 22, 1943 1:40 p.m.

Darling,

Biggest news, outside the moving and DO stuff, is that I've been elected to Phi Beta Kappa in the spring election!! It's really the last thing I wanted out of college, and getting it satisfies me in some strange manner. [Her friend Marie once cracked, "Virginia always wanted to get an A+ in life."] The first woman editor made it, and I wanted to. Also, I wanted it for Mom & Pop,—(whom I called Saturday night to tell them the news)—so I'm glad. Now all I want is to see the DO in good hands so I'll be ready to graduate in peace.

I love you, dearest. Ginny

Elmer – March 23, 1943 9:30 p.m.

My Dearest—

Today I dood it! Yep, I soloed. The reason I haven't written in so long is because I've been worried sick. We must solo in eleven hours or we get an elimination ride, and my time was running out and I still couldn't get my landings down. Today the air was the roughest I have ever seen it and I never thought he would let me

solo. We went over to auxiliary field #1 and I shot six punk landings. After the last one, he taxied over to the wind-sock and got out. "She's all yours" he said and that was all I needed. I gave it the gun and roared off in a cloud of dust. What a feeling to be up there alone! I found myself singing and talking to myself. I shot five landings and then came back and picked up the instructor. You know I really cut it close. I soloed in ten hours and fifty-nine minutes. One minute to spare!

All my love, El

Virginia – March 27, 1943 12:10 a.m.

Darling,

I'm no longer editor of the paper, honey, and it feels pretty peculiar. Don't yet know just how lost I will feel, because it was only this afternoon we elected my successor—Andy O'Keefe, a swell guy. And he's got a very fine staff. But I've enjoyed working with these people and they're wonderful. I'll miss them in more than one way. Can't say how much. And there aren't even all of the has-beens left to console me. Julie Handler, m.e. [managing editor] left for Brooklyn yesterday. He goes in the navy April 5.

I want to get some sleep so that I'll be able to get up *early* tomorrow a.m. The second contingent of air corps students is coming at 6!!

I love you, El. Ginny

Elmer – March 27, 1943 1:40 p.m.

My Dearest—

My flying is on the ball again after a few bad days last week. I have had my three supervised solos and yesterday I took the first of two landing stages. A landing stage, I go on to explain, is an examination in flying. Five men take it together. We take off one after another, fly the pattern around the field and land, then repeat five times. Each time we go around we are graded and must pass each time around in order to pass the stage. What a rat-race our stage was yesterday. One fellow lost his bearings and had to go up to 1500 feet to find out where he was. (We are not allowed to fly above 500 feet on these stages.) The second man tried to stretch a "graveyard glide" and took off the top of a tree with his tail wheel. The third man went into a ground loop when he landed, foolishly applied brakes and flipped over on his back. The fourth man did the funniest thing I have seen since I've been in the army. All the instructors were sitting on the wind "T" in the middle of the field grading the various stages. This fellow got mixed up and came in for a landing crosswind, heading straight for the "T." I have never seen anyone move so fast in my life as those instructors, scrambling off that tee and diving for the ground. He landed before the "T" and bounced over it, so you can see how close he came to them. I just sat up there in the blue, all alone, and laughed myself sick. Luckily, all I did was bounce on one of my landings and consequently I was the only one who passed.

Well dearest, I must get out to the flight line and take my second landing stage. If I pass this one I am free to take a plane up alone anytime.

All my love, always, El

March 29, 1943 – Meat, butter, and cheese are rationed

Elmer – March 31, 1943 11:55 a.m.

My Dearest—

I'm starting this out at the flight line but I doubt if I'll be able to finish it here; the bus will be along shortly to take us back to lunch. I realize I haven't been writing much lately, and I feel badly about it, but there's nothing I can do. I have a twenty-hour check coming up in a day or two and I can't afford to flunk it. I just came in from two and a half hours solo flying and I'm *tired*. Flying is a heck of a lot of fun, but flying the Army way is exhausting as the devil. This twenty hour check includes spins, stalls, "S" turns, elementary "8"'s, Chandelles, forced landings, steep 360° turns and pattern flying, so you see how busy I've been lately.

Darling, I wish you could be down here now. Many of the orange trees are blooming, and the fragrance of orange blossoms fills the air. Makes me think of weddings in June, or any month for that matter. Oh, that this blasted war was over and I could come home and middle-aisle it with you. That is the only time the fragrance of orange-blossoms will mean anything to me.

Every evening they play records on the P.A. system here and there is one record that really sends me. "Black Magic" is the name of it and I think James [bandleader Harry] does it up. Do you know it? First new tune I've heard since I've been away.

All my love, El

Elmer – April 3, 1943 10:05 a.m.

My Dearest—
Yesterday I learned how to do "lazy eights" and was practicing them solo this morning. This is a lazy "8." Start out by diving to get

 air speed, bring the nose up to the horizon and keep climbing and at the same time put it into a turn. As the nose drops below the horizon, level the wings stop the turn and pull the nose up and repeat the process. They are a heck of a lot of fun, you can keep it up all day.

Today I became an upperclassman. Our upperclass moved out last night and our lower class is due in this afternoon. Our ranks sure have dwindled in the past five weeks. At the last count, 52% had already washed and there is bound to be more on the 20 hour check. As a matter of fact three men get their elimination ride this morning. The worst part is over for me now, but I must still be on the ball every minute.

Ginny, dearest, when will I be able to see you and hold you close to me the way I want to? The Seaboard Express runs right past our door and every day it goes by, I think that in a few hours it will pull into Penn. Station and I get an insane desire to hop aboard it. (Get ahold of yourself, El, old boy).

We changed officially to summer uniforms yesterday. I'm wearing khaki now instead of olive drab. They're a heck of a lot more comfortable than the heavy O.D.'s, in this hot Florida sunshine.

All my love, El

Virginia – April 3, 1943 10:00 p.m.

Darling,

I love you so much, sweetheart—and it makes me *so* happy to hear about your flying. Hope you're now qualified to fly anytime you feel like it! Gee, honey, you're wonderful—and though I've never seen you even near a plane, I *know* you are or will be a wonderful pilot.

I've thought of a new way to make me happy without you. I try to dig out of the corners of my mind incidents with you that I haven't thought about for a long time. The other day I remembered, and very happily, the time we went to Belmont Lake State Park—how you kissed me after we'd been resting on the bank. Do you remember darling?

I love you, El. Ginny

April 6, 1943 – British and US forces link up in North Africa

Elmer – April 6, 1943 9:15 p.m.

My Dearest—

I got your wonderful letter of the 3rd this noon just before leaving for the airport. You can't imagine the effect it had upon my flying. I was up solo for about an hour and a half and dearest, you were in the front cockpit all the time. Up about 5,000 feet, with the Florida countryside stretching out below I found myself talking to you, and maybe it was the wind whistling through the outer bay struts, but I could have sworn you answered me.

We had a crash out here Saturday. An instructor and a student (old Maxwell roommate of mine) were putting in some dual time. The instructor had the student do a spin at 3200 feet. When the time came for them to pull out they found the rudder was not working and they couldn't stop spinning. Andy jumped at 500 feet and the instructor at 350'. They just had time to open their chutes before they hit ground. Neither of them were hurt luckily. Monday morning when I went up and kicked it into a spin

I couldn't help thinking of them, but it didn't bother me. I just start my spins at a little higher altitude.

I love you, Ginny darling.

All my love, El

Elmer – April 8, 1943 10:55 a.m.

My Darling—

Your man is exhausted, done in, and generally beat. Yesterday morning I got up at the usual time, had breakfast, tidied up my room, went to school all morning and came back and drilled for an hour. After lunch I went out to the flight line, flew all afternoon came back and had calisthenics for an hour and half. After a nice shower I went to supper, just normally tired, and then it happened. The Captain announced that—"C" flight, section 'I' was starting night flying last night. Immediately after mess we donned our flying togs and whipped back to the airport. We were out there until nearly 1 o'clock this morning flying and learning the fundamentals of instrument flying. Still we had to get up at 6:10 this morning. I could just about drag myself from class to class this morning. Do you still wonder why I don't write more often?

Night flying is really wonderful though. The stars seem to be within reach and the lights below look like diamonds on black velvet. We spent most of our time shooting landings. A row of flare pots are placed along the runway and that is the only thing that guides you into the field. At first I made some awfully bumpy landings, but after a while I got so I could judge how far I was from the ground by the reflection of my wingtip lights. There are six planes flying the pattern and traffic is controlled by a man in the tower with a device called a Biscus Gun. This is somewhat like a flashlight and it is aimed at the pilot for whom the signal is intended. Various intermittent flashes of red and green mean certain things like "remain where you are," "clear the runway," "okay for takeoff," "land immediately" etc. Tricky system.

I start my cross country in about a week. We are plotting courses on our aeronautical charts already. It should be great fun.

You know darling, when I think of how I am plugging away, storing up knowledge in my brain and then realize that this knowledge is meant to be used for destructive purposes, it gives me a queer feeling inside. [While then as now a pejorative term for a homosexual person, queer also meant 'odd, or 'strange.] I don't know just how to explain it. It's just that I have so much love in my heart for you, that it doesn't seem right that I also am being prepared to destroy. Gives me a feeling of being a Jekyll-Hyde character. Not that I'm dissatisfied. I know I have a job to do, the same as everyone else, and this is the only way I want to do it. If only the aviation I'm learning could be used constructively.

If you can't make sense out of this last idea, try to forgive me. I get moody when I'm tired.

All my love, El

Virginia – April 11, 1943 5:25 p.m.

Darling,

I got involved with a camera, taking pictures for my layout for photography (a layout illustrating Syracuse U. at war) and the better part of the day got away.

I'm getting soldiers here in some illustrative situations (cleaning the barracks in the morning, marching into Maxwell for class, one walking guard in front of a former frat house, now a barracks), and in addition to these, I'm going to get pix of gals taking the "commando" course (climbing ropes, jumping over things, etc.) and also some of students in the night course, welding, and learning to work a lathe, for instance. I'm very interested in this assignment. Sometimes I think I wouldn't mind being a photographer. [Virginia later became her family's cinematographer, capturing silent Kodachrome movies of her children growing up.]

Today is beautiful. Marvelously clear, although cold. All I wanted all day long was you, and next a car to float luxuriously around campus in. Both were rather unobtainable, so instead I helped to entertain the air corps students that came after dinner. All the time they get off is Saturday night until one and Sunday until four. It's not very much, so cottages and sororities have open house for them on weekends. The houses were jammed last night and the town got painted pretty scarlet. These boys were raring to go after two weeks in barracks, without even being able to speak to people they knew!

So a whole slew of them filed in here this afternoon and the kids rolled up the rugs for dancing, sang, and Rita Banta [Kathy's younger sister] and I played pool with two of them, and got skunked, by the way. I'm afraid my pool isn't too sharp yet, but I'm trying. I sorta like to do this "entertaining" for them because I figure it makes things a little more pleasant for them. Most of them have girls at home, I imagine. One of those we played pool with did, for which I was glad. He talked about his girl and I talked about you! Another somebody to listen to me talk about you, honey. Gee, I love you.

Did I tell you that I too like "That Old Black Magic"? In fact, I have Charlie Barnet's record version of it. That's the one that begins with a roll on drums—with the knuckles it's done, I imagine. If James has made a record of it, I haven't heard it.

On the other side of this Barnet record is another good one, "I Don't Want Anybody at All" (if I can't have you). There's some wonderfully dirty trumpet rides in it, in addition to Charlie's usual good sax. The dirty trumpet is the main reason why I got the record, so you can see how good it is. I also bought Cugat's "Brazil" recently. Wish you were here to dance with me to it.

Keep up your practice of telling me what you're learning about flying and how you do the various and sundry maneuvers in the air, honey. It may seem to you like a boring letter you're writing but I assure you it isn't. I'm very interested, as you should know, in everything you do. Congratulations to you, darling, all the time— at present for being an upperclassman but also for passing the 90 degree accuracy test. Gee, I'm so proud of you!

I love you always. Ginny

Elmer – April 14, 1943 2:10 p.m.
[apparently sent with photos]

My Dearest—

Your wonderful, long letter came at a very opportune moment. I hadn't heard from you in over ten days, I have a navigation final this afternoon and I think I flunked my forty hour check this morning; so you can see I really needed the lift your letter gave me.

My forty came five minutes after I had landed from an hour and a half cross-country flight with my instructor. The check rider who rode with me today saw me pull a blunder on a 180° accuracy stage (I passed) on Saturday and he was gunning for me. He did everything he could think of to try and rattle me. For instance he did a half-roll, stayed in inverted flight, cut throttle and said "forced landing." He didn't give me anything I had been practicing; instead he gave me new maneuvers I just learned like loops, snap-rolls, slow rolls etc. I may have passed though. He flew with one fellow today and told him definitely he flunked. He just walked away from me disgustedly.

Honey at last here are a couple of snapshots of El in uniform. We took them last week end at Cypress Gardens. I love you, Ginny darling.

All my love, El

April 18, 1943 – The airplane carrying Marshal Admiral Isoroku Yamamoto, commander-in-chief of the Japanese navy and the architect of the attack on Pearl Harbor, is shot down, after US cryptologists intercept his flight plans

---

Virginia – April 18, 1943 5:30 p.m.

Darling,

Oh honey, you don't know how much those pictures mean to me. I've been carrying them around ever since yesterday morning, taking them out every two minutes to look, and sweetheart, they're wonderful. Please send more, quick. I'll have these worn out before long! And would you send the negative of the "air corps poster" pose?! I want to make an enlargement. Gotta have *something* until you get me a big one! And I think that snap is *swell*. [It would end up being his "press photo" throughout the war!]

Darling—I don't know how serious it would be—whether it would mean the axe for you if so—but I hope you didn't flunk your 40-hour check. If praying and thinking and hoping for you does any good, you didn't miss it. Gee, I'm so anxious for you. But—although you must *know* this—it won't make any difference in my love for you if you wash out. Anything you'd do I know would be honorable and good. Dearest, do you know how I love you? But *please* let me know about the navigation final and 40-hour check. I can't wait until I hear from you again.

All my love, dearest—Ginny

Virginia – April 21, 1943 7:30 a.m.

Darling,

This is rather early for me to be writing, but it's all because of Holy week. I'm going to mass every morning and this a.m.

Darling, I'm still glowing about the pictures. Gee, I'm crazy about them—and you! I've showed them to everyone (almost) in the house—you are well admired by the gals.

After dark last night I went up on the roof for a while. It was cool, but like the cool after a warm summer day, and just coming up through the trees was a huge orange moon! Of course, I was dreaming of you, and I remembered that night driving around the north shore. The moon was full that night, and right in front of us as we drove east. There were many other rides in that section. I think I went over them all in memory and it made me feel close to you.

To the west, up there, was the city stretched out and blinking. That reminded me of the first time you came to Syracuse and we sat on Mt. Olympus and watched the lights come on in the city. Sweetheart, everything I do is with you.

I'll have to leave now, honey. May your Easter be happy. I'll be praying for next spring to see us together.

I love you, Ginny

Elmer – April 20, 1943 10:05 a.m.

Dear Mom and Dad—

My best buddy, a fellow I have been rooming with since Nashville, just washed out. I feel pretty bad about it. We were darned good friends. You know, out of twelve of us who shared adjoining rooms in Maxwell, there are only three of us left. That gives you an idea of the washout rate in this place. My instructor only has two of his original five students. Some instructors have lost all their students. I consider myself doggone lucky to have come this far.

Your loving son, El

When he left, El's friend Lee Palser, a talented illustrator, gave him a beautifully drawn message. He wrote, "So long, El. We separate now friend and yours is a long and hard trail to cover but you can do it. You're going to wonder at times if it's worth it but remember it's a job to be done; your job. No one else can do that job for you nor can they do it in the way you would have it done. These will be hard times and you may start to slip but don't fall. You have what it takes so go ahead friend and let me at least say I know a pilot. I know a good pilot." Lee later was an aircrewman on a B-24 bomber that was shot down over Italy in August 1944. Although classified as a POW, he eluded capture by hiding in caves for ten months, until the war in Europe ended.

Elmer – April 22, 1943 11:20 a.m.

My Dearest—

It has been ages since I last wrote, I know, but things have been moving so rapidly around here, I scarcely know whether I'm coming or going. First of all, I am finished academics. I took the last of my finals yesterday. My marks didn't run too badly.

This has been a very eventful, and *very* discouraging 24 hours. I took my 60 hour check yesterday afternoon and the Army deemed it an unsatisfactory ride. Seems the check rider I rode with, was a bug on chandelles, and they are my weakest maneuver. I haven't washed out yet; I get another check today or tomorrow. If wanting to pass has anything to do with it, I won't have any trouble. I have sixty-two hours and 38 minutes behind me. You would think they would take that into consideration. After all I got this far without too much difficulty.

I had a unique experience a couple of days ago. I blacked myself out. Seems I was practicing slow rolls and a *"split 'S'" out of it. (*power dive from an inverted position.) Before I could cut throttle I was diving at 170 miles an hour, and instead of easing the nose up, I sorta pulled it up fast. My stomach went down into my shoes and everything got hazy and then completely black. It's an extremely funny feeling to have complete control of your senses and yet be blind as a bat. The effects are only momentary and there is no danger because blackout comes after you pull out of the dive. I wasn't the first, not the only one to do it. Some fellows have even blacked out their instructors!

Darling did I ever tell you that all the letters you send me go for airplane rides. Maybe it's superstition, maybe it's sentimentality, but I always carry your most recent letter with me when I fly. Makes you seem sorta close to me when I'm up there alone. Honey I love you so much. I hope the next place I go, whether it be Basic or what have you, will be closer to home, so that you can come down.

All my love, El

Virginia – April 24, 1943 12:30 a.m.

Darling—

It's been a week since I've heard from you, and I'm worried about the 40-hour check. But maybe tomorrow (later today) a brown letter will come.

I got started the other afternoon and wrote to Elmer Davis (OWI chief) [famous journalist and head of the Office of War Information], Merz [Charles] (editor of the NY Times) and Haskell [William] (Tribune—whom I met this fall). Of course, I'm not expecting much, but I can't lose more than the postage, and *maybe* something might break. [She tells Elmer in a letter a few days later that she has been invited to meet with both Merz and Haskell.] In the meantime, I'm hearing about a lot of job openings—Binghamton, Watertown—but I want something closer to N.Y.C.

I love you, darling. Ginny

Virginia – April 26, 1943 1:30 p.m.

Dearest,

Honey, I got your letter today, one that I've been holding my breath over, and I'm *still* holding it! After a week of waiting—the last letter said you were afraid you'd flunked the 40-hour—I was tearing my hair. And gee, darling, now I'm still worried. Between you and exams, I'll soon be a mental case. But if prayers do any good, you've passed. I hope so—very much—but you know it won't make any difference in how I love you.

Did I tell you I was elected class marshal (along with a fellow) by seniors at the regular convocation? Well, I was—and of course I was happy. It's an honor that means you lead your class at baccalaureate and commencement exercises. How I wish you could be here. Then everything would be perfect.

I love you, always and always, darling. Ginny

Elmer – April 27, 1943 10:25 a.m.

Dearest—

I'm writing this from the diving raft out on the lake. This morning I got my last 19 minutes of flying and now I have nothing to do but soak up some of this beautiful Florida sunshine.

It is now the 30th of April. This is the first chance I have had to get back to writing. I have been so busy clearing through the flight line and the ground school, chasing laundry around and various and sundry other things connected with leaving a post that I don't know whether I'm coming or going.

[The letter continues on the reverse of the page. Given the information he was about to deliver, I imagine he did this on purpose!]

That furlough idea has been blasted. Today I leave for Basic. My new address is: [Cochran Field, Macon, Georgia].

Yes, now it's Georgia. We are really getting to see the "old south." As soon as I get there, I'll start making inquiries as to how often I could see visitors and what kind of accommodations I could find for you. I want to see you so much, darling, to hold you in my arms again. Will this blasted war never end?

All my love, El

Elmer – May 1, 1943 8:45 p.m.

Dearest—

I lost my temper yesterday. First time in months. It was at dinner and I was sitting across the table from an eliminated cadet. During the routine mealtime conversation, it came out that he had quit. Seems he had gotten a look at a Basic Training plane and he suddenly realized that this isn't going to be any picnic, and that he might possibly get hurt. He readily admitted that he was scared. I told him that he would probably be made a gunner, and his chances of survival would be even slimmer. He said "listen, if they can't make me fight here, they can't make me fight as a gunner. Enough of you guys are eager, you can do all the fighting." Then I blew up. I don't think I cussed so much in my whole life as I did that few minutes. The whole mess hall fell silent before my onslaught. I didn't think there were that kind of people in this country.

You should have seen the last day of flying. Everyone had passed his sixty and it was only a matter of putting in the required time. There are about ten dog-fights going on in the sky at once, and planes were diving on everything in sight; trains, houses, cars, everything. Some fellows were even flying in formation and diving on bombers that fly by every now and then.

All my love, El

Elmer – May 5, 1943 7:20 p.m.

Dear Mom and Dad—

So you are proud of me, eh Pop? I'm glad. I guess last summer when I was running around and drinking like a fish, I wasn't much to be proud of. But see, I can be O.K. if I put my mind to it. I only hope I can make you still prouder when I get my wings and I get into combat.

Your loving son. El

Basic

IN BASIC TRAINING THE air cadets honed their aviation and navigation skills, piloting airplanes more powerful and complicated
than their trainers in primary. They took long cross-country
trips, some at night. And they were beginning to think about
the warplanes they might be assigned to fly.

Virginia – May 3, 1943 11 a.m.

Dearest—

I'm so mad at you I could spit! After a week of wondering, hoping,
and worrying about you and your 60-hour check or recheck—
whether you passed it or not, how you were and if still in the air
corps—I rip open your letter this morning, a few minutes ago,
and find you haven't even mentioned it! No kidding, honey, that
about did it! I'm ready to fall over from lack of sleep, I just got
some *lousy* exam marks, I'll have to stay up all night again tonight
probably for tomorrow's exam—and you don't *mention* what's
been on my mind all week. Aw nuts!

I take it you got through o.k. But I'd really like to understand
it from explicit information rather than guess work.

Jeepers—I'm sorry I'm in such a lousy mood honey. But
maybe you'd realize how I felt if I had written you one week

saying I'd been flunked out, I thought, and the next week I blithely wrote about the commencement exercises. See what I mean? If not, forget it. It's all my mood, then, and these damn exams. I probably shouldn't send you this letter. It will be a helluva thing for you to get at the new post, but it's written now and I won't have time for another very soon.

I will be graduated May 9—this Sunday. Mom & Pop will probably come up and will leave here Monday. So don't write me here please.

I hope you'll let me know about the new regulations soon. *If* I *can* come down, I'll have to come soon—because I have to get a job before very long.

This is awful. I'd better do something constructive—like study for that exam and complete a notebook for the course.

* I love you, honey. Ginny

(*despite this mean letter.)

Elmer – May 5, 1943 8:15 p.m.

My Dearest—

Now I am willing to acknowledge that I am at fault. It was very thoughtless of me to leave you up in the air as I did. I figured that my writing that I was going to a Basic school would make you take for granted that I made the grade. Fact is, I was scheduled for a re-check on my sixty, but the Flight commander and Commanding Officer witnessed a beautiful hurdle stage that I luckily shot the following day, and, since my time was running short, they talked the check rider out of a re-check and he passed me on the first ride.

Darling, I realize you must be under a terrific strain also, but you should have burned that letter you sent me. It made me feel kinda low, at a time when I needed bolstering up more than ever. You see, (I don't suppose I should be telling you this and please don't tell my folks) our upper class has had five fatal accidents in the past four weeks and that doesn't do our morale a bit of good. Suppose we forget the whole thing? I promise to be more explicit in my letters from now on.

I have had two hours and two minutes in a Basic Trainer and by now I am completely confused. I never saw so many instruments in one ship in my life. Trim tabs, landing flaps, prop pitch control, gyro compass, artificial horizon, bank and turn indicator, radio equipment, inter-cockpit phones, etc. etc.

Our first thirty hours in this plane is a transition from a primary trainer. And what a difference! The BT-13A is more than twice as heavy and has more than twice the horsepower than a P.T. It's powered by a Pratt and Whitney 450 H.P. engine and that ain't hay. It's really a smooth flying plane though, when you get on to it.

We're working with radio now. We call the control tower before taking off and we call in again for landing instructions. "7L5 from four zero six, go ahead." "Four zero six from 7L5 (tower) Roger (acknowledgement)." "Calling in for landing instructions." "South-east 'T' setting come on in." "7L5 from four zero six, Wilco." Wilco means "I will comply with orders." It's a lot of fun.

Boy, are they handing us the bookwork now. Here in Basic we get lots of night cross-country, four and five hundred miles long, so we really have to have navigation and instrument flying down pat.

Darling, I have some bad news. You won't be able to come down for four weeks anyway. While we are underclass we don't get any evenings to ourselves and we only get a few hours on either Friday or Saturday evening free. Not only that, but there are no rooms to be had in Macon. Some of the fellows whose wives have been following them around, can't get rooms for them. So I'm afraid it will have to wait awhile.

All my love, El

Elmer – May 9, 1943 9:20 a.m.

My Dearest—

Happy Mother's Day, honey. Yes, I know you're not a mother now, but someday, if I have anything to say about it, you will be.

I am a bad boy. Last night we got open post and another fellow and I went in to see the fair city of Macon. After a good dinner, we bought us a bottle of Haig and Haig Pinch and proceeded to get stinko. One good thing about scotch. I feel fine this morning. I'll bet there isn't another branch of the service that consumes as much alcohol as the Air Corps. Fellows who never touched a drop in civilian life, now are confirmed drunkards. It's amazing. As soon as we are turned loose on a town, there is a mad scramble for the nearest gin-mill. "Nothing can stop the Army Air Corps!"

I see you got my picture o.k. and I'm glad you liked it. I love you very much darling and I am very proud of you. Mom sent me a clipping about you graduating that was in the Review. [It's headlined "Syracuse Honors Virginia Schill."]

I've showed it to everyone in the barracks, and everyone agrees I am very lucky to have such a wonderful woman in love with me. My instructor told me he was going to try to solo me today. It should be quite a thrill soloing one of these big babies. (The B.T.-13A weighs two tons, and as my instructor says, "that ain't fabric.")

A fellow in the next room has a radio and some band is playing "As Time Goes By." The words to that song come closer to what I am trying to convey to you than anything I could say, and I wish I could be with you, especially today. For four years I have thought how nice it would be if I could come up for your graduation. I have been planning on it since I first knew you, and now when the day comes, here I am over a thousand miles away.

They are very mean to us here. They give us our tests in ground school the day before open post, and if we don't pass any of the subjects, we can't get out. Next they will be tying us to the flag pole and giving us ten lashes for every test we flunk. "You too can be an aviation cadet."

Honey, you asked me some time ago if I gave up smoking. I gave it up for Lent, but I am back on the vile weed again. No will power I guess.

I love you darling, and congratulations on your graduation.

All my love, El

Virginia – May 12, 1943 6 a.m. [via Air Mail]

Dearest,

Pop died about 2 hours ago. I can't tell you anymore now. It was coronary thrombosis. I won't be writing for a few days.

Love, Ginny

May 13, 1943 – Axis forces surrender in North Africa

Elmer – May 13, 1943 9:10 p.m.

Dearest—

I don't know what to say. I could say how sorry I am and extend my deepest sympathy, but somehow that sounds hollow and meaningless. I wish I could be there with you at this time. When you need me most, I am never around.

It must have been quite sudden, wasn't it? I mean your father wasn't sick, was he? I still can't believe it. I came back from the flight line, all jubilant because I had finally soloed a BT-13A, and your letter was waiting for me.

There's nothing much I can say now. Please give your mother my sympathy.

All my love, El

Virginia – May 16, 1943 10:55 p.m.

Dearest,

It's been a very long time since you've had a real letter from me. For the first time, perhaps, the excuse is wholly acceptable. Darling, I don't think I realize yet that Pop has gone. It just doesn't seem possible, despite the awful memories of this past week. Every day, I'm afraid, will bring the loss into clearer light. He was such

a great man. And he was thinking about other people until he died. On the way home he asked about you—if I expected to see you. He thought you were a "fine lad" always. Mom and he were pleased when you came to say goodbye before you left. I'm glad you did.

Honey—I could write a whole book on this last week. Things happened so fast. Readjustment won't be so easy, though. But I'm not going to spend pages on Pop's death. I've repeated it as often—mainly to friends who called at the funeral home and it has brought so many tears that I'd rather not. When I see you—please let it be soon—I'll tell you about the whole unhappy affair, if you want to hear it. Here I'll write only that Pop probably knew he was pretty sick, came up for graduation knowing he might not be well, and had a bad heart attack on the train ride home Monday. This was after the weekend was spent in bed, for the most part, with less serious attacks. Mom and I were lucky to get him home, in his own bed where he wanted to be, late Monday night. He was worse Tuesday and died Wednesday morning, early. The funeral was Friday and, dearest, thanks so much for sending the flowers. It was so thoughtful—but I know you liked him and they weren't sent for my sake but for *him*. I'm glad he saw my graduation. I could only wish he could have seen the armistice and our marriage. But if it had had to be as an invalid, I know he'd have preferred it this way.

Seems this letter is pretty sad. You could understand why. There's nothing half so important right now. You may have wondered why I didn't telegraph you the news. It's because I figured it wouldn't do you much good to know any faster and a letter is less abrupt than a telegram.

If I can't see you for 4 weeks, I doubt if I'll be able to until you come here. I hope to be working before then, and I somehow don't expect a vacation right away. Very likely I couldn't come under present circumstances, anyway, but I hate to forget it after dreaming of it so long.

Darling, I haven't even finished unpacking my trunks yet and I've been here almost a week. What a mess my stuff is in! Most of it strewn around the sun porch. You'd never marry me if that were a sample of my housekeeping! But honey, I *can* cook. The kids in the cooperative, who've eaten my pièces de résistance, will vouch for that. They, in surprised tones, say "This is good!"—as if all I should be capable of doing is pounding out stories on my little mill! Wish I could prove it in the near future.

I can never stop telling you you're wonderful. You're always being smart and getting wonderful marks and flying like a good pilot should. Keep it up, darling; I love you and I'm very proud of you.

Ginny

May 18, 1943 – Elmer's twenty-first birthday

Elmer – May 18, 1943 9:10 p.m.

My Dearest—

Well, it's my birthday, but I must say, it's not a particularly happy one. You know the main reason why it's not. I also had a bad day flying. I got a ship, and just as I was about to take off, my motor cut out. I took it back to the line and got another one. This one seemed o.k. and so I climbed up to about 10,000 to do some spins. I did a three turn spin and pulled out at 7,000, about 200 M.P.H. Just as I leveled off, my oil line broke. What a mess. Oil over everything. It was spraying out of the cowling, all over the windshield. For a while I couldn't see a thing. Boy, did I get that baby down on the ground in a hurry. I took it back to the line and got still another ship. This one was o.k.

I had a great time buzzing clouds today. There were nice billowy ones up about eight thousand feet. They are rough on top and it's fun to fly through great valleys in them. I saw a strange phenomenon today. It is called a "Pilot's Halo." As you fly out of a cloud with the sun at your back, there appears directly in front of you a rainbow in a perfect circle and in the center of this is a shadow of your plane. It is amazing and very beautiful.

All my love, El

Elmer – May 21, 1943 3:30 p.m.

My Dearest—

I am bored; I think for the first time since I've been in the army. All student flying has been cancelled until further notice, by order of Colonel Frudenthal. Seems a thunder-storm is roaming around in the vicinity and they won't let us fly until it passes over. So we've just been sitting here twiddling our thumbs until weather clears us.

You have never seen anything in your life like flyers who are grounded. It's amazing. They've always got to be doing something. This ready-room is a madhouse. Two guys rolling all over the floor wrestling, a bunch in one corner singing ribald songs, two more fellows arguing loudly over the relative merits of a B-26 over an A-20 and the poor dispatcher trying to keep order. Me trying to write to the woman I love; and I do love you darling, more and more each day I'm away from you. I have two ambitions in life right now. One is to marry you and the other is to win my wings. Each day brings me closer to my goals, but it's an awfully long wait, especially waiting till after the war to marry you.

Honey, I gotta go now. They've just released solo flying and 403 is waiting for me.

All my love, El

May 23, 1943 – More than 800 Allied bombers attack Dortmund, Germany

Virginia – May 25, 1943 11:50 p.m.

Dearest Carnation Kid,

Remember way back when? Gee, darling, it seems ages ago when you were coming up to Syracuse and writing me letters as a woika in the Chase National! I'm still in the process of getting my "junk" cleaned up, you see, so I've been looking at our past correspondence—your half of it. It was swell. I think I'll read them all, doing it from time to time, whenever I feel lowest. Do you realize, honey, that Oct. 8, 1940, was the date when you first added "with love" at the end of a letter to me? [That date was a few days after the first anniversary of the start of their correspondence. Virginia held out "love" for another three months, but it is clear from other language that she was equally smitten.] All these things are important statistics, y'know!

Heard a program of B.G. [Benny Goodman] records on the Make-Believe Ballroom [popular radio show] last night. One was "Sugarfoot Stomp," reminding me of the Dance Carnival at Madison Square that spring—or summer, if you prefer, and how we walked home! How many times did we run out of gas in that little jalopy of yours? And then they played "Wonder When My Baby's Comin' Home?" That's an important question to me—very important.

This is sort of a drooly letter. I don't mean it to be. Sorry honey.

Hey darling! I love you! Ginny

Elmer — May 25, 1943 8:30 p.m.

My Dearest—

I haven't been in the air since last Wednesday. It has been raining every day. I'm going slowly crazy. You can't imagine what it means to be kept out of the air for so long when it gets in your blood, and it is in my blood. Two things hold prominent places in my heart and mind, you and the plane I fly. Yes, darling, I must admit it. You have a rival for my love. There is a sweet but passionate young lady sitting down at the flight line who answers to my every whim, but whom I must handle with kid gloves or she will dash me to the ground.

By the way, darling, in your last letter, you said your cooking can't be my excuse for not marrying you. Holy Cats! Me having an excuse for *not* marrying you. All you would have to do would be to come down here and say the word, and I'd marry you tomorrow!

All my love, El

Virginia — May 27, 1943 2:22 p.m.

Darling,

I'm being very undressed and absorbing some sun in the back yard. It's a swell day after much rain, and the planes are zooming around again. So far I've seen only B-25's and 26's today. Usually there are several Thunderbolts screaming around. They circle up to their tremendous heights and then back to the field [Mitchel], where, I imagine, a new set of pilots take them up. Anyway, on good days there are Thunderbolts up all day & part of the night. And they whistle so on turns!! Like your imitation of a shell before it lands. But they're certainly fast. Wonder why so many have crashed?

Brod [her brother] & I—mostly Brod—have a garden. Tomatoes, beans, cabbage, and a little parsley. Doing very nicely, too, thank you.

The Thunderbolts are out! Four just passed over in a very lousy formation—but maybe they weren't really trying.

Usually, too, there are B-24's lumbering about, but not today. Maybe too windy.

The Whistling Four just flew over, in much better position. They're improving! I'll give them the nod next time.—Honey, I don't even wink at the loonies that scrape our roof piloting bombers anymore! Good, huh? Still whistle a little, you understand, but that's a hard habit to break.

I hope the sun has come to Georgia to drive the ants out of pilots' pants.

I love you. Ginny

Elmer – May 29, 1943 1:30 p.m.

My Dearest—

Just got your wonderful letter of the 27th wherein you were out in the yard, basking in the beautiful May sunshine. Must be wonderful to have nothing to do but loll about, seeping in vitamin D. I must reprimand you on one count though, dearest. I was very shocked when I opened your letter of the 25th and staring at me in bold letters was the ignominious title "Dear Carnation Kid." I was hoping that that nom d'amour had been forgotten.

This morning I got up at 5:45, had breakfast, cleaned up my room, and came down to the flight line for a lecture on instrument flying. At eight o'clock flying began and I spent all morning shooting crosswind landings and power approaches. Twelve o'clock we took time out for lunch, and now I am back at the flight line waiting for a ship, to go on a 200 mile cross-country trip. I took finals in Aircraft Recognition, Navigation, Radio Procedure, Inspection Periods and Chemical Warfare, this past week. The only mark I know so far is a 95% in Aircraft Recognition.

Just a line; I have to start studying for a final in navigation tomorrow. Today we became upperclassmen. My, how the past four weeks have flown! Seems like I just got here. I've been appointed Cadet First Sergeant for "G" flight, for the rest of my stay here. It's the first chance I've had at a position of importance. May mean the difference between a commission or a flight officer rating when I graduate. Who can tell?

Dearest, so you still whistle at Lieutenants! I'm ashamed of you. I'll have to become a "shave tail" [Army slang for a 2nd Lieutenant] right quick so you'll have one Lieut. in particular to whistle at instead of anyone who happens along. A fine thing!

It is now 5:05 p.m. I just got back from the South Carolina border. Distance means nothing in the air corps. Boy I am bushed.

Darling, I have to get back to the barracks and take a shower.

All my love, El

Virginia – May 29, 1943 11:10 p.m.

Dearest,

It was so gorgeous today it *must* have been *clear*, anyway, in
Macon. I hope you're flying again. I get more letters when you're
not, but you sound more nervous than I ever thought you could be.
What's the corps done to you?

Now look, Honey, don't throw a door at your next bunk
roommate or toss a hangar at the nearest instructor but just try
to contain yourself. A small pail of water thrown at a nearby
sleeper should suffice when I tell you that unless something terrible
intervenes, I'm coming down with your mother and father!! Your
father is going to look up train & bus schedules to Macon.

I've *finally* got your present after consultation with an air
corps major (no small change for me anymore!) on Fifth avenue
Friday. You know every time I've bought you something, since the
army claimed your services, it's just been a guess on my part. So—
send it back if you can't use it. I'll find another air corps officer to
consult!

This major was gazing into store windows like I was, so I
asked him what aviation cadets liked (beside open posts, planes,
& women). He laughed and told me he was in the same boat I was
as his son was graduating from West Point next week & he didn't
know what to get him! But he suggested this (watch the mail).

I'm going to write to the ed. of the Times & the Trib big-wig
& tell them the death of Pop has made plans different for a few
weeks. I don't want them to forget me—but I don't want to miss
seeing you.

WOW! I almost forgot to tell you how wonderful you are
(still) and more so because of the student officer rank you have!
Gee, hon, that's swell. If it were up to me, *your* arm, and not some
other A/C's, would look like a zebra. And you can't expect c.o.'s to
realize how wonderful you are when they only know you a couple

of months—and then only by number, probably. Hey! I gotta *swell* idea. *I'll* write you letters of recommendation! (Sample ↓)

Dearest C.O., ole man,

This Karnation Kid is a wow. If you don't believe me, ask me. I love him.

Ginny

May 30, 1943 – After a land, air, and sea battle, the Americans recapture Attu, the outward island of the Aleutians, which the Japanese had held since June 1942

Elmer – June 3, 1943 9:15 p.m.

My Dearest—

Tighten your safety-belt, honey, I'm going to knock the hell out of your plans. Seems I don't possibly see how you and the folks can come down in the beginning of July. The trouble is that I'm leaving Macon about the 30th of this month and I don't know where I'm going. Even if I did know where I was going, I'm not sure I'd be there when you came, because in Advanced we spend two weeks down on the gulf, in aerial gunnery. So you see it's next to impossible to plan anything right now. I feel lousy about it and I know you and the folks will too. Perhaps in a few weeks, we can arrange something. I wish you and the folks could come down for graduation. You could pin my wings on for me. I'd like that very much.

I flew solo cross-country to Jasper, Florida this afternoon [a 365-mile round trip]. Another fellow flew back formation with me. We sorta got off course and had to buzz a town to find out where we were. Boy did we wake the natives up! We roared down the main street, about 150 feet above the ground. What fun! I fly up to Allendale South Carolina tomorrow [320 miles round trip].

Honey, taps are about to sound so I must leave.

All my love, El

Virginia – June 4, 1943 8:30 p.m.

Dearest,

It's so HOT that although I spent most of today in my bathing suit I felt like I had on my fur coat! But (what fur coat?) beads of sweat from my brow (honest toil!)

nonetheless & undaunted, I cleaned, and washed, and even drove to the village with Mary Margaret to shop. It was HOTTER the

he-aps of places I would have preferred. Like the beach, or a *cool, cool* bar with beer. Instead, though, it was the store. I bought strawberries, and carrots, and cauliflower,

among other things. But I *still* wish some soldier like El or the Carnation Kid would come home to take me to the beach (where poor civilians alone can't drive!) or a bar!

I love you! Ginny

Elmer – June 6, 1943 9:30 p.m.

My Dearest—

Ever since I was in Nashville, I have been going to buy myself
a toilet kit, but I just never got around to it. Then you, with your
unerring intuition, get around to it for me. It's amazing! Yes,
dearest, I like it very much, and I certainly can use it. If you
could see me trotting down to the latrine in the wee hours of the
morning, with my comb, brush, soap, towel, shaving soap and
brush, razor, etc etc falling out of my grasp, you would realize how
much I can use it.

Today three service pilots flew P-51's in and gave us an air
show. What a ship that Mustang is! They'd come roaring in, ten
feet of the ground and pull straight up and do a slow roll on the
way. I've fallen in love with that P-51. What
a beautiful ship! That is the ship I want to
fly. After the demonstration they gave us a
lecture on combat tactics. Combat doesn't
seem so beastly far (split infinitive, tsk, tsk)
off as it once did. Another five or six months
should see 43-H [his flight school class] in
the thick of it.

Darling, taps sounded about 10 minutes ago and the O.C.
will be up here if I don't turn the light out.

I love you. El

Elmer – June 8, 1943 7:30 p.m.

My Dearest—

Gee, today was a wonderful day. First, I went to the flight line
and passed, with flying colors, a combination 20 and 40 hour

check. Then I came home and found your telegram [apparently telling him she was coming down]. Darling you can't imagine how wonderful it made me feel. The week-end of the 19th I have open post on Friday evening and all day Saturday. So if you could arrange to get in town Friday, I could arrange to meet you. Also, if you let me know how long you intend to stay, I'll make arrangements to have someplace for you to hang your hat while in the fair city of Macon.

This letter was interrupted by my roommate who casually mentioned a meteorology assignment still undone. As I again pick up my stylus, twenty-four hours have elapsed and much has transpired. Seems now I am writing from a hospital bed. Yes, I'm in the butcher shop again. Nothing like rubella though. I cut my foot swimming a while back, and this morning when I awoke it was kinda red, so I went to sick call. The doctor shook his head, muttered something about infection and stuck me in a bed. Personally, I feel fine, but I guess he knows his business. Of course this won't interfere with you coming down, I'll be out in a day or two.

Honey, I gotta go now—the doc will be around in a few minutes, and when he comes I am expected to be boiling my foot in hot water.

All my love, El

Elmer – June 12, 1943 8:30 p.m.

My Dearest—

They're letting me out of this place tomorrow and I have an inkling that they will sorta be glad to see me go. Not that I'm any bother, but you see I'm not sick and my spirits, (what with you coming down and all) are unusually high, so the doctors and nurses say I am driving them crazy. I can't understand it.

Funny thing happened to me last week. I was up about eight thousand feet, practicing acrobatics. As I completed the first half of a slow roll and hung there upside down, something black went zooming past my face. I rolled out and looked around but everything seemed to be in order. "Hmm," I said to myself, "something mighty fishy going on here." So I went into another slow roll, hoping to get a better look at the intruder who dared defy the sanctity of my cockpit. Sure enough as I got upside down and my motor began to cough, the same black object whipped into my vision, did a jig on top of the canopy and finally nestled, with a thud, on the back of my neck, over my 'chute harness. "Aha!" I said with all the villainy I could muster, "Now I have ye!" I grabbed it and found it to be a spare, high frequency radio coil that had somehow worked loose from its moorings. This metal gadget is about one foot long and 8" wide, weighing in at five pounds. If it had hit me on the head—it would have broken into smithereens! Some fun.

Honey, I gotta go now. Nursie (2nd lieut, tsk, tsk) is screaming at me again. "Odell, will you put that light out!?" (Taps at 9:00 in the hospital) "Dammit, if they don't put you out of here soon, I'm going to apply for oversees duty." See what us poor wounded soldiers of Uncle Sam have to put up with. It's a crying shame.

All my love, El

Elmer – June 13, 1943 9:20 p.m.

My Dearest—

I was in town this afternoon and reserved a room for you in the Hotel Dempsey. When you get to the station in Macon, walk two blocks straight up Cherry Street and there is the Dempsey. I won't be able to meet you at the station. I'm sorry but I won't be able to get in town until about 700 o'clock Macon time. (Macon is on Central Time, Cochran is on Eastern Time, very confusing.) This will give you time to freshen up after your no doubt grueling ride. Then, too, your train will doubtless be late. I have the room under your name, so all you will have to do is ask for it. I'll meet you at the Dempsey about seven.

Well, darling, I guess that's about all for now. I'll see you Friday night. Gee, that sounds wonderful. I can't wait to see you. I love you so much, dearest, I only wish you were coming to stay. But my makeup in Meteorology is calling.

All my love, El

Judging by the gap in letter dates that follows, it appears Virginia spent more than a brief time in Macon.

Advanced Training

At SPENCE FIELD, IN Moultrie, Georgia, the air cadets would master a more sophisticated trainer and decisions would begin to be made—not by them—as to which aircraft they would fly in combat. The most coveted assignments were to pursuit planes—fighters—like P-51s, P-47s, and P-38s, in that order of preference. Second choices were the bombers—B-17s, B-24s, B-29s and others. The third tier got transport—C-47s and their ilk. The remaining pilots would end up in the Training Command.

Virginia – July 1, 1943 Hempstead again

Darling,

Home—and the past two weeks, at least the time with you, seems like a wonderful dream. Mom was worried—I should have wired her I was staying after Monday—but it's ok, I'm not in the doghouse. Your Mom was worried too! I called her tonight and I'll go over soon to tell her how wonderful you are, as if she didn't know.

The trip home wasn't bad at all, due mostly to the fact that I had a seat in air-conditioned cars all the way. Coming up on the train a happy soldier sang—but loud—"That Old Black Magic." He was in the spell too, I guess.

Funny things, too, like the sign over a garage which blatantly advertised "Ed's Used Parts." Who, I wondered, would care for Ed's used parts. Maybe friends?

And there was an old, OLD conductor, barely able to walk, who'd evidently seen happier days. He'd call out a station and then mutter something under his breath. Probably some deep, dark secret about the town. Rather discouraging to people getting off there, I figured.

Names of towns are always amusing. Two in Virginia particularly so, I had to agree with. One was Hurt, and it looked it. Motley, the other, was indeed, from what I saw. Experiment in Georgia raised the question of whether noble, successful, or otherwise.

I'm listening to Franck's D Minor. I'm very fond of the additional number on the back of the first record—side 2. It's Franck's hymn, Panis Angelicus, Oh Lord Most Holy. Very beautiful thing.

I'm thinking of you, wondering if you're still travelling. But thinking of you is as regular to me as breathing.

I love you dearest, Ginny

While Elmer was tackling new aviation challenges, Virginia was facing challenges of her own. The death of her father, the end of her *Orange* editorship, and her graduation from Syracuse had left her adrift, living at home with her mother, an invalid aunt, and two sisters, and without a job or any certain future. The garden, as before, became a place of solace.

Virginia – July 2, 1943 11:20 p.m.

Dearest,

Undoubtedly I'll be barely able to walk tomorrow. Today I got a job—farmhand at Schill Chateau! Mom had me picking beans—

and more beans. Are they prolific! Perhaps you boys would like to have some beans???

So I stood among the dear growing things, thusly— convincing myself a suntan would look good. But I guess I'll get used to walking on crutches—at least until the beans drop dead from sheer exhaustion—or I do.

Sweetheart, I'm having a tough time making Marie believe we're not married! She says if I'm not, I'm breaking the usual Schill tradition! And, first thing Claire asks me is "Didja get married??" Seems the extra time down there had them wondering.

Mom had a letter from Norm today in which he expressed his sympathy for us about Pop. Awfully nice letter—written June 23 from Alaska.

You have no idea, darling—although maybe you do—how much I enjoyed being with you. For so many reasons, too— for instance I learned so much (for me) about flying and what cadet life is like and even a lot about you as an army pilot. If it's possible, I love you more now. Certainly I understand you better now, if that's not too trite to say what I mean. I know better, that is, what you're doing and I can feel so much closer to you always now. Before, no matter how much you wrote in letters, the things you were experiencing were remote to me. Maybe I'm presuming that I learned a lot, but I really believe I did, even in those few days, and—as I started to say—you have no idea how much nearer to you it's brought me, despite the same number of miles which still separate us.

The boys are getting plenty of night flying these evenings. Beautiful nights, last night & tonight, and it must be wonderful to be up there. And today was *perfect.*—for flying or anything else! Only clouds were a few wispy cirrus numbers just to make the blue interesting. If you 1) don't be *good* in advanced and 2) therefore you aren't made an instructor and 3) thereby (incidentally,

that is) deprive me of the chance of marriage before eighty
and 4) subsequently and consequently you're sent out to OTT
[Operational Training Unit], why, (this is the point) *why* don't you
come to Mitchel? The *weather* is so nice!

Darling, I love you. Ginny

Elmer – July 4, 1943 11:00 a.m.

My Dearest—

Well, here I am, firmly entrenched in an advanced flying school,
and what promises to be the toughest phase of my training.
However, I can almost see my wings. The washout rate here at
Spence is very slight now. If you don't make good in the A.T.-
6, they send you to twin engine school. So I feel that the most
uncertain part of my training is over.

I found out yesterday, that after we get 35 hours in the A.T.-
6 we are sent up to Tifton [Georgia] and get 10 hours in a P-40.
Imagine, in a few weeks, I'll be flying P-40's. I can't believe it.

Darling, you have me in a quandary. I could very easily get
myself sent to instructors school. All I would have to do would be to
make a poor showing in gunnery. Now personally, I would detest
being an instructor, it would bore me to tears, and yet, on the
other hand, if I was made an instructor, I would at least have a few
months of married life with you. Has me going around in circles. I
think that I shall go ahead and do my best in whatever they
assign me to, and let fate decide what happens to me. I doubt if I
could ever bring myself around to purposely do poorly in
gunnery or anything else. Furthermore I don't think you'd want
me to.

You can't imagine what your visit did for me. I have a nice
fresh set of memories to keep me happy for some time.

I wish you were here this afternoon. We're having an open house for the citizens of the local countryside. Big parades, air shows, etc. The main purpose of it is to entice 17 year-olds into the Cadet Corps. Propaganda and stuff. Flag waving, bands playing, etc.

I'm gonna like this place. They feed us amazingly well. They even gave us a pack of cigarettes at dinner. The only fault I have to find here: We have to get up at four-thirty every morning, and you know how I like my sleep.

Strange to say, I am wearing bars already. I've been made a guide sergeant and we wear shoulder insignia. Second lieutenant bars, painted white with two red stripes. Veddy pretty.

Well darling, I have to get duded up for this sharp affair this afternoon.

All my love, El

Elmer – July 6, 1943 8:10 p.m.

My Dearest—

I know—it's been a long time since I've written. Honey, for the next two months, you are going to have to be content with very few letters. Here is my daily schedule. [He details a range of activities—flying, lectures, calisthenics—from reveille to lights-out.]

In a week or two we will have to make room for night flying! Now do you see why you won't be hearing from me very often.

Everything here is done in terms of combat tactics. Gunnery approaches, combat landings, etc. We even get 16 hours of skeet shooting to improve our shooting eye. I can't wait to go down to Elgin Field [Florida] for aerial gunnery practice.

I really feel close to graduation now. Today we filled out formal applications for commissions. Tomorrow they take our measurements and orders for uniforms; two hundred and fifty dollars worth [About $3,700 today]. Only seven more weeks! Long and arduous weeks, yes, but only seven of them.

I'll leave you with a bit of good news. The odds are that I'll get a 2nd lieutenant commission when I graduate.

All my love, El

Virginia – July 9-10, 1943 midnight

Darling,

I'm home tonight for the first time since Thursday morning. Left then to see Merz (NY Times) and I stayed in. Merz was swell, advised me to write him a letter, which he'd give to the m.e. [managing editor] with recommendation, and also said I should take another job while waiting as it's better to be doing something while applying—psychological effect on city editors! He told me to write to all NY papers—keep after them while working— and sooner or later (no telling when, of course) I ought to get something.

His advice wasn't anything outstanding, except for the fact that he does know me now; however slightly, and that's something. [Charles Merz, who was the editorial page editor of the *New York Times* from 1938 to 1961, was from Virginia's father's hometown, Sandusky, Ohio. Perhaps this was why he was so generous to her with his time.]

Just got a bulletin on the radio—Allies have landed on Sicily! Boy—that's news! And good! Golly, how I'd love to have a hand in the reporting of that stuff! And how happy Pop would have been to know about these latest successes. Wish he could have seen the end—but maybe he can see it now, where he is.

As I was saying, I saw Mr. Merz, then tried to contact Haskell of the Trib, but that's easier said than done. Out—so I left a note.

After, a trek down to Barclay Street to the World Telegram office, where I learned a letter to the city editor would be the thing.

Gee I love New York City! It hit me Thursday when I was travelling from one end to the other, almost. Busy, all the time, everywhere, millions of people, all different. And downtown NY is very romantic to me—the biggest businesses and the smallest, right on top of one another, both being equally important in the narrow streets. And Fifth Avenue with all its glory or glamor, if you prefer. I'm crazy about it. Darling, you know what I thought would be great to do? Fly a Mustang right down Fifth Avenue, just off the ground—say about second story level or so—just roar down and scare hell out of the bustling populace!! Wouldn't that be wonderful? When can we do it? Huh? When??

Sweetheart, that's a beast of a schedule you've got! But it is the *last* grind, tough as it is, and it *is* worth it to know when you've finished you've done it the best way. You know of course my thoughts are with you always, and my confidence in you, and my prayers for you.

I love you, El. Ginny

Virginia – July 13, 1943 1:30 a.m.

Dearest,

I was beaming Saturday night, but not with glee or similar emotion. It was only skin deep, being the result of an afternoon at Jones Beach, my first this season. The marine dining room (above the pool, if you'll remember) is now a USO [United Service Organizations social facility], and uniforms are very much in evidence all over the place.

I'm still among the unemployed—that despite the fact that I picked beans a good part of this afternoon—picked beans and violently cursed the Japanese beetles. [She goes on at length about her hatred for these destructive garden pests.]

Where was I? Ah yes—still no job, but I intend to call the Review tomorrow. [This was the *Nassau Daily Review-Star* "Long Island's Greatest Newspaper," a merger of earlier papers that ran from 1937 until its demise in 1954.]

Disjointed letter, darling, but it brings just as much love as always.

Ginny

Virginia – July 13, 1943 11:20 p.m.

Sweetheart,

I don't think I'll write to you tonight. I'm too tired, having just come from 3 William St. where Mrs. Odell fed me beer, cake, and a Tom Collins. [John was in Georgia visiting Elmer.] Delishus, all of it, but now I'm tired and rather warm.

If I don't get a job soon I'll be crawling up the wallpaper with ease. Greene of the Review today said there was nothing at present, as he'd already filled the open job a few weeks ago. (I told you he asked me about it a while ago.) So, maybe I can't get anything locally. The subject isn't heartening. Gee, darling, I wish life was normal and we could be married.

I love you—Ginny

Elmer – July 14, 1943 9:10 p.m.

My Dearest—

You are very wonderful, writing to me so often despite the fact that I only write once or twice a week.

We had a bad accident here yesterday. You remember Bob Loosen, the tall southern boy with gray hair? He was the only one to get out alive. His instructor and a cadet in another ship were killed in a mid air collision while flying formation. Bob 'chuted to safety and was uninjured.

Monday night and last night about thirty of us were in "The Spence Field Aquacade" a dazzling extravaganza put on by the personnel of Spence Field. We cadets gave a demonstration of tactical wartime swimming. Staying afloat with full packs, rescue work, swimming through burning oil, etc. Lots of fun, but I lost a lot of sleep.

Honey, I hate to leave so soon, but my navigation is calling. Damnit, it's always something.

All my love, El

Virginia – July 16, 1943 1:40 p.m.

Darling,

I heard all about your father's trip south last night. Too bad he couldn't have seen you more. And what a town for open posts that must be! Cokes get very tiring after the first! And I suppose cadets can't buy beer on the post. A dirty setup, methinks.

What I wanna know is—how long did it take you to solo? And how's the AT-6? Suppose you don't know yet, but are you going to get leave after graduation?—That's what I thought.

I'm having lousy luck. So far nobody has realized how good I am (?) with a typewriter and no job so far. All day yesterday I tromped around, seeing people. Came to the conclusion that it's better to write. But I still have no job to tell 'em I'm biding my time at. What a vicious circle! A couple more days like yesterday and my morale, which isn't so good right now, will drive me to welding or riveting.

I love you. Ginny

Elmer – July 18, 1943 4:15 p.m.

My Dearest—

Just got home from open post, and after last night, I find Moultrie not quite so dull as would appear at first glance. Seems the local B.P.O.E. [Benevolent and Protective Order of Elks] feels sorry for us drinking cadets who are thwarted at every turn. For the price of one dollar ($1.00) we are given a card which entitles the bearer to enjoy the full privileges of the Order of Elks—viz.—drinking. They have a nice little bar and after a movie last night, my room-mate and I went to the club house and annihilated a number of scotch and sodas. Today I feel perfect.

Everything is peaches and cream. If you were with me, things could never be better. Seems that after about two weeks they make up a squadron of men who do not seem to be fighter material. They are given what is called a standard course, sans gunnery and P-40 time. Upon graduation they go to transport, ferry command, liaison, etc. Today that list was posted and I find myself not on it, so it seems, if I make out O.K. in gunnery, I'll be sent to pursuit O.T.U. They took about 25% of every squadron to make up this new outfit. Eggleston, Mays, and many other of my friends are on it. I really feel sorry for those boys.

We've been flying formation all this week and had one high altitude oxygen mission that was lots of fun. I got the A.T.-6 up to 22,610 feet. The temperature on the ground was about 90°F and when I got upstairs it was 14°F. Man, was it cold! Cold and lonely way up over four miles above the earth. [In the South Pacific war theater, legend had it they cooled their beer by taking it for a high-altitude ride.]

Whenever this war or the weather or something gets me down, I remind myself that there is nothing worthwhile on this earth that you can get without a fight and I tell myself that what I am going through, is the fight I have to put up to deserve you. That makes all this seem worthwhile and pulls me out of the dumps.

Honey, if you think it necessary to get me something for graduation, you will have to think of something besides a ring. Seems Spence has its own graduation ring, and I am going to procure one of the same. [A red stone in a gold setting, it's inscribed "United States Army Air Forces." He wore it the rest of his life.] My mother is extremely optimistic. She is having my room re-decorated, so as to have it nice and pretty when I come home. Speaking of home, in answer to your last letter, I can't even venture a guess as to whether I will get a leave upon graduation. Only time will tell.

You ask about the A.T.-6. Never in the annals of aviation has a better training ship been built. She is beautiful. Handles like a charm only it lands hot and ground loops very easily. I soloed it in four hours, thirty-five minutes, which is about average time.

Darling, I gotta go now. We're having a parade in the hot Georgia sun.

All my love, El

Virginia – July 21, 1943 1:45 p.m.

Dearest,

Most importantly, for today, honey, is that I have a job. Friend of
Mary Margaret's called me last night to tell me the Treasury dept.
(N.Y. office) was looking for newspaper people (reporters, etc.)
for some publicity work. So I came in this a.m. and, after I fill
out about 99 forms for federal employment, I'll have a job. It's
temporary—swell for me because I want to do something while
waiting for a NY paper job—and will last only until the end of the
3rd war loan campaign, which starts in September. They want to
sell several more billions in war bonds and it'll require a lot of
plugging. It ought to be interesting, I'll feel that I'm really helping
the war effort (tangibly, I mean), and it'll be experience in work I
hope to get later on a paper.

So today my morale was boosted, but perceptibly. It could
stood it too!

I love you. Ginny

Virginia – July 22, 1943 11:20 p.m.

Darling—

Guess I didn't tell you much about my job the other day. Well,
I don't know very much about it, but it will start as soon as my
papers (five—count 'em, 5 identical & very lengthy forms to fill
out!) are okayed. I'll be working as a reporter, very likely, unless
he (the city editor—my boss) wants me at something else—rewrite,
maybe. I'll be on the press bureau staff of the 3rd war loan drive
in NYC—the five boroughs. From the looks of the campaign ideas,
it ought to be fun covering the stuff, even in a publicity capacity.
I was in today (RKO bldg.—Radio City) to read stuff on the
campaign's organization, aims, etc.

This weekend, now that I (practically speaking) have a job, I'm going to send letters to NY newspapers to start pestering them. *Maybe* by the time this job is over I'll have convinced *some* paper I'm worth hiring.

Honey, I'm as glad as you are about A/C Odell *not* being in the non-fighter squadron—not so much because I want to see you a fighter pilot as because it means you're succeeding in what you've worked so hard at, getting where you wanted to go, more or less.

It's wonderful to see the 47's soar over the house, on a perfectly clear day, in combat formation. Four of them were up recently, and in really sharp array—But, speaking of nice formation flying, yesterday I saw *five* Forts thunder over in a string, and no matter what you say about those huge babies, you can't say they're not impressive. Boy, what a roar! As far as beauty in those four-motored jobs goes, I think the Liberator is far sleeker, neater in appearance, than the Fortress. I always get a kick out of seeing that pencil-thin fuselage, so silvery and fragile-looking, against the sky. Impressed by their great size & power, though, I'm always reassured by Forts and Liberators.

I love you, dearest. Ginny

July 24, 1943 – British incendiary bombing of Hamburg creates a firestorm that kills more than 42,000 German civilians

---

Elmer – July 25, 1943 7:25 p.m.

Dear Mom and Dad—

When I graduate, I want to give Ginny an engagement ring. So I would appreciate it if you would see Bill Glean and see what he can do for me. I don't want to pay any less than $200 for it. And it must be in a plain gold setting. Nothing fancy. Primarily it must be flawless. The size doesn't matter but it must be perfect. Please do not delay on this because I want it by graduation.

Your loving son, El

Elmer – July 25, 1943 3:25 p.m.

My Dearest—

Had a very enjoyable weekend. A buddy of mine [George 'Pode' Parker] and I drove (he has a '41 Ford convertible) over to Valdosta (about fifty miles away) to see some of our friends who were sent to Moody Field twin engine advanced. Valdosta is a much better town than Moultrie. It has bars in it! Real bars where you get drinks. Real drinks with alcohol in them. Real alcohol like scotch and rye and stuff. Oh happy day.

This coming week is one that I will be glad when it is all over. *That is what I call a sentence perfectly constructed. Anyway all our instrument and acrobatics will be crowded into the next five days. And you know how I hate to fly instruments. Not only that but this week we also start night flying. Shake the feather bed mother, I'm cruisin' in low.

We have a wonderful 1st Lt. who teaches us "Pilots Information File" and how to use it. He used to fly a fighter in Australia and New Caledonia until one day, as he came in for a landing, his wheels collapsed and his belly tank hit the ground and exploded. He got out with a few minor burns but his nerves were completely demolished and they sent him back to recuperate. Anyway he is supposed to give us a 50 minute lecture and then a short quiz. Every day, after about ten minutes of the period has elapsed he'll come out with something like "Dammit, it's too hot to

work. Waddy'a say we take the quiz and get the hell out of here."
So we take the quiz which is a farce and go over and shoot pool.
Good man, Lt. Dunne.

So now you too are working for the government and are
getting a taste of G.I. red tape. I've filled out so many forms I can
almost do it with my eyes shut. You should have seen the lulu they
gave us as an application for a commission. Wow! Page after
page in triplicate.

All my love, El

Virginia – July 26, 1943 11:20 p.m.

Hello honey!

[Here she affects an Irish brogue.] Today I was after goin' up to
143rd St. to see one Mrs. Michael Murphy who has five foin sons
in the serrvus. This, you understand, was sort of an introduction to
my job. From Mrs. M., (a swell person with a *big* sense of humor
and a size to match), I learned that another Mrs. Murphy, also of
the Bronx, has 5 or 6 sons with Uncle Sam. So I'm going to look
into that. Between the two families, the Murphy's are doing their
part!

There must be a balloon barrage battalion about—brother
the *b's* in that sentence! Between Floral Park and Stewart Manor
[two nearby villages] for a couple of days recently the balloons
have been up in numbers. Very pretty! Rather destructive little silver
baubles, though! [Barrage balloons were attached to steel cables
and floated up in the air to interfere with low-flying attack aircraft.]

I love you.* Ginny

* That means intensely, tremendously, certainly, completely, and
always—to list only a *few* of the modifying adverbs.

Hazel Odell – July 28, 1943 8:00 p.m.

My Darling Son—

Now about the ring. Congratulations, honey. I called Bill right away and he says there is no one he would rather do anything for and give a good break than you. So guess what, he is going to let me bring down three or four rings for you to pick from isn't that swell. Does Ginny know she is getting a ring? It sure will be swell when I have my family together again. When Ginny gets her ring I will have to start getting her nice things for her hope chest.

Always all my love, Mother

August 2, 1943 – Lieutenant John F. Kennedy's PT-109 is rammed and sunk by a Japanese destroyer in the South Pacific

---

Virginia – August 2, 1943 9:50 p.m.

Darling,

There was no letter on the hall stand from Saturday's mail. Then I went upstairs & saw the note Mom had written about your phone call!! Oh honey, do you realize how awful I feel to have missed hearing your voice. But I doubt if you felt any better. I won't groan anymore.

The news—I hope it's reliable—that you'll get a leave made missing your call *somewhat* easier to take.

So my feelings are rather mixed up. Sorry to have missed your voice, glad you're flying a P-40 (I really am glad—because it means you're getting to be an honest-to-goodness AAF pilot), but sort of mixed up on the leave stuff. Silly, undoubtedly. I'm waiting to hear what other news you have to add to this—like exactly *when* will you be near enough for me to kiss you?

It may be very well that I won't be toiling for Uncle Sam after all. 'S a complicated story, most of which happened this a. & p.m. But the net result is that I may take a job (in 2 weeks) on the Review instead of the formerly mentioned prospect in NY. I'll give you the latest bulletin on this front (labor, you might say) in the next.

Hey, was I seeing things, or could it be possible that an ordinary (from appearances) buck private I saw in the train was carrying a parachute?? So help me, if it wasn't an air umbrella it sure was wrapped up like one! I was (and am) thoroughly confounded and yet couldn't quite go up and say "Poddon, sir, but is this your parachute?" (Just thought of a crumby pun. Sicilian peasant picks up stray 'chute and asks paratrooper—"Pardon me, but did this just drop you?"—Oh well, just tired, I guess.)

Right now, I have time only to say how very much I love you.

Ginny

Gunnery and Beyond

THUS BEGAN THE LAST six weeks of the air cadets' training. Attrition was nearly nil. Here they would find out what aircraft they were destined to fly—in combat, or not. But whatever that outcome, the most coveted prizes would be awarded here— pilot's wings, and a commission as a second lieutenant in the United States Army Air Forces.

Elmer – August 3, 1943 6:50 p.m.

My Dearest—

Aside from the disappointment of not talking to you Sunday, everything is swell. I have almost four hours in the P-40-F (the British Kittyhawk). What a bunch of airplane! It weighs about 4¼ tons, and is powered by a 1300 horsepower Packard Rolls Royce engine. And what a complicated cockpit! You have to turn on 12 switches before you can start the engine. Reading from left to right: 1. fuel pressure booster switch, 2. prop circuit breaker, 3. prop control switch, 4. ignition, 5,6,7, three miscellaneous

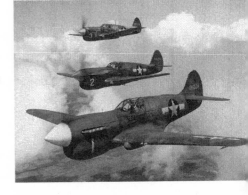

circuit breakers, 8. generator switch, 9. battery switch, 10. coolant shutter circuit breaker, 11. transmitter switch and 12. receiver switch. After all this you can prepare to start.

Today I traveled faster than ever before in my life, and faster than many unfortunate individuals will ever travel. I stuck the nose of my P-40 down at 11,000 feet and at 5,000 feet I was doing 400 (four hundred) miles per hour! What a thrill! Wow! And did I black out when I pulled up! Couldn't see for about 15 seconds. This baby cruises at 220 M.P.H. so it doesn't take much to get it up to 400. The only trouble, when it's going, it wants to roll over on its back. Takes all my strength to keep it level. It really is a wonderful airplane though. Handles like a dream.

All we do here is fly, drink Cokes and smoke. No calisthenics, no school, no drill. Gives us a chance to catch up on our sack time. Honey, I love you very much. If I make out good in gunnery, and there is every indication that I will, I will be sent to combat O.T.U. If this is the case, I am almost sure to get a furlough first. So there is a very good chance of my seeing you by the end of the month.

We leave here Thursday and next Sunday we go to Elgin [an air base in the Florida panhandle] for gunnery. This month will really speed by. Before we know it, the war will be over and we can settle down to a normal existence. Gee, that sounds swell.

All my love, El

Virginia – August 4, 1943 3:15 p.m.

Dearest,

Last night was beautiful. There were so many stars in the sky that it was hard to pick out the plane lights. Wonderful camouflage!

The three I saw were really on the ball as they went over here. Thunderbolts, of course.

This past week's Collier's has a North American ad, in full color, showing AT-6's peeling off. Now I know what you're flying. *Think* I've seen one or two around here.

I might say, though, that I've decided to work for the Review. From what I know now, I'm going on as a sports reporter for a while! Something new for me. Ought to be interesting.

I love you, Ginny

Elmer – August 8, 1943 9:30 p.m.

My Dearest—

How this boy does get around. I'm back in Florida after a two-day sojourn in Spence after Tifton [another air base in Georgia]. We're stationed about five miles from the Gulf of Mexico and forty odd miles from Pensacola, Fla. I've never seen such desolate country in my life. Mile after mile of nothing but water, sand and scrub pine.

This gunning is a lot of fun, though. Barreling down 200 m.p.h. on a ground target and letting go with a burst from a .30 cal. cowl machine gun. We only fly in the morning and the rest of the day is ours. Most of it is spent in sack time, since we have to get up at 4:30 every morning.

I had the strangest feeling Friday night before I started out on a night flying mission. I actually thought I was going to die that night. I don't know how to explain it. Seemed more or less of a premonition of impending disaster. Very foolish indeed, for, as any fool can see, I didn't conk off. Sitting in my room before we left for the flight line, I found myself talking to your picture, trying to tell you how much I loved you before I left. Believe me I was reluctant to get into that ship and mighty relieved when the mission was over. I don't know, maybe I'm going balmy.

Darling, I must say goodbye, it's ten o'clock.

All my love, El

Virginia – August 10, 1943 12:45 a.m.

Dearest,

Out of a long-standing silence, Wally informed me by letter this a.m. that he's classified as pilot and starting at Maxwell.

It's getting so that I'm zoomier than all hell!! (Tsk—such langwich!) But it's true. All I can think about to write you about is what happens in the sky around here! However, I get such a big thrill out of it all—that I'm gonna tell ya, even if it's like hearing me recite nursery rhymes.

The boys at Mitchel are getting gay. Thassall there is to it! This morning they were having a *wonderful* time. It was about 10 and the sky was very blue with only a thin veil of clouds, very high, and they were madly wheeling around, like kids playing tag, making their Thunderbolts roar and whistle and growl all over the place—mainly over Schill Chateau! [Her home was less than five miles from the field.] It was a clubby affair, only six—really only a few compared to the impressive formations of 11 and 14 seen about lately—but awfully gay. Soon they got tired and raced back to the field, seemingly to get their breath.

That isn't the worst, though. Saturday, Marie, Mr. Q. [Marie's father] & I got to Jones beach just in time to see a 47 roar down the beach, just about at the water-line and no more than 100 feet off the ground, pull up suddenly and then knock off a very neat snap roll after leveling off at a nice respectable altitude. He promptly turned around and repeated the performance—and he *was performing*, to a well-crowded Saturday beach—going the opposite direction. By this time every eye on the sand was squinting at him and the sun. Obviously enjoying the audience, this H.P. [hot pilot] gave about 4 encores and then, sighting three other 47's coming in the distance, pulled off and joined them. It was the funniest thing I've seen yet in the aviation line. Playing to the grandstand!

I flew with you last night, honey. Wasn't a very long ride, because the dream, as they all are, wasn't complete, but I *know* it was a twin-engined job. That I know. Wish it were real and you were here with me. The crickets are making a wonderfully peaceful chirping outside, all around, not being drowned out by planes or cars at this time, and I wish so much it *were* peaceful and we didn't have to think in terms of minutes together. When the sky's clear and the sun warm in the yard, making the grass warm on shoeless feet and bare legs and arms, a breeze to ruffle things all over, I think of how very pleasant it would be to enjoy just those things with you on a Sunday, in our own back yard, without being troubled with "tomorrow or the next day or soon I won't be with him" thoughts.

So you'd just better come home—but I'm not even sure if I want that. Can't be an instructor and get leave too, I keep reminding myself. But I *do* want to have you knock on our front door again. Alas, I have tickets to see "Oklahoma," a reportedly excellent musical, on Sept. 2. Even if we don't see much from the seats they probably are, I want to go with *you*! [It's likely they did see it together.]

Guess I won't be a sports reporter right away. Learned today I start Monday on rewrite. That'll be in the main office (RVC) and from 8:30 to 3 (daylight hours). Transportation problem [she didn't have a car] still to be solved.

This is absolutely the last time* I'm going to tell you!

I love you, Ginny

*in this letter

Elmer – August 14, 1943 2:15 p.m.

My Dearest—

I expect to be called out on a gunnery mission any moment. Thursday we finished up ground gunnery and I must be pretty lucky, cause I qualified as expert. However, here in aerial gunnery I think it will be a little different story. Somehow or another I can't seem to catch on. I've only had three missions but the results have been mighty sad. However maybe I'll do a little better. I still have about 1700 rounds and only the last four hundred count for record.

See? Like I said, I was called away. Just got back from firing 200 rounds of .30 caliber ammunition into an elusive tow target. Did I say into? I mean in the approximate vicinity of. Boy for a few seconds while you are coming in on the target you really have your hands full. Aiming the sight, flying the ship, charging the gun, picking up the proper lead, taking the safety catch off, etc, etc,— Busy as the proverbial paper hanger.

All I think about or dream about is walking up the flagstone walk and knocking on Schill's front door, or walking across the lots to my own house. It's been an awfully long time since I've been in Roosevelt or Hempstead, and I have an intense hankering to get back there again.

All my love, El

Elmer – August 15, 1943 9:00 p.m.

My Sweet—

I didn't intend to write tonight but I had to. A while back they played Artie Shaw's "Frenesi" and as I looked out the barracks window, a full moon was coming up over the pine trees. That did it. I just had to talk to you.

There's nothing new to talk about around here. Went swimming in the Gulf this afternoon and my gunnery is slowly improving. But let's not talk business.

Rather let's talk about our home when the war's over. I've been daydreaming up a picture of what it might be like. A few years hence, people will drive along a road on Long Island, in the approximate vicinity of Roslyn and exclaim, "Look! Isn't that a beautiful home. I wonder who lives there" "Didn't you know? That's where the E.W. Odell's live. It's a beautiful place, isn't it."

The first thing that strikes your eye is the sloping lawn, flagstone walk and petunia beds. The house itself is of greystone and white clapboard with green shutters at the upstairs windows. A full length chimney hints of a cheery fireplace in the living room on the right side of the house. On the left side a blue gravel driveway leads up to the two-car garage. The back yard has a wooded section with an outdoor fireplace. More lawn for badminton, croquet or sun bathing. Further back is a well-kept garden. Would you like to live here with me?

All my love, El

Virginia – August 15, 1943 21:20

Dearest,

Hazel Scott just finished batting out an amazingly fast boogie of her own. She's great on the Basin St. program. Why don't you be home sometimes, huh? There's this wonderful music, an' outside the moon's shining like all blue blazes! Some stars, too, but only the most persistent of them can outshine the moon tonight and be seen.—But there you are, in Florida, or Georgia, or wherever you *are!*

Yes, honey, I miss you—or perhaps that's repetitious. But today was gruesomely efficient about making me aware of you— not being here! The weather was perfect. Sorta fallish in texture of the breeze, but still a hot summer day at heart. Then at church I see an a/c—but not you. No, not at all like you, and I wonder like all get-out how come he's home. So I go to the beach with Marie & her father and there I see *five* (you heard me) *more* a/c's!! It's killing me slowly. Where do they come from, I wanna know!!?!

Hey listen to me!! *I love you.*

Ginny

August 17, 1943 – General Patton enters Messina, completing the conquest of Sicily

Virginia – August 18, 1943 3:20 p.m.

Darling,

It's very hot here in the sun, waiting for a bus [to take her home from work]. I missed one a while ago and have to wait half an hour.

The job's o-k. In fact it's too good, as is, to be true. Hours are 8:30 to 3 or 3:30 with an hour for lunch. And on Saturdays, it's only until 12. The work certainly isn't hard and so far I'm not very busy, except in the morning. Things will pick up, though, as the week goes by and when another girl in the office leaves to go back to school. For instance, I did a story on the drafting of fathers and an obituary, among other things this a.m. And if I hadn't gotten the bus situation snarled up, I would have been home now.

Did I tell you that Longines has taken to announcing the "army-navy" time along with the ordinary (civilian) time during their station breaks on the radio. "Seven p.m., Longines Wittenauer watch time, 1900 army-navy time." Wartime changes!

Aug. 19, now and I'm at work. Enclosed is an obit of someone you may know. I always get happy jobs like this. Today I wrote of the posthumous decoration of a fellow who graduated the year before me at Syracuse. He was killed in action in June and I didn't hear of it—I was with you when it ran in the paper. He was a Point Lookout fellow [nearby village].

Things really hummed today. My machine started smoking about 10:30! But I like it that way.

Please don't refer to instructorship as a *racket*. Undoubtedly most of the men picked for this work are just as anxious as you to get to combat, but *somebody* has to teach new flyers, and they're doing an equally important job, (if they do it well a *more* important job) as the pilots on active duty. At least *I* think so. So there!

Gee I wish Halloween would get here! Marie and I have planned a *lovely* piece of wickedness. On Greenwich Street, there's a small private dress shop with a beautiful sign out in front. It reads, in neat blue letters on a white background, "House of Fashion." Marie and I will very carefully change the F to P!! I chuckle every time I pass the place—when I think of the circumstances it might be the cause of!!

Excuse me while I eat lunch.—And by the way, I love you. Keep that in mind, Mister!

Ginny

Elmer – August 18, 1943 915 p.m.

My Dearest—

Back to Spence and damned glad of it. I enjoyed flying gunnery
but the heat down at Eglin took the joy out of everything. Now
about the results. In ground gunnery I qualified as expert as you
know, but in aerial gunnery I don't know. They didn't tell
us which were our record runs. My overall average didn't qualify
me as expert but they might have taken two of my better
scores; so I won't know until I graduate. Quien sabe? [Who
knows?]

Your El has an extremely sore fanny. Yesterday I rode 280
miles in a jeep! Took us ten hours to drive from Eglin to Spence.
We had a lot of fun but it was an awfully rough ride.

Now for the news you've been waiting for! A fellow here in
the squadron knows a G.I. who works over at H.Q. and through
him we found out that an order came through from the Southeast
that everyone should get a 10 day furlough when they graduate,
regardless of where they are being sent. Now there is only one
catch to this. Col. Rodiech, the C.O. of this post has the authority
to rescind this order. Whether he will or not is for speculation, but
at least we have something tangible to hope upon.

Honey I have a good part of my officer's clothes, including
my hot pilot hats. I have three of them. Well, two hot pilot hats and
one dress hat which is really beautiful. It should be, it set me back
$17.50 [about $260]. If you'd told me a year ago that I'd pay that
much for a hat, I'd have told you that you were crazy.

Darling I love you so. When I heard the news that furloughs
were pretty definite, I was really soaring.

All my love, El

Virginia – August 20, 1943 10:20 p.m.

My Darling,

You can write letters like the one you wrote with the moon in the
pine trees any time at all and send them to this address. I know
someone who gets *great* morale and foolishly happy smiles
all over just from reading them. Yes, honey, they're immensely
popular. Maybe it's because I love you so much and they bring you
nearer to me.

Honey, I wish you hadn't planted petunias without asking
me. I don't like petunias. I prefer portulacas and, unless you have
great objections, they'll be the in the yard-wide beds that line the
flagstone walls.

I'm having trouble with the hall, dearest. Stairs are hard to
deal with neatly. They take up so much room, and not very prettily
either! Why don't we have elevators? Then the hall could be semi-
lined with mirrors to give it depth.

The living room is well taken care of, I think, but I don't think
you've seen the sun porch, off the living room and at the back
of the house. It has lots of windows, French windows, I hope—
although I'm afraid our style and periods are getting mixed. The
main idea here, though, is a very open-looking room, cool in
summer and with means of keeping out the sun, and warm, from
gathering the sun, in winter. Could glass bricks be permissible with
greystone & clapboards?

Can't decide either where to put the library, or what-have-
you. Think it should go upstairs? That situation would have
conveniences, seclusion from the more active part of the house.

I haven't been all through it myself yet, but there are bay
windows somewhere and a record library and games downstairs.
No bar, thank you. Very commercial addition to a home, I think,

and not to be desired unless your home is intended to be open to the public. But there will be Venetian blinds. They can be anywhere and I'd like 'em!

It's too dark to look at the back yard now, darling, so why don't we go back inside. It's been a long time since I kissed you and told you I love you.

Ginny

Virginia – August 22, 1943 2225

Darling,

Just tore myself away from my Sunday crossword puzzles (yes—I do them—you might as well know the worst) and I'm feeling very exuberant. [*The New York Times* had begun featuring daily crossword puzzles in February of the previous year, as a wartime diversion for its readers, and Virginia was hooked for life.]

Worked my fingers to a blistered mess of flesh (gad that sounds gruesome—perhaps I exaggerate slightly!) yesterday during a session with the lawnmower and shears. But, I might add, Schill Chateau's grounds are now tonsorially perfect!

Subtle, huh? → I LOVE YOU.

Ginny

August 25, 1943 – After fierce fighting, US forces capture New Georgia in the Solomon Islands

Virginia – August 25, 1943 4:45 p.m.

My Darling,

In my bathing suit, I'm writing the last letter to A/C Odell, and I'm thinking of your mother, almost there, and how happy she must be. And I'm thinking of your wings—how we talked about them and how long you've worked. I'd like so much to be with you tomorrow when you get them—but that's like saying I love you today—unnecessary—I do always.

Involved as that last thought might be, you'll understand it to mean I love you and I'm terrifically proud of you—what you've accomplished now, what you've always been as a person, what you always will be.

The attire I mentioned before, bathing suit, was put on immediately after work to combat the heat and also because I plan to quench, if possible, the thirst of our seared lawn. That entails much water and always I get half of it.

Lots of things to tell you—but all I can think of is "this is Wednesday, and maybe Sunday or Monday El will be home." And then my imagination runs on and I get lost in a pack of wonderful suppositions. Can't do a *thing* about it!! And I keep thinking that maybe tomorrow I'll know whether you're coming home or not. Sech anxiety!

Got an offer of another job yesterday, this one with United Press in the Albany bureau. In ordinary times I'd probably jump at the chance but now I'm quite satisfied where I am. Besides, I want to be home. [This may have been a watershed decision in her life.]

I hereby announce that I've almost completed the regular cross-word puzzle of the Sunday Times, no small achievement for me. Congratulations may be sent to my secretary.

Dearest, always, I love you. Ginny

Elmer was commissioned a second lieutenant in the Army Air Forces and earned his pilot's wings on Saturday, August 28, 1943. His mother was there for the ceremonies. He then got a ten-day leave. While home, he presented Virginia with a rather impressive ring, and made their engagement official. [The cover photo was taken about this time.] He then reported to the 439th Bombardment Group, 3rd Air Force, Dale Mabry Field, Tallahassee, Florida.

September 8, 1943 – The Italian army surrenders; two days later, German troops occupy Rome

Virginia – September 10, 1943 12:50 p.m.

Darling,

How I can do anything with thoughts of you always present. And you seem near to me, so near, all the time. Even coming back to work yesterday, when I knew our trains were going in opposite directions, I didn't feel that you'd gone from me. And they can send you to New Guinea, Oshkosh, or Siberia and in my heart you'll be just as near as you were last week, at home.

Write to me a lot, about everything you do and everyone you know, honey. Then I won't feel that I'm missing part of your life— and it's a life that I so want to be actually part of. Every time a plane roars over I wish I were with you, knowing the planes you're flying (driving!). And every time a plane roars over I feel very frustrated, *very* tied down to earth, and I practically drool.

Last night was a perfect example of that. The sun was setting and making lovely fat clouds a goldish pink color against the bright blue sky. Then the squatty Thunderbolts started tearing around, cutting through the beautiful sky in silhouette in tight 2, 3, and 4 line formations, Gee, I wanna do that!! When are you gonna teach me, honey?

I love you, darling. Ginny

Virginia – September 12, 1943 8:45 p.m.

Dearest,

I think I've hit upon it at last. The continuous, glowing, intense way my love for you fills me had me stumped for a fairly comprehensive method of expressing it. But I'm sure now that the only medium it can be put into, measuring medium, I mean, is light years. Now I've got to find which body is farthest from the earth. Maybe this sounds like literarily flippant exaggeration, but dearest I do love you so much. Everything beautiful I see or experience I want you to have with me—the perfect blue of today's sky and the wonderful warmth of the sun amid cool breeze, the way the setting sun made tree tops gold—and other times I want you, too, because then I'll have something humanly wonderful even when there's not much good about the world.

Oh darling, if only I could be consistent about time. How I want it to drag when we're together, and yet when you leave, I hope the days just stop by to say a brief hello. Whenever I think about you—and that means the whole subject is on my mind *all* the time—I wonder how long I can stand being away from you.

So here I am, getting myself into an uproar, not telling you that Brod said, quote Some rock! end quote, upon seeing my ring—that I keep looking for people to tell the wonderful news to, because it seems to me everyone should know—I feel sorry for anybody who doesn't realize how happy I am!! Guess I'll have to write all the letters I owe and tell 'em all. But I can't *see* how they take it that way, nor can I *show* them! Maybe I sounded, in the first part of this, unhappy. I'm not really. I sing and look at my ring and look at your wings and laugh and whistle and think of you all the time and talk to your pictures and love you immensely. Knowing we are meant for each other keeps me on a cloud, and I guess it's also the fact that I'm so looking forward to our marriage.

Holy cow! All this time and not a word about how I took my eyesight in my hands this afternoon! I went out in the *bright sun*, witnessing Brod's team beat the Camp Hills bunch (softball), and I wore my ring! The glare was awful. I used it to blind the opponents' pitcher!

Tomorrow I shall send you an unglamorous typewritten letter, telling you news instead of *only* how I love you.

Ginny

Elmer –September 13, 1943 11:00 a.m.
[This is his first Army letter with a stamp.
Now that he's an officer, postage is no longer free.]

My Dearest—

Now I'll give you the low-down on this place. Dale Mabry is merely a replacement center for the 3rd Air Force. We will be here for about a week and then be shipped out to various fields for combat training. My flight is being sent to Bartow [Army Air Base], Fla. for O.T.U and we will be flying P-51's. We are extremely lucky because the majority of flights will be sent to P-47's or P-39's. We will be at Bartow for six to eight weeks and then we come back for shipment overseas. So darling, it looks like I'll be out of the country by the middle of November and I won't be seeing you at Christmas as I planned.

Dearest, that ten days home did me a world of good. Somehow I feel differently toward you. I can't explain it. Before I came home I merely loved you but seeing you wrought a change. Now I feel that you are part of me and when I left Thursday, part of me stayed with you. It's hard to try to explain but I feel awfully close to you. The words "I love you" seem terribly inadequate to describe my feelings for you.

All my love, El

Elmer – September 16, 1943 9:45 a.m.

My Dearest—

I only have about fifteen minutes. There's an oxygen lecture in about twenty; but I just had to talk to you. Last evening Parker [George, 'Pode'] and I were sitting in the Forest Inn (a swanky officers club in town) when someone walked up to the juke box and played Artie Shaw's "Dancing in the Dark." Darling, I swear, I almost broke into heart-rending sobs. No kidding, dear, what wonderful memories that song brought back!

There's nothing much of interest going on around here since we're not flying. Yesterday we were issued pup tents, blanket rolls, mess kits and the like for overseas duty. We've all made out our wills and tended to all various and sundry business.

Just got your letter of the 14th and honey, I have very definitely been noticing the moon. You should see it come up behind moss covered pine trees. Really is beautiful and a shame you can't be here to see it with me.

All my love, always, El

Virginia – September 16, 1943 1:40 p.m. [telegram]

DEAREST COMING DOWN. WHEN CAN WE BE MARRIED?
LOVE GINNY.

Virginia – September 16, 1943 8:45 p.m.

Darling,

I hope that by now you've gotten my undoubtedly surprising telegram. Here's how it happened—as I guess you may wonder!

Tuesday afternoon I came home and read your letter [of September 13]. My eyes had been falling out (it seemed) all day, but they felt even worse after I'd cried for 15 minutes. Mom was surprised. She didn't know we'd been talking of marriage, and she wanted to think about it. The whole thing—your going overseas so soon—hit me, and I realized how little anything else matters compared to you. So, being thoroughly exhausted, for some reason (maybe the pint—blood—I gave away Monday), I went to bed at 8:30!!

Yesterday was rather vague. I was thinking about it all the time, and I probably had made up my alleged mind, but I wanted to consult Mom further. So last night I did. She of course didn't disapprove, said she wasn't going to tell me what to do, pointed out all the angles, all of which I knew, and told me to do what I wanted to. Also she suggested I go see your folks.

Therefore I went to 3 William Street and asked for your hand! You know what they would say, and they did, making me very happy.

So darling, today I'm almost fit to be tied down. Don't know whether my head is on or not, and even before I know what cooks with your part of the deal! Golly, I'm so excited honey!

First of all, I talked to Mr. Greene. He didn't explode, was very calm and nice about it, said, in regard to my coming [back] "We'll see what we can do." That's good enough. Then I sent El a telegram, and then I got reservations on the Silver Meteor for Sunday, Sept. 26.

WOW!!! I'm gonna be married to you soon!!!

I keep thinking of things—how will I ever be able to keep my mind in my job for another week and two days??? It was bad enough today, but with each day I'll be nearer the time when I'll be with you and——

Excuse me while I explode!!

Sweetheart, if I don't hear from you soon I really will pop a blood vessel! I'm dying to know you know and I want to know when it will be and where and oh a million things!!

Went down to church to talk to a priest about whatever arrangement may have to be made. He wasn't there, so I'm going back tomorrow night.

Why can't you hear me, honey?? I'm practically screaming with joy!!! Oh hurry and let me know about it! Going in tomorrow to get my ticket to Winter Haven.

I love you—or did you guess? Ginny

Elmer – September 18, 1943 2:10 p.m.

My Darling—

Listen honey, you gotta cut out sending telegrams like that last one. My heart is strong from being so full of love for you, but still it can just take so many shocks. I swear I came very close to passing out cold in the signal office when I read it. Seriously darling, it's wonderful, you're wonderful, life is grand; life is sweet; you are sweet. I love you so much.

Everyone within a fifty mile radius of Tallahassee knows I'm getting married.

I think I told you Mike [A/C classmate] and Lou were married. Mike is coming to Bartow too and maybe we can work up some arrangement whereby you and Lou can get together when

Mike and I aren't around. I wish I knew how much time off we're going to get down there and what arrangements I'll have to make for our wedding.

Darling, I swear, I'm walking around in a daze. I still can't believe we'll be married soon. I should like to have been there when you asked my folks for my hand in holy wed-lock. What did they say, anyway? Gosh, I bet that was good.

We're pulling out in about three hours so shortly I'll be able to let you know what cooks.

I don't know what I ever did to have all this good fortune thrust upon me. You love me and soon will marry me; I got my wings and commission and they are going to let me fly P-51's. What more could any man ask for?

Yesterday morning we went up in the high altitude chamber. We were in for three hours. This time they took us all the way up to 38,000 feet and there we stayed. They wanted to find out who would get the bends. At that low pressure, nitrogen bubbles escape from the blood stream and collect at joints, and can really cause extreme pain. Only two fellows had any signs of them and only because they had been drinking heavily the night before. I was very much afraid my sinuses would give me trouble on the descent but nothing at all happened, happily. I tell you I'm living a charmed life.

All my love, El

This letter has extensive water-stains on its left margin—perhaps they're from Virginia's tears of joy.

Winter Haven

THEY'D GOTTEN THEIR COMMISSIONS and wings, but they wouldn't be effective fighter pilots unless they could shoot straight. In Winter Haven the "newbies" continued practicing gunnery to prove they could consistently hit targets on the ground and in the air. They also were taught advanced aerial combat tactics.

Elmer – September 21, 1943 9:00 p.m.

My Dearest—

You had better get down here pretty quick. I am in an extremely bad mental attitude. I hate this place vehemently and completely. I have never seen such a vivid example of Army inefficiency in my career. We pulled into this hole 2:00 A.M. Sunday morning and what a surprise! Nobody expected us! So they gave us each a cot. (No pillows, sheets or blankets, mind you, just a canvas cot) and bid us a cheery goodnight. Ever since then they have been traveling in circles trying to start a schedule of training for us. Asinine lectures, hemming and hawing, stalking around; and with those beautiful airplanes out on the line, just waiting to be flown. [Fighter pilot hubris on early display here?]

Wrote to Jack and Norm last night and let them in on the astounding bit of good news. Doubtless they will be surprised, especially Norm. Nothing surprises Jack.

Honey, I gotta cut this short and get back to reading tech orders on the operation of the North American P-51. Remember I love you more than anything else in the world. I'll see you soon.

All my love, always, El

Virginia – September 29, 1943

Dear Mom and Pop—almost—

It's usually El I'm writing to in bed at night. Now you're going to get some of my lousy handwriting.

Things are wonderful. El hasn't had time to write—every time he's off the post he's here—so I'm taking over his time. And if there's no rhyme nor reason to this you know why.

I got here an hour and a half late Monday afternoon—the train was late leaving N.Y.—and Lou (Mrs. Mike Kenny) met me. I stayed with her that night and we found this room Tuesday. [Elmer was flying out of Bartow Field, but they lived in nearby Winter Haven.]

Anyway, we have (I have, *we* soon) a very nice room across the street from where the Kennys and a couple of other army pilots and wives have rooms. It's *clean* too, the people are recently from New Jersey and not Southern housekeepers! Our own bathroom, too. Very nice, too. But it seems like Saturday will never come.

So anyway—Monday night we had dinner at the hotel and then went to the officers' club, the only wet spot in town! Another dry spot, doggone it! What is the matter with these people?

Yesterday I took the bus to Bartow to get a marriage license. Had to get El's signature, notarized, etc., and I went back to get the actual license today. And we got rings last night, too. Very pretty. El's is thin, not wide, and matches mine. We have all the arrangements made—saw the priest, too, Monday night—but still have to wait for Saturday morning at 11 o'clock.

The town here is quiet but very nice. People are friendly. And the weather, though hot lately, is not like Georgia and will undoubtedly get more cool later.

The ships are wonderful. Saw them from the bus. El has about 3 hours in the A-36, a P-51 with diving flaps, and will be flying all day Friday as well as tomorrow a.m. This morning he went over the house twice and wiggled his wings!

He got a three day pass and Saturday is their regular day off, so—we have Sat. through Tues.! Think we'll go to Tampa or Sarasota, but I'm not sure which. Lots more to say, of course, but it'll keep.

Love to you—Ginny & El.

Elmer – September 30, 1943 10:30 p.m.

Dear Mom and Dad—

Last night we got the rings. We're going to have a double ring ceremony. Ginny's goes very well with her engagement ring. She spends the daytime with the wives of some of my friends and she was telling me last night that hers was nicer than any of theirs. She's a wonderful woman.

I've gotten so I can fly the P-51 like it should be flown now. [The single-seat, single engine Mustang was the most acclaimed fighter of World War Two, and the one most feared by the

Germans.] This morning the flight commander gave me a ship and told me to take it way out over the gulf and test the homing device. (A system whereby your home field picks you up by radio and guides you home). I got way out over the water and tried the device and the damned thing wouldn't work. It's a good thing I remembered which direction the land was. Every day I fly over the place where Ginny is staying and waggle my wings. She gets a great kick out of that.

I got your package day before yesterday. Thank you very much. Especially for the rice, booties, etc. Hmmm! I may be a fast worker but I'm not that fast.

Your loving son, El

Mom notice

Elmer Odell and Virginia Schill were married in St. Joseph's Catholic Church in Winter Haven, Florida on October 2, 1943. Mike and Lou Kenny were their witnesses.

Obviously, while living together, they didn't write to each other. But the letters they wrote to Elmer's parents survive, and this chapter's narrative is excerpted from them.

October 1, 1943 – The Allies capture Naples following a German retreat in the face of a four-day popular uprising

Virginia – October 7, 1943

Dear Folks,

Tomorrow I'm gonna get a typewriter, I hope, and then I'll write a long letter telling you about our wedding and about what El's doing. Today, though, before the J. Walton [John's middle name] Odells think we've forgotten them, I have a message to send—by order of the lieutenant. Here is the request:

Due to the shattered condition of his nerves and the very *dry* nature of this hyar county, El would *very* much like to find a package in the mail soon with *bottles* in it. The contents of these bottles, (although in the eyes of the post office workers nothing more potent than hair tonic or shaving lotion—postal regulations forbid mailing alcoholic beverages) should be scotch and rye, respectively.

So far I've said *El* wants this. Well, I might as well admit that it would please me, too, to say the least.

Further instructions from the pilot read—the scotch should be Haig and Haig Pinch, Bellows, Ballantines, or Johnny Walker Black Label, in that order of desirability. The rye should be Canadian Club or Carstair's.

There are the details, and though he's desperately in need of a drink (the Haig and Haig I brought down is practically dead), he does remind you to pack it carefully so as not to arouse postal inspectors' suspicions.

To get away from these worldly thoughts—to say we're happy as larks is a gross understatement. Larks or any other kind of bird, beast, or man have never been half as happy. If I were writing to anyone else, I might have to explain how wonderful he is. But you know it as well as I do.

I know a letter from me isn't like a letter from him, but he doesn't have time at the post and when he's off, there I am, distracting his attention. But he will write soon. And I will when I get the typewriter going and let you know all.

Lots of love, Ginny & El

Virginia – October 9, 1943

Dear Folks,

Now I have a typewriter and can write lots of things in record time—at least a lot faster than by pen—so I'll tell you a few of the things which you're probably wondering about. Like the wedding:

Of course it was raining Saturday (we've been married a week!) but not enough to bother us—and it cleared off later in the afternoon. Of course I wore something old, new, borrowed, and blue, and you saw my clothes. El wore his greens. We weren't VERY nervous.

Until just before I left the house I was perfectly calm. And El said that up until 10 o'clock he felt fine. Then he got the same kind of feeling he did when his P-40 engine cut out on him that time just after take-off. We didn't get over it either until some time later. Repeating after the priest, El got tangled and said, "I William Elmer Odell." I wasn't complete master of my tongue either. Quote from me "With this *wing* I thee wed." Ah yes, and though we concentrated on the ceremony at the time, neither of us can remember anything definite at all—except that we both had trouble getting the rings on. Wish you could have been there. We had great fun afterwards—had lunch or dinner or something at one of the hotels, the gang of pilots and wives, and then we went to the home of Mrs. Yonnelly, who owns the house across the street where other wives stay. There we had a drink and then we left for Tampa.

As I may have told you before, Tampa is a very nice town, except we couldn't find a liquor store with any scotch or rye in it. You can get it in bars, restaurants, etc., but it seems to be extinct on liquor store shelves. And we certainly looked! We went dancing at the Tampa Terrace, very nice hotel where the band is good, toured the town. Monday we went shopping and bought ourselves wedding presents. We have a music box (cigarette box) that plays "Roll Out the Barrel" and we've been getting a kick out of that every time we open it. We also bought three statuary pieces, animals from Walt Disney's "Bambi"—Faline the fawn, Thumper the rabbit, and Flower the skunk. They're awfully cute. After missing a bus from Tampa Monday evening (we were eating frog legs in the Tampa Terrace restaurant), we got back here about 9:30 and ran into a party. El had to be at the post at 8 Tuesday morning.

He usually gets in town from the post (six miles away) about 6 o'clock. Then we have dinner and try to find something to do. Usually it's the officers' club at the Haven Hotel. Last night we went to an officers' dance at the civic center. Lot of fun.

Twice this week El and the other husbands have done some "fixing" with the officer of the day and have stayed in over night. I don't know how much longer it will work, but I hope they don't get caught. He has to get up pretty early to get to the flight line by 8. Otherwise, he has to be back at the post by 11:30 p.m.

Until today, El had 14 hours in the planes at the field. He was the first man in his squadron to get formation flying in the 51. Of course he's crazy about the ships, and I can understand why. They're certainly beautiful, if nothing else, but in addition they fly like dreams, from all reports. Wish you could see him soaring over and wiggling his wings back when I wave to him! And one morning he put on a show for me, which had me grinning all over the place out in the middle of a field all by myself. Vertical slow rolls, loops, playing hide-and-go-seek with clouds and everything!

At present, I'm learning Morse code. I know all the letters and numbers. Now I've got to recognize them when somebody else sends them and learn to send it myself faster than my present rate of a letter every minute!

Love to you all, Ginny

Elmer – October 12, 1943 12 Noon

Dear Mom and Dad—

Folks, you can't imagine how extremely happy I am. I swear I never thought it possible to know such happiness. Sometimes it scares me. I feel as though I'm getting more than my share and I'll have to pay for it. I know I picked the right girl and I know we were right in marrying before the end of the war. She's such a wonderful woman.

About church, she goes to hers and I go to mine (when I don't fly Sunday morning) and there is no dissention whatsoever. We are going to have a wonderful married life. We never argue about anything. It's amazing.

Sunday afternoon we went over to Cypress Gardens and went swimming. Lt. and Mrs. E.W. Odell are wintering in Florida. (social item). Saturday evening we went to a swell officers dance in the Winter Haven Hotel. It's great being an officer. The social life is wonderful. Friday night we went to a dance at the local civic club. These Odells sure do get around.

It must be getting sorta chilly up there about now. Still stays as hot as ever down here and the fall crop of oranges are just getting ripe.

Wish Evie luck for me. Tell her to hurry up or that baby will be walking when it's born.

Your loving son, El

October 14, 1943 – US Army Air Corps loses sixty B-17s during a disastrous raid on the ball-bearing factories at Schweinfurt, Germany

Virginia – October 14, 1943

Dear Mom and Pop,

Today I'm in the back yard, under a tangerine tree. Nearby there are grapefruit and orange trees and already I've had the fruit fresh from the trees. What a difference in the taste! They're like different fruits! It's a beautiful day, white clouds floating around in a warm blue sky. What a wonderful place Florida is in the wintertime!

This is wonderful flying weather, nights included, but El hasn't been up in quite a few days. The advanced class has to finish up their flying and get out, so they've been using the 57th's planes, leaving them earthbound and fidgety. But it doesn't annoy me much, except for the fact that El doesn't like it. The longer the advanced class takes, the longer El will be here.

El hasn't seen the letter you sent us which came today, but I know his face will light up and he'll beam the way I did when I read about the Haig and Haig being purchased and the rye being sought after. When he read yesterday's letter he was happier, in the thought that it would soon be coming. Now that it's practically in the mail—well, I guess I'd better go get some club soda!

We do hope the local gendarmes—or the federal men!—don't haul you away to the jug for this kind deed. Neither of you

would look good behind bars and in stripes and it's a cinch the
c.o. wouldn't give El even a one-day pass, even for bailing out
purposes! So you better keep a look-out posted on the corner and
be ready for a quick get-away.

We had dinner at the Haven hotel and stayed there for
another officers' dance. This one featured an army band, and
what a swell band! We, being a stuffy old married couple, almost
knocked ourselves out jumping all night. A couple of people I met
later in the lobby remarked in tones of amazed admiration about
"my dancing partner" and the way he can move his feet! He was
in rare form and we had a wonderful time.

Lots of love, Ginny

Virginia – October 22, 1943

Dear Mom and Pop,

Yippee! Guess what came off a truck for us today! A lovely box
that gurgles! I haven't opened it yet—I'm waiting until El gets
home—but from all appearances the contents are safe. We can't
thank you enough—both for getting it and all the trouble you went
to, finding it and sending it. What can we do for you, huh??

Wednesday we dragged ourselves out of bed at 9:10 to
catch the 9:40 bus to Avon Park. Got to Lodwick Military Academy
about 11:30 and that place is even nicer than the post card shows.
Really a country club! We didn't stay there long, but went out to the
field where El saw his old instructor, who is now a check rider, and
met quite a few other men he knew. Three other pilots we know
from Bartow were there that day too. I practically went all through
the army flying training in one day! I inspected the primary training
ship that they fly, the basic trainer, and the advanced trainer. Both

the BT and the AT (one of each) were on the field too. So now my next step is the 51. I'm going to see that the next time I go out to the post. I'm in no hurry to go there, though, because I'll be going there only when El can't get off the post—when he's officer of the day. And it's not a very enticing post, anyway. Resembles a concentration camp more than anything! All the buildings are painted a sort of olive drab color. But El said all fields such as this one are camouflaged more or less that way.

I don't know what we'll do this weekend, except enjoy a few drinks for a change! There's an officers' dance somewhere, though.

Thanks a million for everything.

Lots of love, Ginny

Virginia – November 3, 1943

Dear Mom and Pop,

El was o.d. Sunday, as I told you he would be. He was "Pistol Packin' Papa" from 1 in the afternoon on. The o.d. has to carry a .45 so that's what he had slung from a holster all day. Vicious looking thing and very heavy, but he didn't shoot anybody. Threatened to enough! Every time anybody said "Pistol packin' papa" or something like that he'd reach for it! He loves that song so!

So we spent Sunday, from 1 on, at the post. I saw the 51, the 47, a navy dive-bomber, and a couple of other ships. That 51 is beautiful, really. Stood on a wing with El and he showed me the workings of the cockpit. What a maze of dials, instruments, switches, buttons, handles, and what-not!! Not an inch of space isn't utilized. And what a small cockpit! The pilot just fits in, and that's all. Compared to the 51, the 47 is a big clumsy thing. But I guess I'm prejudiced. The look of the two planes, however, is a lot different, and the 51 *is* prettier and more graceful. (Better, too.)

El's doing pretty well with his flying. He's been on skip bombing missions and dive bombing missions (one, anyway, yesterday). They were supposed to get in some aerial gunnery the other day but the tow target ship never showed up. His formation flying has been all right, too, from what I know. Yesterday his flight had a bad accident (one of the men in the new group ground-looped badly and completely demolished the plane but got out unscratched) and another of the new group in his flight got lost. So his flight commander had to go to another field and pick up the guy. He'd run out of gas and landed at another field. So they had to get in a mission and there was only one instructor around. You see, the instructors always fly lead ship in formation flying with the student pilots on their wings. So the instructor asked El if he thought he could lead an element. He said he thought he could. The instructor consulted with a couple of other officers, and then told El to lead the element. So he's the first man in the 57th and probably the first in the 56th too, to lead an element! It was a dive-bombing mission, and although his bombing wasn't so hot, the formation flying of the group was really good, he said. Proud of my husband??

I was telling you about Sunday at the post a while back. Well, I saw planes and the skeet range and the field in general, had supper in the officers' mess (very good, too—as are most of the meals, they say)—saw "Corvette K 225" at the post theatre—it was good but not so good as "Action in the North Atlantic"—and THEN, *I got a ride in a jeep!*

What fun it was! Those little buggies sure can travel, and through, around, and over everything! We scooted between trees, ground out of deep sand, turned around on a dime, bounced over bumps and generally went through all the tricks the jeep can do. Another officer drove me and El. Of course I had to duck every time we came near any place where there were other officers to see me as civilians are not allowed to ride in jeeps, or any other army vehicle, I imagine. So I feel pretty unique. I've ridden in a jeep! After the war I think I'll get one & paint it red or light blue and tear around in it. [She didn't.] Sure can tear!

We went to a dance, Halloween dance, at the armory Saturday night and for a dry county that was the drunkenest party I've ever been at! The American Legion was having a state convention in town over the weekend and they were at that dance in droves, drinking as only American Legion men can drink. They were passing out all over the place! So help me, looking at the people on the dance floor, you could almost pick out the sober couples and count them on one hand! We got there, met a few other officers and wives, saw the kind of party it was, and went home for a bottle!! Killed the Canadian Club quite dead, but it wasn't very lively when we brought it so we didn't have to be carried home.

Lots of love, Ginny

Elmer – November 4, 1943 9:55 p.m.

Dear Mom and Dad—

I would like to take the opportunity to thank you profusely for those two bottles of you know what and also for the tennis racket, shorts and shirt.

I am wondering if you got my allotment check for $75.00? Please to keep it for the time being and if we need it, we will let you know.

Ginny and I are living on top of a nice fat pink cloud and it looks as if we will be up there for the rest of our lives. Married life is truly wonderful, isn't it?

My flying is coming along fine, but I suppose my wife keeps you posted on all my doings. Not only is she a good wife, she is also a fine secretary.

I just struck upon a wonderful idea. Seems as though Lt. & Mrs. Odell's liquor supply is nearly exhausted, and, seeing as we got away with it once, I would be very happy if you would try it again. Only this time pay for it out of that seventy five pesos that you have. I know how expensive liquor is now, and it ain't right you should pay for it. You can take out the express charges too. I know it must be hard to get Canadian Club so we will settle for Carstair's but please to make it Haig & Haig *Pinch* bottle Scotch. We thank you from the bottom of our hearts.

All my love, El

Virginia – November 7, 1943

Dear Folks,

Today is El's day off. Ha, ha. He's flying! They want to get them through on time so, day off or no day off, they fly. Guess they won't get another day off until they are finished.

El was one of six trainee pilots chosen to fly in a big mission yesterday. A flock of 51's from Bartow were supposed to be the enemy and were to intercept and "shoot down" some bombers and fighters who were on their way to bomb enemy installations. The mission was very successful. They theoretically shot down all the bombers and some of the fighters (P-40's), too, I imagine. He was flying yesterday afternoon, too, leading an element again.

Was to get in some aerial gunnery but the man before him shot the target off the tow ship and he had to come back without firing a round.

I think El will get in his night flying Tuesday night. I'll go out to the base and watch them take off and land, if I can. Hope he can get the three hours in that one night. There's a good moon, now, and that helps. None of them likes to fly at night.

Lots of love to all, Ginny

November 10, 1943 – Virginia's twenty-second birthday

Virginia – November 12, 1943

Dear Folks,

Wednesday night El was flying and got in the required 3 hours of night flying in one night, thank goodness. It was a good night, too. Everything went all right and we're both glad it's over. I went out to the post and had supper with him in the officers' mess. As I've told you, the food is good. But I couldn't stay there (at the post) long. He had to be at the flight line at 6:15.

He's gotten in two aerial gunnery missions finally and probably will get another today. They have to qualify (get a certain number of hits) three times in succession to be rated as some kind of an aerial gunner. Don't know yet about the second mission but the first was all right.

I don't have to keep telling you how happy I (we) are, do I? It's just as wonderful as six weeks ago—no, more so!

Love to you both, Ginny

Virginia – November 16, 1943

Dear Folks,

This will really be short. I only want to let you know we're moving Sunday to Tallahassee. I hate the thought of packing up and moving again but it's gotta be. I'll be going with some other girls, I guess, as the fellows go in a bunch, army transportation, I think. We expect to get a bus early Sunday morning and get to T. about 12 hours later—yes, I said 12 hours. That's the quickest way, too, including trains. Trains go to Jacksonville and take longer!

As of last night, El had six more hours to get in, but today the weather isn't too good, so I don't know if he'll fly. I imagine so, though. He hasn't called and so he's probably flying.

This will be all for now. You'll hear from us next from Tallahassee, capital of the citrus state!

Love to all, Ginny

Elmer – November 16, 1943 8:00 p.m.

Dear Mom and Dad—

This Tallahassee deal is extremely uncertain. I may be there two days or I may be there two months. All depends on how soon they need replacements in a P-51 unit overseas. In any event I won't be in this country very much longer. There has been much discussion on the subject of where we will be sent. It's pretty certain that we won't go to the South Pacific; of which I am extremely glad. The three most likely places in order of probability are China, North Africa and England. That China deal seems to persist more than the rest. I wouldn't mind going there at all. I am cursed with mixed emotions. After all these months of training I am aching to get into combat, and yet, on the other hand, it's going to be hard as the devil to leave my wife.

Winter must be just about set in up there. I really pity you poor people in the cold. I shouldn't talk, maybe I'll be sent to Alaska or Iceland or sompin'.

Your loving son, El

Virginia – November 23, 1943

Dear Mom & Pop,

We are going to try to call you tonight, but goodness knows whether we'll get you. Probably every pilot at Dale Mabry field, or almost every one, is trying to do the same thing. You see, as El will tell you tonight, they don't expect to be here long—maybe only a couple of days longer. Wish I knew more definitely, but I don't.

Anyway, that's the not-so-happy news El came to town with yesterday afternoon. We (El & I) drove up from Winter Haven Sunday (ran out of gas on the way!) with George Parker and 3 other pilots. If things work out right, Lou, Maida, & I will drive Parker's car home (he's from N.J.) when they leave. Good arrangement, no!

Because we expect to be going by car, I wired home for my winter coat. I'll need it traveling that way. But I'll be so glad to be driving rather than standing in a train.

Love, Ginny

Elmer – November 28, 1943 8:50 p.m.

Dear Mom and Dad—

Well, I got some definite word today. Our shipment has been formed and all we're waiting for is orders from Washington. We're having a swell time here in Tallahassee. Seems we don't do much of anything. We're just waiting around and I get in town to see Ginny most of the day and *all* night. This is a good town, too. Couple of good night spots, good restaurants, three movies and liquor is available! So, having a good room in the best hotel in town, my wife and I have a pretty good setup.

Gee, before I forget. Don't mention to a soul my going overseas soon. *Nobody*!

I know no one would do anything intentionally to harm me but I know of too many cases where the right information at the wrong time has meant trouble. It's funny, none of the boys are worried about combat at all, but they all feel a bit jittery about the trip over [by ship]. They feel o.k. when they're in a position to fight back.

Incidentally Mom, I know it's crazy to tell you not to worry about me, but don't worry about how I feel about going over. True, I will be reluctant to leave my wife, but I still want to go. I've been training extensively for a whole year for one thing and I am on the threshold of doing it. When I go, I assure you it will be in high spirits and all the confidence in the world in myself, my ability, my airplane and my safe return. So if you have any idea at all that I dread the thought of going into combat, or I feel sad about it, get them out of your heads right now.

Your loving son, El.

Virginia – November 30, 1943

Dear Mom & Pop—

Maybe this letter will get to you *after* I do, or maybe it won't. My plans aren't what you call definite. I *hope* to get a plane reservation tomorrow or the next day but if not, I'm coming on the train tomorrow or Thursday, I *think*. Maybe even that won't work out. At any rate, I'll telegraph Mom and tell her. She'll let you know, I imagine.

You see, El got all his equipment yesterday—had a few things to get today—and he expects to be leaving here tonight. But of course he isn't sure. After I know he's gone, I want to leave—but fast—for home.

Have a lot to tell you when I do get there—about the party we had in Winter Haven—the Friday before we left—with the wonderful contents of your box, about the Forest Inn here, where we went last night again, and about a million other things, all concerned with El. I'll talk everybody's ears off, I warn you.

I feel pretty well, except for the peculiar feeling in my stomach and the undependable feeling in my tear ducts! But the final goodbye will be along sometime this afternoon. I'm waiting for a phone call or something. Hope it doesn't take too much waiting. I've finished packing and there's not much to occupy my mind now.

See you soon, then.

Lots of love, Ginny

P.S. Here are some meat coupons you might be able to use.

Elmer was sent to an embarkation location in New York, and Virginia returned home to Hempstead. They were re-united for a short time, in a hotel in New York, before Elmer was shipped overseas, departing from Pier 86 on December 13th aboard the British luxury liner RMS *Aquitania*, which had been converted into a troop transport. Taking advantage of its high speed, the *Aquitania* (like her sister ships, the *Queen Mary* and *Queen Elizabeth*, also converted to troop ships) could evade German U-boats and cross the Atlantic unescorted. Elmer and his squadron arrived in Greenock, Scotland (Port of Glasgow) on or about December 20, 1943.

England

THERE WERE MORE THAN seventy US Army Air Force bases in southeast England, closest to the European Continent. After being moved around quite a bit, Elmer was assigned to the 382nd Fighter Squadron of the 363rd Fighter Group, Ninth Air Force. They were based at Rivenhall, an air base two miles north of the Essex village of Witham, less than twenty miles from the English Channel.

Elmer – December 21, 1943 11:30 p.m. G.C.T.
"Somewhere in England"
[Opened by a censor and received in New York January 4, 1944]

My Darling Wife:

Well, here I am overseas. We're established in a pilots' replacement pool and only the powers that rule know when we will move into a permanent station. For the time being write to the address listed below and please inform the folks of my safe arrival. Today is Evie's birthday so you can wish her a very Happy Birthday for me. Thank You.

We had a very rough but very interesting crossing and I was mighty glad to set foot on solid ground again after pitching and tossing around in the wintry ocean.

I spent the morning censoring the enlisted men's mail.
It is an extremely interesting job and I found that every man is
planning with a woman for a wonderful future, just as we are.
Everyone said to his lady love that he missed her so much, but I
knew none of them miss their wives and sweethearts as much as I
miss you. This may sound foolish but it is an actual ache inside me
and I know if it wasn't for the interesting surroundings, and the fact
that something new is happening daily, I couldn't bear it.

Black-outs around here are no joke. I was walking home
from the post theatre tonight (saw Road to Morocco again) and
ran smack into a major coming the other way. No kidding there
isn't a light in sight.

A very Merry Christmas and a Happy New Year dearest,
although you probably won't get this until after the holidays. If
I can get up to London I promise to get you a present, if not I
promise to make it up to you when I get home. Wish the folks a
happy holiday for me, both your folks and mine.

All my love, El

The first five letters Elmer sent from England bear his signature
over the "passed by examiner" stamp. After that, there's just the
stamp. Letters appear to have been randomly opened, slit on
the left side and closed with a piece of adhesive tape bearing the
words "Opened by U.S. Army Examiner." Only two additional
letters from Elmer were opened, April 11th and July 31st. By
April 18th the stamps had been discontinued.

Many of the letters in this chapter, from both Elmer and
Virginia, were sent by Victory Mail (V-mail), a system whereby
letters written on special forms were transferred to microfilm and
re-printed at their destination. This allowed for very substantial

decreases in the weight and bulk of mail. Elmer's Christmas Day letter is the first V-mail letter in the collection.

Most of Virginia's letters included in this chapter are hand-written on onionskin paper; a maximum of four sheets per letter were permitted.

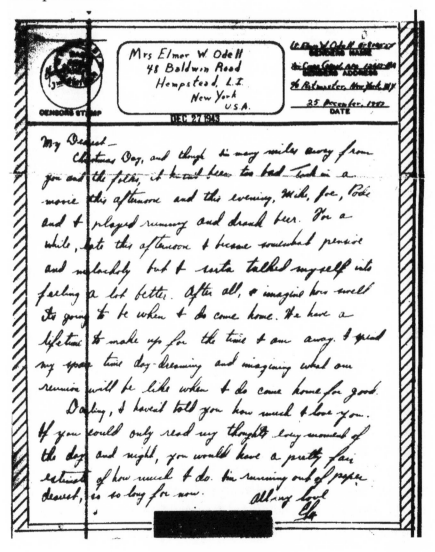

Elmer – December 25, 1943

My Dearest—

Christmas Day, and though I'm many miles away from you and the folks, it hasn't been too bad. Took in a movie this afternoon and this evening Mike, Joe, Pode and I played rummy and drank beer. For a while, late this afternoon I became somewhat pensive and melancholy but I sorta talked myself into feeling a lot better. After all, I imagine how swell it's going to be when I do come home. We have a lifetime to make up for the time I am away. I spend my spare time day-dreaming and imagining what our reunion will be like when I do come home for good.

Darling I haven't told you how much I love you. If you could only read my thoughts.

All my love, El

Elmer – December 30, 1943 [telegram]

LOVE AND BEST WISHES FOR CHRISTMAS AND THE NEW YEAR ALL WELL

ELMER ODELL

Virginia – January 1, 1944 11:20 p.m.
[This envelope has nearly disintegrated, it's been opened so often.]

My darling—

Since we can't be together, I want you to know what happens during my days just as you would were you going to work every morning and coming home each night. When you come back to me, I hope there'll be no gap in our knowledge of one another. I realize you won't be able to write all of what you do every day, but please tell me a lot. I'm so *terribly* anxious to keep up with you, know what you're doing every minute, learn at least a little of what you learn. Remember how I used to ask what you'd done all day? It's the same now, darling, but being unable to ask you makes me even hungrier for such news.

Where to begin? The beginning—or the end, as it was—is perhaps a good place.

When you left me at 2:30 A.M. Dec. 9, at the Hotel Penn, I was entirely surrounded by pink cloud forms, all of which had nothing to do with the rye we'd been drinking. You were there, had been home again, and would be in my arms again in another day or two! That last was what lighted my eyes and gladdened my heart the next day, despite the hangover I had for hours. I should've *known* I couldn't have had a hangover if things were going right! But I got up, gaily, and went to buy your Christmas present (which you'll probably get by Easter!). And I got my baggage, and went home again, arriving in the late afternoon.

Lord knows what I did Thursday night and all day Friday, except imagine you on a 20-mile hike! But by Friday night I was watching the phone, practically, and almost knowing that I'd be called to it soon with you on the other end. But when it got late and I'd had no calls, I attributed it to the 20-miles of walking. Saturday I didn't expect you. You'd mentioned guard duty. But I hung around the corner in the hall, anyway, thinking maybe you could phone. By Sunday I was all but holding my breath. All day long I had to keep busy, manually busy, because I would have crawled up the walls otherwise. So I washed some clothes, ironed some clothes, washed some more clothes, ironed more clothes. That was a gruesome day. Of course, each day would see intercommunications, 3 William Street and 48 Baldwin Road, via phone. Your family and I would make guesses as to why today brought no El and when he might turn up.

Sunday was bad, but Monday was infinitely worse. You see, through Sunday I had managed to maintain hope. After Monday began, though, it was obviously a losing game and I was giving up the hard way. By Monday night I was a "pretty sad bird" in the literal sense and will openly admit to about a quart of tears—if they didn't fill a quart in quantity, they would have in quality, I assure you. Before I went to sleep, though, I had had to admit that the weeping was damn foolish, selfish, and certainly without a good, sturdy cause. Yes, El is gone, I said to me, at least he's gone as far as seeing him goes, but why cry? You knew he'd go, you really were lucky to see him again, very lucky as compared with other wives, and now you're crying for lack of egg in your beer! Tsk! So I shut up and explained to myself that it was mainly the awful disappointment of not seeing you again when, from what you'd said, I fully expected to. (Here I wonder if you knew that was to be the last pass, but I doubt it even as I wonder. If you did know, you would have told me.) I felt that the evening had slipped away without my taking full advantage of it—drinking you in fully, as it were—because I thought there would be another—at least *one* more pass.

I can't remember now when I visited your family during those days, but it was perhaps Tuesday or Wednesday when I had fully recovered my equilibrium. At least, and could definitely not hope for another visit. Your mom told me, when I saw her, of another fellow (infantry, I believe) from Roosevelt who had been home that same night and hadn't been heard from since, of someone she knew who said ships leave *regularly* (seems a foolish thing), and that the Queen Mary and the Queen Elizabeth had left Friday. That is something of the info. she had picked up. I wondered why so many people should know when troop ships left, but then I don't know much about it or even if all this is halfway true. Sure would like to know. We did imagine that you were at Camp Kilmer [an embarkation center in New Jersey], and I suppose that's correct. Funny how you pick up other bits of information that tie in with everything. Heard about a week later that a sister of Betty Donnelly who is an army nurse also had a pass that night or another night around that date and she also had been seen no more.

Perhaps I sound like a young spy, but believe me, honey, I said nothing that was of any value to anybody, even though I did learn these other things. I could see by my experience, though, how bits of loose talk fit together into very interesting information. Me—I just didn't know where my husband was—because natcherly I wouldn't want you swimming about in the North Atlantic in December!!

My dearest, this only begins the conversation. We'll call it Volume I, and, as I did when you were in Nashville, I'll have to send the volumes in separate envelopes, and this time *hope* you get all of them. But the house is getting very cold now—the hour is plenty late—and my fingers grow stiff with the cold. (Oh, to be in Florida—but with you!) Tomorrow I'll get on with the long story of the days since I saw you. If I were to tell you the story of how much, how often, I've felt my love for you during those days, I'd have an endless letter. It would have to be infinite to match the subject.

I love you always, darling. Ginny

Elmer – January 2, 1944 [V-mail, received January 22]

My Dearest—

Well, the holidays are over and people can settle down to normal existence once again. Every one that is except us fellows over here. We never got into the holiday spirit, hence we don't have to get out of it. We're at a very good post now. The food is good, there's liquor at the club and we have a nice warm barracks. What more could one ask?

Darling, I don't know if you have been writing me, my mail hasn't caught up with me yet. I'm not even sure you have my address. As a matter of fact, I'm not even sure what my address is. Maybe about next summer I will start getting mail.

All my love, El

Virginia – January 4, 1944 7:30 p.m

Dearest—

Claire, sitting across from me with that lap dog, Boots, on her lap, says hello to you. She's being quite obnoxious these days about the wonderful Marines [the Marine Corps Women's Reserve]. You see, she took her exam a while back and was sworn in yesterday afternoon. Now, though she won't be in uniform for a month or two, she's already thinking in terms of the leathernecks—to wit they're *the ONLY* service. Ah well, she just doesn't know!

Today I got a letter from Bud Morrison, now married too, who's a sergeant at Randolph field now—ground crew. He sends congratulations and told me what good care they take of the planes "their boys" fly. "You know I never wanted to fly, but I sure like to watch my babies roll out, know that somewhere along there, I had something to do with it." He's inspecting ships now, he told me. And he said, "No better boys ever walked than the boys with the wings. The ground officers are stinko, but the boys in the air are our pets."

My dearest, you can almost *know* that every time your thoughts are with me, I, too, am thinking of you, dreaming of the past few months, picturing the wonderful days when you'll be home to stay.

My love, all to you, darling, Ginny

Virginia – January 5, 1944 9:40 p.m.

My Darling—

First day back with the Review, and, beside a couple of cutlines [photo captions] I wrote, guess whom I interviewed!?!? Ever heard of General Henry H. (Hap) Arnold? [He was head of the Army Air Corps.] Thought so. But wait—not him—but his mother-in-law!! Yup, Mr. Greene hands me a piece of paper with some info on it, tells me to go over to Valley Stream and see her. This I did.

When I came in she said "Now you've just come to see grandmother, so take it easy"!! She asked about you, of course, told me I was a brave child, (for what, I don't know) and as I was leaving she told me to tell you that you had "a darling wife. One good thing about you, you're a wonderful listener, which is fine in a woman!" (Of course I just said, "Sure, I know I'm wonderful," and left.) You must meet her when you come home.

Hope you are praying, dearest—at church services, I mean. You'll feel a lot better if you do get to them, I think. And honey, when you came home that night, your Pop thought you'd been drinking too much. He spoke to me about it later. I told him you weren't—that your eyes looked bad from a tear gas test (?)—but I know how easy you could get into drink habits from lack of other things to do and from nervousness (this last especially). But please don't, honey, (if indeed I have to say even this) because, as your Pop said, the guy you're flying against "isn't going to have a fried egg for a brain"! Please don't be offended. I wouldn't have mentioned it if you will be, although I feel very much at ease now that I have. Understand? It's similar to my saying to you, "Be careful, darling," not because I'm afraid when you fly, but because I want you to *definitely* remember how very much you mean to me.

I love you, my dearest, Ginny

AMERICAN RED CROSS

Jan 5th /1944
11 55 P.M.

My Dearest —

I'm sitting in a hotel run by the Red Cross, waiting for Parker. He and I came into town tonight to get a taste of English night life (and scotch). We took in a movie and then Parker mysteriously dug himself up a woman out of nowhere and now he is in the process of taking her home. I don't suppose I have to say this, darling, but you don't even have to worry about me picking up any English girl, or any other girl, for that matter. I am all yours, Ginny, and I always will be.

I am just beginning to get accustomed to the cold, damp, English climate. It really isn't too bad; it sorta grows on you. We're beginning to get settled here too. I wish I could tell you everything about what I'm doing and what I've learned since I've been here, I know you'd be extremely interested, but you know as well as I that such a thing is impossible. You will just have to be content to know that I am well and happy and very interested in my work. As added consolation, think of the stories I will have to tell when I get home!

Seems I haven't told you in the last few paragraphs that I love you. If only this blasted fracas was over and I could come home to you. That is the day that I am waiting hoping and praying for.

I just saw Parker stagger through the blackout curtain, so I'll kiss you goodnight for the time being.

All my love, El

Virginia – January 6, 1944 11:05 p.m.

My Darling—

I'm at Jean & Charlie's. I was here New Year's eve, too. I came for only an hour and stayed, drinking scotch with them and discussing *everything* until after 3. It was nice, though, and much more pleasant than sitting up alone at home.

We spoke a lot of you that night. Charlie likes you (smart boy, Williamson) and even mentioned an idea of starting a paint store with you after the war [which they eventually did]—or something like that. He asked what you planned to do—if you expected to go back to the bank—and I told him you didn't know, for quite obvious reasons.

I find it a bit disconcerting to think you're in bed when I'm just finishing doing the dishes at night. But even if my waking hours *don't* match yours, my heart and mind are *always* reaching out to you, because, asleep or awake, I love you my darling.

Ginny

Virginia – January 8, 1944 10:40 p.m.

Dearest boy,

News of the day: I started work *Wednesday*, I told you, on the Review, and today I got a full week's pay, $30.10 with all taxes taken out. (I get a base pay of $30 [about $370 in today's dollars], as before, but I get $5 travelling expenses, which is not deducted from, if I make myself clear.) Pretty nice, I thought, for 3 ½ days (?) work. Did I tell you I had to threaten to work for Newsday to get something definite from Greene about when a job would open up for me? Then I asked about money, and managed to get $2.50 more than before. At present, I am very satisfied with the work. Probably when I start on the beat, I'll not only be scared and green, but also worked to death for a while—but it will be only until I become less dumb about the beat, I hope.

This is what I've been meaning to tell you for a *long* time. The day before Christmas, after noon, sometime, John Walton [El's father] knocks on our front door and asked me to go out for a few drinks with him! Though I was hardly dressed to go out, he told me to come as I was and we headed for the West End Tavern. I was so pleased, not only at the event itself but at the consideration and thoughtfulness he showed me. As he said, he got the idea and knew "it's what the boy would want." We had a swell time (scotch & soda) although when the bartender let a Haig & Haig Pinch bottle slip out of his hands, spilling the precious stuff liberally on the bar, I thought I'd cry—or lick it up!

Last Sunday we went ice skating at Tiny's pond and had more fun, but my arches got tired pretty soon, as they always do the first couple of times. Neither of us dusted the ice, though, despite the constant distraction of fighters and bombers flying over. I think everyone at Mitchel was working and every plane up that day—know why?—to celebrate our anniversary, ¼ year! It was Jan. 2!!

After skating last Sunday, by the way, we went to that place on the corner (bowling alley downstairs) and then to Emil's, which, though not very pretty, is a place full of characters and character, somehow. Pop didn't want to take me there at first, but I assured him I wasn't afraid or proud or fussy or what-have-you. We're going to the movies sometime soon.

I'm not taking much *space* to say it in this letter, but it means as much as always, darling.

I love you, El. Ginny

Virginia – January 10, 1944

My dearest,

Jeepers, this has been a good day! I got a letter, a real *letter* from my darling husband when I got home from work!! This was the letter you wrote Dec. 21.

Honey, why was your letter opened by the censor? I thought you censored your own stuff. And, while we're on the subject, is my mail to you also censored? I didn't think so but some people have said it is. Leave me know. If it is, I'll forever feel there's someone looking over my shoulder as I write—which gripes me no end!

We're glad to know for sure you're in England. Guessing gets on one's nerves after a while. Please tell me about it, if you can. I had started fooling with the idea of getting into the Red Cross, hoping to be sent overseas (England, natcherly!), but I learned you must be 25 to qualify. So I won't be surprising you, I guess.

I asked Mr. Greene today about when I would really need
a car and he said probably not for another month or more. I've
been figuring out why he hired me now when the job I'm supposed
to be getting won't be open 'till then. He said today, and it throws
light on the question, that I "might as well be around here, getting
acclimated again, and making some money" while I wait! Pretty
good of him—or was because he thought I *would* take a job with
Newsday? (This last thought doesn't mean that I'm a prize, by any
means. Just indicates how tough times are!!)

Tonight is brilliantly clear and cold and still the moon is full,
and, walking over here, I wondered how that same moon, looking
absolutely frozen tonight, could look so warm and soft in the
summer! I particularly remember how pleasant it was with Spanish
moss-covered trees in the background—what a difference when
the trees are bare black sticks! Sorta like the difference between
life with you and without you. You are all the difference between a
beautiful, warm life and a sharp-edged, barren one.

Always yours, Ginny

Elmer – January 11, 1944 6:00 p.m.

My Dearest Wife—

That word sounds wonderful—"Wife." There is only one difficulty.
A wife shouldn't be three thousand miles away from her lawfully
wedded husband.

I have found a new interest. Parker is teaching me how
to fence. They have foils, sabers and masks in the gym and we
work out with the blades during calisthenics. It's a lot of fun, it's
good exercise and it helps coordination. I got a new job, too. I'm
coaching a basketball team. We have formed a team of fighter

pilots and I was made coach. We have a good bunch of men and with a little bit of practice we should have a pretty fair outfit. It's fun booking games and planning plays and defenses. We played last night in town and lost 38-30. Give us time though, we'll get better.

I'll say goodnight for now. I love you dearest, more than life itself.

El

Virginia – January 12, 1944 10:00 p.m.

My darling husband—

Last night I *was* going to that piano concert in NYC but decided to stay home and get some sleep. As usual, though, I put it off with reading ("A Tree Grows in Brooklyn") and listening to the president. He asked for a national service act to get *all* civilian adults, men & women, doing as much as they're able for the war effort. That, and the crying need for women in the services, *and* the apparent complacency of so many you meet in civilian life all make me feel I'm not doing a damn thing in this war. So I give blood and help out once a week and expect to work with the Red Cross motor corps. But it does seem like such a *little*, darling! Perhaps I wouldn't actually join up with one of the women's services even if you hadn't disapproved, but the selfishness that would keep me out, in that case, would have to withstand an awful conscience twinging!

Over and out for tonight, darling. I love you most passionately, tenderly, sincerely, wholly, eternally.

Ginny

Virginia – January 16, 1944 9:00 p.m.

My dearest—

Tonight I feel very confused and frustrated—mainly the latter. I've
been reading the paper, and the many problems on the fire now
and the various problems in the offing all have me worried. The
Poland–Russia dispute (shall I call it that and still be diplomatic?)
worries me tremendously. Its solution holds so much. If it turns out
badly, the Allied agreements will either be thrown out the window
or the Allies will no longer include Russia. [The question was,
would the advancing Russians sign a peace treaty with Germany
in exchange for part of Poland?] That's the big thing. Then there
are the minor worries—like the trouble with De Gaulle in Algiers.
[He wanted the Allies to arm the French resistance as the vanguard
of the Allied invasion of Europe.] And I feel thoroughly frustrated
because I know *so* little about *so* many things and can do even
less about them!

    Those are my political problems. They'd be easy to take
were they not so closely knit with personal problems—mainly you
and what you are now or will soon be facing. You see I've been
reading of the 51-B's use as an escort plane—first time in the
Battle over Brunswick [Braunschweig] the other night (no, day),
according to reports. Well, I don't much like the idea of escort
work—and maybe you don't either—and even less do I enjoy the
thought of your taking part in the coming offensive over there. I
know it will be, darling, and it isn't that I'm worrying about you
always, either. It's just a sickening insecure feeling, increased
tremendously by the distance separating us.

    As I started out to say, I'm sitting before a fire in our living
room fireplace, and listening to Tchaikovsky's Fifth on the radio,
but what I want to do more than anything else is talk with you.
I want to know more about the 51's work as an escort, how the

pilots talk of it when they return, how bad the opposition is, how the German fliers are, what kind of planes they use and what they can do. And these are only a few. I read all I can in the papers—and I'm glad to be reading about 51's instead of 47's!—but they only told me what I already knew. If I could only talk with you about what you're doing and discuss the coming offensive and what surprises the Germans might be saving, discuss this Russian "division" of Poland with you—then I'm sure I'd feel better. Of course I wouldn't be able to do any more about it, one way or the other, but I like to know what I'm (or you're) getting into. Just knowing helps.

Some droopy letter, so far. But I have one more complaint about me and my mental attitude. I have no power of selection. I read the NY Times book review section this evening and damned if I didn't find, as I always do, several *new* books I ought to read and *want* to read! This, on top of the hundreds of books already written I want to read, the piles of back Time magazines I must read, and the many books in my own library still unread. Gad zooks, El, when will I *ever* have time to read all these things when I can't even find time to *complete* a day's work. For instance, I *never* put all the thoughts I want to in a letter to you. Nor have I started work on our scrapbook. See what I mean? These trifling articles bother me, even if they *are* minor in the great scale of events and what-not. No power of differentiation between important and unimportant. I want to put my short but inquisitive nose into too many things, and the impossibility of the task floors me now & then. Sometimes I wish I'd never learned to read!! Or think—or something, damn it all!

I've been considering going into the nurse's aide business. The gals in the round-robin letter [of wives of some of Elmer's squadron-mates] mentioned the President's request for a national service law—which I think is, or could be, a great thing. It would definitely include me, I suppose. But only if they can find something I can do more efficiently than pound a newspaper office typewriter, I'll gladly do it, if it will end the war any sooner.

My job is working out all right. I worked Friday night, covering a war bond rally in Rockville Centre, so I didn't have to work yesterday morning.

At the rally was a young Russian who'd fought for France in a Foreign Volunteers unit and was taken prisoner by the Germans. He spent nine months in a German prison camp and was finally released because his shoulder, shattered by shrapnel, wouldn't heal. He told the audience that they were like he was when as a small boy, he wouldn't believe the beautiful coals in the fireplace were also very hot. He said that they were like that about the Germans—not believing the awful things they heard of them. Then he told of the prisoners going without water & food for more than 3 days and then after taunting them with fresh water, the German officer gave them soapy, dirty water to drink. He also told of the terrible food they got, how the guards would tease them with pieces of bread and then throw the bread among them, watching the men fight like animals for it. If it hadn't been for Red Cross food packages, he said, he wouldn't be alive now.

Most pertinent to me, because I've been bitter about similar things for some time, was his story about one man in the camp who received a letter from his wife, asking him to sign the papers for her divorce. He said not only that man, in particular, but every man in the camp was sick, actually sick, for 3 days. Couldn't even eat. Every man lost hope, because their only reason for enduring it was the thought of returning to their wives & families. That letter, he said, made every man afraid his wife or mother, even, was forgetting him. He went on to say that no man is fighting for the *words* "freedom" or "democracy," but instead, what those words mean to him personally, and that is usually his home and family.

The story made me even madder than I have been about married women two-timing their husbands overseas. Can't think of anything bad enough to wish for them! You told me once, honey, that you didn't mind my going out with fellows you know, just so I didn't tell you. But I couldn't do even that. If I ever *do* see Norm (he's the only one I'd feel right about "going out" with), I'll tell you about it. You will always know what I'm doing dearest. When I can't tell you how I spend my time, I'll have grown two heads, or something equally monstrous.

I love you, all ways, always, Ginny

Elmer – January 18, 1944 8:00 p.m.

Hello Darling—

Gee, but I love my wife. I haven't received most of my luggage as yet and my big picture of you is with it, but our wedding picture is looking over my shoulder right now and you can't realize how much it means to me.

The mail situation isn't any better. I have received exactly one piece of mail since I left the states and that was a Christmas card from a buddy of mine in the Air Transport Command in Illinois? [Letters through February 18th did not have Elmer's correct address and had to be re-directed, sometimes incorrectly. He didn't receive any more mail until he reported to his squadron on February 4th. A stack of it was waiting there for him.]

Funny thing happened Sunday. I was coming in for a landing. As I circled the field my canopy opened about two inches, the weather moved in and my radio went dead—all within the space of about five minutes. The weather was so thick I lost the field when I peeled off to land. They finally brought me in by flares. This damned English weather.

I've enjoyed this little chat. I hope we can meet again real soon. So long.

Your loving husband, El

January 27, 1944 – The Soviet Army ends the nearly two-and-a-half-year German siege of Leningrad

---

Virginia – February 2, 1944 1:55 p.m. [typewritten]

My darling,

After your letter of yesterday, written on the 18th, saying you'd had no mail from us, I called the Red Cross. They offered to get in touch with their field director in your vicinity and let you know we're writing. But they said it would take about a month before they got an answer. Thereupon, I decided to take a chance on your getting a cable sooner. Sent one this noon and got a kick out of the various messages you can send by piecing together their brief phrases. Like "All well, children evacuated. Can you lend me some money? Kisses." Or "Son born. Keep smiling." Or maybe "Daughter born. Good luck. Keep it up." As I said, I got a chuckle out of some of these imaginary cables. What I did send was "Letters and parcels sent. All well at home. All my love, dearest." Hope you have gotten it. [He did.]

Have I told you that this job is very helpful in getting me used to being Mrs. Odell? For the first few times when I wrote a slug line and my name at the top of the story, I'd start in on sch— but then remember. Haven't made that mistake in a long time, now. Odell comes out of the typewriter just as easily. Of course, Marie sometimes calls me "Miss Schill" as she used to and I don't catch her, but then, that's a privilege she has after so many years. One thing I'm glad of—seldom do I have to repeat my name over the phone. When it was Miss Schill, I was Mrs. Shell, Miss Scholl, Miss Shawl, and every other possible misinterpretation. Odell goes over the wire very easily—but when anyone spells it, I still have trouble. Before they'd leave the c out. Now they put an apostrophe in. Oh well, makes conversation on dull days. "No apostrophe?" "No, no apostrophe." "Oh, then it's not Irish." "Nope, not Irish." "English?" "Nope, French Huguenot, I understand." "Oh." Pause for corrections. "Rather unusual name." "Yes," I say, and it sometimes, if I'm lucky, stops there. But if I'm being accurate, that day, I have to say, "No, not very," or something, and then it continues.

[She describes being sent on an interview assignment to a local park.]

We took off for the Belmont Lake State Park! Oh goody, I thought. More happy places! It looked very bleak, of course, and wintry, but beautiful even so. King's [the interviewee] office window looks out over the lake, very near where we sat that summer day—and you kissed me—and we sang "Bewitched, Bothered and Bewildered" all afternoon. I bet we have nicer memories than any other ten couples laid end to end, or something!

Jeepers, no more room. But enough to tell you I love you. Ginny

Virginia – February 4, 1944 1:45 p.m.

My dearest,

Again I'm writing to you on a typewriter, but this method gets a lot of information to you quickly—at least it gets on paper quickly, saving wear on my pen for the less fascinating bits of info. More important things, more personal things, I'll write in *blue* on white.

Yes, still at work, but with nothing to do for a few minutes anyway—until Greene discovers my idleness. Pat and I went to eat at Eddie Hall's old place (on Sunrise highway, just down the road apiece). We walks in and what begins to play on the radio but "Bewitched —"!

I was all set, practically, to take the nurse's aide course when I found out that Bill Kennedy, whose place I expect to take on the paper, would be going soon. So I called a halt to preparations to start the course. Besides my admitted dislike for the whole idea of being a nurse's aide, I also really doubt if I could complete the course entirely. When I do get this reporter's job, I'll probably be up to my neck in work (being as I'll be very green) and I'll have to work more than ordinarily necessary at first.

Of course as soon as I started this yesterday, Greene tromped up with a pack of releases for me to rewrite, plus a bunch of info about Dogs for Defense, with which I'll have to do a feature. [More than ten thousand donated household pets were trained to be sentries, scouts, messengers, mine-sniffers, and more.]

The baby-bearing is quite popular. The girl who took my job here when I left has told Mr. Greene she's expecting and will have to leave. I haven't heard how he took it. (He had said something about having me and Agnes, the girl expecting, to worry about these days—meaning worry as to when we'd have to leave because of enlargement. I told him he damn well didn't have anything to worry about in my case, that an ocean between us was a stiff proposition. *I* didn't tell him this, really, but the girl he was talking to about it said as much.)

Darling, I love you, always will, completely. Wish you could know how *very* much.

Ginny

NASSAU CANINES HELP K-9 CORPS

Raise Cash For Buddies On Fighting Front, Get 'Ratings'

Most of Nassau's dogs may be 4-F in regard to the K-9 corps standards, but hundreds of county pets already are serving on battlefronts by proxy as enlisted personnel "behind the lines" in the war dog fund.

War Dog For A Dollar

The system gives 4-F dogs—those unfit for military service—a chance to help in the war, and it works through the owner's pocketbook. Dogs for Defense, inc., procuring agency for armed forces dogpower, instituted the fund about a year ago to keep the procurement service functioning. Before the army or navy gets a dog, the animal must be processed—registered, examined, crated, and shipped—and the cost runs to about $10 a dog.

Now, for a dollar, any dog can become "a dog behind the dog behind the guns" and wear a private's tag in the canine civilian army. If the dog is the seagoing type, the owner can request a seaman's rating for him. For larger contributions, the rank increases; $5 for a sergeant or chief petty officer, $10 for a lieutenant or ensign, $20 for a colonel or naval captain, and $100 for a general or admiral.

This system will allow all of the country's estimated 20,000,000 dogs to help, even though only about 2,000,000 are believed fit for military duty. Some of the requirements are a height of 20 inches or more at the shoulder, weight of 50 pounds or more, age of one to five years, and perfect physical condition. The dog must not be gun shy or storm shy. But rigid qualifications eliminate most dogs from frontline service.

Nassau Dogs Enrolled

Nassau county pet owners are already well represented on war dog fund lists at 250 Park avenue, New York city. James M. Austin of Old Westbury, the organization's chairman, enrolled his famous Champion Nornay Saddler, three inches too short for battle, as a general, and he asked other dog fanciers to spread the idea. Now there are about 20,000 enlistments, generals to privates, with many army and navy mascots in that number. Letters of enlistment have come from Hawaii, Africa, Australia, and every section of the nation. Nip and Tuck, comic strip characters, are also in the ranks.

"Lieutenant Snooper," shown in

4-F's But They're Fighting

John W. Leech, 11, of Bellerose, above, is teaching "Lieutenant Snooper" to salute, in keeping with his army title in the war dog fund, Dogs for Defense, incorporated. The lieutenant is a fox terrier, grandson of Nornay Saddler, and is the inseparable pal of young John, son of Mr. and Mrs. John H. D. Leech of 14 Hudson road. At right, top photo, is another from the James

Austin kennels in Old Westbury, "Seaman Duchess," fox terrier owned by Mrs. Charles Thill of 11 Downing street, East Williston. Mrs. Thill's husband is a chief petty officer in the navy, photography division. Wearing his war dog fund tag, at lower right, is "Marine Sergeant Corso von Albersdorff," boxer, owned by Nicholas Meyer of Orchard drive, East Williston.

the accompanying photo with his master, was enlisted early in the drive and was made official recruiting officer in Bellerose. "Seaman Duchess" joined when her owner's husband left for the navy.

Other local dogs, unable to go to war, but serving in the war dog fund as recruiting agents are: "Chief Petty Officer Peter," owned by Miss A. C. Pratt, 35

collar are mailed to the owner. The K-9 corps began with 200 dogs privately trained through the Dogs for Defense organization. The military branches now do the training at special K-9 camps, but Dogs for Defense is still the only "induction center" and to which donated dogs are sent. Through the war dog fund, Dogs for Defense officials will continue to send dogs to the armed forces' K-9 corps which is expected eventually to save 300,000 dogs.

Feb. 10, 1944.

Elmer – February 4, 1944 [V-mail received February 16]

My Dearest Wife—

Came to my permanent post (or supposedly, explanation later) recently and found some mail waiting for me. Four letters from you, some from Mom, Evie, Aunt Emily etc. Got the one with one picture (keep this up I like it) the one with Norm's pictures in it, the one with the Arnold interview and another.

Now to try to answer some of your questions. First of all, your letters to me are not censored, so don't be afraid of someone looking over your shoulder. Secondly, darling, tell Dad, and this is for you too, please don't worry about me drinking too much. I drink hardly anything over here; an occasional scotch and soda. I've heard of too many guys who dove in from high altitude from over imbibing the night before. The one thing on my mind is coming home to you and anything that will keep me from doing that, namely alcohol, I'm staying away from.

I'm running out of paper and I must tell you how very much I love you and miss you.

All my love, El

Elmer – February 6, 1944 [V-mail received February 17]

My Dearest Wife—

I received the first volume of your letters yesterday—about four days after the second volume and many after. I was never so glad to get mail in my life. I will soon be able to get some air mail paper and I have been storing up interesting information to write a long letter.

Living only for you.

All My Love, El

Virginia – February 7, 1944 2:50 p.m.

Darling—

Good news from the Bureau of Internal Revenue Saturday. Called on them in their Hempstead office to find out if I have to file a return this March. The nice man said I didn't have to until my husband came home!! (But come home soon, darling, even if it *does* mean we'll have to make out an income tax report!) Also I asked him how much should be withheld from my salary, being married now. He told me I should claim the exemption of a "married person living with husband or wife." "You live with him in your dreams," he said—and he wasn't fooling.

Today, getting your clipping about the P-51B from Stars & Stripes and nothing else but the envelope, it was quite a disappointment to put it mildly. [She writes at length about how upset she is by this. For weight reasons, Elmer had sent two envelopes simultaneously, one with a letter and one with the article. The latter arrived a day before the former.]

Honey, please remember that as much as the 51 means to *you*, *no* airplane or anything else means as much to *me* as you. And when I can't have you, I want something you've written.

Lou and Rose will be in NYC this weekend. We've got tickets to "The Merry Widow." And we'll probably bat the breeze for hours. Gonna stay over at the Hotel Penn. I'll never forget that place and the entrance where we happily kissed goodbye, I thinking you'd be out again in a day or two. But if I'd known, I suppose I wouldn't have let you go.

Always, all my love, Ginny

Elmer – February 8, 1944 18:30

My Dearest Wife—

A short while back, I was the most miserable specimen in the E.T.O. [European Theater of Operation]. You see when we came over here we were assigned to a group that was flying 51's.

All well and good. The group had not arrived, so we were sent elsewhere to get in some more training. Still all well and good. After a while we were sent back to the group and to our horror and chagrin, the group was flying [P-]47's. You have never seen morale ebb so low as that of the "Barton Bums." After a while we sort of became resigned to our fate and tried to find the good points of the ship we were to take into combat. No use. Finally one morning we woke up and the birds were singing and the sun was shining. Something was definitely up, for sun shining in England is so uncommon, that, it is believed in some rural sections, it heralds some great day, and in our case it did, for later that morning word came, by carrier pigeon from the higher ups, that we were to be transferred to a new group and fly our dream ship. So, as I think it was Shakespeare who said "All's well that ends well."

All the pilots in our flight live in the same barracks; a cozy little Nissen hut. (I'm not kidding). There are nine of us in "D" flight. I will probably mention the boys from time to time so I think now would be an opportune moment to introduce you to them. The fellow with the moustache sitting on the end bunk writing is Asbury; "Gremlin" Asbury to the boys. The two guys drooling over the pin-up girl in this week's "Yank" are from left to right "Mr." Deeds and Ed. Pawlak. The fellow on my left is Ben Pollard the flight commander. He's a swell fellow. The two fellows on the bunk the other side of the stove are Stew Sullivan (he was in Bartow with me) and "Hicky" Aldrich the asst. flight commander. Down at the far end reading tech orders is Edwards; "Eager Ed" as he is affectionately known. The eighth guy "Bull" Bullard is in the hospital with tonsillitis. So here you have the swell fellows that

make up the best flight in the best squadron in the best group in England.

Well darling, I think that just about covers all I am allowed to say, except, that I love you, so very much. I think when I get home I won't even leave you to go to work.

Your ever-loving husband,

Always, El

Elmer – February 14, 1944 "You Know Where"

My Dearest Wife—

Got the pictures of Mac and Maida and the Cypress Swamp. One complaint though; Want more pictures of you. You're the only one I want in my English Album.

You mentioned my letter being censored. Let me explain that. When officers' mail reaches New York it is spot checked. That is about one in twenty is censored. No doubt my brown envelope stood out in the bunch and that's why it was opened. However, never fear, your mail to me is never opened until I get it.

Let me tell you about an air raid we had recently. We were sitting in the barracks playing penny ante when the sirens blew. Presently he heard the boom of ack ack [anti-aircraft artillery] and the occasional thud of a big one. We went out into the open to watch the show. It was really an awe-inspiring sight. Search lights all over the sky and the flashes of ack ack bursts plus the glare of dropping flares. All the action was a good distance away but most of it we could see quite plainly. Once in a while they would catch a bomber in the lights and it was fun to watch his frenzied attempts at dodging. These raids are nothing to worry about though. Just an occasional meager attempt at reprisal on the part of the Germans. Nuisance value mostly. They break up our poker games.

We have a little motto stuck up on the wall of the Operations room which I think is cute and you might be interested in. Goes something like this.

"If you get out of formation
Give your soul to the lord;
'cause your ass belongs to Jerry" [Allied nickname for the
    Germans]

In the near future I expect to get my back flying pay for December, January and February, so you can be expecting a good sized money order. By the time I get home, we should be about ready to set up housekeeping.

Well, dearest I got a flight scheduled. I'm writing this down at the line and my name just went up on the operations board.

All my love, El

Virginia – February 14, 1944 – V-mail

Dearest,

Remember the plans we'd dreamed up about getting a cabin far away from everybody when you come home, and going there for a month, with no interruptions or separations or formations to meet or to go to? Well, the arrangements are practically all made. All I need is you. Mrs. Quantrell's sister, Gladys Berg, who goes with me to the USO every Wednesday night, has a cottage at Mastic [eastern Long Island]. That is, she and her husband have a cottage. Well, the description of it is swell, and she was telling me all about it and then said, "When Elmer comes home, you can have the key and go out there." I told her that she could be sure we'd take her up on the offer. Gee, it would be swell. The cottage is on a sort of lagoon, I understand, with Fire Island within rowing distance. Then you can cross the narrow Island and, presto, you have the ocean and beach all to yourself. Now please, honey, use your influence to end the war and come home, but most important is the latter.

All my love, Ginny

Elmer – February 17, 1944 –
"There'll always be an England"

My Dearest—

It was raining and snowing all day today. Naturally no flying so I got a jeep and took a trip down to my last station to check on the mail situation. I picked up quite a stack for the boys, and one for me. I straightened out the snarls in the mail problem, so mail will be coming here regularly. When I got back this afternoon there was a letter from you dated Feb. 5th, so things are looking up.

There isn't anything new around here to relate. Quite a bit of activity getting masks fitted, radio set installed, ammunition belted, lectures and stuff, so we aren't exactly idle. Although yesterday I slept until 11:30 A.M. (War is hell).

Just took time out to eat a hard-boiled egg, (part of our weekly rations) and get in a discussion on old motion pictures. All the old blood and thunder jobs were re-hashed; "Charge of the Light Brigade" "Cleopatra" "Bengal Lances" "Beau Geste" and all the rest. The boys are kidding me about my New York accent.

All my love, always, El

Virginia – February 17, 1944 10:10 p.m.

Dearest El—

Please continue to tell me about the fellows you're flying with and *everything*! You know how *much* I'm interested. I *live* on news about you as much as I do on food. Really honey!

Da news from Schill Chateau: Claire is very disappointed and feeling that life is quite bitter. The marines discovered that she'd falsified her birth certificate to show she was 20 instead of 19—and rejected her. The poor kid had made all plans, of course, but you can't give her too much real sympathy. She should never have tried it, underhanded as it was, and whatnot. But she'd left Sperry's, made lots of plans, as I said, and was all ready to go. She'll get over it, but it's tough, nonetheless. It's good that she's out of Sperry's, though. That place is really full of *NO GOODS*. [Claire was a very attractive young woman, and likely got 'hit on' quite regularly.] She's talking now of getting a civilian job at Mitchel field.

Mitchel, by the way, is entirely a bomber base now, I understand. I see very few fighters, even 47's, zooming around these days. Talking to an anti-aircraft man at the USO last night— and I'm afraid I scared the poor guy talking so blithely and *continuously* about planes!—I learned there were a couple of 51's over there Sunday. I wish I'd been over to see them. He said there was a 38 there too. That's one I'd like to see, too. Wish you were here to tell me about the new night fighter, the P-61, Black Widow. But then, I wish you were here—period!

D flight sounds great, honey, and *of course* it's the best flight in the best squadron in the best group in the *army air force*!! Couldn't I come over and make your Nissen hut even cozier? I'd do all mending, cooking (?), and even put up chintz curtains if you'd like! Ask the flight commander, huh?

I love you always, always. Ginny

Virginia – February 20, 1944 1:30 p.m.
[on Hotel Pennsylvania stationery,
at a pilots' wives' 'get-together' in NYC]

Darling—

Rose and I are both sitting here in our room, quietly writing to our husbands. The weekend has been nice. All we talk about is you and Joe and flying *and* you and Joe.

Went to 11:45 mass at St. Patrick's [Cathedral, on Fifth Avenue].

Wish I could get to mass in a church like that oftener. The size alone makes me feel small—which is a good for my usually far-from-humble attitude—and the organ music is gorgeous. It could easily have brought tears—it was that beautiful. The masses of people, too, all so different yet all gathered for a single purpose, are very inspiring to me.

Honey, I hope you go to church services regularly. Your Mom and I, I know, pray for you always, but you've got to be on our side, too—and openly so.

I got a pint of Ballantine's scotch for this weekend, figuring on a large, raucous reunion in our room. But things turned out quietly and I still have the pint. Guess I'll give your Mom & Pop a present for Valentine's day (but I gave it to them the day before). I got them a quart of Schenley's rye. All this liquor was obtained through Charlie. He knows liquor dealers, who won't sell it to just anyone in these days of scarcity.

Darling, I love you! Ginny

Elmer – February 20, 1944 9:00 p.m.

My Dearest—

Just got back from a lecture in Group Intelligence. Gee, but they're interesting lectures. Some day when this is all over I'll tell you what they're about.

I didn't get any mail yesterday or today, but my private Gestapo [German secret police] has informed me that a huge amount of mail found its way to the post office this evening.

The air raid sirens just this moment began to wail. I wonder what they're heading for tonight? The ack, ack should start rumbling any moment. Probably trying to reciprocate for a big raid we made today.

Dearest, I'm gonna say good-night for the time being. I want to write to Norm and get to bed early. I have a flying mission scheduled for tomorrow.

All my love, always, El

Elmer – February 21, 1944 8:15 p.m. –
"Guess What? Still in Eng."

My Dearest—

Tonight there was cause for rejoicing in the group. The new bar officially opened in the officers club. I went in and sampled their stock to the tune of five double scotch and sodas. So if this letter becomes illegible after a while you'll know why.

This Wednesday being the beginning of Lent, I have decided to give up drinking and smoking. I give these up every year as you probably know by now. And if I do say so I stick by my decision; so you don't have to worry about me becoming a drunkard for the next six weeks or so. I'm kidding honey, you know I don't drink too much.

Yesterday I mentioned a ferry mission I had scheduled for today. About noon ten of us took a truck over to another field to pick up some planes that were assigned to our group. The field we went to was operational and the boys were out on a mission. We spent some time listening on the radio to some of their conversation as they flew deep into Germany. Sure was interesting. The ship I flew back was a different type than I've ever flown before and I really sweated that thing out flying it back. I'll tell you more about it when the war is over.

In that letter from Jack today, I find that he is out in Montana flying mostly C-47's [cargo plane]. His main run is from Montana to Fairbanks, Alaska. Doesn't sound too interesting to me. I've ridden in a C-47 over here and I'm sure I wouldn't want to fly them regularly. Perhaps I'm a bit prejudiced.

I love you dearest—
Your loving husband, El

Elmer – February 21, 1944 8:20 p.m.

Dear Mom and Dad—

One of the letters from Ginny was an old one that just caught up with me, and in it she told me how good she felt when you came over the day before Christmas to take her out, Dad. It made me feel awful good too, when I read it. I swear, tears came to my eyes when she quoted you as saying "it's what the boy would want." And it's what I would want, Dad. I realize what it must be for a young girl to be tied down by a wedding ring and I sure do appreciate you taking the time to take her out. I know you and I have never been really close as father and son, Dad, but it's taken a war to make me realize what a swell Pop I have. Things are going to be different when I get home. You and I are going to go hunting and fishing and take in ball games, like we never did before.

Well folks I guess that's about all for now. I gotta get some sleep. Big day tomorrow.

All my love, El

Virginia – February 23, 1944 4:50 p.m.

My Darling—

My hair is standing on end and I'm sitting at the edge of my seat! You said "my name just went up on the operations board." Come, come now, Lieutenant. I gotta know more than that. *Please* tell me *some way*, when these "flights" you mention so casually are combat missions. I'm *not* going to worry. I just wanna know! So there! And I won't tell anybody *atall* if you say not to.

Reading about the reportedly big air raids the Jerries have been pulling on London, I figure you've had plenty of fireworks to watch. I hope you aren't more involved than *watching*, although it would mean you're damn close to London.

Did I tell you about my Lenten regulations? I'm skipping desserts and most cigarettes. My smoking will be curtailed almost entirely. First I was going to quit smoking, but I'm sure I'd probably start eating sweets then too much. So—a combination. I'll leave you know how it woiks.

Honey—what's this I keep reading in posters in barber shop windows about "Odell's American Beauty"? There's a picture of a glamorous, mostly naked gal, a bottle (hair tonic, I guess) and "Odell's American Beauty." That's about all. Come on, you've been holding out on me!! Who is she? I see that sign every morning in that little "tonsorial parlor" on South Franklin—then I go by Feldi's florist. Seems wonderful to see daffodils and beautifully colored flowers blooming behind the glass when outside it's so cold you can see your breath. The daffodils help me to believe spring is really coming. Florists' shops are such wonderful places.

I love you darling, always, Ginny

Virginia – February 24, 1944 [V-mail]

My dearest—

Brod also dropped in tonight to bid his civilian life adieu. Got his "warning" notice Wednesday (yesterday) and he leaves at 9 a.m. tomorrow from Penn station. Goes to Ft. Dix [New Jersey], he says. But that's fast work! Of course, he's been *in* since Jan. 22. He quit work today! Now I'll have somebody else to write to, although I know right now I'll get damn few, if any answers! Also, now I have a car for the duration. Sometimes I wonder whether that's good or bad.

Always, Ginny

First Blood

FIGHTER AIRCRAFT IN WORLD War Two had three main functions. They were to conduct "fighter sweeps," escort bombers, and strafe or bomb targets of opportunity. A fighter sweep meant destroying enemy aircraft before they could get to you, by attacking them on the ground, as they took off, or as they slowly climbed—heavy with fuel and armaments. In addition to its machine guns, the single-seater P-51 'Mustang' could carry a five-hundred pound bomb under each wing. These could be jettisoned if engaging in aerial warfare. If not, pilots returning from a mission went after airfields, railroad junctions, bridges, depots, and other targets, with bombs and/or guns. To protect their rear and flanks, the fighters normally flew in four-plane diamond formations. The pilot in the rear, the most vulnerable to attack, was referred to as "tail-end Charlie," and was usually the junior man.

The fighters were originally intended primarily for ground attack and close infantry support because Army brass believed the bombers, especially the B-17s with their heavy armament, would be able to successfully defend themselves against German fighters. They were spectacularly and tragically wrong.

Elmer – February 24, 1944 9:20 p.m.

My Dearest—

It's nine-twenty now and I want to be in bed by ten so I'm afraid
this is going to be short. There is another reason I'm not writing
a long letter. Seems my right wrist is wrapped up like a mummy. I
dove, head first, off the tail end of a G.I. truck onto a cement road.
Not on purpose, I assure you; my foot slipped. I broke my fall with
my hand and wasn't hurt. The only trouble, I sprained my wrist,
and having it taped up, makes my writing sorta difficult.

My wrist had better be a lot better by tomorrow. You see, I
have a date to fly over Germany. Yes, the big day has finally come,
and for me to miss out because of a sprained wrist would really be
hell. I am surprised at my emotions. I'm not in the least bit worried
or scared. The only feeling I have, is one of extreme and intense
excitement. Like the way I felt on Christmas Eve when I was a kid.

Seems like every time I write to you, the air raid sirens blow.
They just blew again. I really should put the lights out. Someone
just put them out. I'm now writing by flashlight.

I haven't told you I loved you in this letter yet. I do darling,
you know I do. I want to go out and watch the raid so I'll say good
night for now. I'll be thinking of you on my trip tomorrow.

All my love, to you, always, El

Virginia – February 25, 1944 [V-mail]

My dearest—

Yesterday and today have been beautiful, spring-like days, and
today your Mom & I went to the Farmingdale Aggies school to
the 25th annual country life show. I was covering it and if *working*

were that every day, it would be great. Wonderful day for a drive. I wanted to go anyway, and I was able to go on company time.

Of course, Greene said something about making me Victory garden editor for the summer because I evidenced interest in covering the show, but maybe that too might be fun. I'm interested in Victory gardening, plan to have a *marvelous* one myself, and perhaps it would be beneficial to all concerned. [These were home vegetable gardens planted to help the war effort.] I'm thinking I'd like to write a weekly column or something. Wonder if Greene would like that idea?

Always, Ginny

Elmer – February 28, 1944 11:15 a.m.

My Dearest—

Sitting down at the line, sweating out a call to report to group for a briefing. There should be a mission today—the weather is perfect.

I am happier now than I have been since I left the states and you, my darling. I am getting mail regularly and we're at long last in the thick of it. (Time out while I watch a P-47 buzz the field. That will call for reprisals). Speaking of mail honey, forget what I said about V-mail. Air mail is much better and it is getting here fast enough.

Please send me some candy and chewing gum. I'm dying for candy and chewing gum. Thank you also for the photos of Mom and Dad and especially that "cheesecake" one of you. (Long low whistle).

(I'll be back, got a ferry mission). [He was moving aircraft from one field to another.]

It is now 7:20. After that ferry mission I had another short mission so when that was finished, came time for supper.

Now to try and answer some of the questions you asked in the Feb. 17th letter. A fighter pilot gets home after 200 combat hours, the frequency of missions depends upon weather conditions and the decision of the higher ups. As for the length of missions, you wouldn't want me to tell you that. After all the general public doesn't know the range of the new 51 and I'm afraid it's not up to me to release this information.

Remember before when I said that buzz called for reprisals. The debt has been repaid. Jack Wenner and I really beat up their field on this ferry mission. No numbers on a ferry ship.

Let's get back to Seversky. [She had sent a clipping about Alexander Seversky, a Russian-American aviation pioneer and an outspoken advocate of strategic air power.] I think he has a one tracked mind. All he can think about is super-bombers and great big flying battlefields. He seems to think he knows everything about escort. He should talk to escort pilots, and find out what the bomber pilots think of the boys who fly escort for them and how effective they think escort ships are. Not so long ago a crippled fort [B-17 "Flying Fortress"] set down on our field. When the crew came in for interrogation the first thing they asked was "Was that you boys up there." When they found out it was they nearly fell to their knees and "allahed" us. Gone is the friction between bomber and fighter boys. We have great respect for the courage of the fortress boys, and the fortress pilots practically worship us fighter pilots. Not only that but if señor Seversky would interrogate a few fighter pilots he would find, to his astonishment that we are very satisfied with our materiel and the majority of us wouldn't fly one of his multi-place super-fighters if the army had them. So there.

Darling, if you don't stop sending me pictures of nightgowns, your legs, etc., I'm going to blow my top. I read a line somewhere, "A man can get mighty lonely in a crowd of men."

Honey, I'm lonely. All I'm going to dream about now is that month out at the Quantrell's cottage when this mess is over. Sounds really wonderful.

This is about all 6¢ will cover so I'll kiss you good night for now.

Your devoted husband, always, El

Virginia – March 1, 1944 [V-mail]

Dearest—

There has been an interruption. Suddenly Mr. Greene yelled, "Ginny! Ferchrissakes, you've gotta get over to Lynbrook to talk to Major Torgerson!! [Torgerson was a hero of the action at Guadalcanal, in the south Pacific.] Inside of 15 minutes I had found out, a little, what the score was, got a ride over, and was standing flat-footed in this marine's house trying to get some orderly information from him. But he was nervous, and he had a million things to say, and he was very willing to tell you all about it, but all so quickly and unchronologically that it was a hell of a thing trying to get a story put together. I don't think I'll worry about it right now. I'll worry about it tomorrow when I have to write the story. He was very nice. I wondered how a man who's seen so much of horrible things can maintain any normalcy at all. But, except for his continually doing or saying something, he was, it seemed, normal and happy.

All my love, always, darling, Ginny

Elmer – March 1, 1944 6:30 a.m.

My Dearest—

I'm mad. I was all set to go on a raid to Germany, only to find that I am Airdrome Officer for the day and consequently I couldn't go on the mission. See why I'm mad. Grrrr! Airdrome Officer has to stay in the control tower all day and check time on all take-offs and landings. Also decide on what runway to use and if the weather is flyable. It's a very interesting assignment to pull but it came at the wrong time. Oh, well, there'll probably be another one tomorrow.

What a crazy place this barracks is. Poker game in one corner, barber shop trio in another, two guys arguing over the legs of pin-up girls on the wall. Bedlam has busted loose.

The Baron Molen [squadron mate] is now a member of the "caterpillar club" [so named because parachutes were then made of silk]. He bailed out yesterday when his ship refused to come out of a dive. He's laid up in the hospital with a broken arm. Hit the ground swinging [meaning the 'chute had just opened to slow his freefall]. Lucky guy.

I wanna get to bed, I might be on a mission tomorrow. I love you, darling, oh so much.

Your loving husband, El

Virginia – March 2, 1944 10:20 p.m.

Darling—

Wrote to you (V-mail) about being sent out to talk with Major Torgerson. I'm enclosing the story that ran in today's paper. He's a very nice fellow, awfully pleasant about giving you some of his

Lucky To Be Alive Marine Hero Says

Major Harry L. Torgerson shows his niece, 4-year-old Patricia Hilms, his rifle and a picture of Commander Roy Harris of the Bougainville Seabees, "wonderful workers." In the picture, Harris is standing next to a sign which says, "So when we reach the isle of Japan, with our caps at a jaunty tilt, we'll enter the city of Tokyo, on the roads the Seabees built."

"I'm alive. I'm lucky."

In these words Major Harry L. Torgerson, Lynbrook's favorite hero, summed up his most recent exploits in battling Japs in the South Pacific.

The marine major got to his sister's home at 25 Clifford street, Lynbrook, yesterday morning and had hardly closed the front door when the phone began to ring. Word of a hero's return gets around quickly, although Mrs. William F. Hilms, Jr., his sister, can't understand how people found out this time.

Landed On Bougainville

Home for a few days last year around Christmas time, the six foot two officer hardly had time to visit with his family. That time the newspapers, organizations, and his many friends had him telling how he blew Japs out of their dugouts with 20 cases of TNT when the first United States forces landed at Guadalcanal to recapture the territory.

This time the major has stories of the marine landing at Bougainville to establish a beachhead, and neutralize the island with bombings. Major Robert Vance, in command of the unit, was wounded

and Torgerson was put in command.

"Of course I wasn't up at the fighting front much in this campaign," he said. "Most trouble I had at Bougainville was from Jap snipers," and he took a .31 calibre Jap bullet out of his pile of souvenirs. "This went through my helmet. The Jap was up in a tree and I was in a foxhole.

"Another time a Jap sniper was pestering headquarters. Sergeant Major John Abbott went out and got him. Our job at Bougainville was to extend the perimeter defenses and establish outposts of resistance. This was tough because the enemy resistance was heavy. In an hour and a half we had 43 casualties.

"The Seabees laid the main road and a fighter stri there and we had to neutralize the island by bombing attacks. Saved a lot of lives this way. We left Bougainville January 17, the last ma-

Continued On Page 2. Col. 6

leave time to give you a story, but he was awfully nervous, too. He walked up and down, talking continually, rushed from place to place in the house getting things to show you. And it was terribly hard to pin him down long enough to get anything chronologically straight. If I'd had to stick around him long I'd have the twitches. He was very swell, though, about it all. Poor guy probably gets about 24 hours to himself on the entire leave. That's the trouble with being a hero.

[An excerpt from the article]: "Continually Major Torgerson mentioned his officers and men, giving them credit rather than take any himself. The battle at Bougainville lasted 42 days for the major, most of that time spent in foxholes. 'We were being bombed quite a bit so I had to make the men stay in their foxholes most of the time. Because they did, we had only one casualty from bombing.' His clear eyes brightened again when he picked up his rifle. A very efficient-looking weapon named 'Daisie Mae, the 3rd.' Specifically made with a short stock, handy for jungle fighting when shooting from the hip is important, the rifle has done a good job for the major for a year and a half. He wouldn't estimate how many Japs it had sent to another world."

Tomorrow morning I'm going to Farmingdale State Institute of Applied Agriculture again. They're having a hearing for potato growers about what restrictions should be placed on the distribution of potatoes to prevent the spread of the golden nematode, potato pest. Me, as garden editor,—I get the assignment! But I like work outside the office.

Always, I love you, Ginny

Elmer – March 2, 1944 9:15 p.m.

My Dearest—

Missed out on today's raid again today. You see, all the squadrons are over strength and naturally everybody can't get on every mission, but I'm awfully anxious to get over Germany. Joe went today and you should have seen him when he came back; looked like he'd been through a war. It sure does take the starch out of you. The boys flew over the Ruhr valley today. Most of the time everyone tries to avoid it, the flak [anti-aircraft fire] is so heavy. It's so bad that the pilots have nicknamed it "happy valley."

I had a close call today. Four of us were doing a little dive bomb practicing. I was just coming in on my pass when I saw two bombs drop in the target area. I looked up to see where they were coming from, and here comes a 47 like a bat out of hell, directly at me. I just pulled up in time. Someone got his signals mixed. (It wasn't me).

Remember, I love you more every day.

Your loving husband, always, El

Elmer – March 4, 1944 10:10 p.m.

My Dearest—

I probably shouldn't be writing, I'm all mixed up inside, but you want to know what I think and do all the time and what I feel now is part of it. You have heard me mention "Eager" Joe Edwards and "Herky" Aldrich. Well, they're not with us anymore. They, and four other swell fellows in the squadron didn't come back from the mission today [their group lost ten that day]. It's the first losses the squadron has suffered and it has hit most of the fellows pretty hard. One of the flight leaders (of another flight) is down at the club getting blind drunk. He's really feeling bad. Seems he's grounded and he couldn't lead his flight today, but he scheduled it. The other four men who are missing are his flight, that he sent but couldn't lead. Things like this make things like books and music and things seem unimportant. Herky and I were going into hear the London Philharmonic the next time we got a leave together.

Joe Edwards

"Herky" Aldrich

Darling, I'm sorry but I can't write anymore. I had a lot of things I was going to tell you but they have eluded me.

Your loving husband, El

Virginia – March 4 & 6, 1944 [V-mail]

My dearest—

I'm almost as excited as you must have been about your first combat mission. I'm dying to hear about it. You said your emotions were those of excitement. I guess that's what mine were too. I can't say that I've been more nervous or worried about you lately, although I guess I've thought about you more in a worrying sense than usual, but essentially I've been no more afraid than ever. Harping on the subject, in one's own mind, doesn't help at all, so although there may be a twinge of tenseness, or whatever it can be called, in my thoughts of you now, it's not hand-wringing worry, ever, dearest. I have too much faith in you and God. So honey, f.y.i., when you think of me, I'll certainly be *thinking* of you, and it won't be *worrying* about you, either, so your mental picture of me can exclude furrows in the brow! (I thought you'd like to know this. As I tell your Mom all the time—or whenever she begins to worry—we'll hear soon enough if anything goes wrong.)

To be honest, I've been bragging about you even more than ever after your last letters. I'm so stinking proud of you, honey, that I just can't help it. Visiting Kathy over the weekend, I went to church with the people next door. They have a young son, about 10, who's ordinarily not that interested in me. His mother told him, coming home from church, that my husband flies a fighter plane. Immediately there was interest in his voice. "Yeah??" he said, "A

P-38?" No, and I told him a P-51B. And don't think he didn't know what that is. These kids know more about it than most adults you talk to. He has great respect for me now, I think, this young Bobby!

Your very loving wife, Ginny

Elmer – March 5, 1944 1:20 p.m.

My Dearest—

I'm sitting down at the line waiting for the boys to come back from a mission. I feel a lot better than I did when I wrote you last night. Went to church this morning and the chaplain said a few words in behalf of our boys who didn't come home yesterday. You have been asking me about how often I go to church. Honey I go as often as I get a chance, but over here, Sunday is the same as any other day and the war goes on as usual. Only if there's a mission and I'm not scheduled to go on it, can I get to services. That's what happened today.

Was in London again, not so long ago. Bought myself an overcoat and a pair of shoes. Saw a couple of movies, too.

We were walking along Oxford Street and a Canadian WAAC came walking the other way and tossed us one of the smartest and most military salutes I have ever seen rendered by anyone in any service, man or woman. It really increased my respect for women in uniform.

Dearest the boys are starting to come back from the mission and I'm going out in a jeep to pick some of them up from the dispersal area.

All my love, El

P.S. I didn't tell you our squadron has one destroyed and three damaged to its credit. First claims made by any squadron in the group.

Elmer – March 7, 1944 9:00 p.m.

My Dearest—

The outfit had a party Sunday night, thrown by the officers who have recently been promoted. It was a gala affair; much drinking up until late hours. There was a band and some American nurses and British A.T.S. [Auxiliary Territorial Service, the women's branch of the British Army] girls were invited. I danced a couple of dances but I didn't enjoy it. I used to be a pretty good dancer. How come I can't dance with anyone but you? I'm glad. I had great fun watching everyone get drunk while I stayed sober. Remember, I gave up drinking and smoking for Lent. Nother good thing about the shin-dig; the colonel got us excused from the mission the following day.

Nother funny thing happened today. We had a meeting down at group. There were about fifty officers there and we all left at once. I was the last to leave and as we filed down the road an enlisted man came up the road, saluting as he came. When he reached me, he must have been tired because instead of saluting, he extended his hand, shook hands with me and said, in dead earnest, "consider yourself saluted, sir." I thanked him and went on, but when I got out of earshot I very nearly died laughing.

Darling, I'm getting mighty tired and probably will be flying to the continent tomorrow, so I'll kiss you goodnight for now.

Your loving husband, El

Elmer – March 8, 1944 8:00 p.m.

My Dearest—

I missed out on that mission today but I am *definitely* going on the one tomorrow; my name is already on the board. I'm flying Ben Pollard's wing. I really sweated out Parker ["Pode," his friend since pre-flight school] this afternoon. He and his leader got lost and were the last ones in. Really had me worried.

You mentioned something about Charlie Williamson wanting to go into business with me after the war. It sounds like a good idea. At least it gives me something to plan on. I've sorta been groping in the dark lately about what I'm going to do after the war.

In that Jan 9th letter, you also wrote something that gave me a laugh. You said, "Much prefer you in England. At least there you don't have the weather to fight in addition to the enemy." You probably don't realize that we worry more about the weather over here than we do enemy action. To prove that this is a tougher theatre, five missions give you the air medal over here, to twenty five missions in the Pacific Theatre.

Tomorrow night I'll give you full details of the mission.

All my love, always, El

Elmer – March 9, 1944 8:45 p.m. – England

My Darling—

Last evening I said I was going to tell you the details of my mission today. Went to the briefing this morning and I see that Berlin was our target. "Oh goody" I said "I've always wanted to see Berlin." I was sadly disappointed though; when I went out to the ship I was flying, it was not in flying status. The starter solenoid was out. So I stayed on the ground again today.

Since I have no experiences of my own to relate, I will tell you some of the stories that came back from yesterday's and today's missions. I'll start with something Joe Santarlasci did that brought repercussions all the way down from 9th Air Force. Seems he aborted* from the mission and rather than land with two full drop [fuel] tanks, he dropped them in what he thought was an empty field. There were some men working in the field and they had piled their coats and tools around a fire. "Old Eagle Eye" Joe dropped one of his tanks plumb in the middle of the fire. Burned up all the tools and coats. I thought that was very funny.

* Did I tell you that "to abort" means to come home before a mission is complete.

Another funny story was one that a fellow in another squadron tells of his trip home. You'll have to excuse the language but I'm trying to relate this word for word. "I ran out of oxygen just as I left the target area, so I went down to the deck. Coming across Germany, I saw a flak tower in front of me, so I gave it a short burst. (In a surprised voice)—and the sonsa bitches fired back; so I turned around and gave them another burst. Longer this time, but the bastards still fired back. I made another pass at them and gave them a long burst. They didn't fire back this time—musta all been dead."

The funny part was the way he said that they fired back at him. He was surprised and hurt, but mostly hurt to think that someone would actually fire back at him.

Flight Officer Bruce Carr was the first of the Bartow Boys to get a victory. He got an ME-109 [Messerschmitt fighter] yesterday. I was talking to him last evening and he seemed sorry he shot the German down. It was under unusual circumstances; that's the reason for his feelings. Details—"I flew at about 3,000 feet and as I passed over a German airdrome, four 109's took off. Just as the fourth ship got his wheels up, I slid into position for a stern attack. I gave him a short burst and observed hits. He opened up his canopy as if to bail out, but apparently changed his mind so I gave him another burst. This time he did a half-roll and dropped out of the ship, but the dope pulled his rip cord too soon and the chute caught on the tail of his ship. The chute finally broke loose, but it had torn a big hole in the top of the chute and the poor devil dropped like a rock."

And there you have an idea of some of the individual stories that combine to make up the great drama that is taking place over here every day. Each pilot's experiences would make an interesting book in ordinary times, but they get lost in the multitude.

Your loving husband, El

Virginia – March 12, 1944 7:10 p.m.

Darling—

I want to ask you *again* what you think about my coming to England if I can?? I've gotten application blanks from the OWI [Office of War Information] and, when I've filled them out (3 of them!) I'll "be granted an interview." But I don't want to do anything more until I've heard from you! Please, leave me know about this! *If* I should leave (if I should get the chance to go overseas with the OWI) it wouldn't be a very nice trick to play on Mr. Greene, but if I could be with you at all, and if you think things would work out in any worthwhile or convenient manner, I'd leave the Review anyway.

I want to write a long letter—about that letter you wrote me after losing 2 men from the flight—but this is no time. How I wish I could be in England, if only to see you during this awful business, and maybe help a little! Maybe it will be possible.

Having to be away from you is bad enough, but when you're undergoing such hell, it seems far worse—and far more important for me to be with you, at least knowing what hell is, too, if not helping to lessen it.

Always loving you, Ginny

Virginia – March 13, 1944 [V-mail]

My dearest—

It's "too late, too late to say you're sorry" you told me to use V-mail. My husband told me to use V-mail. I didn't want to but he *tole* me. So I got a *huge* supply so's I could write a *lot*. Now he says to forget what he said about V-mail. Air mail is good, he says. Ha! And what am I to do with my lovely box of V-mail stationery, I ask you??

All right, honey, so I won't write very often this way. Mostly it will be air mail, but there will still be some this way until my stock is gone. I'll also try to use it on other people.

I love you, El. Ginny

Virginia – March 13, 1944 10:10 p.m.

Darling—

Heard from a youth, talking to his girl, as they got off the train in Hempstead—in loud tones: "I yam an aviation cadet, apt to become a second lieutenant!" Poor lad, I murmured to myself.

When I saw "Othello" a while back, it definitely reminded me of the day you sat in on my English (Shakespeare) class and the substitute prof for the day read passages, carefully leaving out the more lurid parts. And we snickered slightly. The Broadway production is not delicate, but puts every last bit of the play to good use. Robeson [Paul, the groundbreaking Black actor], of course is marvelous.

As I started to say, I thought of you in a definite place during "Othello." When Kathy, Marie, Fran, Carol and I saw Helen Hayes in "Harriet" Saturday, I thought of you, but this time in a general way. The play—the story of Harriet Beecher Stowe and her novel, "Uncle Tom's Cabin" and its results—put me into one of those thoughtful moods. One part of the play is provocative of much thinking as it portrays another war, another period of horror, men and women being torn apart, men being killed. Whenever I try to get at the details of this, I get very discouraged, hopelessly entangled. The play, of course, takes the long-run view, which I suppose is the logical and best view of war.

Guess this is all for one envelope. The APO doesn't realize how much love I get into every letter! More than ½ ounce by far!

Ginny

Elmer – March 15, 1944 7:20 p.m.

My Darling—

Last evening about fifteen of us borrowed one of the ambulances and went into town to a movie. Just as we came out of the show, the sirens blew, so we had to come home without lights. It was an especially heavy raid. A plane was shot down not far from here. We saw him go in. It was amazing. Just a light in the sky spiraling down and an engine winding up. Then a dull rumble as he struck. They dropped a lot of incendiaries last night.

This afternoon, Sam Proctor and I, not having anything better to do, went rabbit-hunting with our .45's. We saw a couple, but the .45 isn't the best weapon in the world for hunting rabbits. Our meanderings took us to a field about ½ mile the other side of the far runway. There were a lot of white patches on the field which called for investigation. They were incendiary bombs and we found some that didn't go off. I have two now that I intend to bring home as mementos of England. [He didn't.] Jerry came too close for comfort last night.

Dearest. If you could only know how much I long for you, to take you in my arms and tell you how very much I love you.

Your loving husband, El

Virginia – March 15, 1944 10:10 p.m.

My dearest—

Glad you like the gen [possibly short for general news?], darling. I'll keep sending it, you can be sure, but let me know if the stuff becomes uninteresting, or I'm duplicating things you get through English newspapers or Stars & Stripes. Maybe you'd like more juicy news from Da News—rape, murder, and divorce? There's certainly plenty of it being printed every day in that rag! I read it for Terry ["Terry and the Pirates," Milton Caniff's classic adventure comic strip of the time] and for the clever features they often run. Otherwise, and particularly editorially, it STINKS! [It's likely she's referring to the tabloid *New York Daily News*.] Their editorials get me so hoppin' MAD!!! [Then, as now, very conservative.]

In a previous letter I mentioned that newspaper reports say the 51's are being used for escort work. Guess you got that letter because you commented on it in yours of Feb. 21, saying it's not going to be escort work you'll be doing. This has me thoroughly confused, because alla time I'm (finally) reading in the papers about 51's escorting (on the Berlin raids, etc.) and I'm thinking maybe El was on that one. Then you write of having a date to fly over Germany, I put 2 + 2 on paper, get four, then you say it's five. Now I take it that you're doing things in your Mustang that isn't written up by our illustrious war correspondents—or did you get fooled? Holy smokes, let me know!! As I said, I want my imagining to be the right category, anyway!!

Also in answer to your amusement at my blithe remark comparing English and South Pacific weather: When I said I was glad you didn't have to fight the weather too, I was thinking not of *bad* weather, because *everyplace* has some of that, but of the kind of weather that breeds bugs—germs, flies, gnats, heat, and general discomfort if not disease. Unless I'm depending too much on newspaper reports again, the South Pacific has it all over England for that kind of weather.

Today was one of those *bad* days that make me feel I'd better get the hell out of the newspaper business, get back to school and learn a few more things, or just try to keep the gray matter functioning. Greene gave me a *lousy* story which had been written on what looked like a swell source—a Fort tail gunner home from England. There were a *few* meagre facts in the story, but nothing of what should have been told. No phone, I found, so calling the guy (staff sgt.) was out. Greene, grumbling "that's what we get for sending a woman out on a man's story" (a woman had written it) and I grumbled back that it depends on what woman he sends out, hands me the keys to his car, tells me to go over and talk to the fellow.

I got there, but he's in bed. Natcherly his mother doesn't want to wake him and I certainly wouldn't ask her to. So I query the mama. He's nervous, bashful anyway, and doesn't want to talk about combat. But I got a few details. HOWEVER, I *didn't* check on the fact in the story Greene had given me to "rewrite." So, not only do I put two t's on his name, Nesbit, throughout, but, and much more importantly, I give him the DSC [Distinguished Service Cross, the second highest American military award], which, of course, it is foolish to *think* of him having! He has the DFC [Distinguished Flying Cross]. Rewriting, the woman made a *slight* error (DS instead DF) and I jumped on the bandwagon. Things like that gripe me so—because it was so damn dumb of somebody else in the first place (the society editor this time) and because it was *doubly* stupid of me.—Every day I learn something, usually the hard way. Today: check everything that you didn't hear yourself from the source—and then even check! (P.S. Wrote a letter of apology to the poor fellow & his mother.)

Darling, here I am at the bottom of page 4, and I've hardly begun to talk to you about everything that's on my mind. I'll come back tomorrow, though, and chatter further.

Your loving wife, Ginny

Virginia – March 16, 1944 7:45 p.m.

Darling—

Thought I loved you all I could. Then you wrote that you'd given up smoking and drinking for Lent, as usual. I'd thought you might do something, but figured you'd want to smoke pretty badly. I know you must, honey, yet you gave that up and drinking too. Gee, I do admire you so much. Oh honey, you've just got to come back! Two people like us, loving each other so much, so *very* much and having such fun together—well, it doesn't happen often. But as

I've said before, El, my dearest, I have faith in God and in you. All three of us together, we can't lose.

I'm happy like larks that you and the boys like my scrap books. Tonight I'm going to knock another together. More pin-ups as soon as I can get them.

I wrote to you about yesterday's "bad" day. Forgot to tell you what our photographer, Lou Wharff, said to Mr. Greene (in front of me) about the whole mess. "Know what's the matter with Ginny today? She hasn't got her bobby socks on!" Sure enough, for a change I was wearing shoes (real ones—heels and all) and stockings. But I don't often go to all this trouble unless I know I'm going out of the office. Waste of time, stockings, and comfort! So I take a ribbing all the time about my "bobby" socks. And the "paratrooper's" shoes, my favorite for office wear, scare people all the time. Walking (softly, of course) around in them, I sound like John Greene stomping about, and as I turn corners in the office, I'm forever meeting relieved sighs of "Oh, I thought you were Mr. Greene!" You'd think he was an awful ogre but I guess, on second thought, I wouldn't care to be on the wrong side of him, having his stomping ending at *my* desk!! There aren't many times when you can't kid with him, but I've run into a couple of his grouches: not seriously in combat yet, however. I've heard from Pat (the gal in the office, on the desk, whom I eat lunch with, as I've told you) that he was mad as a hatter when I left to get married. I didn't notice: I don't think I would've noticed if he'd snapped my head off at the time!!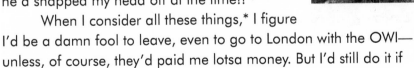

When I consider all these things,* I figure I'd be a damn fool to leave, even to go to London with the OWI— unless, of course, they'd paid me lotsa money. But I'd still do it if you think it would be worthwhile and so forth. I'm waiting to hear from you.

    * his taking me back, putting me on the job, making money, while I waited for the reporter's job to open, and lots of things.

    I love you always, sweetheart, and I'm living during this awful present only for the wonderful future with you.

Always yours, Ginny

Elmer – March 17, 1944 7:30 p.m.

My Darling Wife—

In your V-mail of March 6th you went to great length to prove to me that you don't worry about me and it makes me feel good to know that you don't. An incident happened recently that showed me that God is watching over me and I have no fear for the future. I ferried in a plane from higher headquarters and as is customary, it was completely overhauled when I brought it in. During the course of the overhaul, engineering discovered that one of the engine bolts was sheared. Any violent maneuver or a hard landing, and the engine would have fallen out. The engineering officer was very surprised that it hadn't. As he said to me when he

told me, "brother, you're living on borrowed time." I know I'm not though. I know the Lord was watching over me.

    All the pilots in the squadron had their pictures taken yesterday for a "History of the 382nd Fighter Squadron." Doubtless I will have a couple of extras and I promise to send them to you. Had them taken in my leather jacket and no doubt they will be real hot.

I have more to tell you, but it all can wait, except for the fact that I love you, Ginny darling, more and more.

All my love, El

Elmer – March 18, 1944 8:30 p.m.

My Darling Wife—

It is only by the grace of an all-powerful, ever present, understanding God that you are not a widow tonight. This is no exaggeration honey; today I came as near as I ever want to dying. Explanation: I was flying Ben Pollard's wing on the mission today. It was a long mission and we were carrying a drop tank (extra fuel) under each wing. At exactly 11:42 o'clock this morning, the flagman gave us the high-sign and Ben and I poured the coal on. Everything was going fine until we got about ½ way down the runway. Then—Wham! My ship blew a tire and I swerved toward Ben. I slammed opposite rudder to avoid a collision and lost control. When I got the ship under control again I was off the runway, heading out across the grass at about 100 miles per hour. And not enough field to take off, nor any chance to stop in time. I knew I must crash so I cut off all the switches, held the stick back to try to prevent nosing over, and closed my eyes. When I opened them, I was in a farmer's yard and the nose of my plane was in a chicken coop. Gasoline was all over the plane and I shudder when I think of what a small spark would have done to me. Events are sort of hazy from then until I was back in operations. I went back to the scene this afternoon and the plane is a complete wreck. The whole fuselage is torn and twisted, both wings are broken, the prop is wrapped around the engine, I lost both wheels when I hit the embankment, demolished the tail on a stump and squashed about 150 gallons of gasoline under the wings. So you see what I mean when I say I'm lucky to be alive tonight.

Now I shall try to describe my reactions. When I realized that it was inevitable that I crash, I did everything possible to save my neck, and resigned myself to my fate. Either I'm too crazy to be scared or else I haven't any nerves, because I wasn't in the least bit scared. When I closed my eyes, (I didn't want to see it coming) I said to myself "This is it, El, and there's nothing you can do about it. If the Lord wants you, he'll take you, if not, you'll come out all-right." Then, I swore softly to myself and felt badly because I thought I'd never see you again, and this was my last thought till the plane came to a screeching halt and I opened my eyes.

This had a funny side to it. When I collected my wits and started to open the canopy, I looked out to where my left wing should have been and there were two English farmers just standing there looking at me. Finally one of them took a step forward and said "I say, can we do anything?" As I sat there in that cockpit expecting the gas fumes to explode any second, I couldn't help but laugh to myself.

I don't feel like writing this whole story again, so would you tell the folks. And you and the folks can cease worrying. God is taking care of your husband and their son. It really gave me a good feeling when I found I could face death without fear. This may sound melodramatic but you can't realize, as a matter of fact neither can I, how close I came to getting it.

I'm going to bed darling. It's been a big day.

Your loving husband, El

March 19, 1944 – German forces occupy Hungary

Virginia – March 20, 1944 9:50 p.m.

Dearest—

Honey, today is some kind of occasion because I got my first byline
with my new name!
So you can see it in print—and maybe feel as good about it as I
did—I'll enclose it.

Driving over to Simonson's [the subject of her interview]
to get some pictures, I was tremendously alive to the spring-like
warmth, blue sky, and almost audible growth of grass and flowers.
It was a swell day to be starting out somewhere wild (natural,
I mean) with you. Then a couple of Thunderbolts came batting
across the light blue, fast, sure, and practically singing of power
and freedom. So help me, darling, at that moment I could hardly
stand the loneliness, the deep longing for you inside me. I actually
groaned aloud, as if in some kind of pain, and shifted into second
with a fury, trying to help my spirit get away, somewhere, closer
to yours. That's the way I feel all the time, darling, but it's only
now and then that I can catch it, see it as it is, with causes and
effects. Most of the time I keep it smothered, about to burst, inside,
because I'd probably go nuts if I didn't.

Darling, I love you, lieutenant, and will always,

Yours, completely, Ginny

Elmer – March 22, 1944 7:30 p.m.

My Dearest—

I haven't written in about four days. Since my accident as a matter
of fact, but I've been somewhat busy and somewhat taking it easy.
I was busy making out accident reports and answering questions to

an investigating committee. Final decree hasn't been passed down yet but the major says I'll be charged with 50% pilot error. This may sound bad but it's not. It is very seldom that a committee ever passes any decision but 100% pilot error. Major MacWerter the CO still can't believe I did it on take off and am still alive to tell it.

Stewart Sullivan

We got a bad break on our flight yesterday. "Things must come to a screeching halt" [Stewart] Sullivan and "Pappy" Watkins collided in mid air and both went in without a chance. Watkins was one of the new boys in the flight. He was married and had a baby boy. That makes four men we lost out of our original flight of nine. The rest of my time being busy was packing up their belongings to send home. Haven't been busy flying; I was grounded until today for the investigation. I won't be flying tomorrow either. I am airdrome officer for the day.

I haven't said it yet, but you know I'm thinking about you all the time, dearest.

"Pappy" Watkins

All my love, El

Elmer – March 22, 1944 9:00 p.m.

Dear Mom and Dad—

We had quite a raid last night. I went to sleep just about the same time as the air raid siren blew. About an hour later I was rudely awaken by a helluvan explosion which damned near blew me out of bed. I thought the Jerries were bombing our base, but it was a German bomber that was shot down with all its bombs about three miles away. It was quite a show, but they've become so common around here, that I didn't even bother to get out of bed.

Gotta hit the hay now. I'm airdrome officer tomorrow and I have to be wide awake.

Your loving son, El

Virginia – March 22, 1944 10:00 a.m.
[a workday, but she's home with a cold]

My dearest—

Feels peculiar to be writing at this hour. Usually when I'm writing to you, you're asleep, but now maybe you're flying—over Germany perhaps. Anyway, I think you'll be able to hear me better now, since you're awake as I write!

Seriously, darling, except for not saying whether or not you've been in combat yet—and I take it you haven't or you would have told me about it—your letters are wonderful. I love to hear the stories of combat, of just plain flying, and colorful incidents that happen on the post. You tell them so well, and it makes me feel so much closer to you—almost as if you were telling me "what happened today" back in Winter Haven. Gee, by all means keep it up. That most recent long letter, with the stories the other boys told of the raid, was swell. It made me feel less like I was missing out on all you're experiencing. And always your stories give me such a thrill because they're so thoroughly air corpsish—colorful, spirited. I'm so proud of you and the whole damn branch!! The recruiting service could use me!!

Always yours—Ginny

Elmer – March 24, 1944 7:15 p.m.

My Dearest—

We have acquired a radio in our barracks and the differences between European and American broadcasts are amazing. First of all there is no advertising over here and their planning (or lack of it) of programs is so different. They just seem to amble on playing music or announcing news or whatever comes into their heads. Being so close to the continent, we can pick up German broadcasts as easily as British ones. No doubt you have heard of Lord Haw Haw [English-language Nazi propagandist]. We listen to him regularly and also to news bulletins put out by the "German Supreme Command" in English. They really must think the Allies are a bunch of morons to believe some of the things they say. My favorite expression of theirs is—"On the Eastern front our troops are carrying out an effective disengagement with the enemy." Some days, when we darken the German skies with great masses of bombers, the German radio will report it thusly, "This morning a few allied nuisance raids dropped bombs on targets in the Berlin area." Very humorous. Another thing I get a great kick out of is German swing. It's amazing what a few kraut-heads can do to ordinary musical instruments. Sounds like a mixture of Early American Jazz, a military march and a Bavarian folk-song.

If you are like me, no matter how interesting a letter may be, the best part is when you express your love for me.

Your loving husband, always, Elmer

Virginia – March 26, 1944 8:20 p.m.

My darling—

The pilot's wife is tired, but good and. Yesterday and today have been beautiful days, speaking in meteorological terms,—warmish and clear and hinting of spring, complete with buds, green grass, and flowers. And yesterday the weather got the best of me. I came home from work, stood outside and breathed a couple of times, and then's when it happened. Hardly gave myself time to eat lunch before I was garbed in slacks and suede jacket *and* spade. So all afternoon I battled bushes—the ramblers on the side of the garage, and that *huge* forsythia bush.

Now, after all the back-breaking labor, I hope the young hellions who pass here daily will agree to leave things in the ground. I have vowed to frighten or beat them off, whenever possible. And I guess I'll have to. I'd no sooner completed the planting when 3 little darlings came by, sampling each shoot—thinking, I believe, about whether it would be more effective to pull them out all at once, quickly, or slowly tromp and taunt them to death. I bellowed viciously at them, with full intent to kill, and they retreated. But the looks in their eyes gave me a very uneasy feeling. My only hope lies in the hardiness of the plant. If they grow, it will be through their own strength, and no help of the passersby.

As I started to say, honey, I've been missing you like hell, darling, and I don't know how—if this is a sample of what all the coming days will be like—I'll be able to stand it without becoming crazy, alcoholic, or slightly queer. What I mean is—the weather is warm and pleasant, and I dream of how nice it would be if you were walking with me; I'm trying to keep busy, digging in the garden, and the planes roar over me all afternoon, filling me with a longing to fly but more than that, it's a longing for you, because with you close to me, I can fly with you; I come inside, tired, but still ready to burst with this deep, unabating desire, and turn on the radio—"Bewitched, Bothered & Bewildered" taunts me further.

You do know it, very definitely, don't you dearest?—How very much I love you?

Always, Ginny

Elmer – March 28, 1944 7:45 p.m.

My Dearest—

First of all I will answer your question as to whether I think you should try to get sent to England with the O.W.I. When I first read of your idea, I became all enthused and it seemed like a wonderful setup. Now after I have thought it all out in a serious and practical light, I see it wouldn't work; for many reasons.

First of all I don't know how often I could see you. If I stayed where I am, and you were in London I could see you two days a week at most. But I am moving in the near future and will doubtless be further from London. Then too with an invasion imminent [It was clear England was gearing up for D-Day.], who knows how long I'll be in this country.

Secondly, this country has felt the pinch of war much more than ours, and even in a big city like London, life, even at its best can't at all compare with life in the states. There is plenty of food but there isn't the variety or quality that we have at home. No fresh fruit, or milk, no eggs, no white bread, etc., things you take for granted back home. Summing the second point up, I wouldn't want my wife living under wartime conditions when she didn't have to.

Thirdly, I think you would worry more about me if you were over here. If I were late for a meeting I can see you suspecting everything. And when we parted each weekend we both would be wondering if it would be our last meeting. Just imagine the strain it would put us both under! I know I would worry about you if you were in London, far from all your relatives and friends, and in a strange city. Let me cite one example. A friend of Bill Bullard's was a co-pilot on a B-17. Whether by accident or arrangement, this fellow's sister, a W.A.A.C., was stationed in London. Day before yesterday, Bill and I took a cross country to this guy's base, just for a visit, only to find he failed to return from a mission two days before. Just imagine how tough it must be on that fellow's sister, over here, all alone, when she should be home comforting and getting comfort from his folks. Not a very pretty picture.

Lastly, because of worry and thinking about seeing each other all the time, I doubt very much if we could do justice to our respective jobs. I know I couldn't. Flying over here isn't like flying back in Florida. Darling, I made this so long-winded because I want you to fully realize why, although I hate to do it, I must say, "no, I don't want you to come over here." Ginny, dear, the one thing I want in the world is to be with you, to take you into my arms again, but under such adverse conditions, I doubt if it would be the best thing for both of us.

Got a letter from Charlie Simonson [flying buddy from Long Island] today. He is over at another 51 base not far from here. Some time after Easter when I fall *off* the wagon again we're going to get together and go on a roaring bender. He was assigned to a reconnaissance outfit and had to buy his way back into a fighting group. Paid $160.00 to a guy to take his place.

Now to talk about myself for a while. You keep saying how proud you are of me. As yet I haven't done anything to be proud of. I'm the only one in the squadron who hasn't any combat time at all. Since that accident the doc thinks my nerves have been a little too ragged for combat flying. However Ben Pollard says I'll be on the next mission or the one after that, and I promise to let you know as soon as possible, when to be proud of me.

Honey I got your letter of the 11th today, with the picture of you in front of a Gin-mill enclosed. I think I recognize that joint. It's on 7th avenue between 34th and 35th streets, name of "Commuter's Bar & Grill." Tell me if I'm right.

Now this is going to sound like a cross between a Dutch Uncle, a Puritanical Father and a W.C.T.U. [Women's Christian

Temperance Union] devotee, but frankly honey, I don't like the sight of an unescorted woman in a barroom. I may sound old fashioned on this point and probably am, but I still think it's not quite the thing. My mother has done it with her bridge club and I know you do it, all of which proves to me how harmless it is, but I still can't bring myself to call it proper. Since I started making the rounds with the boys a few years ago, I've been in quite a few gin mills; some of the best, some of the worst and have seen all sorts of unescorted women in them; some of the best and some of the worst, and never, in any case has it appealed to me. There! It's off my chest. You'll probably be somewhat angry, but darling, if I didn't love you so terribly much I wouldn't have said anything.

And I do love you darling. All my life I have been sorta self-centered and had been living for El mostly. Now all that has changed. I don't give a damn about myself, but live for you and you alone. Darling, I would do anything in the world to make you happy, and if the Lord sees fit to let me come home from this war, the happiness in the rest of my life will come from trying to make your life happier.

I want you so, darling, El

Virginia – March 30, 1944 8:45 p.m.

My dearest—

No mail in more than a week, but Rosey [squadron mate Joe Santarlasci's wife] hasn't had any either and last night I heard [from a friend] that all mail to & from England has been held up. She heard it on the radio, read it in the Times, and Rosey heard likewise from Mrs. Parker [Pode's mother], so perhaps there's something in it. At any rate, it's made me feel a whole lot better—and your Mom, too, when I told her a while ago.

Your Mom gave me a few twigs from Uncle Jim's peach & apple tree last Sunday and the apple blossoms are out now. They're so dainty, in color and odor. Wish we had some fruit trees in our yard. We'll have fruit trees in our yard some day, honey, won't we?

In case you've forgotten since I told you three minutes (reading time) back, I love you, darling.

Ginny

Virginia – April 2, 1944 3:25 p.m.
[returning on the train from a reunion weekend in Syracuse]

Dearest El—

Dean Hilton (Miss H. is dean of women here) spoke at the banquet, as is her unalterable custom, and I took great exception to what she said. Talking to all these "outstanding" coeds, she gave them a harangue (I use that term out of bitterness) about women holding their own, getting equal rights in all fields, and forging on ahead to greener fields. It was, in short, a pep talk for the career woman. She said something about their greatest job ahead was to do something big in their field. She didn't mention anything about women's truly important job, the job nobody else can do, and the job that's capable of bringing them the greatest real power and greatness—the job of being good wives and mothers.

From all the talk that's heard now about juvenile delinquency—and although it's played up a lot, too damn much of it is true. I think the home as an institution must really be going to hell in this country. There seems to be a great shortage of skilled mothers and homemakers. They've all transferred to other, more glamorous branches of the service.

Sound like a grandmother—or a gal who herself didn't want to do something on her own hook. You know that's not true. I still hope to write something someday beside newspaper stuff. But I hope I'll never get to thinking that my most important job here is making a name or money. If you ever see me getting that way, refer me to this, or just bat my ears back. It would be justifiable wife-beating, honey, if ever anything is. More than anything else, darling, I want to be a good wife to you and a good mother to our children.

Having polished off that subject pretty well for today, I might get on with the weekend.

Yours—Ginny

Elmer – April 2, 1944 10:30 p.m.

My Dearest—

It's been a few nights since I've written, but so much has happened, I am still not thinking straight. The good news of my flying my first combat mission yesterday is overshadowed by some news that still has me dazed and I still can't believe. "Pode" went in day before yesterday.

I was listening in on the radio in the tower when the rest of his flight reported what happened. I'm sorry but I'm not permitted to divulge details. It was quick and he never knew what hit him.

[His fuel load wasn't balanced properly, so when he pulled out of a steep dive, the plane broke in half.] I would appreciate it if you wouldn't offer your condolences to his family until you are sure the War Dept. has notified them. Joe and I are going to his funeral day after tomorrow and we'll write his folks and tell them about it, but neither of us will write for a  week or ten days just to make sure. Boy, I thought I was hardened to this sort of thing, but when I heard about it, I went off in a corner and bawled like a baby. When it's acquaintances, you can take it, but when it's your close friends get it, it's a little different.

Yes, I've been on a combat mission. No doubt the papers carry an account of what raid took place on April 1st, so you'll know where I went. Later on I'll write a long letter describing the whole thing, but I don't feel much like writing now.

Honey, I haven't written to my folks in a few days. Will you tell them I got the big box of candy & nuts and thank them.

I love you Ginny, El

April 4, 1944 – General Charles de Gaulle takes command of all Free French forces

---

Elmer – April 5, 1944 8:30 p.m.

My Dearest—

Joe and I went to Pode's funeral yesterday. (Again, I ask you to save your condolences until you know that his parents have been notified, I shouldn't write so soon after it happened.) It was a nice funeral as funerals go. The cemetery is located on the side of a hill overlooking a vast expanse of beautiful English countryside. The ceremony was short and simple. A short talk by a chaplain, a volley of three rounds from the honor guard and taps. Very impressive. When this first happened, I was bitter and felt lousy that a good guy like him should get it when there are so many heels left around. (That's why I haven't written you in so long, I couldn't write in such a rebellious mood). However after thinking things out I realize that the Lord must have wanted him for something and his death fitted into a scheme of things beyond the scope of the best of us. I miss him, but I don't feel bad about it anymore; just an awful lot of pity for his folks and Nella [Pode's fiancée].

Lt. Parker, Fighter Pilot, Dies in Crash

BURLINGTON, April 7.—Lieutenant George F. Parker, 22, a fighter pilot with the American Air Forces in England, was killed March 30 in a plane crash. The War Department's notification last night to the parents, Mr. and Mrs. George M. Parker, of Stevens Station, gave no details of the accident.

A graduate of Burlington High School and a former employe of the Florence Pipe Foundry & Machine Company, Lieutenant Parker enlisted in November, 1942. He went overseas last December and participated in a number of combat missions over enemy areas in Europe. He was engaged to Miss Nella McNally, of Burlington.

I was going to tell you about the mission Saturday. Briefing was extremely early, so we knew it was to be a long mission. I flew Ben Pollard's wing and Asbury and Bullard made up the other element in the flight. The take-off was on schedule and the trip over the channel was uneventful. We came to the rendezvous spot on time and there wasn't a sign of the bombers. After about five minutes of circling they appeared, hundreds of B-24's, glistening in the sun and headed south. This was strange because we were already in S.W. Germany and the target area was north. We escorted them for a while and presently the Swiss Alps were rising above us and the Swiss lakes were sparkling below. I guess the bombers were lost and here they found their position for we headed northwest and somewhat later they started on a bombing run. The group we were protecting were not the ones that bombed Switzerland, I know, but they might easily have been. [The accidental bombing of Schaffhausen, Switzerland by Allied aircraft on April 1, 1944 destroyed large parts of the city. Fifty people were killed and some 270 injured.]

The most awe inspiring sight I know is to witness from about 25,000 feet, the bombing of a large city. I was flying in a position where I could watch the whole show. First the lead ship signals that this is the run; the bomb bay doors open and what seems to be ages later, tiny flashes appear on the toy town below. Almost immediately these flashes bloom into puffs of smoke and soon the whole town is obliterated. This may sound ruthless but I feel good inside knowing that somewhere far below a factory, that has been manufacturing war material to keep me away from you, has received a major setback. We escorted the bombers halfway back across the continent and then were relieved by another fighter group. You should have heard the boys grumble when we got home. It was the longest mission (in actual flying time, not distance, our outfit has been to Berlin) our group has ever flown and we were mighty pissed off because no one had so much as seen an enemy fighter. You can't imagine what sitting cramped up in a fighter for a couple of hours can do to you. Without a bit of exaggeration, I couldn't walk for ten minutes after I landed. My legs were actually paralyzed from poor circulation, cold, and working rudders. They're good as new in 15 or twenty minutes though.

It's getting late and I've about run out of paper. Room enough to say I love you Dearest—El

Virginia – April 6, 1944 9:00 p.m.

My darling,

It's hard to tell you how I feel. Today, at last, I got your letter of the 18th, telling me about the accident. [She got mail *referring* to Elmer's accident *before* the letter describing it.] Calling it by such a simple name as *accident* seems like an awful understatement. Of course, from things you said in later letters (which I got first) I knew it was no wing tip you got, but even then, realizing it must have been serious, I found your complete description a shock. Oh, darling, I can't tell you how I feel! It's the delayed reaction kind of thing. To say how thankful I am for your safety seems silly.

So I keep telling you all those details, leading up to my receiving the letter you wrote March 18, but when I get to tell you what I thought, it's almost impossible. Perhaps, if it's even *slightly* possible, I feel something of your feelings—great wonder at your escaping unhurt (entirely?) and deep thankfulness to the good Lord for what was a near miracle. Dearest, you must know how I love you, and this thing makes me feel the way I might had someone snatched you away from me for a second, but definitely away from me, then returned you, safe. I know it sounds impossible—(2½ weeks later!) but I'm stunned. Only certain thought in my mind is that God certainly was with you. Prayers for you were answered, but I feel that I now owe the Almighty an awful lot for what he has done for me—this greatest thing of all, I mean, he has given me in addition to the rest.

I want to know how you are now, how your flying is, and what in hell they mean by charging you with 50% pilot error ?!? I know it's a great concession from the usual "100% pilot error" decision, but exactly where did your "50% error" lie ?? It beats me. Any explanation?

Riding downtown with Marie & Leo Hanning, I told them and Leo said, "His guardian angel is going to be putting in for overtime!" That puts it into words, too! But nothing can explain how I feel entirely. All I can think of is you, as usual, but now with an uneasiness in my heart.

Always yours—Ginny

Virginia – April 7, 1944 8:15 p.m.

My dearest one—

Guess you took one of these weekend pictures the wrong way.
That one of me with "Beer" in the background probably was taken
where you said it was. Frankly, I wouldn't be sure, but we were
walking around that section, so it very likely was the "Commuters'
Bar & Grill" that you recognized. But, honey, we were *not in* the
place! As I recall it, it was a rather dark and dirty-looking gin mill,
and I can see why, if you gathered from the snapshot
that we'd been *in* there, I got that lecture about going
unescorted into bars. Actually, we took that snap plus
the one of Rosey at the door of a bar just to kid you
and Joe. And the one of me made me think of what
you used to say—"My wife is a stew"—that I used to
get such a kick out of, and you always got a comeback
out of.

   Maybe that explains the pictures. About the
lecture in general, though, honey, I was angry about
it, somewhat, as you expected I might be. No, I wasn't
really angry. Slightly annoyed, more amused though,
because of what you evidently understood from that
snapshot. Here's what I think. I can understand why you dislike
the idea of women in bars without escorts. Usually—well, a lot
of them—are there for one purpose—to pick up a man. Not a
pretty thought. But darling, I don't go *often* to bars, escorted or
not, and I don't go then to *any* old bar. In NYC, for instance, with
the gals, we go to someplace like the Hotel Penn cocktail lounge,
which has always been the "correct" place for unescorted women.
Home, here in Hempstead, the only place I've been is Ye Olde
Corner, really a very quiet, neighborhood place, where Marie and
I go, sit at a table, have a couple of beers and talk. There are

usually about six or seven other people in the place—all being very respectable.

So darling, I hope you're not worrying about my behavior. There are *very* few times these days when I *am* escorted (I doubt if you'd *want* me to be with one (escort) more often!) and when I'm not, out somewhere, you can be sure I'm not *looking* for an escort!!! If I were, I've been going to the wrong places!!

If you're afraid what people will think, I have no answer except that I do things the way *I* think is right, and to hell with the neighbors' idea on the subject. That's rather harsh, but I mean it in the sense that "what the neighbors might think" doesn't govern my actions. My conscience is the c.o. and it's still on the job.

You say you've seen some of the worst and some of the best sort of women in "barrooms." I've already said I go to very few "barrooms." Only one I could term thus is the Old Corner. But further, if you are to judge all women by some (majority or minority, I can't say) and their actions, then I can also say I don't like the thought of men in barrooms because I, also, have seen some pretty sad sights with *men* as the disgusting characters. Yes, I suppose that's a silly argument as far as being escorted or unescorted goes, but not in regard merely to *being in* the bars. I hope you understand what I mean. Discussing anything at length by letter is pretty hard.

I'm glad you told me how you feel, honey, but I don't think what I've been doing is wrong. If you do, I disagree, and you'll have to explain further to me why it's so improper—particularly in these times—if you expect me to stop.

Helluva letter this is to my very dearest of husbands. It shouldn't happen—a waste of paper when my love for you is so much more important—but you undoubtedly expected a reply to your mention of the subject.

Yours—Ginny

Virginia – April 10, 1944 10:25 p.m.

Darling—

I can't tell you how bad I felt when Rosey wrote to me that Pode
had been killed. I wanted so to be with you, maybe help you, but
there's nothing to be said now when I'm so far away—from you
and the event itself. I had told Rosey I'd come to Philly this past
weekend, not realizing it was Easter. So, when I finally woke up
to the date, I told her we'd postpone it. She had arranged for us
to go visit Pode's folks, so she called Mrs. Parker Friday morning
to tell her we wouldn't be there. Mrs. Parker's sister answered the
phone and told Rose they'd been notified of the accident—at least
Rose gathered that it happened in an accident and not combat.

I got home from mass Saturday morning and found Rosey's
note—and it almost floored me. Every day I read of some poor
boy's death and wince inwardly, though I don't know them all. But
I couldn't take this. Tears don't help the dead, but they help the
living sometimes. I wasn't very close to Pode, as a friend, I mean,
and never knew him as well as you, but darling, if hearts crack
in sorrow, mine is for Pode's death. I can't believe it—death of
someone at all close never seems possible—but I can imagine how
terrible you boys, who knew him well, must still feel.

I wanted to know more about it, but if you can't tell me,
that's that. I hope you can tell his parents. I've often wondered
whether the boys in his flight could write details to the parents of
someone killed. Seems to me little enough that can be done. A
telegram is brutally brief.

Between Pode's death and your accident, I've been definitely
down in the dumps. My "No worrying" spirit has had an awful big
slice taken out by these events, and I can't help it. Nothing but time
will heal these bruises—time and your return.

I won't dwell on this subject—although ever since Saturday
morning Pode's face has been in my mind—the way that one lock

of hair fell over his forehead and his rosy cheeks—Joe's kidding, calling him "Pretty"—that time he sat brooding over his drink at the officers' lounge at Winter Haven—when we all sang ourselves hoarse coming up from W.H. to Tallahassee and Pode wouldn't buy gas—oh my darling, everything is so clear and the life in him so very sharp in my memory that death seems an impossibility.— oh my darling, you know how I feel. I hope I haven't made it worse by writing these things I'm thinking and *thinking*. If we were together I would tell you. But letters, coming so long afterwards, sometimes do more harm than good.—I'm going to have a mass said for Pode and will send his parents a sympathy card and the mass card from us. Is there anything else you want me to do? Also, when I visit Rose this weekend, we'll go see Mrs. Parker, although that's a task I don't look forward to, because I'm not sure I can do her any good since I've never met her. But we'll go nevertheless.

Oh darling I wish I could do something or say something or write something that would be a gift to Pode. I'll try. I wish you were here to help me.

Nothing seems very important compared to this topic. I can only think of the news of Norm's heroism, and he's being recommended for the Soldiers' Medal for rescue work in a burning bomber. It did my heart good to hear about it—and my heart, these days, could stand much more of such goodness. By the way, I didn't tell your mother about Pode. If she knew him at all, it would be tough, and if she didn't it would make

To Get Medal

SGT. NORMAN HILMAR

NORMAN HILMAR CITED FOR MEDAL

Hempstead Sergeant In The Aleutians Aided Plane's Trapped

Sergeant Norman Hilmar, 22, 14 Seaman avenue, Hempstead, has been recommended for the Soldier's Medal for heroic action in the Aleutians. Two others, one of whom was killed, have also been recommended for the medal.

Pulled Injured From Plane

The action happened at an advanced Aleutian base when a Liberator bomber was caught in a gust of wind as it was taking off and got out of control and rolled down a stony hillside. Halfway down a 500-pound bomb broke from the bomb rack and exploded.

her worry. I told Pop, but unless you mention it in your letters home (as perhaps you already have) [he didn't] I won't tell her about it.—After saying that, about keeping something from your Mom, I suppose this will sound unfair, but I don't want you to hesitate to write me all the bad news as well as any good news. If you don't want me to tell anyone, just say so, but darling, I want to be near you. Since I can't be actually, I want to be in spirit. Your letters— with as much of you and your daily life in them as possible—are the only things that keep me close to you.

How can I tell you how terribly I want you, how very much I love you? The love and longing well inside me, but find no outlet on paper.

I'm yours, darling. Ginny

Elmer – April 10, 1944 9:40 p.m.
[heavily censored with a razor blade]

My Darling—

This won't be too long—I'm pretty tired. Made two sweeps today. Neither was very long but with briefing for both and preparations, it's been a full day's work. Then too I find I'm scheduled for tomorrow's mission so I really have to get some sleep. Yes, at last my talents are being recognized and my combat time is starting to build up. Just an old fighter pilot from way back. But these missions haven't been without their losses.

[Name excised] failed to return from the mission. No one knows what happened—no one saw him go down. Yesterday [name excised] was forced to bail out over enemy [the rest of this page was completely excised].

Speaking of flak, today I came closer to it than is comfortable and I never want to come any closer. As we left the enemy coast, (Ashbury, Jabara, a new man, Schmitty and Odell as tail end Charlie) we saw that our course took us over a well defended town, so we altered course and made landfall out over countryside. About two miles at sea, when we thought we were safe, the stuff broke so close in front of our prop spinner that we could hear it explode and we flew through the dirty black smoke it makes. Didn't last long, but when we landed, Asbury's ship had a foot long hole in the wing and Schmitty had a hole in the air scoop.

Well, dearest, I'm getting mighty sleepy, and the sack looks mighty good, despite the fact that you're not sharing it with me.

All my love, El

Virginia – April 11, 1944 12 midnight

Dearest—

I was awfully glad, and very interested, to hear about your first combat mission. *Escorting*, now wasn't it?? No further comment about this from here. You can enlarge on your earlier theory of different type missions if you will. (Hyuh, hyuh!) But that's an aside, really, darling. It was fascinating to read your letter. You do so well at making me feel near you on this combat job.

But in reference to my being proud of you before you'd been on combat missions: dearest El, I'm proud of you now, I was proud of you before combat, before overseas duty, before your being commissioned, before any army service at all. I have always been proud of you as a most wonderful man, a sincerely fine person, and always will be so. The additional greatnesses supplement a cup already overflowing. There is nothing I can remember your doing, ever, that detracted from that respect for you, nor will there be in the future. So don't ask me to be proud of my husband for a certain time, for one single thing. You are already the most wonderful man in the world, in my mind as well as in my heart, and every day, by things you do and say and think, I am assured that this is true and not only a wife's opinion.

For you, darling, always—Ginny

Virginia – April 12, 1944 9:50 p.m.

My little boy—

I love you. I love you. I love you. And you can keep saying that Ginny loves El until it rings in your ears. That's what I'd like. No chance for you to forget for even a second. BUT, don't let me sit around on your shoulders in combat, heckling you or taking your mind off the big thing—doing your job and keeping a whole hide. I love you *and* I want you back. Ya hear? I'll kiss you goodbye at the flight line and wait for you there. Always come back to me there, though, and I promise not to haunt you at work. Not even a short buzz on the telepathic phone.

Your loving wife—Ginny

Elmer – April 12, 1944 9:30 p.m.

My Dearest—

Up until today, when the weather closed in, I've been flying every day, for a goodly number of days. All combat missions too. Yes, I'm quite a veteran now. But so much flying takes something out of you, and lately, when intelligence finished their interrogation, I've been eating and flopping into bed.

I have some good news. First of all I have my own ship now!
Yep, a beautiful new silver job. Gee, it's pretty. Honey, I can't get
anyone who knows how to paint a skunk for "Skunk and Soda"
[what they called scotch and soda] so I was thinking of naming the
ship "El's Belle." If you don't like it or you really want "Skunk and
Soda" let me know immediately and I'll change it. Another hunk
of good news. When I came down from a mission yesterday I was
notified that I had been appointed Asst. Squadron Operations
Officer. It's quite a responsible job, I guess, and I can't see why
they chose me over a bunch of guys who have been with the
squadron since it formed. Guess no one wanted the job. Seriously
though, I have a lot more confidence in my flying than I had
before. For instance, day before yesterday we started on a mission.
"C" flight included Lt. Robertson (our new flight leader) Clark,
Bullard and Odell as tail end Charlie. We ran into overcast at
6,000 feet and didn't break out until 28,000 feet. When we got on
the ground, Robertson had nothing but praise for and amazement
at my ability to hold number four position through 22,000 feet of
overcast, on instruments. I didn't think it was so hard but the other
fellows in the flight thought it was quite a feat. More about the
mission though. At about 18 thousand, Bullard's engine developed
trouble and he couldn't keep up, so we lost the rest. When we
broke out, there wasn't a ship in sight. The whole group was
scattered so the mission was called off. Our field was socked in so
Bill and I let down through the stuff and got a heading to another
field. I landed first cause Bill had to drop his tanks. The only way
I knew where the runway was, was by flares that control was
shooting through the fog. I never want to make another landing
like that one. When I got on the ground, I couldn't see the other
side of the runway and a truck had to lead me to the parking area.
It was so bad when I landed they wouldn't let Bill land, but sent
him up north. When he got back, he congratulated me on being

able to fly his wing through that stuff, especially when he had a bad engine. Made me feel good.

All my love, El

April 15, 1944 – Royal Air Force and US bombers attack the Ploesti oil fields in Romania

---

Virginia – April 15, 1944 7:35 p.m.

Darling—

Got here about 6 yesterday (Friday) and, after supper we went into Philadelphia and took the bus to Burlington [New Jersey]. Nella and Mr. Parker met us and drove us to Pode's home—a very nice home. Mrs. Parker was feeling better, but you can imagine how they both must feel, losing their only child. I feel worse for Mr. Parker, (He's a very nice person—as is his wife.) because a man has to take it, can't break down and release his grief. He usually has to stand it and help his wife. Nella seemed to be all right and getting over it. She too is helping Mrs. Parker, who, though she tried to get interested in us, appeared listless and still somewhat dazed.

We got there late. They asked us to stay for the weekend, but we hadn't realized we'd been invited, so weren't prepared. Rose had to work this morning, anyway. But they asked us to come again to stay for the weekend, and we'd like to. I imagine it will help Mrs. Parker to have people around, especially those who knew Pode.

At times there were lulls in the conversation, but it wasn't as hard as I expected it to be. Both Rose and I told them all we knew about it. They'd been informed he died of a fractured skull—and at Mistley [a village in southern England near where they were based]. They were afraid he'd lingered in a hospital for a while, so I told them what you'd told me—that it was quick. They were also glad to hear about his burial. Mr. Parker said after the war they're going to England to bring his body home [which they did]. I know you'll write them all these details and they'll be *very* glad to hear anything you can tell them—if he was in a hospital at all, if he was badly injured, and everything else. As you can imagine, every little bit of information is a help to them. And perhaps you can tell them some incidents concerning Pode that will please them. They talk of the little things, remembering him, fondling the memories, and more bits of his life, in England particularly, will give them at least a little comfort.

I noticed Nella wore a diamond on her third, left, but I didn't know she & Pode were engaged. Were they? I don't like to ask.

Oh, sweetheart, I want you and love you! Can you feel this yearning over there? It's strong enough, I'm sure.

I love you, El darling.Ginny

Elmer – April 18, 1944 9:30 p.m.

My Dearest—

Had to abort from a mission today, and in my own airplane too! Got about halfway across the North Sea at about 15,000 feet when oil started pouring all over the canopy. I had to land with my head out the window so I could see where I was going.

It was a beautiful day in England today. Pawlak and I took a walk in the country. Should have seen us, flying jackets and caps baggy pants, no ties, G.I. shoes and a trench knife on our belts.

After we got tired of walking, we hitched a ride on an army truck into town and spent the afternoon dodging M.P.'s. Slightly out of uniform, you know. But I was talking about the English countryside. We have a wonderful view from where we are. Boids is continually singing and everything is green. Daffodils and other kinds of flowers which I don't know the name of, is blooming all over the place. Many farmers have sheep around here and all the momma sheep have little sheeps which frolic in the afternoon. All is quiet and serene. Spring has come to the E.T.O.!!

It's even beautiful over Germany. There are some beautiful mountains and rivers in Germany. When I fly over there, it's hard for me to realize that down below there are thousands of people who hate our guts and we are at war with.

Many times I find myself talking about or to you without even realizing it, and the spell will be broken by someone exclaiming, "Gee, you must love your wife." And I do darling, so much.

All my love, El

April 19, 1944 – Warsaw ghetto uprising begins

Daily Combat

As WINTER TURNED TO spring, and the weather in Europe improved, sporadic raids turned to daily "shows," pilots' slang for missions.

Elmer – April 21, 1944 8:45 p.m.

My Dearest—

If I don't get home before many months pass, the army will have a raving maniac on their hands. No kidding Ginny, when I think of us two, wanting nothing in this world but each other and yet having to be separated for such long periods of time, it makes me see red and I fairly blow my top. Then I tell myself, "El, the Lord is looking down at you and saying, 'there's a lucky fellow, he's found the only girl in the world for him, but he can't have her for nothing, or he wouldn't appreciate her, so I'll just make him work a little for her, then when the war is over and he goes home to her, he'll *really* be happy.'" This makes me feel better and my vision loses its scarlet hue.

Now, I'm going to do a little moralizing. Today, I got your letter dated April 10th, just before I started out on a mission. Needless to say, it didn't exactly bolster my morale any at all. Not because it started me worrying about my own neck, or because

377

it made me think of poor Pode, (that subject is a closed chapter), but because reading your letter I realized that you had been hurt and stunned by Pode's death. That is what makes me feel bad; when I know you're not happy. Your happiness is all that matters to me. You may think me hard and brutal by that parenthesis two sentences back. That's not the case at all. Pode was the best friend I ever made in the army, and for a short while after his death I felt crushed and nothing seemed worthwhile, in a world where such good fellows as Pode get it. But honey I realize, and you've just got to too, that we're in a bloody war, and good men are getting killed every day, and doubtless they all have good friends here and at home. The only thing we can do is forget deaths as soon as possible and work harder to get this mess over as soon as possible. Of course you're far from the front and don't see death as often as we do, so consequently it's not as easy for you to pass these things off. But you just have to do it if you want any happiness at all, and by the same token, if you want me to have any.

Now we take up the question of Lt. Odell's morale. Let me tell you flatly. My morale is damned good. I have lots of confidence in my plane, my flying, my organization, and most of all in my Lord. I don't worry at all about my life and the only slumps come from little incidents. Don't worry about that accident I had. In my opinion, it was the best thing that could have happened to me. Took a helluva lot of cockiness out of me and made me a much better pilot. As for my morale or nerves, it didn't *affect* them in the least. And you can repeat this paragraph to the folks.

Now a little something for *your* morale. I have finally decided on a fitting name for my airplane. "El's Belle, Ginny" it is going to be, with the "Ginny" in prominence, something like this— *El's Belle, Ginny.* How does it feel to have a ship named after you? And what a ship! It's all silver, trimmed in black. I have my name, my crew chief's and my armorer's names on the side in black and my mission symbols under the side window in black. I have an umbrella for each escort mission, a bomb for each dive bombing mission and a broom for each fighter sweep.

Around the guns I have a black patch trimmed in red and the name will be black, trimmed in red. Really an artistic airplane.

But comes now the big surprise! Yesterday your husband received word that he has been recommended for the "Air Medal" for "valor in flight over enemy territory" or some such rot as that. So has Joe, but don't tell Rosey, maybe he wants to surprise her. Don't tell the folks, either. Let them be surprised. No doubt public relations will send some sort of notification. There, does that help your morale any?

Darling, four pages is about enough for 6¢, so I'll say goodnight for now.

All my love, El

Virginia – April 21, 1944 9:15 p.m.

My darling—

Got your letter of April 10 today, after a week of sweating. But damn it all, I'm mad at the censor. He not only opened it but chopped it indiscriminately so I don't know what two boys were lost—except that one bailed out—nor could I get the sense of what I guess was radio conversation before he bailed out. The eager beaver also cut out where your fighter sweeps were—as if I couldn't refer to the newspaper for that info!

I thought it was funny when I got Norm's beribboned letter, but getting one from you is very different! Your letters with your very interesting stories of post life and combat flying are the only pleasant things in this damn war. Then an eager beaver cuts one up!

I suppose they're getting on the ball because of the coming invasion, but I don't see what harm there was in the things you were saying. I hope you'll tell me the story again, honey, and more important, I hope this doesn't make you stop writing me interesting things. I enjoy your letters so much!

All this grousing—when I really am so glad to have a letter, even a holey one. And thanks for the card showing Westminster Abbey. I'm waiting for pictures of you, though. Any interesting scenery is secondary.

You mentioned your combat time, that it was building up. How's about a regular box score? And what's the squadron's score now?

Darling, you must know, that my heart is full of love for you.

Always yours—Ginny

Elmer – April 23, 1944 7:30 p.m.

My Darling—

The Ninth Air Force is really putting the "bee" on the 363rd Fighter Group. Man, have we been busy. Yesterday a dive bombing mission in the morning, a fighter sweep in the afternoon. Same thing today. No, no escort! Hyunk, hyunk, hyunk! This in answer to your letter of April 11th. Incidentally, I didn't say I wouldn't be doing any escorting. Only that this wouldn't be the only thing we do.

Was our faces red yesterday. Our flight, Robbie, Deeds, Bullard and Odell as tail end Charlie went screaming down to strafe an airfield in Belgium. As we leveled out to start our run, we could see that the place was deserted and sheep were grazing on the runways. What a laugh!

Honey, I'm enclosing a shot of myself, taken by the squadron intelligence section. Quite the picture! [This is an "escape and evasion" photograph, for use in creating fake civilian IDs if shot down and eluding capture.]

All my love, yours always, El

Virginia – April 23, 1944 10:45 p.m.

My darling—

Dearest, your letter of the 17th got here yesterday, in record time, perhaps in atonement for the long delay the last one met. I was glad to get a letter and *so* pleased about your getting a plane and also the assistant sqdn. Operations officer job!! And hearing that you're "flying right," even getting official nods for your flying, makes me beam like anything.

And "El's Belle" is a very good name for your ship. "Skunk'n Soda" was all right but being as nobody can draw a skunk—and also "El's Belle" is more personal. See that she takes good care of you and vice versa.

Yesterday was full of effort, and as a result, my garden has in it already, onions, peas, carrots, beets, cabbage & broccoli. [This was her "Victory Garden."]

The family doesn't believe I have a job. But when I work Thursday night (from about 9 or 10 to whenever everything's in)

I don't have to go in on Friday or Sat. morning. It's confusing to everyone but me. And don't ask me what I do on the R.S., either. I still don't know. But I guess I'll be a reporter soon. Selective service, I think, has decided to take 26-year-olds now.

Honey, I know how damn tired you must be after flying most of the day. Don't let the thought that I'll worry keep you from getting sleep you need. I like letters but not that much. If it would bring you back sooner or assure me that you *will* come home safe, I'd settle for no mail at all.

I love you, El—Ginny

Elmer – April 25, 1944 2:00 p.m.

My Darling—

There isn't anything new or different going on. Just flying, flying, flying, day after day. I'm really building up the combat time. We've been going on two shows a day for the past two or three days. I'll soon have a cluster for my air medal.

My airplane will be ready for a test hop tomorrow. I just had a new type engine put in it. It's a helluva lot better engine than the old one was. I say old but it really was a new engine. Had the same number of hours as the ship. About a week ago the coolant jacket broke on a pre-flight and ruined the engine. I'll be able to take it on a show day after tomorrow. I'm expecting great things from that "kite," since it has your name on it.

One of our boys was lucky as hell on that show this morning. An ack ack shell hit the drop tank under his wing, and exploded inside the wing. The drop tank fell *off* and the shell tore a hole in the wing about 1 foot in diameter on the bottom, and about three feet in diameter on the top. Completely took out one of his guns and broke the main spar that holds the wing on. It's amazing that the wing didn't fall off.

I dreamt about you last night. Gee, it was wonderful. I could see you as plain as day.

All my love, always, El

Virginia – April 27, 1944 7:15 p.m.

My dearest—

Gadzooks, the air medal already!!! Oh honey, that's wonderful. I was so happy I could have weeped—felt like getting myself a P.A. system, spreading all over Nassau, to tell everybody. Yet you won't even let me tell your folks. O.K. I won't—but if your wife is reported in the papers as having suddenly and inexplicably exploded, you'll know why.

Honey, will you please lemme know when you actually get the medal? And send details—like the c.o.'s name who awards it? I can't stand waiting for public relations to come through—and if I do, Newsday will have it at the same time, and we certainly should beat them on this!!

Jeepers—it's swell! I still wanna know how many missions you have, and how many are necessary to get the air medal. It's five for the big boys [bombers], but is it the same for you "little friends"?

And I'm thrilled at having the "Ginny" added to "El's Belle" for your plane's name. More than I can say. She better take care of you now!!

My morale is fine, darling, and better than ever since your letter today. To take the curse off this short letter, a coupla pitchas of guess who are enclosed.

Always, Your Belle, Ginny

Elmer – May 2, 1944 4:30 p.m.

My Darling—

Before I married you, I heard that a married man did not make a
good combat pilot because he tended to be over-cautious. That is
not the case with me; you and your love has been the only thing
that keeps me going over here.

Would now like to relate to you an incident that happened a
few days ago. Robbie, Odell, Pawlak and Deeds in that order were
flying out over the channel on a routine non-operational flight.
We were about four miles off shore and Robbie had just started a
shallow turn into the element. I glanced over on Robbie's left wing
where two ships were supposed to be. There was nothing there
but a mass of wreckage. Couldn't even recognize anything that
resembled an airplane. Deeds and Pawlak had collided in mid-air.
I cursed softly to myself and said, two good pilots and two ships
gone. As I watched the wreckage fell in a ball and then broke in
two large pieces with bits of flotsam floating down toward the sea.
Then an amazing thing happened. Two parachutes blossomed
from the wreckage. Robbie called into Air Sea Rescue to get a ship
out there. We circled the spot, saw the chutes hit the water and the
boys inflate their dinghies and climb aboard. There was a fishing
boat in the vicinity and we guided it to the spot. We saw the boat
pick them up, so we headed home. That afternoon Doc Foster and
I took the ambulance down to pick them up. Deeds got a whopper
of a black eye and Pawlak got a bump on the head. Outside of
that neither was hurt. Their numbers just weren't up, but I shall
always have in my memory the sight of that mass of wreckage
falling earthward.

This morning Robbie, Jabara, Asbury and I were coming
back from a mission and we went down on the deck to strafe
an airfield in Belgium. We took those Heine bastards really by

surprise. Caught a bunch of German soldiers bicycling down a road near the field. When they saw us coming their actions made me bust out laughing. Most of them fell off their bikes and crawled into a ditch. Others fairly flew off the cycles. One unfortunate creature couldn't find a place to hide and took off across a field like a shot. I was so low I almost hit a truck watching these guys. Some fun.

Well dearest, I have to get some chow.

All my love, El

Elmer – May 4, 1944 4:05 p.m.

My Darling—

Got three letters from you this morning! Wonderful, absolutely wonderful They came at the right time too. I was glum because I had to abort from a trip to Berlin. Seems like I got way out in the middle of the North Sea and my engine quit completely. I lost about five thousand feet of altitude and 11 years of my life before I got it started again. Sure would like to have gone on that show.

Darling, I'll have to cut this short. I'm writing this down at operations and I have quite a bit of work to do.

All my love, always, El

Virginia – May 7, 1944 9:45 p.m.

Jeepers, honey, but today was a gorgeous day. I want you to see such lovely days, and even if England is beautiful in the spring, it can't compare to the splendor of Long Island, familiar places magically changed from drab winter appearance. After a lot of rain, the trees were filmed, just faintly misted over, with pale green. And today all the maples had their small green umbrella buds out, and for the first time this year, the trees cast a solid shadow all around.

Did I tell you that brother, told of your picnic in the chicken coop, was duly impressed and then wrote, "But I wanna know what happened to the chickens?"

The peas are up, onions doing nicely, and today, when Pop brought me a lilac bush & some lily of the valley (from your grandmother's, I think) we discovered that the carrots & beets have pushed through. Feels good to see things growing, I only wish you were here, that it was *our* garden. But that's only a few of the things I wish.

Yours alone, Ginny

Elmer – May 8, 1944 4:15 p.m.

My Dearest—

Took a nice trip yesterday. Bunch of us fellows got up bright and early to go. The scenery was beautiful, the air, fresh and clean, and the sun shining so brightly that it was worth getting up at 6:30 to go. The only trouble was that the people we came in contact with were none too friendly. We went to Berlin.

Today I got your letter of April 21st in answer to the one that was hacked up by the eager censor. Ben Pollard was the one that bailed out over enemy territory and his last words before he left the ship were "I'll see you guys when this thing is over, watch out for the flak." Swell guy. The other fellow that we lost was Jack (I don't like your wife) Wenner.

Again you ask me to ask for something and this time I have
an answer for you. I should like to have a couple of good books.
There must be something interesting on the current best-seller list.
Probably when you get this, you'll say "Hmmm, he can find time
to read, but he can't find time to write to me more often." Simple
explanation.—At night, after I get into the sack, I like to have a
smoke and read for a while. Wonderful way to relax. Makes one
sleep good. Anyway reading material is at a minimum over here
and I find myself browsing through "Better Homes and Gardens"
or "Crocheting Made Easy."

I gotta go get some chow, so I'll kiss you on both cheeks,
then full on those luscious lips of yours and say so long for now.

All my love, El

Virginia – May 8, 1944 9:00 p.m.

My Darling—

This evening I have a hash mark in adhesive tape on my arm. Put
out the service flag mother! I've given my fourth pint to the Red
Cross. (That *pint* doesn't mean rye, either. It's blood to which I
refer!)

The process was as usual. They poked around with the
needle trying to get a good foothold in my thin and cringing vein.
That's usual. They always have trouble finding them—and when
they find 'em, they about as wide as the needle. No cooperation
in the vein department. Then, comme toujours, also, the blood
wunt come out. After several nurses & doctors all taking a turn at
wheedling (by pumping) it shamefacedly (I know it was *red*!—Ooh,
such things I say! If you hear a panther—) came out. At first the

tourniquet was too tight, and I was unable to rumple a tissue in my hand—yes, no strenk. So a doc loosened it. That was that.

But I'm afraid I'm just a sissy. Didn't get faint afterwards. Got up and walked in for coffee under my own steam. But then my head felt like I had it in a steam bath and I took a rain check on the coffee & took a turn on the cot. That was a pretty good deal anyway. Got a ride home.

Meant to tell you that Lou said Mike "hates it"—meaning flying combat, etc. Is this, as I think, just Mike, or do you, too, "hate it?" I realize it's no picnic, you miss home (putting all this mildly), but I had an idea the boys still enjoyed flying, even, combat, and got some excitement, even fun over there. Or am I fubar on this? I'd like to know.

Darling, I wear your wings almost every place but to bed. I love you more than anything else in God's world.

Always yours—Ginny

Elmer – May 9, 1944 8:00 p.m.

My Darling—

I can just see you mumbling to your self when you get this thing. "What the hell is this? Now comes it tripewritten letters from my man." I know that you feel the same way I do about getting typewritten sheets from my love, so now comes an explanation. Seems that in my job as ass't ops officer, a lot of typing is necessary, and since it takes up time to get the clerks to do it, I decided to learn it myself. Just wrote to my folks this way and the results were not too bad. As a matter of fact I am already beginning to pride myself on my typing. So I hope that you won't mind getting a letter now and then that is not written in my very illegible longhand.

Now for the events of the day. This morning we went on a very uneventful, but none the less enjoyable show. Escorting Liberators [B-24's] this time. I say it was enjoyable because I was really in the mood for flying, but something happened that wasn't so enjoyable. The bombers had just finished their run over the target and were just pulling away from the area, when we noticed one of them pull away from the formation and head off on a tangent. He must have been hit by flak, (there was a lot of it in the area), for as we watched, flames started shooting out all over the place. The next moment he exploded in mid-air and three flaming hunks of what was a beautiful airplane spiraled lackadaisically earthward. The worst part of it is that none of us saw any chutes leave the plane. As I've often maintained,—I really have respect for those bomber boys.

Just turned the radio on and what do I hear but T. Dorsey's "Boogie Woogie". Doggone does that bring back fond memories! Remember the night we were walking back from dinner at the Haven Hotel and the juke box at that sandwich shop on the corner was playing it. Just now as the music stopped, some joker started drooling in German! Imagine! A German station playing "Boogie Woogie".

The fellows are about due back from night flying so I gotta get busy on the amount of flying time they logged, and get the report down to Group. It's ten to eleven already and I've been up since six-thirty this morning. Maybe I'll get to bed by midnight. I'm flying on a long range mission tomorrow, and on the Major's wing.

All my love, always, El

Virginia – May 11, 1944 5:30 p.m.

Darling—

I got a letter from Jack yesterday. He's ferrying still, seeing a lot of ocean, but he said little else about his work. It's obvious that he'd like to be in something more active. Gotta give these boys credit. They do all the dull work, the uninteresting and hard work, with little in return. That is, nobody pays much attention to them, whatever they do. And, say what you will, public acclaim, glory, or what-have-you means a lot in any kind of job.

I wanna know what the hell is the matter with that winged buggy of yours?? Coolant jacket, oil line busts, and now an abortion (yipe!) and from a big B raid too. STINK!! Or do alla boys have as much trouble with their kites off and on? With the name your plane has, I feel partly responsible for her temperament and tantrums!

I forgot to say before, talking about your new engine conking out on the raid May 4 that I don't like the idea at all. Your losing 5,000 feet of altitude is bad enough but the 10 years off your life I don't like *at all*, atall, atall! But seriously, darling, I hope the thing ticks right from now on. I have only one husband, you, and I want only one, you.

Always yours, Ginny

Virginia – May 13, 1944 10:40 p.m.

Dearest one—

I can't say that the weeks haven't sped. It really is almost summer, and perhaps soon it will be fall and then winter and I can hope then, at least, for your return. Can't I?

I knew tonight that summer was knocking on the door. Could even hear it! Coming home I drove into flashes of lightning and booming thunder. *And* the smell. Yes, honey, *Roosevelt* has begun to smell again. So what with the thunder & lightning storm (gee, I love them!), pelting rain, and that lovely stink from the edges of *Roosevelt*, [a running "wrong side of the tracks" joke between them] how could one not help knowing summer is here?

I wuz visiting yore folks for a short time tonight. Doubted if I could get over tomorrow so I took Mom a gift from us for Mother's Day. We gave her a box of Barracini candy and a quart of Schenley's! Fine thing to give your mother—liquor—but it's hard to get, and she likes rye, and I could get some through Charlie, so—mother gets a bottle of rye!! And she certainly ought to get whatever she likes. Darling, she's a wonderful person, a swell mother-in-law (I couldn't want anyone nicer) and I'm one lucky girl. Not only the best man in the world, but undoubtedly the best mother-in-law, too!! All this brought out (into writing) because tomorrow's Mom's day, but that goes for your father, too. They're wonderful, and they make me feel so much at home whenever I'm with them. A lot of people when they marry find they've

also married a family, and aren't particularly happy about the family part of it. But honey, even if the saying weren't true (that you marry the whole family), I'd want it to be so, in the case of a family as nice as yours. It has occurred to me as I write this that I've never before told you how much your mother and father and Evie mean to me. Guess I sort of took it for granted that you knew, since I go over so much

John, Virginia, Evie, and Bud

and have such good times with them. In case you never knew it, though, this is written to make it very definite.

Hardly surprising that your folks are so wonderful though. How could so marvelous a man come from anything but people like yours are?

Oh my darling, you must never go away from me when you come home! Every day, all day long, there are so many beautiful things I want to see with you. Spring, in all its loveliness, is something that makes me feel good inside, and not having you with me to breathe cool morning air that's sweet with the smell of new leaves, the delicate fragrance of apple blossoms and lilacs, to watch the tree break out in pale green after a rain, to see the lawn almost turn green in a day—oh so many wonderful changes that make me sure there's a God, there's good in this world, that life is worth struggling for—and all these things I want to see as I'm standing by your side. All these natural beauties, everything that's clean, good, and beautiful I classify with you.

I'm yours, darling—Ginny

Virginia – May 15, 1944 10:00 p.m.

Darling—

I thought of you so much and so vividly before going to sleep last night, yet I couldn't scrape together even a dream about you! Somebody ought to invent a dream selector—a gadget that would enable you to tune in on dream subjects before retiring, as you would on a radio. Then, If any dreams were in the air (or should I say subconscious mind?), you'd get the kind you wanted.

That collision Deeds & Pawlak had has my mouth hanging open still. It is absolutely *amazing* that they got out with only those injuries, but I suppose it's no more unbelievable than your escape from the chicken coop crash, unhurt. These things always remind me of and emphasize the truth of St. Paul's words in one of his letters: "Oh the depth of the riches, of the wisdom, and of the knowledge of God! How incomprehensible are His judgments, and how unsearchable His ways! For who hath known the mind of the Lord? Or who hath been His counselor? Or who hath first given to Him and recompense shall be made him? For of Him, and by Him, and in Him are all things. To Him be glory forever."

That epistle happened to be the one in the prayers of the mass in the prayer book I was given in 1933. (The epistle changes every Sunday, as does the Gospel and as do a few other prayers of the mass.) I read that prayer book every Sunday for years before the full meaning of those words were understandable. And since that time—I don't remember when it was—when I almost suddenly knew the meaning of those words of St. Paul's letter to the Ephesians, it has been my favorite epistle. Hurry home, sweetheart.

Yours—Ginny

Virginia – May 16, 1944 9:25 p.m.

My darling—

Just heard on the radio what I already read in da newspapers— that Wrigley's gum is going to servicemen only hereafter. Now I'll be forced to get a pass to Mitchel if I want to get you any double mint!

I can't remember if I ever wrote anything to you about your opinion of my travel-to-England idea. Your reasons for answering no weren't surprising. I realize what you said as fact before I wrote, but I still thought being over there, nearer you and certainly a helluva lot nearer the war, would be better than sweating and seemingly doing nothing here at home. So often, darling, I feel so damnably useless, like the parasite, sitting down and living on what so many are fighting for.

Somebody, I tell myself, has to keep the home fires burning, but a small voice asks then if I add any fuel here at home, if the blaze wouldn't be just as bright without me around. And I can't definitely tell myself I *am* any particular cog in this war, at home *or* abroad. This doesn't help the morale.

Anyway, the sum of the whole thing: I respect your judgment, and I haven't done anything more about it. But I think of it, naturally, particularly with continuous talk of invasion, and I think you can understand how I feel.

I love you—Ginny

Virginia – May 17, 1944 10:05 p.m.

My dearest—

Gleeps, you have been convoited! Yes, I said convoited to the use of that vicious weapon, the mill, the machine, the tripewriter! Your letter of May 9, arriving today, was quite usual on the outside, but inside! Who's writing to me disguised as my man? What wolf has usurped my husband's envelope? Whassa score here?

Honey, I like a hand-written letter (from you—it don't matter nohow with anyone else) better'n a typed one, but I don't dislike typed ones in the least. And if using the machine is easier (and gets me more letters!) everything is copasetic that way.

Honey, you oughta see what happens to my disposition on letterful days as compared with letterless ones. Yesterday I came home from work, sans much enthusiasm for anything but seeing if I had any mail from you. Mom said no. First I checked the mail box, then, finding she was right, I returned into the house and started resetting the clocks, all of which stopped and threw up their hands in horror at my lengthy face. Then I proceeded to growl at anyone who was foolish enough to speak to me.

Today, though, I called home to find out what chances of life the mailman had. His hide was saved. Mom said there was a letter from you. Like a lahk, happily, I skipped home; bright like little Miss Sunshine I whipped something into the oven for dinner. I had read a letter from you and you had told me you love me and things were as good as possible (without the one I'm living for). You are my only happiness, I love you, my husband.

Yours—Ginny

May 18, 1944 – Elmer's twenty-second birthday

Elmer – May 18, 1944 3:30 p.m.

My Dearest—

It has been an awfully long time since I last wrote, but I've been pretty doggone busy and in part it has been indirectly your fault. You see, one of my letters to you was censored and the censorship department sent a letter to my C.O. in protest. As a result I have been spending a lot of time in research of army regulations on censorship in preparation to giving a lecture to the squadron. So, darling, I'm going to lean over backwards in my letters to keep out of future trouble and I'm afraid from now on my letters will carry little more than my love for you.

Little bit of good news that I won't be able to go into detail about. Now I have a swastika painted on the side of my ship. Got a Jerry at last! Wish I could tell you more than that. [On a May Thirteenth mission, Elmer had destroyed a Junkers Ju 88 twin engine dive bomber sitting on a runway— obliterating it with machine gun fire.]

Now let me tell you about Teresa. Don't get excited, you don't have a rival, heaven forbid. Teresa is a combination waitress-hostess at a little joint a few of us hang out in when we get to town. She's an Italian woman about forty five years old and she acts like a mother to us. No kidding, she really treats us fine. Every time we go there she invites us to her house for a home cooked meal. We've always declined, because of rationing, but last week-end, we took her up on it. Went to her home in the suburbs for a spaghetti dinner. And what a meal! Started out with a glass of wine, and then gorged ourselves on spaghetti, washed down with pale ale. Then she brings out broiled pork chops and mashed potatoes. Then came dessert of sliced peaches and custard, topped off with a coffee royale. I swear I could hardly move. About an hour later, she insisted we have a cup of tea and a piece of home-made raisin cake. Yes the English (Teresa's married to an English fireman) are a fine people.

I love you so much, Ginny darling. Let's hope and pray we're together on my next birthday.

All my love, for you always, El

Virginia – May 18, 1944 9:10 p.m.

Darling—

The place is the Freeport cop house, I'm waiting for somebody (one of the cops) to come in with info on a drowning this afternoon. You get letters from the damnest places!

Called the first precinct before leaving home. Some guy blew his top in Roosevelt this afternoon—but with a gun. I don't know who yet. Tell you later if I think you might know him.

Jeepers, hey, almost 50 hours combat by May 8! That's good, no? *Now* what I wanna know is, does that 200 and then home still go??

I was shocked to hear that the other fellow lost with Pollard was Johnny Wenner, not only because he was a nice guy but also because just a couple of nights ago I wrote him a V-mail letter, telling him our usual conversation piece, "I don't like you!" When I started to write it, I thought perhaps I shouldn't as you hadn't mentioned him recently and he might have been the one you told

me about in the censored letter. Then I thought that I was getting to be morbid, thinking a guy's dead when I didn't know. Then today your letter (May 8) told me. As I recall, in the censored letter I gathered that Pollard bailed out, but didn't Johnny? Or doesn't anyone know? I'm still hoping that he's all right, hoping that letter won't come back stamped "DECEASED." [He was listed as M.I.A., but presumably killed.]

I love you so much, dearest! Ginny

Virginia – May 26, 1944 1:10 a.m.

Dearest—

At the office, waiting for a final, slow story to come in.

Maybe you're writing to me now. I hope so, even though we shouldn't bote talk ta oncet. I felt worried about you last night, as I was writing to you the announcements of the day's pasting of Germany and the occupied countries came over the radio. It sounded like every flying craft the Allies have went into action, and no small number were lost on the raids. I thought of you in it, all too vividly I thought of it, and I was worried. I hope I can get a letter to make me feel better tomorrow.

You tole me not to worry, honey, when I don't hear from you, but damn it all, I just can't help it. Try to transplant yourself over here with me over there, batting about flak-infested skies, and as you listened to daily (hourly!) reports on the radio about "today's raids, today's losses" and read the papers with figures, pictures, what-not, wouldn't you just now and then be troubled with one or two nasty old worry thoughts? Like I said, darling, I don't wring my hands all day, but when I get home from work and there's no letter—since a week ago, I simply can't be expected to forget it. Long letters from you about what you've been doing are wonderful, but if they can't be long, they'll still be wonderful to me. Three words, plus regulation frills, would mean a lot to me right now. It would be a thought from you, telling me what I most want to hear and letting me know you're all right—or you were a week ago.

The story came in. I must write same. Be back tomorrow.

All my love, darling—Ginny

Elmer – May 27, 1944 12:00 Noon

Dear Mom and Dad:

Got your latest letter just before I started out on a mission. That's the time I like to get letters. When I get a letter at this time, it makes the mission a cinch. I read it sitting in the cockpit of my ship, waiting to start the engine. It was a very nice mission, took a nice trip to Paris. Paris is beautiful in the springtime.

It doesn't seem possible that I'm twenty-two. These past few years of my life have really sped by. When I think of it, it sorta scares me. If the rest of my life goes as fast as the last couple of years, I'll be an old man in no time. You know, I bet that when I get home, you won't recognize me. I am really changing. My hair is falling out at an alarming rate and I'm looking much older. Wearing an oxygen mask on every mission, pulls your face downwards and gives you wrinkles. I went to a dance on my birthday and happened to mention that it was my birthday to a girl that I was dancing with. She asked me how old I was and I told her to guess. See looking at me for a moment or two and then said, "Oh I should say about twenty-six or twenty-seven." I almost fell through the floor, and so did she when I told her I was twenty-two. Just an old fighter pilot from way back.

I'll say so long for now,
with all my love—El

Virginia – May 28, 1944 9:30 a.m.

Darling—

Auntie Anna [Virginia's mother's sister] died early this morning. We were expecting it, praying for it, to relieve her of the agonies she's been suffering for months and months. [She had never recovered from a skiing accident when young.] But it's a little hard anyway. Getting used to an absence is sometimes more difficult than becoming accustomed to a new presence. After 30 years—of course I wouldn't remember all of them—it's hard to rearrange your thinking habits when it's a question of counting noses. She was with us a long time, doing so much for us all those years. Lord knows why she had to suffer the way she did.

Friday afternoon I weeded the garden—much bending from the waist and oh my aching leg muscles!!— I've been weeding, planting, putting down a mulch in the garden, spraying—oh my aching back, what a dead bunny I am!

In addition to working, keeping my mind occupied thoroughly and getting myself filthy dirty, I was acquiring a peachy sunburn on same aching back. Trouble with a garden tan—it's always on the back. Bending over the good earth doesn't allow for a frontal attack by the sun. I'm thinking of working out a system of mirrors, or a clever acrobatic arrangement whereby I can weed with my face up!

Friday night Marie and I roared at Danny Kaye in "Up in Arms" and were much impressed with "Memphis Belle," the story of a Flying Fortress [B-17]. I told you I wanted to see it and it really was wonderful. I realized it before, but this picture brought very vividly to my mind that I—and all other civilians at home—can never know, never really understand what you and the other fliers are experiencing. It doesn't make me happy, either, realizing that there's a big part of your life I'll never be close to or even nearly understand. Maybe it's best that I don't.

Wally sent me an article from a recent Sat Eve Post on women in newspapers. His father (now m.e. of the Phila. Record) was quoted in the article and didn't give much credit to the gals. Wally wants me to write an irate letter or something. I'm working on it, mainly in mind only. I read it and was amused. I failed to get mad. Don't much care what the hell anybody thinks of newspaper women. All I can say is, I'd like to know what they'd do right now without 'em!!

All my love, darling—Ginny

Elmer – May 29, 1944 2:25 p.m.

My Dearest;

You have often expressed a desire to know all my thoughts and reactions while I'm away, so now I'm going to try to tell you how it feels to go into combat. Not so long ago we were on a bomber escort job and somehow or other the squadron got split up and there were only four of us protecting one box of about sixty bombers. Robbie, Schiff, me and Jabara. Suddenly, we saw above us, about twenty 109's stooging up for an attack. The odds were about five to one against us, but our job was to keep them away from the bombers, so we poured on the coal to it and started to pull up to their altitude, to try to break up the attack. I have heard that when you go into combat, you don't have time to be scared. That is so much bull. Never before in my life have I been so scared. My throat went dry, and cold chills went up and down my spine. Then things began to pop. As we went up into them, they broke towards us, and then changed their minds, apparently thinking we would not attack such a large force. I was flying Robbie's wing and had to stay with him, or I probably could have gotten myself one. Robbie picked out one of the lead ones and away we went. (Just got word of another mission this afternoon, and I got a helluva lot to do. So I'll see you later.)

Here I am again and it is now 8:20 p.m. Just got back from a mission and a very good one. Nice and short, and no trouble whatsoever. That's the kind of a mission I like. Well to get back to my story. As we went after the two lead ships, the rest of them broke into us, head on. Boy, if you want a thrill, you should have that happen to you some time. We fired at them, but the rate of closure was so great, that we did no more than scare them. All this time, Robbie was on the tail of a ship, that he was determined to shoot down. The outfit made a circle and came at us again, head on. By this time, my nerves were about shot, but there was nothing for me to do, but to hang on to Robbie's tail and keep it clear of enemy fighters. Just about this time we went into a tight turn, and the number four man spun out, so the number three man joined us and left the ship that he was chasing. For what seemed ages we chase this guy, and the 109's were swarming around. Suddenly out of the corner of my eye, I see a ship coming at me from about 90 degrees, and there was a big black cross on his wing. He slid in astern of me, and I knew I was a gone duck if he stayed there. I was about to call a break, when the Nazi that Robbie was chasing inadvertently saved my life. At this particular time, he decided that he had had enough, and dove for the deck. We went screaming after him, and in this way, I was able to shake the Hun off my tail. Robbie got the one he was after, we saw him bail out, but by the time we caught him, we were far below the scene of action and to try to climb up into that mess would have been suicide, so we headed for home. Out of the mess, we shot down one Nazi and broke up an attack on the bombers, so we considered it a day's work well done. The whole action didn't take more than a couple of minutes, but in that couple of minutes I was really scared. When I got back, I asked the other fellows if they were scared too, thinking that maybe I was a coward or something. But it's a natural reaction, all of them were shaking in their boots.

Incidentally, that guy who spun out, finally got back with us. So now you know what combat really feels like.

I'm getting tired and I'll have to kiss you goodnight for now.

All my love, for you, forever. El

Elmer – May 30, 1944 4:30 p.m.

My Dearest;

If I keep telling you of my close shaves, you will begin to think I am throwing the bull, just a bit, but Darling, everything I say is the gospel truth. Last night I told you how combat felt, now I am going to tell you of another experience of mine. If I have any more close shaves, my nerves won't be worth a damn. You seemed to make quite a fuss over that chicken coop deal, well this was just about ten times as bad. As Joe Santarlasci said when I got back on the ground, "If I were you, I'd stay on the ground after that." I can't tell you the date or the place [May 30th over Berlin], but we were on a bomber escort job deep in enemy territory. We had just met the bombers and had spied a couple of 190's [Focke-Wulf fighters] queuing up on the other side of the big friends [B-17's]. We broke into them, and none of us saw a bunch of them above, that were providing top cover for the ones attacking the bombers. I was tail end Charlie again, and consequently the one to get it first. I don't know what it was that hit me, but suddenly 20 mm shells[from an ME-109] began to explode all over El's Belle Ginny. I started violent evasive action and just at that moment, a shell hit my wing tip and threw me into a spin, at twenty thousand feet. When I finally got the thing under control, I had lost fifteen thousand feet of altitude. Then was when I really got scared. About two feet of my right wing had been blown away and my left horizontal stabilizer was in ribbons. Not only that but I was all by myself and about five hundred miles from home. I headed homeward, hoping that I would not be bounced again, and fervently and shamelessly praying that my ship would hold together. I sorta doubted it because it took all the strength I could muster to keep the doggone ship on an even keel. [He had the control stick jammed all the way over to the left. If he eased up on it at all, the plane would do a snap roll.] About halfway home, my heart sank again. About three miles off to my left, I saw seven 109's in a rat race [holding pattern]. Praying that they did not see me, I dove to the deck. My prayers were answered, and then what seemed like a miracle happened. I heard someone calling me over the radio. It was Robbie, wanting to know my position and if I was all right. I told him what my difficulty was and my geographical position. He came back on the radio and said "Hold on Odee boy, we'll be with you in a jiffy." By maintaining radio contact, I was able to direct him to my position, and sure enough, about three quarters of an hour later I saw three ships approaching from the rear. Robbie, Asbury and Jabara, came up alongside and did slow rolls around me. I was so happy to see them that I almost cried. After that, things went pretty smoothly. When we got back to the field, Robbie called in and had an ambulance and a crash wagon standing by, but they were not necessary. My landing gear wasn't damaged and I made a pretty good landing, everything considered. When I got on the ground, everyone came crowding around. Two majors from the group and my own C.O. were there and offered congratulations for doing a good job in bringing it back. Doc. Foster came roaring out in the ambulance to make sure that I was o.k. I was alright but I was shaking so bad that I could hardly hold a cigarette. [The ground crew patched up the plane, and Elmer flew it a few days later. While making the repairs, the crew discovered a long groove just below the right-hand side of the cockpit, where a German 20-mm shell had ricocheted off. He brought home this piece of the wing as a souvenir.]

All this leads me to one conclusion. God, by getting me out of these scrapes, is proving to me that he is on my side and protecting me from harm. It's a doggone good feeling too, to *know* that he is on your side.

Darling, I have to make up a mission schedule for tomorrow, so I'll kiss you good night for now. Don't worry either, I'm all right.

All my love, always, El

Elmer – June 1, 1944 9:30 p.m.

My Darling Wife—

All I'm going to talk about in this letter is our plans for our post-war world, (if I may borrow an overworked phrase), because that's all I've been thinking about of late. First of all, in one of your recent letters, talking about good times in Tallahassee, you expressed a desire that we might be reckless and crazily carefree for a while after I get back. I was hoping that you would feel that way, for that is what I planned to do for the first couple of months after my return. Just doing what we felt like, going where we felt like and when we felt like and just raising the devil in general and the heck with anything and anybody. During this time we could be sorta planning the immediate future such as finding a place to live until such time when we can build our own home, and finding me a job. Which brings me up to my second daydream. Our life immediately after we pass the rowdy stage. Probably living in a small rented cottage. We will be sorta semi-settled down in this stage. I mean we will start to take on the responsibilities of managing a home and getting a line on what it will be like when we get our own home. I say semi-settled down because I still will feel sorta carefree. You know, jitterbugging at dances and going on an occasional bender. During that period we can be planning on the next phase. Doing things like looking for a good spot to build our dream home and drawing up plans for the house itself. This will take some time because every room, every window, every closet, every foot of wiring will have to suit us both to perfection. After it is built I don't want either of us to say, "darn it, that closet door gets in the way every time I turn around." This home of ours is going to be flawless in every respect. After we get some dough saved up, we'll start the actual building. And what fun that's going to be. I can see us now—pestering carpenters, arguing with architects, cursing contractors. We're going to get our money's worth out of that house. After that stage of our life, when we get our home built and are actually living in it, I think, will be the happiest days of our life. I can see us on a winter night, in front of the fireplace, sipping scotch and sodas and necking, *and* planning a future for our children.

Throughout all this time we will be also having more fun outdoors. Fun shopping for fishing tackle, and guns. (A nice light 16 gauge upland game gun for you. Maybe if you're real good, a 12 gauge duck gun!) I can see us planning weekends—fishing trips to a lake in the Catskills or a pheasant hunt on a brisk October morn. Maybe we'll try skiing and certainly ice-skating in winter. Then in the spring time the flounders and weakfish will be running and the Trout season opens April 1st. It's all going to be

such fun, darling, and only because I'll be doing it with you. You're
not only a wife to me (and the most wonderful wife any man ever
had) but you're also a buddy and a swell one at that.

I get such enjoyment out of merely planning these things.
Just imagine the infinite happiness we'll get out of actually
doing them.

All my love, forever, El

Elmer – June 4, 1944 5:00 p.m.

My Dearest;

Went to church this morning and this being the first Sunday in the
month, I took Communion. I love the Communion service. Every
time I go to church, I come out, feeling a glow inside, but there
is something more inside when I come away from a Communion
service. I don't know how to explain it, but it is as if I suddenly find
something in me that I didn't previously know was there. It's a
doggone good feeling, anyway.

I almost forgot another thing that I am happy about today.
On that mission this afternoon, El's Belle Ginny was up there flying
combat again. With a new wingtip and a new tail, she's as good
as new, if not better. This may seem crazy to you, but it seemed
to me that that ship was glad to be up in the air again. I felt it by
the way she flew. Handled like a baby carriage. I felt as if she was
thanking me for bringing her home that day instead of bailing out
and leaving her to her own devices that day over Germany. And
believe me I was seriously contemplating doing that very thing for
a while there.

Yours forever, El

Virginia – June 4, 1944 10:55 p.m.

My Dearest—

Mary Margaret [another sister] told me of a story that makes me green with envy. Friend of hers was in New York, met a couple of fliers, took them to dinner. They kept looking at their watches. He thought they wanted to get away, so he told them if they had to leave, go ahead. Then they told him that only a few short hours before they were bombing Berlin. Their colonel had given them 48 hours leave, to go to New York, no doubt with a plane flying over here, and they had to return shortly. Why don't you talk to your colonel? ?

At the USO Wednesday night & floated off by myself for awhile. They played Jimmy Dorsey's "Green Eyes" on the radio, and without even closing my dream-filled eyes I was dancing with you at the Point Lookout pavilion. You were in summer worsteds—it was Labor Day last year—and I probably had only that red & white bathing suit on. We'd had a couple of beers, and before that we'd walked to the end of the beach. That was the day I asked, rather told you that you were hungry, and you explained that after nine months in army camps, what else? When I think of you coming home from months overseas—!!!—but, honey, I'll probably bark at you before you so much as growl at me!

Seems very physical to be telling you this so definitely but you must know that I love you completely, darling, and that means with my body, my mind, and my soul.

Adding everyday conversation at this point seems very pointless and trifling.

Honey—I'm punchy. It must be when I can have dreams like that. But when a gal's obsessed with one love, one man, one dream, one hope, all interrelated and dependent upon one another, you can't expect much else. You know what that dream and hope is, who the man is I love so much.

Always yours—Ginny

After D-Day

A T FIRST LIGHT ON June 6, 1944, the amphibious assault on the beaches of Normandy, France marked the main Allied invasion of Europe. And although Germany held out for another eleven months, this spelled the beginning of the end for the Nazis.

Virginia – June 7, 1944 10:30 p.m.

My darling—

What can I say of Tuesday's—yesterday's most important news—invasion? Anything I say is as nothing to what it must be to you. I was getting dressed yesterday morning about 7:45 when I had a phone call. Sleepily, I learned it was Don McCarthy, Lt. AAF. He was on his way to Richmond to fly P-40's, he thought. And he asked about you. I told him I'd heard nothing in a couple of weeks and then he said, "Good news from there this morning" After I'd asked what he meant and he told me, at first I thought he was joking and then I got excited. After the call, I turned the radio on and damn near forgot to get dressed, listening to the reports. I was furious to think that I had been *sleeping*, quietly sleeping in my bed, when these things were happening! And I had been dreaming of crossing bridges—bridge after bridge I crossed in that dream! (You can figure that one out!)

So I went to work, and the sound of the place was wonderful—teletype machines rattling full steam, typewriters pounding just as noisily, nobody talking but everyone busily at work. I was busy too, but disgustingly enough I didn't do one damn word of invasion stuff! By noon, when the paper was gone, I figured I may as well be the janitor around the place for all the use I'd been for Tuesday's paper, carrying the biggest news the world has ever read.

When Greene came back, after lunch, he called me over and said he had something for me to do. "You're the wife of one of the boys over there in this," he said. "Give me about 2 ½ pages of your reactions to the news." I got excited inside, as I do whenever there's something unusual for me to work on, and I told him that it wouldn't be easy. "Of course it won't be easy. I don't give you jobs that are cinches," he answered. So I started thinking about it, in the darker parts of my gray matter, and continued with my routine work, knowing I'd never be able to write such stuff at the office, particularly as he said he wanted it in the first person.

Going home on the bus, I jotted down a few notes for myself, and last night, on that lousy typewriter of ours, I sweated the thing out, wondering if you would mind, wondering how accurate I would be, wondering frankly darling, if you were alive as I wrote. As I told Mr. Greene, it was far from easy. Then this a.m. I handed it to him, telling him I hoped it was something like what he wanted.

When the paper came out I was definitely surprised. I had an idea he'd use a by-line, since it was first person, but had no inkling he would slam it above the flag [the newspaper's nameplate] this way. I was pleased—though I have no reason to be, as I don't know if that had been his plan all along—but I was nervous about it, too. Mostly because I still didn't know how you were (and still don't) or how it would hit you. I'm enclosing it, natcherly, after all this discussion.

Of course it doesn't say everything—or even half of what I feel. You know that. But it was for publication, and I couldn't tell Nassau how I feel about you—for one reason, because I can't even tell you, fully, how much you mean to me. But the people in the office liked it. I hope you do.

Silly, I guess, to write so much about a small thing. It's because this little event is my public part in the biggest news of this and any year, and also because I wanted you to know about the whole thing.

Before writing this thing last night, I'd spent the early evening weeding and watering the garden. My D-day was very eventful!

All my love, Ginny

A Fighter Pilot's Wife Writes Her Invasion Reactions

By VIRGINIA ODELL

Nassau Daily Review-Star

LONG ISLAND'S GREATEST NEWSPAPER

VOL. XLVI. No. 134   HEMPSTEAD TOWN, LONG ISLAND, N. Y.—WEDNESDAY, JUNE 7, 1944   ——PRICE FOUR CENTS

GLIDER-BORNE TROOPS SEIZE KEY POSITIONS AT CHERBOURG

"Not many hours have passed since the start of the Allied invasion of Europe, undoubtedly the greatest military operation of all time. The news quickened the pulse of the nation, put dread fear of the days to come into the hearts of thousands. I am only one among those thousands. My husband is a fighter pilot based in England.

The fear inside me is nothing new. I have almost become used to it, as it's been there since he began flying combat early this year. But as raids over Europe increased in number, grew in size, so grew my tense feeling, and yesterday marked some sort of a climax. Now holding their breath with me are the families of the invading land troops.

What a pilot thinks of "when he's up there in the blue" is definitely not what the song indicates. What a pilot's wife thought of yesterday, when the invasion was announced, is much the same as what she has been thinking every day for months, only more so.

You wonder, for instance, if the armorer for his Mustang fighter plane did a good job when he checked and loaded the guns, and you hope the crew chief continues to be "eager," keeping the ship in perfect operating condition. Then you pray that both your pilot and whoever is flying his wing are on the ball today. It doesn't take long for things to happen when they're flying faster than 400 miles an hour.

As I have wished so many times before, I wished I could be experiencing some of what he has been going through, even though I know that very likely I couldn't take much of it. But yesterday he probably went out on more than one mission. Maybe he was flying just above the armada of landing vessels and then went in "on the deck" to pick out some shore batteries to bomb or a few Nazi air strips to strafe.

Instead of going on a bomber mission or a fighter sweep, he might have been one of the escorting fighters for a group of heavy bombers with a big target to knock out. Or his outfit may have been used in an efficient use of combined operations, with landing vessels and ground troops calling for protection, or asking to have some annoying resistance bombed out.

Whatever it was, I know that he was cramped into the small, hot cockpit of his P-51, and part of the time he was wearing the very important but equally uncomfortable oxygen mask. He was a plenty tired pilot after yesterday's missions. He was tired from straining to spot enemy planes, from concentration on the flight, keeping his plane in tight formation, and tired after the careful calculation required if there was any bombing or strafing to be done.

Despite the very personal interest I have in the invasion force, many other thoughts were in my mind yesterday—thoughts for friends who were in on it, but also for the thousands, strangers to me, who faced dangers and death with them.

I have great faith in the young men, only recently unimportant clerks, delivery boys, students, who are now making the world's history. Taken from ordinary jobs, they are now asked to do the heroic. They are doing just that, daily overcoming tremendous difficulties, making heartbreaking sacrifices, and treating it all as commonplace.

So with the invasion started, my schedule will be the same. I wonder about him, worry about him, write to him. And praying for him, victory and lasting peace, I am assured and comforted by such things as the tremendous roar of friendly bombers making huge shadows over neat neighborhood gardens— Victory gardens."

■

In a note, her city editor wrote, "I liked your story. The introspection which one expects to find dominant in a story of this type benefited from your extraversion, the projection of your thoughts in the direction of Cherbourg. Perhaps as you wrote it you did not realize the literary 'West Wall' you breached successfully—the job of making a civilian's reactions interesting on the military's greatest day."

Elmer – June 8, 1944 "D+2" 7:40 p.m.

My Dearest—

In the light of what has been going on for the past couple of days, I think you will forgive me for not haven't written. We have been on the go continuously for the past seventy-two hours. On the alert continually and grabbing & snatching a bit of sleep when the chance presented itself. Last evening I was scheduled for a mission but I just couldn't make it. Doc. Foster gave me a couple of sleeping tablets and I slept for fifteen hours last night. Now I am fresh as a daisy and ready to go again. I wish I could tell you what I have seen the past day or so. The gigantic size of operations is breath-taking. Anyone who hasn't seen it, just wouldn't believe it.

I wouldn't have missed this show for anything in the world. History is really being made. I'm writing this while waiting for another mission and this little bit of time is exceptional. You will have to get used to not much mail in the next couple of weeks. Every chance I get, I will write, but I'm afraid these chances will be few and far between. However, dearest, know that I will be thinking of you continually in all these operations and working a little bit harder to hasten the day when I'll be coming home to you.

Yesterday I got your semi-typewritten letter with the two pictures in it. Keep those pictures of you in a bathing suit coming. They're good for morale. Why couldn't that have been me sitting

on the warm sands with you, instead of Claire? That other shot of Dad with the new car was good too. He's a swell little guy, isn't he. I never realized how much I liked my Dad until I left him. He's hard to make friends with, and I was never as close to him as I should have been. However I expect to be when I get home. I've got all sorts of plans to take him to ball games and hunting and fishing—the things he likes to do. [His father

was not a demonstrative man, only writing a
handful of letters the entire time Elmer was away,
explaining that Hazel reported all the news and
he had nothing to add. Elmer's mother wrote to
him almost daily, even with little to say.]

Well darling, just got alerted for a mission
so I'll kiss you goodnight for now. Don't worry,
darling.

All my love, for you, El

P.S. I quote tonight's "Stars and Stripes" on a sentence I like—"The
curtain has risen on the last last tragic act of Hitler's play."

Virginia – June 10, 1944 11:35 a.m.

My darling—

The make-believe ballroom just finished—with Charlie Barnet's
"Pompton Turnpike" (oh, Syracuse weekends with you!) and then
I heard for the first time that the 9th air force has established
headquarters in France. I'm wondering if you're there yet, and if
not, how soon they'll have fields ready for fighters. As with you,
it's "never a dull moment" with me and "something new every
day." The excitement of these times is, admittedly, stimulating,
but stimulation is stimulating just so long!! I hope I will never

complain, when we're old and calm
(?) of just ordinary living. If I do, you'll
please boot me in the drawers!

Thinking, as I do always, of the
day you come home, I'm enclosing this
snap of the Gladys Berg (and family)
cottage at Mastic which we've been
offered when you come back. The

thoughts of such wonderful aloneness with you and the absolutely thrilling thought of just seeing you and being in your arms again is almost more than I can stand.

Yesterday the first letter from you in 3 weeks arrived. You can imagine how glad I was to get it, and particularly as you told me of the swastika on your plane. That's *great*, honey, and of course I'd like to know all about it, but doggone that damn eager so-and-so censor!! And now I won't hear anything of what you're doing. Damn, damn, damn!! But I suppose it's gotta be that way. I hope you'll tell me *something* anyway. My imagination is good, but it needs a little directing for *some* accuracy. About your swastika, though—Honey I wouldn't care if you never got one if I got you back. Please don't take foolish chances, darling. I don't think you will, but I love you so much, I just gotta tell you to be careful every now and then.

Always, my love. Ginny

Elmer – June 13, 1944 4:05 p.m.

My Dearest—

I've made a new friend, yesterday. A Red Cross Clubmobile (a mobile unit that comes to all the army posts and gives out doughnuts and coffee to the boys) started using our field as a home base. I walked over there yesterday, cause all of those units have a record player. I got to talking to one of the girls and had a dance or two with her. When I got back to operations, someone said to me, "What are you doing, bucking for a first?" "What do you mean"? I asked? "Dancing with Gen'l Spaatz's daughter" he answered. [Carl Spaatz was commander of Strategic Air Forces in Europe in 1944.] You could have knocked me over with a feather.

She's a very nice girl and is really doing a good job over here, and has been for the past year. There was an article in Life magazine about her and Ginny and Dooley, the other two girls on the trailer, perhaps you read it.

Weather lately has given us a short rest from flying, but it's cleared up now, so we'll be at it again shortly. I've got over ninety combat hours and soon will be starting my second hundred, but after that I'll just start on my third. No more tours for fighter pilots in the 9th. So it looks like I'll see you when the war is over.

All my love, for you, El

Elmer – June 15, 1944 8:00 p.m.

My Dearest—

Hello Honey, how are you this beautiful evening And it is beautiful. A sky polka-dotted with pink cumulus lackadaisically floating nowhere in particular. Listen to me waxing poetic. I must be getting flak-happy or maybe too much high altitude is getting me. Did I tell you about the beautiful night before last? We were coming back from a late evening mission and the sun was just relaxing in the west as we crossed out of the enemy coast. There was a haze close to the ground and the whole Cherbourg Peninsula was tinted pink. This in contrast to the many shades of blue in the evening sky was breathtaking. It was hard for me to realize that not far below me, men were savagely killing and being killed. God must really be disgusted with the way the crowd on this earth are conducting themselves.

Got my air medal today, along with quite a few other fellows including Joe. Brig. General Weyland [Otto P. Weyland, whom Patton called "the best damn general in the Air Corps"] made the presentations at an extremely informal ceremony. He gave a brief but interesting talk beforehand, lauding the 9th A.F. He wasn't the least bit brass-hatty and seemed like a swell fellow. I'll send you the hunk of bronze (with ribbon attached) as soon as I can tear myself away from it.

Got your wonderful article yesterday and since then I have read it at least twenty times and have showed it to practically everyone in the outfit. You asked me how I felt about it. Well, it left me with sort of mixed feelings. Mostly pride in you and your ability to express yourself so eloquently. Also if possible it deepened my love for you, to know that you have such feelings inside you to write such things. It sort of left me a little uneasy inside. I don't know just how to put this—it seems that the American public have nothing crammed down their throats but the "glorious American Airmen." The theme seems just a bit overdone. Hell, we have a soft racket compared with those poor devils in the Infantry and Armored Divisions. I'm not talking about your article, mind you, you were told to do it and did what I call a fine job of it. I can't explain what I mean but I hope you know what I'm driving at. I showed it to Taddy Spaatz and she thought it was swell and said I must have a wonderful wife, to which I emphatically agreed.

All my love, for you, forever, El

Elmer – June 22, 1944 3:30 p.m.

Dear Mom and Dad;

I got your latest letter yesterday, Dad, just before going on an exceptionally tough mission. I remembered what you had said about hitting them hard and hitting them often, and I swear, I went into enemy territory with murder in my heart. It would have been suicide for any crazy Kraut to get in front of my guns then. I don't know how to explain it, but I felt like you were a football coach and I was the quarterback, and that letter was a pep talk, just before the game. This may seem foolish to you, but after reading that letter I felt like I could lick the whole Luftwaffe, single handed.

Had about the best time on a mission this morning, than I have had since I've been flying, I think. I can't tell you much about it, but you will read about it in the papers, I think. [The headline from the *New York Times*: "Cherbourg Assaulted After Heavy Barrage; Nazi Lines Pounded; 80-Minute Air Blasting Opens American Drive to Take French Port."] I was flying right on the tree tops, about three hundred and fifty miles an hour. There was flak all around, and I guess, it was pretty dangerous, but I was having so much fun that I found me singing to myself. [He never described this mission in any letter to Virginia.]

It looks as though there might be another mission soon. Always on the go, never a dull moment. Take care of yourselves and keep the letters coming.

Your loving son, El

Virginia – June 24, 1944 11:45 p.m.

My darling—

The letters today got me down in the dumps like you didn't want me to be. That no tours for the 9th air force fighters is not pleasant news. It sorta knocks my future into dim distance, and when the future is all you're looking for, that's hard. I'm mad, because I think it's unfair, and very let down. "The end of the war"— although I know it can't be forever—sounds like such a terribly vague and distant date. What I wanna know is how do you expect me to take it that long?

Oh honey, if you were only home! I can't go on when I think of what that would mean.—anyway, I can understand how you might get to thinking queer things. Just so you remember how queer they are, and how illogical and untrue.

Gotta stop trying to tell you how much I love you—realizing when I start it's quite impossible. Love was never meant to be shown, for the satisfaction of the lovers, in writing.

The atmosphere at the office is very chilly these days in the editorial part. We're trying to get a Guild (American Newspaper Guild) contract, unionize, in other words, and Greene is taking it as a personal insult from all of us. It's not pleasant, but if we get it, the contract ought to benefit us all, one way or another. Every other newspaper, NYC and LI dailies (NY Sun excepted) is already Guild-organized. The great Stiles [the publisher] probably figures he can be different and keep his organization a big, happy, underpaid family.

All my love, always—Ginny

P.S. Awfully glad to hear "El's Belle, Ginny" is flying again!

Virginia – June 29, 1944 10:45 p.m.

Darling—

I just gotta discuss a problem which is becoming more and more serious. It concerns my pants. Yes, honey, I said pants. I'm faced with the question of how to keep them on. This is an all day problem. Y'see, this is war, and women's drawers, most effective with elastic, have suffered considerably. I find my present stock of pants has reached the stage where almost every pair is as wide or wider at the top than at the bottom!! I hope you will concede that this is a threatening predicament, because *I* am *not* wider at the top (or waist) than at the bottom (bottom).

That's the situation, and elastic-topped pants are not to be bought. The ones that are available are either of such quality as would render them similarly ineffective after a few workouts *or* are the button-top variety, which have many evil features. (These we'll not discuss here and now.)

Considering all these things, sir, couldn't you please talk with the fellas, bringing such hardships as these into the light, and get this war over with hurriedly? The bloomers of the nation are fast falling!! It's growing late!! Mothers, wives, and sweethearts will thank you, perhaps even let go their determined hold on unsteady unmentionables to throw their arms about you to thank you. This is a great cause for which we fight.

Gee, honey, this is a screwy sort of letter, but I must kid around sometimes, trying to forget how much I miss you, Uppermost in my heart is you.

I love you, El,Ginny

Virginia – July 2, 1944 9:20 p.m.

My darling—

Called your Mom this a.m. and found they got your letter of the 22nd [about the Air Medal]. She told me how swell it made Pop feel. He's certainly all fire fond of you, boy, and even though he tries to be quite modest and attempts to keep his pride in you to himself, it bursts out the cracks and spills all around. Can't say as I blame him, to be the author of gross understatement!

"If you were home"—well I wouldn't be sitting on my bed in shorts and sweater with thorn scratches on my hands. We'd be celebrating, some way, our ninth (month) anniversary. (Any day, now, I can legally have a baby!) Jeepers, honey, but it's been swell. Even the seven months you've been away have been better than if we hadn't gotten married. Knowing my *husband* is coming home to me, waiting for my *husband* is lots better than waiting for my fiancé. Remember this, darling, whenever those crazy ideas—that maybe you shouldn't have married me and "left me"—start kicking themselves around your head.

The above thorn scratches resulted from a battle with our ramblers along the driveway. They'd decided to ramble all over the driveway. I had to convince them that the trellis was a better place to travel. I was anxious to get it done soon because those *@!!* Japanese beetles are emerging again, and soon they'll cover the roses, making me afraid to work in them. The doggone things fly so aimlessly and light on anything when disturbed—and I donwanna have Jap beetles on me! Caught the first one I saw— dropped the little bastard in a jar of water—but I know they'll soon outnumber me by hundreds.

I don't know whether I told you how *very* much I enjoy your letters. Your description of combat missions, how you feel, what you do, makes me feel closer to you, and also gives me a better idea of this damn war. You're always telling me you can't write interesting letters, yet I have letters, written by Lt. E.W. Odell, that are more graphic and exciting than a picture. You can complain of not being able to write all you want, just so you keep sending me letters like these!

All my love, darling—Ginny

From France

As soon as it was prudent and logistically feasible, the Allies began moving their air squadrons across the Channel to captured German airfields in France. Being more than a hundred miles closer meant they could fly further into enemy-held territory and stay on targets longer.

Elmer – July 9, 1944

My Dearest—

It's been a week since I've written a line to anyone. Main reason is because I've been so busy I've hardly had time to sit down since the first of the month. I neglected to put, at the top of the paper, the place of origin. No longer is it "somewhere in England." From now on, it's "somewhere in France." Yes, the 363rd has moved across the channel. This explains the vast activity that has kept me from writing. First stepped on French soil on the fourth of July, so our celebrating had a two-fold purpose. Except there was nothing to celebrate with.

We moved into this field shortly after the Krauts moved out, and all the free time the fellows get, is spent souvenir hunting. I have a German rifle, helmet, and belt buckle, and no doubt could get more. [He was *not* permitted to bring these home with him.]

The French people are extremely friendly, only I can't understand what they say. Just this afternoon Bill Bullard and I were driving down a road and saw an old farmer plodding along. We stopped and offered him a ride, but couldn't make him understand, so he had to keep on plodding.

Darling, this has been awfully short, but the place is still in a state of confusion, and I have lots to do. Remember, even though a letter doesn't come every day, that I love you more than anything else in the world and am only living to come home to you.

All my love, El

P.S. Let the folks know you heard from me. Thank you.

Elmer – July 10, 1944 8:30 p.m. – "Somewhere in Normandy"

My Darling—

Today I got my first hunk of mail since I've been across. It was your letter of the 25th and I detected a note of disappointment in it, due to the knowledge there being no tours of duty for fighter pilots in the 9th. Well, I have some news that might gladden your heart. I know it gladdened mine. Seems that the 9th has adopted a new policy. After 200 hours, a pilot goes home on a 30 day leave. This thirty days excludes traveling time. After that time the pilot returns to his old outfit for another tour. There is a catch to this setup though. It seems that a good many of us in the group will get 200 hours at the same time, and since we can't all leave at once, most of us will have nearer 300 hours when our time comes to get the leave. However it gives us something to work for. You can plan on seeing me probably sometime in the spring. I have about 125 combat hours now and it will be around 3 or four months before I get 200 hours. Now that we are based in France, we lose all that time it used to take us to cross the channel, and consequently time doesn't build up quite so fast.

Honey, you seemed to be hyped up again on the subject of getting overseas. I realize you want to do something, but in my opinion, you're doing plenty. After all, war isn't a woman's job and you are doing a man-sized job on the paper. I consider the newspaper an essential industry. Aside from that, you're buying bonds, giving blood and keeping a victory garden. You're doing as much or more than is expected of any woman in war time. Also, since I'm not in England any longer, the chances of you seeing me, even occasionally, if you did come overseas, are mighty slim. So, Dearest, I guess you'd better stay home and sweat out a 30 day leave with me.

It's getting late and I see by the bulletin board that I'm scheduled for the first mission in the morning, so I'll kiss you goodnight for the time being, my sweet.

All my love, all for you, El

Virginia – July 12, 1944 10:15 p.m.

My darling—

Missing you like this is worse than a continual headache. It really hurts. We had a beautiful moon recently, but I didn't dare write about it while it was still around. Can't take it any more. I'd come in after dark, notice the roses and hydrangea blossoms, all white in the brightness, and then quickly come inside.

This moon business is only one thing. Tonight you're so *definitely* far away from me that I could bite people's heads off, swear without cease for minutes, or crawl into a corner and cry. But none of these would help much. I want you, now and always.

Say, Bud, who ya gonna vote for in November, Roosevelt or Dewey? I ask, not wishing to coerce you in any way (fat chance at this distance!) but merely to find out what you think about this election—also to ask if you've written for your ballot. But about *who* to vote for, I dunno yet. It really is a bit of a problem. I don't want to vote for Dewey, although he'd probably make a good president in *some* years. And besides, I don't much like the Republican platform—against a "world state" and "armed forces" to keep the peace. Don't like that at all. In other words, even though I really would prefer to get another man in after so long, I'm afraid of Republican reactionary policies, their "back to the good old days" ideas, and "throw out the bureaucrats" stuff. And more important, even, is their international policy. I'd sooner trust FDR's.

I love you darling, with all my heart and soul—

Always, Ginny

Elmer – July 13, 1944 10:15 p.m.

Feldpost

Feſtgeſtellt und gerechnet
Leutnant und Rompanieführer
II./Flieger-Regimen.
5. Kompanie

Feldpost

My Dearest—

What thinkest thou of my new stationery? The ink stamps are some the Krauts left behind in their hasty departure and the stamp is a free stamp for mail from soldiers.

Had a field day yesterday. Twelve of us bounced ten FW-190's. Destroyed five of them and damaged three. I got credited with a damaged, but I had more fun than I have had in a long time. There was a low overcast and as we made a tight turn, I got thrown up in it. There were a lot of planes milling around in the soup, and rather than risk a collision, I climbed up through the stuff. It was as smooth as a blanket on top and I circled, for that was where we were going to rejoin, after the fight. I was pissed off because I thought I had missed out on a good scrap, but in a moment my spirits soared. A ship peeped out of the cloud bank and I saw it was a 190. Zoom, I went screaming after him, but the Kraut saw me coming and ducked back in the stuff. Then it dawned on me that a lot of them might try to escape this way, so I kept a sharp lookout. Sure enough, it wasn't long before another one came out, but before I could get a shot at him he was back in the clouds. This would never do. All I was doing was chasing them back down where my buddies could get them, and not getting any myself. So I went down right on top of the clouds where they couldn't see me so soon. Almost immediately one popped out, right in front of me, going straight up. I pulled my sight through him and squeezed the trigger. Wham! Bam! And I could see hits on his wing roots. Then he must have known something was wrong cause he did a quick wingover and disappeared in the clouds. I chased one more down and then the fight was over and the squadron got together and went home. Good day's hunting. And we didn't lose anyone. Some fun! I'm flying tomorrow, so I'll kiss you goodnight for now.

All my love, all for you, always, El

Virginia – July 15, 1944 9:30 p.m.

My dearest—

Just now I came back from Lagakis', fetching ice cream. That place is full of reminiscences. They're all over the place. There was one sitting at the counter—you and I guzzling a soda. We had roller skates with us. You'll remember that one. And there was another lounging on one of the tables. It looked very like the first one, only older. We were again going through a soda and I was gazing over at you, most fondly. I pushed my way through all these (there were others) and said hello to Mr. & Mrs. L. They asked about you.

About now I've figured that there must be something cooking over your way. No mail since July 3. [She didn't get any until July 17.] It makes me feel lousy, even when I know there's an excellent reason for it. I don't get any for a while and I look around and find I'm in a big blue hole. Getting out isn't easy. Usually end up by letting go with enough tears to enable me to swim to the edge! Good thing I can swim!

I sat in the living room and looked down Baldwin road this afternoon. Daydreaming, of course, I thought how wonderful if you were on your way home and would suddenly come into sight and walk up to Schill Chateau. Even the thought of this made me whirl around inside. If it should ever happen I really believe happiness would overcome me. I just can't imagine such joy.

All my love, Ginny

Virginia – July 17, 1944 6:15 p.m.

My darling—

So you're in la belle France now. Never a dull moment. Your mention of trouble with the language gives me the fascinating idea of sending you French lessons so's you can communicate at least to some degree with farmers, for instance, to whom you wanna give a lift. Of course, I don't guarantee they'll understand you and

I practically promise you still won't be able to understand them, but you could try, no? And it may help me remember some French, which I've practically forgotten completely in the last few years. You know, I think, that yes is Oui, pronounced "wee" and no is non, pronounce like our no except for a nasal *n* (slight) sound at the end.

So you wanted to ask a farmer if he wanted a ride. The expression is Voulez-vous promener en auto? Voolez-voo prumnay on auto? And to tell him where you were going—Nous allons à San Lo (We're going to Saint Lo).

That à (meaning *to*) is pronounced like our expression of disgust, Brooklynese, a gowon (oh, go on!). It is a flatter *a* than it is in the English borrowing, à la mode.

I can hear you laughing yourself into a fit over the above. O.K., so you have a "Traveler's Handbook!" How did I know? Seriously, honey, if these things may help at all, I'll throw in a few in each letter. Think I will anyway. If nothing else, they'll hand you a laff!

From reference in the July 5 noospaper, I figure that perhaps you're near La Haye du Puits. This because the Yanks were near there at that time, and I imagine you'd be used to support American troops. If not that maybe near Carpiquet (?) where there's an airfield the Canadians took around that time. But I got a funny idea you'll never tell me how close my guess is to the troot.

By the way, honey, don't think you're gonna clutter up our house with pieces of German equipment—souvenirs! The only souvenir *I* want of this damn war is *you*, and having you decorating the house will be all I'll ask.

Like you imagined, darling, I was made happier to hear you'll get a leave after 200 hours (theoretically), but still the spring looks so far away now, especially when I remember how long the winter *always* seems to me. But I really didn't expect to see you before 1945. Last Wednesday I was given (for 50 cents!) a charming gold USO pin, signifying my completion of 50 or more combat hours down there. Wonder will I get oak leaf clusters for it as time goes on??? Think so honey?

Wish I could kiss you, but you know that. And you know, too, how much I love you, darling.

Always yours, Ginny

Elmer – July 18, 1944 9:10 p.m. – "Somewhere in France"

My Darling—

By the way, did I ever tell you that I have acquired a new way of drinking scotch and soda? Well, you know how we used to drink it. One shot of scotch in a tall glass and then drown it with ice and soda. They don't drink it that way over here. Take a smaller glass, put a double or triple scotch in it and just add a dash of soda, no ice. Makes a fine drink, especially after dinner, and you'd be surprised how quickly you can get drunk on nine or ten of these. Try *one* some time. I say one, because they hit you suddenly, like a 109 out of the sun.

I knew sooner or later I'd swing the conversation to airplanes. Some noteworthy news. The 382nd has been doing some wonderful things lately, and so that publicity could be pin-pointed on us alone, we felt that the squadron should have a name. We finally agreed to call ourselves the "Pied Pipers." This name has two sides. First, you know the Pied Piper drove the rats out of Europe. And that's what we're doing. Driving the Nazi Rats out. Secondly, a swell fellow, one of the best in the outfit, named his ship the "Pied Piper." Reason he named his ship thusly was because he went to a small college in Minnesota, name of Hamline, and the student body called themselves the Pied Pipers of Hamlin [the mascot of Hamline, now a university, is still the Piper]. He [First Lieutenant Dale H. Rook.] went down on that show I was so badly shot up on [May 30, 1944]. So if you should read anywhere about the exploits of the "Pied Piper Squadron," know that your husband is one of them.

One of such exploits happened today. The squadron sent out eight ships on a show. Dammit all to hell, I wasn't one of them. This eight got bounced by from seventy-five to one hundred enemy aircraft! We shot down ten, damaged four others and sent the rest scattering! Can you imagine, eight slugging it out with from 75 to 100 and coming out on top! Old lady luck sure was riding with the 382nd today. [They lost one, Lt. Bullard, later listed as a POW and repatriated after the war. In a July 30th *New York Times* article that Virginia sent Elmer, and also in the squadron report of that battle: "There were head-on encounters at minimum range, chases, and deflection shots at all ranges, at altitudes varying from the deck to the top of the overcast. Lt McGee lined up on one ME 109, saw it crack up after hitting a tree with its wing, without having fired a shot. Lt Asbury's guns jammed after killing one, damaging two. Lt McGee joined him, shot up the two he was chasing, saw them crash. Lt. Palmer destroyed one, saw its pilot hurtle chuteless into a farmhouse. After twenty minutes of combat and weaving, twisting, turning, the Messerschmitts had decided it was a rotten day and no more were in sight."]

Now I take up a very serious matter. The trouble you have been having with elastic in your pants. I have considered the matter very thoroughly, and though I feel deeply for you, and realize the gravity of the situation, at the moment there is nothing I can do for you. However if you will take this letter to the nearest Chaplain, it will entitle you to one hour of condolences and sympathy.

All my love, all for you, always, El

P.S. Leave us be careful what we print about the exploits of Lt. Odell, fighter pilot, extraordinary. You know, all that information has to be O.K.'ed before it can be released for print.

Virginia – July 18, 1944 7:40 p.m.

Dearest,

I'm having a cigarette in my boudoir after a shower. The shower served to take the mud off me but it also made me tired as hell, and I still have a night of work ahead of me. This business of working at night is good in that I have all day, almost, to push a hoe in the garden, but I sometimes forget that I'll be tired by night. Oh well, I can hope the cops won't have anything.

The picture of me with the gloves was meant to include my feet. Claire misjudged. But it shows my usual gardening costume. The gloves were bought to save my lily-white hands, but they're still quite white & my hands aren't. The darn things (gloves, not hands) were so clumsy that I don't use them much. But I think they're quite sharp, anyway.

For gardening shoes I wear a beat-up pair of saddle shoes that used to belong to Jean. They're lovely, though somewhat scuffed, and have a picturesque or gnomish(?) (gnome-like would be a better word.) air about them since they turn up at the toes! The curly quality is due to the fact that they're too long for me and also because they've been soaked so often and then used in a bent-ing position (as I'm squatting). You can imagine by this description & the picture what a lovely view I am at work.

My darling, I can't ever say how much I love you.

Yours—Ginny

Elmer – July 20, 1944 9:55 p.m. "France"

My Darling—

Right now I am as happy or happier than I have ever been since I left you, way back in December. And if you will look at the return address on the envelope, you will see the main reason. Yes, I am no longer a shavetail, but a full-fledged First Lieutenant. Last evening I went over to the orderly room to see if there was any mail from my wife. There was no mail for me except for an important-looking envelope from Headquarters, Ninth Fighter Command. I was scared as hell. I thought I was in trouble, something like getting caught "beating up" an airdrome or something. So with quaking heart and trembling fingers, I tore open the envelope. There was a raft of important sounding words, but the gist of it was that Elmer W. Odell is hereby appointed to the rank of First Looie. Swell, huh?

There are a lot more reasons why I am happy. Joe, and a few more of my buddies made "First" too, and last night we had quite a celebration on the post. To help us celebrate, "Doc" Foster gave us a bottle of scotch and a bottle of good French wine.

Third reason why I am happy. Got two packages from my wonderful wife today. Box of many kinds of candy, raisins, etc. and a box with books and mags in it. Thank you dearest.

Other reasons for my joy are manifold, but sorta intangible. Took stock of myself today. Kinda added up my assets, as it were, and came out way in the blue. Realized how lucky I am. Got the best wife in the world, got the best folks in the world, got a swell bunch of buddies, and I'm doing the things I like. What have I done to deserve such good fortune.

Last but far from the least reason is hard to explain. It's a feeling of well—being inside, which stems from a fierce faith and confidence in God. This feeling welled up inside me this morning, while flying. We took off at 5:30 on a dawn patrol. It was dark when we scrambled. The winking navigation lights on other ships, keeping us in formation, promised a good flight. And it was; the best I have ever flown. Some day you and I are going to take a hop, early in the morning, and watch the sunrise from above the clouds. No one, witnessing this spectacle, can ever afterwards, carry a shadow of a doubt about there being a God. And that sunrise this morning was the most beautiful that I have ever seen. It's a hopeless task, but I shall try to describe it to you. We flew at about five thousand feet. The whole countryside, except an area around our field, was completely covered by a ground fog and looked like a well-slept-in white satin nightgown, tossed carelessly on a bed. Below us and to the east, there was a line of dark, fluffy cumulus, contrasted against the light blue dawn. To the west and above us were wispy cirro-stratus and the sun, shining on them, painted them every shade of pink and salmon imaginable. These clouds were set in a deep blue sky. If Jerry had bounced us, I think he would have gotten me. I was at peace with the world and couldn't possibly conceive wrath and destruction on such a beautiful morning. Don't worry though, my eyes were ever-alert. I think this alertness, which we acquire after flying combat for a time, enabled me to fully appreciate such breath-taking beauty.

You wonder why I'm happy?

I love you so much, darling; I think it is this love that has strengthened my faith and made me capable of appreciating the *really* beautiful things in life.

All my love, for you—El

July 21, 1944 – US troops invade Guam, eventually liberating the American territory from Japanese occupation

Virginia – July 22, 1944 10:00 a.m.

My darling—

In a newsreel last night there was a scene of little French school girls singing "My Country 'Tis of Thee." They had a very decided accent, of course, and couldn't pronounce "mountainside" (they put two syllables where the first is) very well, but it was very touching to see and hear. It brought tears, very suddenly. I wonder at my sentimentality, trying to find a definite reason for such feeling, but it's quite indescribable. Just one of those small human events that make war seem even more cruel and bitter by comparison.

Got your letter of July 13 yesterday. I could just see you sitting on top of that cloud layer, waiting for Jerries to come out. Reminded me of a cat after mice! But always be careful, dearest. I want you back more than I want anything else in the world. A big kiss for your "damaged," honey. (what shall I give you now for the "confirmed"?) See that no one claims you as damaged. I wouldn't like that.

When I opened that letter with the German stamps on top, for a minute I thought my lieutenant was in a prison camp or something! It looks very official!

Jeepers—haven't given you your French lesson for today. Lemme see. Suppose you wanna ask how much something costs. It's "Combien coute-il?" pronounced *Combyen* (very little *y* sound) *cooteel*. Or asking for a glass (or *some*) water it's "Donnez-moi de l'eau, s'il vous plait? Doonay mya de low, see voo plé (short e, as in *end*) Like I said a long time ago in a letter, you *don't* say "Je vous desire" or "Je vous adore."! But I'll say those things to you and mean them all, but plenty, chèr garçon, parce que tu êtes tout de ma vie, maintenant et toujours.

Translated it reads—dear boy, because you're all my life (my whole life), now and always.

I love you, darling—Ginny

Elmer – July 25, 1944 10:00 p.m.

My Darling—

Sitting here in my room, with naught but a towel girding my loins. Feel pretty good. After a day of quite a bit of flying (and no more action than a bit of accurate flak), came home, played a game of ball after supper and have just stepped out of a warm tub. Cleanliness is a wonderful thing. No matter how low I may sometimes feel, a warm tub puts a rosy hue on everything. Got a letter from Dad yesterday! Dad's letter contained that clipping about me. [The brief article quotes from Elmer's June 8 letter to Virginia describing D-Day.] I was very pleased and flattered. Thank you very much. Only one catch. That copy you sent Rosey. She sent it to Joe and he got it a couple of hours before I got mine. He passed it around the barracks, and I got quite a bit of friendly razzing about it. Fellows now call me "Ace" and "Hot Rock." I don't really mind though. [The article had incorrectly credited him with 'shooting down' a Nazi plane, when he had destroyed it on the ground.]

Despite the fact that there wasn't any action today, I had a lot of fun. We were flying this morning, Robbie, Jabara, Pawlak and I. Patrol can get very boring at times, and Robbie, realizing this, started doing slow rolls. That was a signal to the rest of us. You should have seen "D" flight. All kinds of acrobatics imaginable, all over the sky, and in formation. Pawlak and I have been flying together quite a bit lately. We fly second element [a two-plane formation]. There's no element leader and wingman. We fly mutual support and in case of a fight, the nearest guy gets first crack. We've worked out a set of visible signals so we can talk without radio chatter.

My mind is tired and I don't feel witty or sharp. So I'll kiss you goodnight.

All my love, for you, always, El

Hazel Odell – July 27, 1944 7:00 a.m.

My Darling Son—

We received your lovely letter yesterday written the 20th in which we learned of your promotion.

I wish you could have seen me when I read that. My head and heart swelled about three inches and I told everyone I met and believe me dad was just as proud as a peacock. Gee El, you have us all puffed up with pride. I told you many times you could and would do something big and I know you will continue to reach the top in anything you do. We have always been proud of you and the older you get the prouder we are and let's hope you hurry home so we can show you off. Well honey I hope your helmet fits you after all this but it's really swell to have a son like you.

Good luck and all my love, Mother

Virginia – July 27, 1944 12:30 a.m.

Darling,

I love you, *first* lieutenant, like mad, and I'm about to bust with
happiness for you, pride in you, and love for you. Don't know why
I should have been lifted onto a cloud when that letter came this
afternoon. I knew that one day they'd break down and give you
those silver bars, that my lootnint is a full-fledged one,—I dunno;
it's like that time you were put in charge of 7 or 8 people at the
bank, only this is even better.

But aside from the good news in your letter of the 20th, that
was one of the most beautiful things I've ever read. I've told you
this before, darling, but you don't seem to believe me. Your letters
are wonderful, and I don't mean because they're your letters to
me, either. That description of the sunrise almost had me up there
with you, and your elation was so evident in the letter that it almost
bubbled out of the envelope.

Be sure to kiss Joe on both cheeks for me (you're in la belle
France, aren't you?) in the customary congratulatory manner.

Honey, Rosey was telling me that she & Joe have started a
"Fun Fund" for having a great time on when he gets home without
using any of their bank savings. Think I'll start stacking all my
dimes in our "Roll Out the Barrel" cigarette case (I have it out for a
morale booster but don't use it for cigarettes).

Did I tell you? The Jap beetles like petunias, damn them all!!
Come home & give 'em some low level attack from your 51, huh?
I'm afraid of them.

Never mind the strafing, Just come home, darling. I miss
you terribly.

All my love, Ginny

Virginia – July 28, 1944 2:00 a.m.

Darling,

We had a heap big storm today and the rumbling of thunder was heard for more than an hour before the storm hit. I always like storms. Gives me a very satisfied feeling, a feeling that I'm very small in this world where men can do nothing but just watch the elements whip themselves into a frenzy, watch and wait for them to calm themselves.

And the color everything takes, an intensified color, before the storm—I get a kick out of that. Looks like a view through peculiar-colored sun glasses. The wind started wrapping itself around everything, and then, suddenly, the clouds let loose in an effort that appeared to be aiming at knocking everything flat with the force of the rain. Baldwin road outside our house was flooded from curb to curb when the rains finally ceased, after not very long, too. Then the clean, cool smell of the earth is really good.

In the last short thunderstorm we had I got an idea of how it must feel to have a shell burst outside your plane—or did I tell you? Driving home the lightning struck so close that the flash and the thunder were simultaneously heard and seen. My heart went on the double for a while.

All my love, always, Ginny

Elmer – July 29, 1944 9:00 p.m.

My Darling—

It won't be long before I'm back in England. I have a seven day leave coming up this Tuesday. Now maybe I can get to see something on the British Isles. You can't see much on a 48 hr.

pass, and that's all I ever got when I was over there. I hope to get up to Scotland and play some golf.

In a letter not so long ago, you asked me about my political choice. I'm sticking to Roosevelt, for four more years, anyway. I don't know too much about either platform, but after all he *is* my boss, and it wouldn't be good to desert him now.

I am sitting down at the club drinking a scotch & soda, and a guy is knocking out Blues in the Night on the piano. Gee but I wish I was home with you. I've had my fill of this war.

All my love, for you, always, El

Virginia – July 31, 1944 [Addressed to "FOIST Lt. E.W. Odell"]

My leetle boy,

Honey, I'm so glad my letters give you a laugh now and then. I got yours of July 18 today and in it you wrote out my permission to see the nearest chaplain. It was sweet of you, and it did me a world of good. This very afternoon I rushed over to Mitchel, waving the letter in one hand and holding up my pants with the other. That, I thought, was the necessary, though not so neat way to handle it. At first there was a bit of trouble with the M.P.'s at the gate, but a hasty explanation resulted in my being rushed to the chaplain's office in a jeep.

It was slightly before the hour when I arrived, so I had to wait. Someone else was getting a full hour of condolence. On the stroke of four, however, his door opened, a smiling GI stepped out, and I, corners of my mouth and pants drooping, entered. He was very sympathetic, of course. That's what Holy Joes are made for. First I told him the whole long tale, beginning with my batch of new, springy drawers when the war broke out, concluding with a careful description of their present fate. Then I showed him your letter, and he began to weep with me. I explained that with you gone and my pants going, I had a tough time keeping a grip on both me and my undies.

He was swell, saying, "Of course, I know just how you must feel." Then he told me that things were tough all over, that only yesterday his last garters gave out and the PX was fresh out. Delicately lifting the cuff of his trousers (the cuffless cuff, natcherly), he showed me his wrinkled socks. This did it. I was impressed and knew that these things were indeed T.S. And with everything so bad, even in the chaplain's office, better times must come soon. As I was thanking him, the clock moved toward five and he reached for his punch to nick your letter. That done, he ushered me, smiling, to the door. The spring was back in my step, honey, even if it's still out of my pants.

But no kidding, my darling, I love you more than anything in this gummed-up world. If it weren't for you, the whole of it wouldn't be worth the red six cents pasted outside.

All my love, Ginny

Virginia – August 2, 1944 11:30 p.m.

My darling,

Rain, rain, stay right here,
We've had enough of warm and clear.
This poetic mood lingers. The above is to indicate that this aft, it began to rain and as I listen, or attempt to listen above the racket of this machine and the linotypes outside, I think it's still raining. Mitchel field predicted it would do this very thing when I called to ask 'em this morning. Great thing. You call the county meteorology

office and they don't predict a thing. So you call Mitchel and they tell you! The county must maintain military secrets!

So glad for the rain. Farmers will be most happy. We had a Hellcat [Grumman Navy F6F fighter] crash land in an Elmont farm yesterday and when I was talking to one of the farm folk, asking them if it wasn't a pretty exciting day, she said they weren't interested in that kind of excitement. What they're looking for from the skies, I gathered, was rain. The Hellcat, by the way, was being tested by a British naval flier and no one was hurt, but of course I couldn't get a word about it from the navy officials. Got all I had from the farmer folk, who had a good batch of crops ruint.

You're the best sweetheart, and I know it well.

Always yours, Ginny

Elmer – August 4, 1944 9:55 p.m.

My Darling—

It's been a number of days since I've last written and I'm sorry. I've been in London four days and every evening when I say I'm going to write, someone comes with a bottle and I get drunk. Last night it was Bingham, the night before, Jabara and the night before that, I had my own bottle. A pint of good Bourbon that "Doc" Foster gave me to take on my leave. Nice of him, I thought. This evening I steered clear of the fellas. Went to a show by myself and came back here determined to write. My leave has for the most part, been pleasant, but I heard some news that sorta took the joy out of it. I found out that Lee Mayo is missing in action. "Pee Wee" Malone is also missing. The old gang has really been getting the axe.

I was going up to Scotland on my leave, but travel conditions are not much good and it wouldn't have been worth it for five days. Going up north tomorrow to see a few of my buddies at a Thunderbolt base.

Now I am going to ask a couple of favors. First of all, I would appreciate it if you would send me a dollar bill. Reason I ask is because I want to start a short-snorter bill. [A short-snorter is a string of banknotes taped end-to-end and inscribed. During World War II flying travelers would sign the local currency of each country they stopped at, creating a token of good luck while crossing the Atlantic.] It should be a nice remembrance of the fellows in the squadron when I get home.

This has been rather short, but short or long, you know that my love goes with it.

All my love, all for you, El

August 4, 1944 – Anne Frank is betrayed, discovered, and arrested in Amsterdam

Virginia – August 6, 1944 10:40 p.m.

Most wonderful husband,

Getting back to civilization & news, after only a day & a half [from a weekend at Mastic beach], I find the Yanks are almost in Brest and St. Nazaire and the predictions on the war's end are more optimistic. Even I, as I told you, a confirmed pessimist in the matter, feel a glimmer of hope that perhaps I'll see you this year, and just the thought makes my heart race. However will I stand such happiness?

The thought alone, that you, the finest man God could give me, love me, makes me supremely happy and content to sweat out 10 wars for you.

Yours alone, Ginny

Virginia – August 9, 1944 10:20 p.m.

My dearest—

I got your letter of the 29th today and I thought of last week when I suppose you were on your vacation. Frankly, honey, I was burned to think of you on leave without me. Now why didn't you leave me try to get to London, hmmnn?? But I hope you got to Scotland and enjoyed some golf and first-hand Scotch. Golf, I always thought, is prolly a nice game, but who has the money to buy clubs? That $26 you're getting as a first looie (is it $26?) is going to your head, I can tell! Here I was having it spent on a new set of eyelashes and a permanent, but no, you're squandering it on the golf course. Hey, can I come too??

Some bad news to get told. Today the Ackerly's got a telegram saying that Bob [high school classmate] is missing after a July 26 mission. I wrote the story just a while ago and I hope like the dickens I'll soon have a better one to write about him. [Ackerly's P-51 was hit by anti-aircraft fire over France. He bailed out and survived the war.]

Just told Monsieur Greene that you were probably in Scotland last week on a seven day leave, and also mentioned that gee, he coulda come home in that time. Greene agreed and said "I'd bawl him out if I were you." Consider yourself bawled out— ha, ha.

Mom was pretty upset today; she found out the price she'd have to pay in inheritance taxes. She hasn't told anyone else this, but the tax amounts to almost $13,000!!! [About $175,000 in today's dollars.] I was amazed. That is indeed a neat piece of change. It's almost 30 per cent. *Everything* gets taxed. She was upset thinking how Pop saved, denied himself things all the time, always thought a good long time before he bought a thing for himself, and when he's gone, Uncle knocks a big hole in it. Of course, the war has a lot to do with it, and it's gotta be, I suppose, but it makes Pop's efforts seem a bit wasted.

I could tell you tonight that I love you as much as is humanly possible, but I know that tomorrow I will love you more.

All my love, always, darling, Ginny

August 11, 1944 – The Nazis bombard the ancient cloisters at Cluny, attempting to dislodge the French Resistance

Virginia – August 11, 1944 2:05 p.m.

Dearest,

I got home from da office and found your letter of August 4th, requesting the dollar bill and 35 mm. film. Hopping onto my white charger, who was tethered to the back door, still sweating from the race from Rockville Centre, I galloped to the village and fetched home three (3) 35 mm. rolls, 36 exposures per roll.

The other request is enclosed, and I'm wondering when you're going to get to be a member of the Short Snorter club. I thought they had to fly acrost the ocean to be eligible, or am I sadly confused.

Of course I'm ready to blow my top because you didn't write more often when you wuz on leave, but at this distance, my ire is hard to vent. *If* I can remember to, I'll chew you out good when you get home for this neglect. Please remind me.

I was doggone sorry to hear about Lee's being missing, but as with Bob Ackerly, I have hopes that he may turn up, soon or after the war, o.k. You hadn't told me about Peewee, but from Lou, as I wrote you before, I'd heard he'd been killed. I hope she got it wrong and he's only missing. With the last, there's hope.

Heard something from a 15th air force gunner today that made me very happy. Called this Hempstead kid, friend of Claire's, who's home after 51 missions on a Liberator, operating from Italy. I asked him about the German fighters, etc., and he said the FW 190's and the new ME 109's were good, "But nothing compares with the 51." He said. He said that captured Germans told them that the German fliers had been told to keep away from the 51's and the Spitfires. They'd seen what happened when they tangle with them. I thought that was very nice, and natcherly incorporated it in my story! After all, since the Mustang had its debut over there, there has been too little said of it, for my money. Around here, anyway, all you hear about is the Thunderbolt, due of course, to Republic's plant nearby.

Norman dropped in yesterday afternoon just as I was preparing to catch a nap. He broke up that idea very effectively. We batted the breeze all afternoon.

It's good to have him around. Except that it emphasizes your absence, it makes things feel like "the good ole days." Recalling the good times you have had together, he remembered in particular one afternoon when you both rolled down a slope at Morgan Memorial park, wrestling. He said that was perhaps one of the happiest moments of his life. It grew quite nostalgic for a while.

Then we got into a discussion of religion. As I've said to you before and as I told him yesterday, I can't understand how a fellow who so appreciates the beauty of the world, the goodness in people, can attribute it to nothing. He enjoys so much, finds so much simple pleasure, that he believes that is his heaven. To me, his philosophy has no beginning or end. Perhaps I'm too methodical or something to understand such thinking. I tried to get from him what it was, and then told him how such beliefs registered with me. It was terribly interesting. If we get the chance, I think we'll continue the discussion before he goes back to camp.

I love you, El, always. When are you coming home, honey? I wanna know when to put the corned beef and cabbage on!

Yours, Ginny

Elmer – August 12, 1944 9:00 p.m.

My Darling—

Back to war again after a very enjoyable leave. Didn't do half the things I intended to do, but had a fairly good time nonetheless. Finally got to see "For Whom The Bell Tolls." Thought it was pretty darned good.

(Honey, I'll finish this tomorrow; the lights just went "out)"

Now I'll tell you why I didn't finish the following day like I promised. The morning was foggy and I slept late. In the afternoon we sweated out a mission and finally took off at four-thirty. Getting back about seven we found the field socked in and had to go to another field. The weather kept us there until late the following afternoon (yesterday). Last evening we had a dance at the club and I got stinking cause we were released all day today. Slept till noon today and went swimming in the afternoon.

As to the pictures I promised you, unfortunately, they took all our pictures away when we left England. However I expect to get them back soon and I'll get them to you as soon as possible. And you're all wet on your guessing where I am.

I fly 1st mission tomorrow so I'll kiss you goodnight for now. Oh, if I could only do it in person.

All my love, for you, always, El

Virginia – August 13, 1944 7:55 p.m.

Darling—

The Schills have a batch of clams from the Odell fishing trip Friday. Guess Mom will make chowder tomorrow.

Came close to knocking myself out yesterday. From 1 pm to dusk I labored in the garden, most of the time working on the border along Baldwin road. Sometimes I wonder why I ask for all this work. I didn't *have* to make a border there!

I feel that I'm still young, honey, a truck driver whistled at me while I was working out there. Or doesn't that prove anything??

George Hall [remember George?] was driving by and stopped for a while. He's newly commissioned from Aberdeen OCS and is home on leave. He's been there ever since he went into the army, 2½ years or more ago! George, by the way, hasn't changed atall, atall. No comment, other than that.

Despite the awful loneliness of these days, it'll be more than worth it, having you home when they're over.

All my love, Ginny

Virginia – August 14, 1944 9:45 p.m.

My dearest,

I was going to tell you about the smell that permeates the house. NO. It is NOT the smell that comes from Roosevelt. It is the smell of clam chowder. Like I said last night, the Schills got some of the Odell clams, and as your Pop tole me, I laid 'em out on the cellar floor yesterday to keep until today. Got home from work and asked Mom about them. "OOOoooh—I forgot all about them," she said, almost horror-stricken. Maybe she thought they'd do awful things down in the cellar. Well, she was right. I went down to fetch them and as I picked them up, they hissed at me! They did!! I was scared. Thought they might bite me! But I got them upstairs without getting so much as a nip and we steamed them open. After they were all off the floor, however, I noticed that they were not house-broken, as your mother later told me. They had leaked.

Scrubbing the damn things almost cost me the use of my right arm, but it was finally finished and Mom proceeded to get the other stuff ready for the chowder. In it went onions, tomatoes, parsley, and carrots, all from the farm outside. We're gonna have the chowder tomorrow, and it certainly smells good. It was quite interesting to me—seeing them being first just as tight as clams are reported to be and then wide open from steaming. And it was fun, because Mom hasn't made chowder in so long that I called your mother for directions in the middle of the process.

One thing I still don't know, however—the anatomy of the clam. I'm wondering which end is which, how they operate, etc. Must take that up with an encyclopedia some time, or if you'll please come home and tell me, I'd like that ever so much better.

Darling, I wish you were here to hear the noise of the summer night. When I stop typing, I am amazed at the multitude of sounds coming from outside. They're made of crickets and katydids and I don't know what else, but the combined sound, never ceasing, seems like some kind of engine, incessant and steadily the same, that's keeping the earth going while the sun is down. When one of the noisy bugs stops for a while, it sounds like part of the engine shut off, or else something needs oiling. Fascinating to listen to so many calls.

All ways, I love you, Ginny

Elmer – August 15, 1944 3:20 p.m.

My Dearest—

Got another fairly good action story for you. Day before yesterday morning eight of us boys were out and jumped twelve Jerries. One boy got three and another fellow got one. The rest of us were moaning because we weren't in the show. That evening eight of us went out; I was flying Red #2, on Heberlein's wing. It had been an uneventful mission and we were just heading home when Heberlein called and said we were going down to investigate two bogies on the deck. On the way he called again and said "No, there's three of them;" and a moment later he called again and said, Gee, there's lots of them. On the final count there were twenty-five of them, and they were ME-109's & FW-190's, streaking for home. They were flying line abreast, and since we had diving speed, we caught them easily. I looked up and saw two of them in my sights, apparently an element leader and his wing man. I took a bead on the leader and even before I shot, I knew I had him. Don't ask me how I knew. I just felt it. For the first time I was absolutely calm in a fight. I took my time, put the right lead on him, and made sure everything was right. Then I gently pressed the tit. Wham!, and almost immediately his engine was on fire and pieces started falling from his ship. Next minute he bailed out. When he got out, his wingman did a chandelle [an abrupt, climbing turn] to the right and leveled off 90° later. I followed him up and when he straightened out, I started shooting. He must have been a badly frightened Kraut, because I had no sooner started firing, than he jettisoned his canopy and got the hell out of there. So I got two and the outfit got eight and damaged four. It was a pretty good day. One squadron ("Pied Pipers") destroyed twelve and damaged four. And no losses on our part. [In a late-night and martini-fueled conversation some twenty years later, Elmer expressed his remorse about this incident. "The kid was just trying to get home, and I killed him." Given the severity of the damage he describes above, his first victim in the attack may not have gotten out or survived, and Elmer may have sanitized this account for Virginia's sake.]

Darling, I dreamed about you last night. Gee, it was wonderful. Remember I love you and am living for the day when we can be together forever.

All my love, El

Virginia – August 15, 1944 10:25 p.m.

My darling,

You are about to receive some of the most gruesome pictures yet taken. Oh don't try to get out of it! You asked for it. "Send me pictures," you said, not caring for my difficulty at finding someone to take pictures with Charlie's tricky camera. So here are a few of the latest horrors. Do you *still* want more?

Frankly, and I wouldn't mention this to a soul, I believe these were bollixed up (by enemy agents) in the process of developing and printing. These agents attempt to make all servicemen's wives

Written on the back side: This is Glamour! Coiffure by Salt Water and Breeze Salon. Ain't I the lovely thing? Oh well, try not to be too frightened.

Exhibit—Uggh! Leo does not catch me at my very best. So I stick out my teeth, kidding like, and he makes with the shutter!! But looka the nice background—channel, boat, houses—good, huh?

look like bags, so as to convince the fighting man that victory, which would mean having to return to this mess, would be hell, so he surrenders. Whaddaya think?

Been meaning to send you this for some time. Now comes one of my latest attempts at poetry.

Second Fiddle
My husband's in love with another.
She's modern, and smooth, and slim.
Though I hear she's a hard one to handle
She's a slave to his every whim.
His new love's a gun-totin' mama,
A high-flyin', hard hittin' queen.
They travel all over together
Seeing places that I've never seen.
My husband's in love with another,
And she's dangerous, fast as they come.
Am I jealous? Why no, I'm all for her,
His battle-scarred P-51!

All right, so you guessed the ending. But you are acquainted with the author, so maybe we can discount your opinion.

Know what? You do so! I love you darling, and want you very much, all the time, for always.

Yours, Ginny

On August 18, Virginia sent Elmer a compilation of goofy personal news items and photos she called "DA NEWS FROM HERE," typed and formatted to look like a newspaper. It was humorous stuff, except for this editorial.

I've been wondering, lately, how people could possibly have gotten over the last war so thoroughly as they seemed to. When I think of all the real hardship and horror men are going through now, I feel that men in the last war must have known similar times, yet as I think of those men who saw service in world war I, I feel that they recovered and forgot far too quickly for the country's good.

For instance, maybe, as the men of this war are thinking, they thought only of getting home and getting away from it all, forgetting everything connected with it. Perhaps this was necessary before they could become normal people again.

But if this happens after world war II, we can most certainly look forward to world war III.

It's hard for me to say, "When El comes home you must not think that here is all that is to be wanted." Actually, that *is* all *I* want. But it's a selfish attitude. Instead I must try to keep alive to the world, open to new ideas. The tendency to crawl away into a comfortable shell is what will make this country again unprepared for war.

This is brief and mixed up. But I do think that to preserve peace the US should have a large, but *large* standing military machine, army, navy, and air corps. Perhaps compulsory military training would be a good idea, to prevent the services from becoming the resting places for most scum of the nation's men, to keep the people aware that the country must be defended at all times.

The ability to forget is one of man's most fortunate gifts, but it also works to his ruin.

Virginia – August 21, 1944 12:05 a.m.

My darling,

Today reminded me of those wonderful September days when there's a cool breeze but the sun is scorchingly hot. It was clear, today, perfectly clear. The sun didn't have a bit of interference. Sky was never bluer or brighter.

But I had a lousy feeling inside me which detracted more than a little bit from the peace of the day. Seems I haven't heard from you since August 4th when you were in London. Being in London was perhaps a vacation, but thoughts of the robot bombs made me more than a little anxious to hear from you again. A week goes by with no word, and even though I try, there's no stopping the awful fear that grows inside until you feel there's nothing there but just fear.

Since I sent you Da News From Here—and I got a great kick out of doing that— I have had some fun with your folks. Last night I dropped in after spending the day in the garden. Told them you were buying us a couple of drinks. So we went to Paul's and had a couple of aforementioned drinks. Also had much talk, to go with it. As always, each drink was to you and your safe return.

Pop said something I got a kick out of. We were talking about watches and he mentioned going to see the Waltham watch company in Mass. one time. As they were shown the place, the guide said, "They employ 2,000 girls here just to make faces."

I love you more than I have ever loved you before, but I know it is not as much as I shall love you tomorrow. I'm tired of existing. Life will begin again when you come home.

For you, only, always—Ginny

Elmer – August 21, 1944 8:45 p.m.

My Darling—

Got your letter of Aug 6th today. Those pictures are doggone good. Especially the one of Mom. She seldom takes a good picture, and this is one of the best I've seen.

For the past couple of days I have been living an agony of waiting, of hushed expectations and hope. Two things that mean more to me than anything I can think of, with the obvious exception of you. First of all, the Ninth is changing its leave policy and if things go as is expected and hoped for, it will mean that I will be home before Christmas. Wonderful, isn't it? That's the thing I'm hoping and praying for. The second thing, although lesser in importance, came yesterday with the knowledge that I had been recommended for the Distinguished Flying Cross. Whether it will be accepted or not, I don't know, but at least knowing that the recommendation is in, still makes me feel good. So for the next five or six days, I will just have to be a bundle of jangled nerves.

We've been weathered in for a number of days. Did have a U.S.O. show at the post tonight but it wasn't much good. Had a cowboy singer who did some fine yodeling and a dancer with a nice pair of gams (not as nice as yours) but the rest was routine.

Ginny darling, I've already commented on the pictures you just sent but I want to devote a paragraph to the one of you. When I looked at that one, something inside me went "click", because for an instant it brought you to my side. Don't know why this shot in particular. Maybe because it expresses the things about you that I love most. Your warmth, vitality and cheerfulness. If I don't get home to you soon, I think I'll die from sheer longing.

All my love, all for you, always—El

Virginia – August 24, 1944 2:50 a.m.

My darling,

I'm sure beat, but with reason. Been going on this job today since about 2 p.m., with interval for supper and a fling at dishwashing for an hour or so at the USO thrown in. But this territory (the branch) I find is plenty busy, with war casualties, if nothing else. Every night I've worked so far there have been at least two, missing, wounded, or killed. Going to see the families of the latter is no fun. Again tonight that was on the schedule—Italian people, and very nice.

Running around Inwood, which is composed of Italians and Negroes, isn't too appealing, if you know what that section is like, but I don't mind it at all. I find that people are pretty nice if you're nice to them, and I'm certainly not going to add fear of my own townsmen to my list of worries. (Sound like I'm becoming gray with them all, don't I?!!)

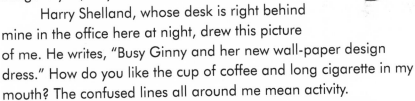

Hon, the enclosed is a portrait of me at work tonight, and believe me I was busy. I still could do a feature, but I'm just too dead to think. Wish I could tell you about some of the things. I like to bat the breeze about things to you, as you well know, but not tonight.

Harry Shelland, whose desk is right behind mine in the office here at night, drew this picture of me. He writes, "Busy Ginny and her new wall-paper design dress." How do you like the cup of coffee and long cigarette in my mouth? The confused lines all around me mean activity.

Darling, I got another rejection slip from SATEVEPOST yesterday. I really shouldn't try to sell my tripe to them. [This probably refers to a piece she wrote based on Elmer's adventures.] Better I should start on the Police Gazette and work up. Sometimes I think I am nothing more than a hack, and worse, will *never* be anything but. This last because I am so lazy. Ah well.

Keep in mind the fact that you are everything to me. Everything, darling.

All my love, Ginny

August 25, 1944 – Allied armies liberate Paris

Virginia – August 25, 1944 2:10 a.m.

My dearest,

High as a kite, that's what my morale is about this pernt. Your letter, telling me about the two Jerries and enclosing two pitchas, did it this afternoon. Honey, what a boost for the war-weary we— meaning me, and our families. I've managed to show the pictures to all the better people in Nassau county already. Anyone who escapes seeing them will have to get out of town for the next two weeks. Jeepers, I'm proud as all hell of you, but in usual modesty, I lower my voice to a dull roar to tell everyone how wonderful you most certainly are.

The pictures are swell. I don't think they're so hot of you— much prefer the other one you sent me from England [sitting on the wing, shown in a previous chapter] as a picture of you—but they show you with the ship, almost in action, so to speak, and what more can I ask, except for you yourself? The one with the helmet etc. on, in the cockpit, is better than the other. Looks more like you, considering the unflattering appearance the helmet has. But doggone, I like them both. And I love you.

There has been a great long interval between paragraphs. It's now 3 a.m., and I'm the last one in the newsroom tonight. But Bill Thompson, one of the oldest reporters on this rag, was telling me about old Long Island, around this section. And we discussed the ills of the R-S, which are many, believe me. We, it was decided, would run a paper a whole lot different. But then, we don't have a paper to run. I like to talk to people like this. He's seen an awful lot, and it helps to show how much I have to learn. He usually tells me a joke, too, if he's heard one.

It was Bill who told me the story of a lady who was to have a baby. The baby turned out to be triplets, and as she wheeled the three of them in front of admiring neighbors, she told them that this could happen only once in 57,965,243 times. Then from the crowd one old woman says to another, "Wonder when she gets time to do her housework!" [Bidda-bing, bidda-bang, bidda-boom!]

I got a great kick out of that one. Most of his are a lot tamer. He is, like I said, a great guy. Newspaper people are a wonderful lot, for the most part.

Do I miss you? Do I think of you all the time? Do I love you, El? Darling, "YES" is hardly emphatic enough.

All my love, dearest boy, Ginny

Elmer – August 26, 1944 7:30 p.m.

My Dearest—

We have been moving again. Still in Normandy and still have the same address but the place isn't the same as the last one, nor as good. That's one thing I don't like about the army—moving. Can never remember where I put anything.

No word yet on that new leave policy. Still sweating it out. No news on the D.F.C. either. I think it will go through, though. Joe and a couple other fellows got theirs and those of us who have been recommended haven't had any rejection notice. So I guess it's just a matter of time.

Bunch of us older pilots [he's not yet twenty-three, Jabara is twenty] are going over to England in the near future for a routine physical check-up. Long overdue, I might add. Pilots are supposed to get a 64 exam [Form 64, Physical Examination for Flying] every six months. I haven't had one in over a year. Don't know what the outcome will be. If I'm O.K. I'll come back to combat. If things are O.K. but not as good as they might be, I might be taken off combat status for a while, and fly non-operational in the U.K. Or I might even be grounded for a short period. I'm a bit worried about my eyes. They've given me trouble on every 64 I've taken. Who can say, though. I'll let you know the outcome as soon as possible.

Honey, that poem you wrote [about the Mustang] I thought was really good. You're so doggone wonderful, I can't realize I have the good fortune to be married to you. Darling, when I get home I promise to make up for the bad time I've given you by going away.

All my love, all for you, always, El

Virginia – August 27, 1944 1:45 p.m.

My dearest,

Autumn is coming, the nights are quite cool, and I'm getting worried. Cold weather & I don't agree, especially living alone like I am.

Living alone—you know what I mean—and you'd think by now perhaps I'd be used to it, but doggone, honey, I get lonelier every day. Last night I had dinner in NY with Bardo (Eleanor), who used to live in Wilbur cottage with me. She & another girl have been seeing the sights. We just had dinner together. They had tickets to the ice show at the Center Theater & being as it was impossible to get another at that time, I went home. Walking through the crowds in the theater section, on my way to Penn station, I was as lonely as I might have been on a desert island. I'm getting bored with heroes—not really bored, but quite tired of writing stories about them. I shouldn't, I suppose, but in the past week I've had 3 or 4, sometimes (like Friday) two a night to see. It is annoying me most, I think, because it seems to me that my stories all sound alike. Talked to a fellow Friday who's home for the first time in 5 ½ years! He was in the regular army at Pearl Harbor when it was attacked. I feel sorry for the guys who come home in sort of a bunch. To me, they're all heroes of a sort, but most of them won't ever get any public recognition (the publicity kind) at all. Maybe they won't mind at all, but I will.

The stars these past few nights have been *gorgeous*. Orion is beginning to show above the horizon in the southeast. I like to see Orion, but when I can find him low in the south I know winter is on the way. I want to learn more constellations. There are very few I can recognize. But even without knowing what they're called, I can be completely awed at them. After staring for a while, I thought they reminded me of those fluorescent animals in the water, lying along the shoreline at night, some shining continually and others blinking.

Haven't told you in a long time, & I guess you don't mind it every so often—please be careful, honey. I won't breathe right until you are right here beside me again, even if the Germans said uncle tomorrow.

Always yours, Ginny

Virginia – August 29, 1944 1:15 a.m.

My darling,

Jeeps, it was so good to get another letter today, and with another picture. Hope you have some idea of how good these things make me feel. Because if you haven't, there's nothing I can do. I couldn't describe it to you in a letter. I was glad to see your ground crew, honey. Kindly leave them know I salute them, curtsy politely at the introduction via letter, and wish them well.

Questions: Do you have the new swastikas on your ship? Where are the umbrella and broom symbols you first wrote me about? All I see are bombs, 60 of 'em. Does this mean, my good man, that you have simplified the process of recording missions by using bombs for everything, HUH? And have the Pied Pipers got an insigne yet?

I won't try to guess where you are anymore. But I figure from what you said (something about the channel) that you're near the coast. That covers plenty of territory. It doesn't really matter. What I want to know is, when can I kiss you again?

I'm waiting for you, darling, Ginny

Virginia – August 31, 1944 11:30 p.m.

My little fruit-face,

The mood is jovial, sweetheart, even though I try to suppress it. And the reason why I suppress, or try to, this exuberance, is because of the flimsy reason for it. Your letter today with its wee small hopes of getting home before Christmas. Darling, I tried to take it very soberly, and inwardly I realize that when you wrote it, it was just a chance. But despite the grumbling from the sensible part of me that I should say quietly that I hope this happens, I can't help but wish like fury that it does happen, that perhaps already you know that it will happen. Lord love a duck, but I can hardly wait to hear whether or not the ninth has made up its mind yet! Hurry, hurry, baby, I can't hang on much more, as the song goes.

Not only this do you thrust temptingly at me, via letter, this leave (perhaps soon), I mean, but also you dangle the DFC at me.

Great guns, she shouted, I hope you're busy with yore pen these days. I must have late reports on this stuff.

I was very glad to get the picture today. All these pictures seem too good to be true after such a long dearth. Nice to see the nose of your ship with the name. Made me feel very good, of course. What I wanna know now—what are the stripes painted under the plane? Or is that US insignia. [They were 'invasion stripes,' painted on Allied aircraft for D-Day and beyond, to quickly distinguish them from enemy planes.]

So I'll leave you now, darling, assuring you that I will love you like this, and more, always. Always.

All my love, Ginny

Virginia – September 2, 1944 1:05 a.m.

Darling,

Bad news today. Lou wrote that Mike [Mike Kenney, the best man at their wedding] was missing, since Aug. 17. She wrote to me on the day she heard, August 30, and I try to imagine how she must feel. There is hope, of course, and that helps a lot, but the awful fear that must be inside her is beyond imagination. I don't know whether I should visit her, but I think I will. Maybe it will help. Hope she hears he's a prisoner soon, but it often takes a few months. And she was planning on seeing him soon, too. This war, as you said recently, has taken an awful slice out of the Bartow boys.

The news today wasn't all bad. Kathy called me tonight from her home and I'm going to Maplewood for the weekend. She's in, probably for the last time before going overseas, from what she said on the phone. Going across [to India] will please her no end, and I don't blame her. Gosh, hey, I wanna see the world, too! But with you.

I want to drop Lou a note before going home, so this'll be all. Don't know what to say to her, because I really can't imagine how hard it must be, with the kid and all. Must make a stab at it, though.

I love you more all the time, dearest, and the best thing I can dream of is having you home again.

Always, yours, Ginny

Mike *was* a POW and returned home, but of the twenty-seven pilots in Elmer's advanced gunnery class, only nine survived the war.

Virginia – September 2, 1944 9:40 p.m.

My dearest—

Here we are married 11 months, officially engaged a year, and unofficially almost two. In your letter today you said you'd try to make up "for the bad time" you've "given me by going away." Oh, honey, you'd never have to *try* to make me happy. Just being you, and being near me is enough to make my life wonderful again. And darling, you didn't *give* me any bad time, & certainly I have the better part of the bad times we're both having.

I'm worried about you, too, about the 64 coming up. *I* wouldn't mind your being put on non-operational flying or even being grounded, except that you probably would be unhappy. But if this should happen (you are taken out of combat flying), would you still be in on the chance of getting home before Christmas?

If I told you my every thought begins and ends with you, it would be nothing new. You know that. And if I should tell you how terribly I long to share with you every sweet part of living—from smelling coffee in the morning and lying in bed late to seeing the unexpected colors of petunias in the garden and watching clouds drift past a full moon—all these things I enjoy *so* much, but always feel it's incomplete without you—but I've told you this, too, before. And how often have I explained what you mean to me— considerably more than the world and then some—how often? You must know it now.

So I try to say, make more emphatic, to you that you are the most wonderful husband any girl ever had, that I am most terribly proud of you, of being your wife and belonging to you. It all sounds the same, though. I can't write it boldly enough, or just enough, to encompass it all. But it all means the same, too, darling—that I love you. And that you know.

Yours, always, Ginny

Elmer – September 3, 1944 9:00 p.m.

My Darling—

It's been a week since I last wrote, but so doggone much has happened since, I have scarcely been able to keep up with myself, let alone with letters. First of all, you can stop worrying about me. I won't be flying at all, much less combat for about two months, and here is the story. You remember I told you we were going to England for a physical check-up? I was supposed to leave France last Monday morning. Well, things began happening last Sunday evening. We had a soft-ball game with the enlisted men and I was playing second base. A fellow attempted to steal second. As the peg came out from home plate this fellow slid into the base and me. I was knocked for a row of tin cans, and when I tried to get up, I knew there was something radically wrong. Someone sent for "Doc." Foster and the ambulance and half-hour later my leg was under an x-ray machine. You guessed it. I am now sporting a beautiful plaster cast. It isn't a bad break and it's a simple fracture (which I attempt to illustrate on the back), but it will keep me from flying for a couple of months.

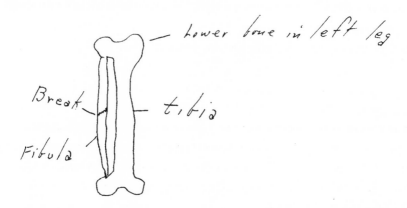

Knowing I was supposed to go to England, Monday morning they put a walking cast on it, and Tuesday, with the aid of a pair of crutches, I departed for the United Kingdom. Took my 6-4 with Joe and the rest of the fellows and passed it with flying colors, (except for the leg). I will remain in England a couple of weeks for observation and then go back to my outfit. You'll find my new address on the envelope. What the squadron will do with me, I can't say. Probably sit around censoring mail or something until I can fly again.

But now for some better news. About that new leave policy. It's been adopted and is even better than we hoped for. Even with this time I'm losing, there is still a good chance I'll be home before Christmas. Good, no? And my recommendation for the D.F.C. has not been turned down, so I should be getting that soon. All in all, even with a busted gam, things are looking pretty bright.

Darling, something happened over here, that made me almost cry, with love for you. I met Quent Regan [flight school classmate] over here, (he's recuperating from a pretty bad crash) and in the course of a bull session about old times, he told me about you on the day I left Tallahassee. Said he'd never forget how unhappy and forlorn you looked, sitting on the steps of the Colonial Hotel, crying your eyes out, and how, in spite of all their attempts, you wouldn't be cheered up. When he told me this, I could feel my love for you just welling up inside me.

All my love, all for you, El

P.S. Would you mind telling the folks about my accident. Impress upon them that it isn't serious and tell them they can stop worrying about my flying. [His mother, born in 1900, was terrified at the thought of flying, and never set foot on an airplane in the ninety-three years of her life.]

Virginia – September 6, 1944 11:10 p.m.

Sweetheart—

Got a few things to tell you, in a hurry, like. Your always loving (and usually thirsty) wife made a poichase. Through Mrs. Q., who knows a liquor dealer, I have cornered two pints of Canadian Club and we're working for a bottle of scotch to go with it. Won't be able to get Haig & Haig, but maybe something else fairly good. Rye, these days, is quite easy to get. Scotch is next to impossible. But both these bottles (if I finally get third, that too) are for us when you get home—soon, I hope.

Our fun fund (my half), by the way, now has about 7 dollars in it. The bank account, when I put in the latest check, will be $1775, plus $200 some odd in the Hempstead bank.

Got a couple jokes from Mrs. Q. tonight at the U.S.O.

Abie comes home and tells his wife he bought a new pair of pants. "Look, Reba," he says, "I'm getting pair of pants wit 14 inch zippa."

Reba is unimpressed, just says, "Yeah," and doesn't even look at the pants.

"Leesten, Reba, I got 14 inch zippa with da pants! Ain't dot good?"

"Sot vot?" says Reba. "Da neighbas got a two-car garage, and vot comes out??—a bicycle!"

Not much room left for the other one—and besides, I shouldn't be telling you these nasty stories. Tsk! Poisoning an innocent young mind!

> I love you, all ways, darling, always.
> Ginny

Virginia – September 8, 1944 9:15 p.m.

Dearest—

Oh boy am I proud of a purchase I purchased today! Oh boy! Remember I tole you how impossible it is to find scotch in retail quantities (bottles for sale, to be explicit)? Awright. So it's next to impossible. Chas. W. Williamson (who is *really* W. Chas, Wmson.) Esq. himself said as how even *he* couldn't find anyone with scotch.

To quit beating about the forsythia, I, the little (?) wife, have now a fifth of this precious liquid in my possession. And the brand? J. Walker, Black Label!! Kindly congratulate me, honey!

Of course, I used pull. Gotta admit it. I used Mrs. Q., who knows the guy in Clare's Liquor establishment in Baldwin. She asked him to save her some scotch when he got it. (She also got the Canadian Club for us.) Today she called, found he had some, sent me over. I come into the store saying, "Mrs. Quantrell sent me," just like in the prohibition days. (Don't you remember?) I laughed to myself when it came out, but the laugh grew into a big broad smile when he returned from the back (safe, no doubt) with the wonderful oblongish bottle for me to approve. Approve is mild for what I did, paying him the $6.99 [$95 today!] very quickly lest the mirage vanish. So now, honey, we got scotch, one bottle, anyway, and I will endeavor to get more.

I enclose this leaf, darling, which is the first beautifully colored leaf I've found on the ground, although the trees are beginning to switch makeup in some sections. Found the leaf today, and soon they'll be thick underfoot. This morning, walking to the bus, I had goose pimples on my arms and could smell a wood fire from someone's fireplace—just a hint of smoke in the air. It's almost fall, and I dread the thought of what follows then. But autumn is indeed a wonderful time.

All my love, Ginny

And indeed autumn *was* a wonderful time. That was the last letter in a correspondence that began with a postcard in October 1939. As you, dear reader, may recall, about seven weeks before this letter, on July 15, Virginia wrote, "I sat in the living room and looked down Baldwin road this afternoon. Daydreaming, of course, I thought how wonderful if you were on your way home and would suddenly come into sight and walk up to Schill Chateau. Even the thought of this made me whirl around inside. If it should ever happen I really believe happiness would overcome me. I just can't imagine such joy."

Well, that's what *did* happen. After Elmer got to England and had his exam, the Army apparently decided there was little sense in keeping him there for six weeks or so, then sending him back to France. And he had submitted the paperwork for a thirty-day "stateside" leave, which was in the approval process. So they flew him home. Virginia's last letter was postmarked at 1:00 p.m. on September 9th, and Elmer showed up at 48 Baldwin Road the next day, ahead of his letter telling her about his broken leg. Now you couldn't ask for a more beautiful story ending than that, could you?

Epilogue

IMAGINE THE SHRIEKS OF surprise and delight that accompanied Elmer's arrival at the Schill Chateau that September afternoon. After, I suspect, attending to the business of conceiving me, I'm guessing Elmer and Virginia headed to Roosevelt. Knowing Virginia's sense of humor and drama, she very likely would have left Elmer in the car and greeted her in-laws at the door by saying, "There's someone out here I'd like you to meet."

FOUR

NASSAU DAILY REVIEW-STAR–

LT. ODELL HOME, HIS LEG BROKEN

Mustang Flier Survives 60 Missions, Hurt On Ball Field

Without a word of warning, First Lieutenant Elmer W. Odell, whose wife lives at 48 Baldwin road, Hempstead, appeared at the front door of his home, early yesterday morning. He wore a cast on one leg—the one he had fractured in a baseball game, recently in England.

The young Mustang fighter plane pilot, son of Mr. and Mrs. John W. Odell, of 3 William street, Roosevelt, who has flown more than 60 combat missions flew home on his 21-day furlough, several months before the earliest he had expected it.

In his Mustang, "El's Belle, Ginny," part of the famous "Pied Pipers," Lieutenant Odell went all out on a recent mission to knock down two "Jerries" in less than five minutes of the aerial encounter.

Odell was flying the squadron leader's wing as they went out on patrol in the Le Mans area. Shortly after arriving over the patrol area, planes thought to be bandits were spotted flying close to the deck. The flight leader told his squadron he was going down to investigate. The closer he came to them the more he saw until a total of 25 enemy aircraft were spotted, or odds of three to one.

Lieutenant Odell describes the encounter by saying, "We were about 1,000 feet above them as we dove and were closing fast when they spotted us. I say they saw us coming because all at once black smoke began to pour from their engines as they gave it full throttle and they got right down on the trees. They seemed to want no part of a fight with us and seemed quite intent on getting home. However, we had diving speed and soon overtook them. As they came into range I lined up one, an element leader and picked him off like a wooden duck as he flew a straight, unerring course. He bailed out. His wingman then broke to the right and up and as he leveled out 90 degrees to his original course I began firing. Hardly had I pressed the trigger button when his canopy came off and he bailed out. He must have been scared to death."

Lieutenant Odell, a former bank clerk at Chase National in New York city, began his flying training in December, 1942, at Maxwell Field, Ala., and graduated from advanced flying school at Spence Field, Ala., in August, 1943. Since February of this year he has been flying combat. He

Gets 2 Nazis In 5 Minutes

Lieutenant Elmer W. Odell of Roosevelt in the cockpit of his P-51 Mustang, added two German planes to his score in a recent fight in the Le Mans area. The fighter pilot, now based in France, has flown more than 60 combat missions.

has been awarded the Air Medal and six bronze Oak Leaf Clusters.

Lieutenant Odell is a graduate of Hempstead High school, and studied at the American Institute of Banking. His wife Virginia, after whom his Ninth Air Force Mustang is named, is a reporter for the Nassau Daily Review-Star.

WAR BONDS will help to back the WACs WAVES and SPARS.

I can almost hear the peals of joy as the news rippled for blocks through this neighborhood, close-knit with extended family and friends. "Elmer's home!!"

He had been flown back via France, England, Iceland, and Canada, so he got to have his "Short-Snorter." It has bills from

those four countries signed and taped to the US dollar Virginia sent him. An outpatient call he made to the Mitchel Field infirmary for his leg coincided with a visit from the then First Lady, so his "sawbuck" also is autographed by Eleanor Roosevelt.

Elmer never returned to war. His separation citation reads, "Flew 67 combat missions in European Theater as a P-51 fighter pilot. Participated in long range escort bombing missions over Berlin, Hamburg, Koblentz, and Franfurt. Specialized in dive bombing and straf-ing of enemy airfields, bridges, railroads and other targets of opportunity. On 23rd combat mission over Berlin had 2 foot of right wing shot off and all movable surfaces of left horizontal stabilizer. Is credited with 1 FW-190, damaged in air, 2 ME-109's destroyed in air and 1 JU-88 destroyed on the ground." His dec-orations included the Distinguished Flying Cross, the Air Medal with eight Oak Leaf Clusters, and the European–African–Middle Eastern Campaign Ribbon with three Battle Stars.

Elmer and Virginia took the hunting and fishing trips they'd promised each other, stay-ing at that cabin in Mastic they'd dreamed about. These were likely among the few vaca-tions they had, as the demands of work and family all-to-soon intervened.

In early November they drove south. Their destination—DeRidder, Louisiana, and

Elmer's assignment as a flight instructor. They called it "Dead" Ridder, for Beauregard Parish was a *dry* county. They vowed to bring back plenty of booze when they returned from holiday leave.

Elmer was awarded his DFC at a ceremony there. The citation read, in part, "During the course of the flight, they observed far below a group of ten plus enemy aircraft engaged in the strafing of our front line troops. From an advantageous position in the sun, the eight of them bounced the strafers so successfully that eight of them were instantly destroyed, and a further three damaged for the loss of none of our number. Lt. Odell, himself, pressed attack so fiercely that he succeeded in destroying two of the enemy to aid in the total score. Such superior flying ability and heroic devotion to duty is a credit to the Army Air Corps."

He would proudly wear that ribbon on his jacket lapel for the rest of his life.

Although they owned a car, they traveled by train home and back for Christmas, because gasoline was in short supply and tightly rationed.

Sporting his medals and accompanied by a pregnant wife, Lieutenant Odell could not pay for a drink in the bar car.

In early February 1945, the DeRidder base was closed, partially due to citizen complaints about loud bombing noises and close calls. They moved to a base in Stuttgart, Arkansas, where they resided until the war's end. On May 8, Germany and Italy surrendered, ending the war in Europe. Elmer and Virginia's first child, John Mainard, was born at the Army Air Corps Hospital at Barksdale Field, Shreveport, Louisiana, on June 24. Japan surrendered on August 14, after the atomic bombing of Hiroshima and Nagasaki on August 6 and 9, ending the Second World War.

Elmer was released from military service on September 7, 1945 and we returned to New York. As one might expect, there was a glut of pilots, and the airlines were only taking applications from those with college degrees, so the economic success my parents fantasized about in their war correspondence did not come quickly.

Elmer and Virginia bought a small house in Roosevelt, two blocks away from his parents. They kept both flower and vegetable gardens, and one side of the garage was a riot of dark red climbing roses. Over the next five years they had three more children, Janet, Daniel, and Mary Ann. Daniel was given the middle name "Parker," as were—years later—a granddaughter and a great-grandson.

Elmer got a job at a paint store in Rockville Centre. After seven years of night school, he got his bachelor's degree in business administration, and then operated his own successful paint stores.

Virginia never resumed her journalism career. To help with the household budget, she worked for a time as a teacher's aide at the Cerebral Palsy Center in Roosevelt. After her children were grown and off to college she went back herself, got her M.A. in English, and taught that subject at her alma mater, Hempstead High School.

Elmer stayed in the Air Force Reserve and flew fighter jets from 1946 to 1956, retiring with the rank of Captain. In 1958

Elmer and Virginia finally bought their dream house, a 1914 six-bedroom one-of-a-kind, in neighboring Garden City. It was a far more prosperous village than Roosevelt, and it was where Elmer had his business. Here they celebrated fifty years of happy marriage and lived out the rest of their lives.

■

About the Author

Courtesy CCSF/Monica Davey

JOHN ODELL IS FACULTY emeritus of the Broadcast Electronic Media Arts Department at City College of San Francisco. Prior to teaching, he spent more than twenty-five years in television news as an award-winning video editor; also doing stints as a writer, producer, and reporter. John holds a BA from Columbia University and a Master's in Mass Communications from San Diego State University. A U.S. Navy Vietnam veteran, John served on aircraft carriers as a photo intelligence officer.